D1230104

The Crisis of Responsibility

The Crisis
of Responsibility

Man as the *Source* of Accountability

by William Horosz

University of Oklahoma Press : Norman

WILLIAM MADISON RANDALL LIBRARY UNC AT WILMINGTON

By William Horosz

The Crisis of Responsibility (Norman, 1975)

The Promise and Peril of Human Purpose (St. Louis, 1970)

Escape From Destiny: Self-Directive Theory of Man and Culture (Springfield, Illinois, 1967)

Coeditor and contributor, *Religion in Philosophical and Cultural Perspective,* "Religion and Culture in Modern Perspective" (Princeton, 1967)

Library of Congress Cataloging in Publication Data

Horosz, William.
   The crisis of responsibility.

   Includes bibliographical references.
   1. Responsibility. I. Title.
BJ1451.H67   170   75-2104
ISBN 0-8061-1281-6

Copyright 1975 by the University of Oklahoma Press, Publishing Division of the University. Composed and printed at Norman, Oklahoma, U.S.A., by the University of Oklahoma Press. First edition.

BJ 1451
.H67

To My Wife, for love and care, for having discovered that marvelous alchemy of blending human vitality with responsibility.

144314

Preface

At the height of his literary career in the late 1930's when he produced his masterpiece, *The Grapes of Wrath*, John Steinbeck revealed a passionate image of man as self-transcending, as one who stood above and beyond the conditions of labor and environment. It was an empathic glimpse of man. He said, in effect, that the task of man was "to create beyond a single need" and "beyond his work." This was what gave man a sense of responsibility and directionality. The author said at the time, "For man, unlike any other thing organic or inorganic in the universe, walks up the stairs of his concepts, emerges ahead of his accomplishments." Modern existentialists support this vision of man as being "ahead of himself," as being self-transcending.

But four decades later modern man is not so exuberant or self-confident as Steinbeck envisioned him. He is neither certain of his directionality nor clear about the sensibility of his responsibility. The world is in social turmoil. Watergate, the nearly successful political coup which threatened democratic values, in fact reveals an image of man as moving down the stairs of responsibility. This downhill democracy has shocked most Americans beyond belief and has brought about a reexamination of social responsibility in high places. The foundations of responsibility having been shaken, man is no longer so exuberant in mounting the stairway of responsibility, of transcending his work and environment. Nor is he certain about his sense of directionality. Is self-transcendence a functional directionality of man's purposive life, or is it a fundamental characteristic of totalities which would control the behavior of man? The thick gray foliage of totalities has obstructed man's vision about the human genesis of responsibility and self-transcendence.

The paradox is that although man lives in an affluent society, he has the feelingful awareness of having lost his hold on life, his *human claims* on responsibility and self-transcendence. His sense of responsibility has been numbed beyond belief, he no longer shows, or cares to show, a sense of "responsibility for" some of his choices and goals. He has been conditioned as part of the system, part of the organization, and these entities alone have the power to perform the needed tasks in an overly organized and administered society. Why, then, express the sense of "responsibility for" in a highly structured world where it doesn't count anyway? Thus against great odds man learns to live as part of a system of totality and gives his consent reluctantly to the overriding considerations of a highly structured and organized society. But it does absolve him from exhibiting in his being and actions a certain sense of "responsibility for." What has brought about the loss of personal and social responsibility where man has lost his enthusiasm to walk up the stairs of responsibility and ideality?

A large part of the blame for the gap between "responsibility for" and "responsibility to"—what I call the *crisis* of responsibility—can be attributed to submergence philosophies and the conditioning by totalities. They have assumed "responsibility for" man. Although man exhibits a certain nervousness about this cleavage in his personal and social life, he does what he must for survival. Can man reestablish his claims on responsibility and directionality in modern mass society? Can he establish the primacy of *human claims* over the *totalistic claims* upon his life? An affirmative reply may not be necessary to man's survival, but it certainly is essential for quality living. Shall we be content with a view of man where he is no longer the claimant of his powers, both personal and social?

My concern in this book is to offer a diagnosis of the crisis and a partial solution for transcending it. A more comprehensive solution of the problem is called for, but this will require a separate argumentation in another book. The plan here is to offer some specifics about the breakdown of the human sensibility of responsibility and its possible restoration. More specifically, what *is* the crisis of responsibility? That we are confused about the *source* of human responsibility. Does it have its sources in systems of totality, or within man himself? If in the latter, what is its proper locus? This line of questioning is ignored in modern deliberations on responsibility, because the concept of responsibility is always dealt with on the level of action. But it has deeper roots. In this volume I hope to show that the question of sources of human responsibility is not a muddled question, that its solution is the only way of overcoming some of the personal and social problems in our day, of exhibiting the renewed composure of man.

It is understandable, historically, why we have attributed or entrusted the sources of responsibility to systems of totality. The models of man as the sources of responsibility have failed us generation after generation. Obviously, we have lost our faith in the possibility that the "human orderer" is really the source of *human* responsibility. Having been unnerved by these failures in the past, our new trust in totalities as the sources of human responsibility has become the order of the day. After all, only large organizations can perform the required tasks on a large scale which the individual cannot even approximate. Having been shaken by our attitudes toward human beings and models of the "human orderer," we have sought more secure foundations for human responsibility, above or below man. But responsibility can mean only one thing when man is merged with systems of totality: that man is a "responder" or merely a set of "response functions" in such a submerged system. Are we content to pay the price for such an attitude toward man and human responsibility? Once we submerge the part in the whole, the meaning of responsibility is clear: it becomes a *unifying principle* for that specific totality. The focus is placed on the totalization of experience rather than its humanization. Man now owes primary allegiance to the specific totality in terms of "responsibility to" its criterion. Each system of totality has its own model of the "responder," and such totalistic systems are mutually exclusive. The responder in Marxism is one life-style, the responder in Christianity another. If man is merely a "process of reaching out" (self-transcending), eventually it is the totalities which set the standard for the responder and not a purposive being in quest for his wholeness. The choice is clear: either man becomes a responder in some system of totality, where he is responsible as an *answerer* to that totality, or man as a purposive being, as in some sense a "human orderer" of his choices, goals, and ultimate goals, is the source of such total systems of responsibility. My preference is for the latter, where man has the opportunity to show "responsibility for" systems of total responsibility, and not only show "responsibility to" such systems of totality.

Who decides the vital issue? Do we leave such a decision to our feelingful awareness—to our "dumb responses" which, according to William James, are the real guides of life? Do we give the priority to our heads or wills, or to collective man oriented toward the worker, as in Marxism? Do we attribute the choice or ontological option to the sovereignty of the subject self, as in Sartre, who has yet to explain the source and meaning of human responsibility in his promised ethics? All these models of man, and many others, have failed in the course of history, and they, too, like the systems of totality, have a blanket of thick gray foliage between us and the truth about the real source of human responsibility.

It is my contention in this book that while on the level of action and experience responsibility is a culturally conditioned term, its source in man has a singular locus. This is not the case when its sources are placed in some system of totality. The very effort to anchor the source in systems of totality raises the question of pluralism and relativism which is insurmountable once this path is taken. Which totality is the final source of responsibility, if they are mutually exclusive totalities? It is just at the point of locus in the problem that the issue comes to a head—where claims of ultimacy abound, as to which totality is real and which a fabrication. It is here that human pretension and power behave at their worst: "mine is real and yours is false." Such antithetical totalistic claims have had disastrous consequences for humanity in the history of thought. Once the problem is seen in its relativistic form, compatibility systems are out of reach; they merely multiply the totalities on hand. For such mutually exclusive systems of totality have no common meaning or structure. Instead of answering the question of sources, they tend to obscure the possibility of an answer, or else they "bracket" the issue and choose to ignore it, a favorite tactic of the conciliators.

If the issue of anchoring the sources of human responsibility in some system of totality is taken for what it is—an impasse, an insurmountable problem, or one of those "treacherous imponderables"—then the alternative is clearer. Man's claims on responsibility and self-transcendence must be reestablished at all cost. It should be made clear how through objectification and reification man has allowed his powers to slip away from him, how they have been usurped by systems of totality. This requires a new definition of responsibility that goes below the image of man as "responder" and as "self-transcending." *Responsibility is man confronting the "human orderer" in himself and society.* In society he shows this ability in *purpose-bearing institutions*, policy-making and rule-making—a social alternative to totalism and totalitarian claims. This is apparently the only way to avoid the myriad models of the responder offered by systems of totality as the alleged sources of responsibility and self-transcendence. *The simple but enigmatic definition of responsibility is what this book is all about.* But it is from a positive perspective and vantage point from which we examine and interrogate other theories of responsibility: philosophical, psychological, secular, and religious models of the responder.

Special attention is given to humanistic psychology, which has made great strides in understanding man but refuses to let go of its cherished images of the *whole man* and the *whole of reality*, refusing to part with "holism." Yet the holistic image of purposiveness is not the primary meaning of human purpose. Here John Steinbeck's image of man as self-transcending, as moving ahead of his accomplishments, does not suffice as a model of man. Unless man as a purposive being is in control of the power of self-transcendence, it remains an unharnessed power that totalities use for their own particular ends. The problem here is the same as with responsibility, whether we anchor it in systems of totality or within a specific locus of man. Unless man is capable of such purposive ontological options, there is no point in discussing either the concept of responsibility or that of self-transcendence. It is man alone who can revitalize both concepts, give new meaning and content, by reestablishing the human claims to them over the totalities which have surreptitiously reversed the role of claimant from a human to a totalist one. In the perspective of this volume, the humanization of experience has priority over the totalization of experience. Such methods of totalizing human experience at first go unnoticed but later do not even require human consent. The humanization of experience means that man's sense of directionality in life is the primary source of human responsibility. This always has priority to some totalistic directionality of human existence.

Of course there are many problems in finding the locus of responsibility in a theory of man, but these are surmountable. Do we look for the source in some form of human vitality, such as feeling, or in man's purposive nature? Is there a need to escape human participation to come up with an adequate notion of the "human orderer"? It is my contention here that a strong sense of the "human orderer" is amenable to a philosophy of action and participation. Twentieth-century thinkers have doubted this merger; instead they have sacrificed a significant model of man for a submergence philosophy which gave man a "turning space" in some totality. Such an absorption of man into systems of totality is no longer a requirement in this volume. While natural and sociohistorical factors do mediate man's life and influence him greatly, man is still a purposive being in existence who practices model-making, human reality–claim-making, and who has a say about his experiences.

One may object that man can't be "responsible for" everything. After all, he is a finite creature. But there is a significant area of human life—in choice-making, goal-making, totality-making, responsibility-making— where man is decidedly a "human orderer." Totalities, after all, are nothing but the projections and productions that derive from man's search for wholeness. There is no claim made here for an omnipotent "human orderer," for he remains infinitely finite in his self-direction and search for wholeness. But this fact is ignored by philosophies of submergence and systems of totality. Yet they are all shabby claimants when compared to a purposive being that is the claimant of his powers in existence. We are not discussing here the isolated individual. Man is in the thick of experience exhibiting his purposive gifts. Both the isolated individual and the total individual are but abstractions from man's purposive life; they reflect our attitude toward human beings and to ourselves. The "responder" in some system of totality is also such an abstraction. He, too, is one of the attitudes toward ourselves and about human beings in general. The concept of the responder derives from human typology about human beings.

In analytic philosophy and the social sciences one frequently observes apologies for the concept of responsibility. This is rather sad and unfortunate. In our technological age one can be so distracted and numbed in his sensibilities that one is not even aware of the fact that his human powers are eroding rapidly. A clarification of the question of sources will be of some aid in overcoming such apathy. Once responsibility is disconnected from the human claimant of his powers, the concept of "control" will take its place, and then totalities will be more alienating and distancing than they are now. This threat should not be taken lightly, because it affects the very fiber and quality of human life. There are no apologies for human responsibility in this volume. Anchoring it in a new model of man will make it just a little more difficult to bypass it for the planned life in a technological age. Thus the crisis of responsibility is more than an academic issue. It affects the very fiber and quality of human life.

It is time once more for man to assert his human powers, not just in business and industry, and to walk up the stairs of his concepts and powers, to make new *human* reality claims for his human gifts. If man fails to assert himself in such a manner, totalists are ever ready to totalize human experience without human consent. Are you willing to consent to such a life-style? The task in this volume is to show how man as a purposive being can be liberated for responsibility in an age of mass society and technology.

When personal and social responsibility is made *anonymous* by the big organizational complex of modern society, schemes of totality are given a free license to practice their dictatorial claims upon human life. Awareness of such alienation is the first requisite for becoming human and of staying human in modern society with its external and internal pressures and sanctions.

In short, totalities should be seen for what they are; namely, *human projections and productions of man's search for wholeness.* That is to say, models of wholeness for which certain *human* reality-claims or claims of ultimacy are made. The entire problem centers in man's claim-making capacity, which modern schemes of totality have ignored.

The crisis of responsibility comes to light, with vital urgency, when it is seen first as human problem rather than in the context of totalities as it has been presented to us in the course of history. The "responder" must first be seen in its relation to the purposive being (I have called him a human orderer) before it is related to schemes of totality. In the light of this new perspective, totalities are given their proper place as projections of man's search for wholeness. Without such an understanding there is no way to clear up the confusion about the source or sources of human responsibility, and no way to reduce the tension that people experience in facing responsibility in the complexities of modern society. In such a spirit of awakening modern man will turn utopian thinking into critical thinking when he is promised emancipation from one totality to another. For what man truly needs is emancipation from all totalities, be they religious, social, or philosophical, if he is to retain or regain his human dignity. Thus emancipation for responsibility, and a broader awareness of its import for life, is what is required of modern man, if the crisis of responsibility is to be met. This book is offered with the hope that it will give the reader this broadened awareness of what is required of us to face the problems of modern society in a *human* manner. Ours is an age which demands responsible purposive being.

WILLIAM HOROSZ

Norman, Oklahoma
January 23, 1975

Acknowledgments

I wish to express my appreciation and thanks to Miss Leona Barnett, my typist, and to Mrs. Suzan Taylor for competent typing assistance. Sincere thanks is due also to several of my colleagues for helpful references and suggestions on some of the topics in the book. They are: J. N. Mohanty, Robert Shahan, and J. C. Feaver. Dr. Edward Crim, Dean of the Graduate College, has given financial assistance to help complete the final draft of this manuscript. I also wish to express my thanks to those graduate students in philosophy who have expressed concern for the theme of this book and contributed much to its dialogue.

Contents

PART ONE: Six Models of Human Participation

It is not the ordinary course of life that wears us out; but the impossible burden of the imponderables is the responsibility that finally defeats us. I have a recurrent dream about this. It is a large, dark, empty house. Apparently empty, for the halls are long and wide, and soundless; there are numerous doors that even in the stillness give the sense of tumultuous life; and occasionally a man or a woman, strange to me but familiar, as if I had known the person in another life, comes out of a door, and gives me a menacing look. I have it over and over again, and I think the dream is a symbol of what I have said, the treachery of the imponderables.

—ALLEN TATE

1. Youth's Discovery of Responsibility in Spontaneity

One could attribute the upsurge of immediacy as a rallying point for youth to conditions of alienation in an advanced technological society as a forced option. That is to say, they have no other recourse but spontaneity, but to withdraw to an inward castle of personal delights, in a social structure where the personal life is in peril. But there is a point of no return in considering the problem of youth in terms of alienation. As a term of social analysis, some scientists consider it next to useless. However, many books about the radical left are still being written which concern themselves with "The Abuse of Discontent" and how this alienation colors their social views. From the standpoint of our theme, we shall be concerned with a more positive relation between spontaneity as a direct form of immediate experience and that of responsibility. The concept of alienation will be momentarily set aside. While alienation is an understandable psychosocial fact, it is not the most important thing considering the source of human responsibility. More important is the fact that there is a subjective choice of values involved, a positive vision, if you will, linking responsibility to its source in direct experience—utopian as that may sound to those who prefer a more ordered life.

My concern here is to examine the relation of spontaneity to responsibility as a mode of participation by youth in modern society. We shall call it participation by social immediacy. Although this chapter is not a case study of youth, it is a model of social participation, competing with many other models of participation. Undoubtedly, this is a new phenomenon which we are not accustomed to, and for this reason it is necessary to examine some of the claims being made about the source of responsibility in the medium of social immediacy. The directives of immediacy have played a much greater role in conditioning the youth of the New Left than any other source. Since it is a form of youthful commitment, the view of

3

the radicals as being uncommitted or alienated seems like an oversimplification. The fact is, there is commitment to a lyrical quality of life that appears to be absent in the antiecstatic technological society with which they part. If there is complete absorption in the immediate realm and in the revolution of totality, then a positive view of the matter should disclose some of the connections between spontaneity and responsibility.

The New Left has resulted in a new life-style for the individual and for the liberated community. There is high regard for the phenomenon of spontaneity, utopian as it seems, among the anti-intellectual and anti-authoritarian youth. They view it not merely as a condition, but a source of a new sense of responsibility that will usher in the healthy society. Others may view this as alienation, as having its source in estrangement and resentment, such as W. P. Gerberding and D. E. Smith in *The Radical Left*. Smith, for example, attributes all the social pronouncements of the New Left to this twofold alienation: "The answer is that the most characteristic feature of the radical Left is the blatant alienation of its advocates and this alienation has set the general tone of the social and political criticism of the past ten years."[1]

The radical left continues to believe that spontaneity is the proper guide to a life of adventure and promise. Although the radicals are not the first to derive a sense of direction, a vision, and a sense of responsibility from immediate experience, they are the first to use it as a community-building agency on a global scale and in establishing affinity groups or communes. For the first time in history, spontaneity is given a social and activist dimension which may even surpass the claims of Romantic individualism. That such social immediacy is a requirement for successful revolutions is a strong belief for most radicals.

The intent of this chapter is to demonstrate that the connection between spontaneity and shared responsibility is an untenable one. The reason for this thesis is that the phenomenon of spontaneity is itself a derived form of directionality. Spontaneity is not its own. It has a gathering focus in the human orderer or in the orderings of a system of totality(s). Most radicals derive this elemental mode of responsiveness to social conditions from some system of totality: Marxian, neo-Marxian, anarchist, etc. If this is the case, responsibility cannot be derived from spontaneity, which is itself a functionary of other things. Where responsibility is rooted in a

---

[1] W. P. Gerberding and D. E. Smith, eds., *The Radical Left* (New York, Houghton Mifflin, 1970), 354–55.

system of totality, it always functions first as a unifying principle in that system.

What has prompted this high regard for spontaneity as the source of responsibility or of the healthy community? Alienation, in the form of estrangement and resentment, has already been mentioned as a cause; other causes are historical. One of them is the Marxian distinction between abstraction and immediacy which Herbert Marcuse exploits in *Reason and Revolution* (1954).

ABSTRACTION AND IMMEDIACY

Immediate experience is used to justify man's constructions and abstractions, but it is held by many not to be in need of justification itself. Marx shared this view of direct experience. In his desire to "change" the world, in contrast to Hegel's attempt to "understand" it, Marx made an absolute distinction between abstraction and immediacy and thought thereby he brought about the "negation of philosophy." Philosophical categories were transmuted to social and economic ones. It is obvious that this change shows a preference for the appeal of direct experience to reason. Marcuse states that

Every single concept in the Marxian theory has a materially different foundation. . . . Marx's theory is a "critique" in the sense that all concepts are an indictment of the totality of the existing order. . . . History and social reality themselves thus "negate" philosophy. The critique of society cannot be carried through by philosophical doctrine, but becomes the task of socio-historical practice.[2]

In replacing the Hegelian form of rational totality, Marx substituted for it the real, immediate totality of history, free from human projection, construction, and abstraction. The social forms in this totality were the actual bearers of the tendencies located in collective immediacy. Once the totality was located within immediate experience, with dialectical social forms as its inevitable structures, the whole was operative in every moment of history, bringing about the needful, desired future. The negation of philosophy was accomplished. There was no longer any need for human projection, construction, and abstraction on the primitive level of experience. Within the context of immediate experience, there was reconciliation of idea and reality, of models of existence with existence, of the possible with the

[2] Herbert Marcuse, *Reason and Revolution* (New York, Humanities Press, 1954), 258, 261.

actual. Thus was dispensed the belief that reason's abstractions were needed to mediate a given social reality. Reality was now made accessible by an appeal to direct socioeconomic experience rather than by reason's abstractions. There were many countermovements to the Hegelian world-view contributing to the historical upsurge of spontaneity as the source of human responsibility. The Marxian perspective was one among many.

How valid is the absolute distinction between abstraction and immediacy? In relation to man's intellect, there is a significant difference with immediacy as a direct form of experience, for it requires man's elemental modes of response as the condition for interaction. But with respect to human purpose, understood as man's capacity for self-direction on the level of being, the distinction between abstraction and immediacy breaks down. What I am suggesting is a broader use of abstraction so as to include model-making on the level of participation. Abstraction on this lower level of human participation can be viewed as another order of abstraction, other than mental abstraction. Human participation in existence, no matter how fully one is absorbed in concrete experiences, is perspectival. It is not only the human mind that is perspectival. I should like to call this fact of interaction abstractionism by participation. This would equally apply to social participation and to participation by social immediacy. When such participation is related to larger wholes, we have the further right to call it perspectival holism. The Marxian view of totality in terms of economic classes is precisely such a model of existence by participation, rather than by mental abstraction. No amount of ideology critique can be rid of abstractions for good. In fact, I shall show that it is the biggest abstraction of all.

In terms of my theory, it is impossible to banish the concept of abstraction from the realm of immediacy, the domain of unmediated experience. We merely replace one abstraction with another. Abstraction has many lives. Consequently, when Marx rejected Hegel's model of totality as having too much the structure of reason in it, he was not banishing the role of philosophy in toto. By negating philosophy of the Hegelian variety, postulated on the basis of universal reason, Marx was not negating philosophy as a whole. He was merely pointing to the false identification in Hegel's system between reason's power to universalize and man's intellect itself. How was Marx certain that his view of economic, class, and historical totality was not another model of existence replacing a previous one that had significance in his day? How can the Marxian critique be "an indictment of the totality of the existing order"? Hegel's rationalist view of reality is displaced by an experience-oriented view of totality which has its own abstractions. The very fact that Marx chose economic and class modes of response to history, selected from other possible modes of elemental response to history, which he equated with his model of totality, indicates the abstracted nature of his model of existence. These abstractions are of another order of response because, after all, he was pressing for the perspective of dialectical materialism against idealism. But they are abstractions by participation, which are always perspectival both by way of actions and by way of postulated totalities.

This brings us to the crux of the matter: the line between abstraction and immediacy is an artificial demarcation needing further explanation which does not rationalize the problem. If direct experience is a model of existence and nothing more, then it cannot be identified with existence as existence or with existence as totality. Direct experience in Marxian usage is already an abstraction from experience, especially in its collective usage. It serves more as an instrument of apologetics than as a truth about reality. It is an abstraction which results from the perspectival nature of social participation, which the idea of the whole does not rescue. The reality of immediate wholeness is itself the biggest abstraction of all because it, too, is perspectival participation.

Marx failed to realize the designing qualities of the human orderer in participation. He failed to note that man creates abstractions, models of social life, models of totality, by economic participation, by social action, and by other elemental modes of response. These primitive ways of responding to life are always perspectival and in most cases specific. They need, therefore, a gathering focus either in man or in some system of totality. Marx, in opposition to Hegel, merely launched another philosophy about reality that relied more on abstractions by participation (changing the world) than on the abstractions of the mind. From this perspective the "negation" of philosophy does not take place because Marx's philosophy is exhibit A of this ongoing process. As an object of human participation, the "concrete," as opposed to the "abstract," bears the designs of man's participation in experience. Marx failed to realize that man fashions experience not only by his mind, but by his actions and his being. After all, the distinction between ideology and fact, abstraction and concreteness, is posterior to purposes of being.

The attempt on the part of Marcuse to banish abstractions from the

7

Marxian theory of totality is thus ill advised. I view it as another claim to ultimacy by another totalist in the competition for the understanding of existence by different models of totality. The appeal to experience to confirm totality as real is simply a case of apologetics. No totalist in history has succeeded in demonstrating how he moves from his perspective of totality to cosmic reality. The "totality of class society" cannot be designed without the model-making capacity of man's purposive nature as a participant in existence. This holistic use or tendency of human purpose is an inextricable part of one's model of totality. To call this forming capacity of man in the matrix of participation an ideology, or an abstraction, is to miss the point.[3]

The Marxian claim to ultimacy about his model of existence has not gone uncriticized. In *Christianity and Class War*, Berdyaev thinks there is much evidence of abstractionism in the Marxian view of totality:

He attributed an absolute significance to "class" and it has certainly played a very big part in history, but its importance is relative, it is a constituent but not an integral part of man. . . . On the higher level, society is a function of class; on the lower level, personality is such a function: class is, in a way, the substance, the *noumenon*, the thing-in-itself, and everything else is only accident.[4]

What does one do with such a plurality of totalities, each making claims to ultimacy for the one of his choice and each ruled by a dialectic suiting its structure and goals? There appears to be no way out of this relativism but the claim to ultimacy for the totality of one's choice. The appeal to socioeconomic history, which is an appeal to direct experience, is a way of claiming ultimacy for the Marxian view of totality over the Hegelian totality of reason and subjectivity. These examples would show that human participation in some system of totality is a limited kind of participation. There is also perspectivalism and relativism among totalities, as well as the perspectivalism of human participation in them. Surely, reality is broader than that, or at least open to many such schemes of participation in totality.

---

[3] *Ibid.*, 314: "The totality that the Marxian dialectic gets to is the totality of class society, and the negativity that underlies its contradictions and shapes its very content is the negativity of class relations." The alleged separation between the Marxian dialectic and Hegel's ontology is read by Marcuse as the absence of all abstractions and model-making in the Marxian view of totality. It is not a metaphysical state of affairs or the forming power of human purpose, which belongs to the superstructure rather than to the basic structure of life.

[4] Nicholas Berdyaev, *Christianity and Class War* (London, Sheed and Ward, 1934), 33, 36–37. Berdyaev has his own system of totality in the Christian framework, which has another rationale and makes other claims to ultimacy.

The fact is that totality cannot be separated from man's search for wholeness. If this is the case, abstractionism by participation is present in every vision of human totality. The dialectic is merely the servant of each system of totality, making man "responsible to" the system of totality but not "responsible for" it. This would lead us to conclude that because every system of totality is but a temporary and tentative view of existence (a part of man's search for meaning in life), that claims of ultimacy for one's system of totality are unwarranted. The claim that Marx's system of totality is model-free because it rests on direct experience—indeed, on the whole of reality—is just the claim to ultimacy mentioned above. The appeal to experience is nothing but a weapon of apologetics to launch the priority of his system of totality in history. To identify one's system of totality with total historical reality *qua* reality is the pretentious claim to omniscience I mentioned earlier. Marx does not demonstrate sufficiently how he goes over from his system of totality to cosmic reality *qua* reality, to "the ultimate totality." Immediate wholeness is thus not free of the mixture of abstraction and immediacy mentioned above.

As noted above, the absolute distinction between abstraction and immediate experience is a rather tenuous one. The problem can be clarified some if the issue is related to purposive being rather than to reality or totality. We must square off the relation of these terms with human orderers, who are capable of immediatizing and mediatizing—and, therefore, of model-making—in order to solve some of the real problems in their relationships. From our point of view, hidden abstractions infect the area of immediate experience at every turn. If the human orderer is effectively related to participation in existence, model-making on the level of participation, just as on the level of thought, is unavoidable. This is at the heart of the issue between the virgin quality of spontaneity and shared human responsibility.

Human history is not free from abstractions and from models of participation when it is understood as the result of human participation. Even when it is understood in terms of a system of totality and its participation in history, this must be conceived as the result of human participation. When schemes of totality are given a status beyond human participation, they are nothing but abstractions, and in some cases nothing but fictitious entities. The course of history can be viewed from three perspectives: from above, from below, and from within ourselves. I call these perspectives three different models of existence or of history. The Marxian view of totality is a prepurposive model of history. The fact that it is dialectically ordered betrays its directionality as coming from below. The model of totality controls both the form and content of his comprehensive world-view, which Marx mistakenly believes is the real order of the universe.

Marcuse believes that the Marxian progress over Hegel indicates a shift in categories from Hegel, a shift to material foundations (that is, model-free) for the categories. What Marcuse fails to realize is that both thinkers were postulating models of totality, each respectively believing that his model was the whole of reality. The difference between the two models is not the question of whether one is abstract and the other real, but in their claims to ultimacy. The only way to make an abstraction like totality real and immediate is by claims to ultimacy. There is no way of verifying totalities, especially the real totality of cosmic reality. The fact that every totalist in the history of thought has made his case for real totality by identifying his model of existence with existence as existence does not make this procedure valid. In fact, this procedure of mistaken identifications is illicit because it presupposes omniscience on the part of the totalist. It is time we get wise to this game. What has encouraged such practice is the appeal to immediate experience, which justifies other constructs and abstractions but which does not require justification itself. This assumptive practice of taking model-free immediate experience for granted is itself only another claim to ultimacy. Both are a way of claiming "absolute participation" in existence in the midst of perspectivalism. There are, then, two basic problems in the phrase "direct totality." The term "direct" and the notion of "totality" are in need of reexamination because, through their unjustified assumptions, totalists have assumed "absolute participation" in the sphere of temporality.

THE PARADOX OF SPONTANEITY

The paradox of spontaneity is that the more we emphasize self-expression in a free and spontaneous being as a life-style, the more we give our life over to a system of totality(s). If spontaneity is not its own, but only a derived directionality from totality, self-expression can only serve the intentions of direct experience and its connections to totality. The intention of spontaneity is to supply complete absorption in life, without the mediation of the intellect. Spontaneous living is the practice of immediate living in all its connective interactions. But the more one emphasizes these primal connections to nature, to being, or to life, the more there is a sense of directionality experienced that appears to be coming from below the human orderer. Man can only be responsible to spontaneity, not for it. We are not responsible for our feelings and emotions and primal interchanges with life. We are advised merely to follow their directives. The human orderer is not the gathering focus for these elemental responses to life. Among the radicals of the New Left, spontaneity is the servant either of a naturalistic or a social totality(s), or a mixture of both.

The paradox derives from what I shall call the philosophy of the divided will. The will has the capacity to alienate itself, to divide itself, to say no to itself, and to submit its directives to another power, such as a system of totality. It is an elemental mode of response in life, and one which no longer has its gathering focus in the human orderer. This is, in essence, the paradox of will-less thought and will-less participation. The phenomenon of the divided will is thus an elemental mode of response to social existence which denies itself, never to recover its form of being or its capacity to order and reorder the choices and goals of life. While this phenomenon enables one to be responsible to something or some system of totality, it has a basic incapacity to be responsible for them. This is essentially a dialectical ordering of the will which enables it to be a servant of totality.

That is precisely what is involved in the notion of social spontaneity. When the will decides to throw in its lot spontaneously with the directives of social totality, it experiences complete absorption in the revolution of totality, for which it is not responsible, but only responsible to its directives. The appeal to immediate experience is merely the rationale for justifying the will in its immediate course of action, of giving itself over to the directives of another power, such as totality. It becomes part of the "elemental upsurge" experienced in the developmental course of history. Will forgoes its own directives to be guided by the directives of immediacy, which, in turn, is guided by the directives of totality and its dialectical intentions.

The Social Dimension of Spontaneity

There is an implicit assumption on the part of the New Left that subjectivity in all its manifestations is of one piece. Whether one speaks of the subject self, the situational self, or the universal self, subjectivity is believed to be *sui generis*, a seamless robe with no patches of abstraction on it. It is in the light of this assumption that there is ready identification of spontaneity with the social dimension of existence. I believe that the analogy for all these uses of subjectivity has its model in the individual subject self. One of the features of subjectivity so defined is spontaneity. With this analogy as its base, various forms of social subjectivity are postulated which reflect the organismic theory of collective life. At the base of social subjectivity is the notion of freedom, which is defined as relation to. Social spontaneity takes three forms: the whole-man notion, situational or contextual immediacy, and universal spontaneity. One is most free and spontaneous when he considers the whole man in his total experience, or the total situation in social experience, or universal immediacy where the part participates fully in some scheme of totality. All three forms of spontaneous subjectivity, when youth is characterized as a "stage of life," can be described in terms of the value that is placed by youth on change, transformation, and movement. There is at this stage of life, as Kenneth Keniston reminds us, "the consequent abhorrence of *stasis*":

To change, to stay on the road, to retain a sense of inner development and/or outer momentum is essential to many youths' sense of active vitality. The psychological problems of youth are experienced as most overwhelming when they seem to block change: thus, youth grows panicky when confronted with the feeling of "getting nowhere," of "being stuck in a rut," or of "not moving."[5]

There is an intensity of experience in such movement, whether it is the need to be moved, the need to move others, the need to move through the world, or to move with the revolution of totality. Such immersion in being is marked by completeness and fullness. The human orderer is no longer in charge of the intensity of such experiences. This is true of both the mark of the personal and the social in youthful experiences. Is such fullness of participation model-free? Is it free of model-making in the context of such participation? Or has one already made a preconceived ontological commitment to a model of existence that enables him to read off direct experience in terms of spontaneity? Can we talk about individual and social immediacy on the same level of discourse?

I think there is an uncritical transfer of spontaneity from the individual to situational and then to universal immediacy. All three models of subjectivity are conceived as having a base in the socio-organic structure of life itself. The analogy of organic spontaneity, when imposed upon the mass, becomes superorganic in function—or, as it is called in political

---

[5] Kenneth Keniston, "Youth: A 'New' Stage of Life," *The American Scholar* (Autumn, 1970), 638–39.

theory, the organismic model of unity. There are many problems that arise when we move from one kind of spontaneity to another. However, my main objection to social immediacy is that direct experience is conceived on a universal rather than an individual basis. This, to me, is immediacy by consent and not by the direct flow of life in and through the collective. When social spontaneity is fused with the concept of totality, it is really a plea for absolute participation in social forms of behavior, which I believe is another myth. Thus the specter of "absolute participation" haunts the participatory model we have labeled the social dimension of immediacy. While we have largely stopped playing the game of "absolute knowledge" in philosophy, we have not learned to spot the same practice in participation. Absolute participation may be regarded as a correlative notion of absolute knowledge and functions as its foundation.

Social spontaneity is also paradoxical in nature because it is not its own. It serves instead the intentions of a revolutionary totality, as in the case of the New Left. The paradox is that social self-expression or mass immediacy or fusion, cannot be stated in terms of self-activity, self-management (as, for example, the workers creatively in charge of their own products), because it is still lacking directionality in spite of all its vitality. Whatever directionality is given, such vitality is usually attributed to an external order, like the party. All three forms of social immediacy—the notion of the whole man, situational immediacy, and universal immediateness—are problematic because of the paradoxical nature of spontaneity. To make it our own we must follow it through the mediation of totality and identify with it.

The Whole Man in Leftist Literature

The case for the "whole man" is stated in terms of an appeal to immediate experience that is allegedly free of construction and abstraction. The effort to label this, as some do, as a bad case of anti-intellectualism or a resurgence of the cult of feeling due to alienating conditions in modern society, is somehow inadequate. However, there is a modicum of truth in it, the belief that the intellect alienates man from the intensity of lived experience. Such a dissatisfaction with the rationalism of liberalism on the part of the New Left is understandable because it wants to get things done and be on the move. It despises the calculating delays of the intellect. Spontaneity, in this context at least, means the doer, the actor, or agent on the level of immediate social encounter. Spontaneity is thus the passport to the new land of historical action and absorption through which the agent is constituted as a whole. Historical immediacy authenticates the man and cures him of intellectual alienation. Thus there is a distrust among the radicals of reason's efficacy in experience, just as Marx showed mistrust of Hegel's universe of rational totality.

But can one buy immediacy at this cheap a price? As long as the issue is merely the contrast between intellect and immediate experience, and the latter is taken to be the foundation of rational constructs, the problem is oversimplified. But if we relate the problem to the human orderer and ask the question, Why is the whole man whole?, the reply is that it is the sociohistoric totality that makes him whole. Man's search for wholeness takes place in the medium of immediate experience. This is where the transformation or transfiguration takes place, from a personal search for wholeness to the all controlling wholeness of dialectically ordered history. It is this medium of transformation which transforms the orderings of the human orderer to the orderings of totality that I am questioning. The whole man is whole not because of his ordering capacity or because of his search for wholeness, but because of what the historically real whole does for him and to him. The whole man is a social man, the species man of Marx, in modern garb. Yet it may be so only by social consensus and not by immediacy or by social spontaneity. The whole man is only one of three models of subjectivity; he is not man as man, or the real man. Out there in history he is competing with other images of human nature, all claiming to be unitive in their experience and wholeness.

The "whole man" theme is that he is a participant in total immediacy. He is inside global immediacy with its revolutionary upsurge in history. His wholeness, or search for wholeness, depends on how he commits himself to this historic totality with the principle of contradiction that dialectically motivates it. The whole man wins his spurs from totality as it rides through history. He is not his own; he follows the spontaneousness of totality at work dialectically in history. He lives by the principle of "coresponsiveness," and his "freedom in community" is defined by totality. The whole man is the social participant, and the social participant is a participant in a model-free totality that is the source of all spontaneity in history via social forms. Consequently, the whole man is not "responsible for" spontaneous directionality; on the contrary, he is "responsible to" such directives originated by the totality moving in history.

It has been noted by way of criticism that the intensity of experience does not make the whole man, neither does the attempt to alienate him from his rational and purposive life, nor does the alleged real or immediate totality make him so considered a part from his own search for wholeness. In the light of my theory, the whole man theme can only be stated in terms of man's search for wholeness, a search which produces comprehensive models of human nature that support his quest for meaning. In fact, in the sphere of spontaneity, the human agent only feels his way around in the structures of connective totality. He is not the source of human actions in such a connective realism. Man's fusion with a sociohistoric totality is a secondary and mistaken identification to human participation in existence or in history. It involves a prior purposiveness, namely, the human or-derer's ontological capacity for self-direction in the thick of participation. If the whole-man theme is only a model of man and not man *qua* man, then it presupposes a gathering focus either in man or in a system of totality. The New Left chooses totality in a preconceived manner, that is to say, as something prior to purposive being whose intentions it identifies with the subject of being when it is immersed in being spontaneously.

Situational Spontaneity

Situational spontaneity is also alleged to be a direct form of participation in history or a social encounter therein. Sartre gives a classic example in his major work, *Being and Nothingness*, when he depicts the "situation" as the relation of freedom to the given plenitude of being. Although the author claims that the given does not constitute the notion of freedom, "since freedom is interiorized as the internal negation of the given,"[6] we should be wary of such a dialectical relationship. The reason for caution is that freedom is already in a prior way goal-directed to the given and re-ceives movement and directionality from the given. Sartre's view is, after all, a system of totality, whatever else it may be. The For-itself is goal-directed to itself in a system of totality that is immediate. The fact that freedom "supposes all being in order to rise up in the heart of being as a hole"[7] is an indication it lacks directionality of its own and depends on the directionality of totality.

Its very definition as "a lack of being in relation to a given being," as "a hole in being" or as the "nothingness of being," would seem to indicate

---

[6] Jean-Paul Sartre, *Being and Nothingness*, ed. by H. E. Barnes (New York, Philo-sophical Library, 1956), 487.

[7] *Ibid.*, 485.

its need for directionality by a system of totality. Freedom, as a lack, is not its own. It follows the directives of totality, which comes from the initial commitment of the For-itself as that which is goal-directed to itself in a system of totality that is immediate and dialectically structured and ordered. Perhaps this is what is meant by the phrase "condemned to be free." Situational freedom, then, is the freedom that totality allows in its spontaneous march through history. The given plenitude of being is its foundation, to which freedom is goal-directed in its choice of projects. The very fact that it needs the "resistance" of the given plenitude of being in order to operate, or to come into conception, indicates just how much the For-itself is goal-directed to itself by the dictates of totality, the given plenitude of being.

What is the implication of Sartre's perspective for the social dimension of spontaneity? For Sartre, the subject of being is a human agent, a doer, or actor. What kind of action, then, is situational being? It is my contention that this kind of "situationism" is not its own but is governed by the intentions of totality; that is to say, it is a form of totalistic participation requiring comprehension from above or from below the situation. Situational immediacy is thus the bearer of totality and its directives. One cannot simply add up the two terms of a situation in the principle of coresponsiveness and come up with the qualitative meaning of such situations. There is surplus meaning in such situations that involves the participation of totality in and through social forms. Put in different language, it means that before we can have social encounter, there must be social self-direction (not in the sense of superorganic directedness), such as purpose-bearing masses, purpose-bearing organizations, or purpose-bearing groups or parties. Social encounter presupposes social self-direction, even in the prior commitment of equating situationism with subjectivity. This is what Sartre denies in situational encounters. The alternative he chooses is directedness by totality, which the author relates to man's drive for wholeness or totalization.

Let us examine the subject of being that Sartre calls the situation. In Rossana Rossanda's interview with Sartre conducted in Rome in 1969, the author struggled with the paradox of spontaneity and institutionalism (or the party). In the resultant article, "The Risk of Spontaneity and the Logic of the Institution," Sartre remarks:

In sum, I have attempted to deal with such matters as mass, party, spontaneity, serialization, groups, etc., all of which represent a preliminary answer to this problem. What I attempted to show is that in relationship to the masses, the party is a necessary reality, insofar as the masses themselves do not have spontaneity. When the masses are left to themselves, they remain serialized. On the other hand, once the party becomes an institution, it invariably becomes, with minor exceptions, reactionary in relation to what it seeks to create or help develop, i.e., the fusion of the group. In other words, the contraposition of spontaneity and the party is a pseudo problem. In terms of self-consciousness, the working class does not appear to be homogeneous, but a conglomeration of elements and groups which ultimately become "fused."[8]

While the entire mass is not capable of situational spontaneity, affinity groups and various elements in society can experience this "first nature" or "primitive liberty." All it involves is a kind of primitive class consciousness. In the masses one may find serialization or massification. But here and there in the midst of the masses one may find a few "fusing groups," or situational immediacy. The relationship of reification and serialization among workers in the mass is quite common. In such cases they are "constantly other than themselves" because they are determined by others, managed instead of self-managed (the latter would be a case of situational immediacy). Sartre goes on to say:

Thus, we are confronted here with various forms of class consciousness. On the one hand, we have an advanced consciousness, while on the other, practically nonexistent consciousness, and between these, a series of mediations. It is for this reason that I think we cannot speak of class spontaneity. It is correct to speak only of groups produced by circumstances which create themselves according to particular situations. In this process, the groups do not regain some kind of profound spontaneity. They do, however, experience similar situations as a result of specific conditions of exploitation and specific wage demands. In so doing, they see themselves in a more or less correct perspective.[9]

Thus Sartre rejects the notion of mass immediacy and class immediacy, both of which lack this fusing identification with consciousness. And yet when he speaks of Czechoslovakia in his article, "The Socialism That Came in from the Cold," he thinks of that nation as having had a "first nature" because it was a fused nation—"socialism with a human face"—which, the author claims, "the string-pullers in Moscow, manipulated by their own manipulations," spoiled in the process of becoming.[10] In the

---

[8] Arthur Lothstein (ed.), *All We Are Saying* (New York, Putnam, 1970), 285.

[9] *Ibid.*, 286.

[10] Jean-Paul Sartre, "The Socialism That Came in from the Cold," *Evergreen* (November, 1970), 27–73.

process of becoming, then, we must allow for varying sizes and shapes of situations, even as large as national groupings, as being in possession of subjective being, or in possession of unitive, fusing, and streamish experience.

But this kind of subjectivity, shot through with feelingful awareness on the part of groups and situations in face-to-face encounters (social encounter), is meaningful as a form of direct social experience only if it can be shown that it is free from the intentions and directions of totality. Sartre does not succeed in demonstrating this. He is first a totalist, then a situationist, and last an individualist. But if it is the case that self-consciousness is not its own but belongs as a field to a system of dialectical totality, then how can it be the immediate defining characteristic of spontaneity as the source of human responsibility? If it can only be given direction by "resistance" in the given plenitude of being, and be the result of these "specific conditions" or "produced by circumstances," can it be the source of human directionality and shared responsibility? The complexity of the problem turns into an enigma when the author remarks, "It is correct to speak of groups produced by circumstances which create themselves according to particular situations." Is this statement close to Heidegger's "destiny that destines"? Or does the principle of coresponsibility, suggested by the two terms of the situation, indicate the workings of totality in the situation? For example, if Sartre is talking about "freedom in community," then there are many different models of this theme. Such freedom in situations is only one kind of freedom in community. There are also many models of totality, and each totality dictates the form and content of freedom in community or of situational spontaneity.

The Communist "party" as the vanguard of the revolution of totality is capable of such group fusing, of such organic linkages on the collective level, of saving the masses from serialization. Is this mediated immediacy? Is this manipulated spontaneity? Or is it simply the immediacy of action free of model-making, abstractions, and mediations? Although the party is more structured than the mass, it is capable of more spontaneity than the mass or class. That is the reason it has the function of being a vanguard. The function of vanguard, however, is mediational. How does this mediation relate to unmediated (immediate) experience in the form of spontaneousness? The party has problems fusing the masses because of its ever-increasing need to institutionalize itself in the form of a vanguard function. It is incapable of fusing the masses without corrupting them. It has an ambiguous role.

This is why the thinking of the fusing group which originated in the heat of a specific situation and which is not "spontaneous" has a stronger function, a much more critical and original function, than that of a structured group. The thinking and actions of groups reflect their structural makeup. Insofar as the party is an institution and its main concern is its own organization, it thinks as an institution and thus becomes removed from reality. It becomes an ideology and degenerates in the same way as does the experience of the struggle. On the other hand, the fusing group thinks about the experience as it occurs, without any institutionalized mediations.[11]

While Sartre is concerned to show the relation of situational groups to institutions or to external order, I have been concerned to show the relation of situational subjectivity to the orderings of totality. Totality, too, is external insofar as it states the case for the whole of existence from beyond human participation and from beyond the situations. The directives of such totality(s) impose upon man an even more stifling order than institutions. When the individual or the situation are identified in their interests with the intentions of totality, this is an inward imposition of external order; totality is both beyond the individual and the social situation.

Sartre sees the contradiction between spontaneity and institutionalization as being located in the heart of the party itself. To free the masses and give them guidance, the party must progressively become institutionalized or else it will fail in its function. Sartre's answer to this problem of "active mediation" in the midst of the serialized masses is to show the way "how to go beyond the contradiction inherent in the very nature of the party." In order to produce a unitive situation, the party would have to unite in its efforts both receptive and assertive roles—"become capable of receiving the impetus which originates from the movement, and instead of pretending to direct this impetus, it would interpret it both for its own benefit and for that of the movement."[12] The masses would have to match this effort by the upsurge of elemental responsibility by actually becoming the subject of collective action so they could feed the party (that would direct them) some sense of directiveness and shared responsibility.

If one reflects on the broader implications of Sartre's philosophy of social

[11] Lothstein, *op. cit.*, 287.
[12] *Ibid.*, 287.

encounter in and through situations, some issues and problems appear in clearer perspective. I shall enumerate three such critical areas.

First, Sartre's situationism implies that a philosophy of social encounter can give us unitive experience that is free of model-making and abstractions. Sartre's very language prepares the reader for this expectation. The situation, then, is the "For-itself's engagement in the world." That is precisely where freedom and action meet on the proving ground of facticity. That is also the place where human responsibility comes to light and offers its guidance. Such situations of immediate experience, where real choices are made, are not on the same level of consciousness. There are various forms of class consciousness in these contextual situations, all requiring varying stages of mediation to come to full consciousness and spontaneity. But the situation is where the action is. This would imply that purposive being—or the human orderer, as I have called him—is reduced to the level of action, engagement, and involvement. Sartre himself states the case for such a philosophy of direct encounter:

But if human reality is action, this means evidently that its determination to action is itself action. . . . The existence of the act implies its autonomy. . . . We shall never apprehend ourselves except as a choice in the making.[13]

In the light of my thesis, such a philosophy of direct encounter may be a myth because it presupposes a level of unmediated behavior with all sorts of covert forms of abstractions in it. Is it true that actions have their own given perspectives, their own intentions and goal-directedness? Can the subject of being be reduced to the subject of action? If such a move is advisable, it presupposes a purposive being in existence capable of self-direction in such intentional behavior, to whom such a reduction from being to action is an interesting game. Sartre does not provide for such a self-directing human orderer in existence. He stays on the level of goal-directedness with the subject and its projects in the world. It may well turn out to be that the autonomy or neutrality of action that Sartre supports may well be an illusion, like Husserl's autonomy of the *ratio* and its implicated transcendental, disinterested spectator. American linguistic philosophy, with its study of intentional acts, has adequately shown that action, unlike motion, is not its own, but that it needs a human agent as the self-performer of its actions to distinguish these from simple motions.

If we add to this the further alternative we have been developing—that

---

[13] Sartre, *Being and Nothingness*, 476–77, 479.

action belongs either to the human orderer in existence or to the orderings of a system of totality, with no middle ground of neutrality or autonomy presupposed—then the philosophy of social encounter is a dubious venture. For such spontaneous social action is at the mercy of a system of totality. Social subjectivity does not give us an adequate notion of the human orderer to be self-directing in its encounters. When such encounters are too direct they are at the mercy of the orderings of totality. What is interesting to note in Sartre's case is that actions are autonomous or neutral only with respect to the human orderer. They are not neutral with respect to the system of totality. The situations are implicated in the system of totality in the sense that their goal directions are sustained by the self-directives of totality. Situations are servants of totality. The autonomy of actions is thus an assumptive position because such self-making through choice-making already presupposes a purposive being, or the presence of a human orderer in self-direction, in choice-making. It is clear that Sartre does not take this alternative. He prefers to order human life by situations that already implicate the orderings of totality in human life.

Second, what clues does Sartre give us to indicate his leaning toward totalism? The evidence for unitive experience discovered in situations that reflect direct encounter is always dialectical. The method of dialectics is the servant of totality and a commitment to its immanent workings in and through situations. The dialectic is prior to purposive being in existence and serves the development of history. As Sartre views it: "True, thought is one, but its unity is dialectical. It is a living and developing reality."[14] It has the quality of a necessary historical process about it, and this quality gives the directives to the phenomenon of spontaneity in situations. Thus social encounter is not its own. It is dialectically ordered, even though it is believed to have its own social forms, its own inherent tensions and contradictions. Sartre believes that the dialectical tension which he sees in the party will eventually lead us back to Marx's developmental scheme for history, and this is free of ideology, as Marcuse earlier informed us. After all, what Sartre and Marx have in common is Hegel, the master dialectician. Neither does Sartre suspect that his situational totality may just be another model of the whole of existence, as were the models of Hegel and Marx. The belief that all three totalists were on the same track of totalization even Sartre would find hard to believe. Although the principle of permanent

[14] Lothstein, *op. cit.*, 299.

contradiction as the real mover of social encounter is present in all three writers, it is dialectically ordered by each model of totality.

Third, the paradoxical nature of the party has a permanent tension and contradiction in it. It is the interplay of spontaneity and institutionalism, receptive and assertive freedom. The party is instrumental to the dialectic that guides it in history. It is the tool of revolutionary struggle acted out on the plane of becoming. The party's participation, like all human participation in situations, is dialectically ordered. If this is the case, human responsibility has its source in totality. The lone subject self is responsible to the situations implicating totality, but it is not responsible for such total systems of responsibility. The role of the party is to overcome the massification of the masses, its tendency for massification and contentment with aggregateness. Its positive function is to fuse the masses into more intense unitive groups. It is thus the tool of mediation bringing about spontaneousness among the disparate elements, members, and groups in society. However, in performing the series of mediations among the masses, both the party and the masses have a higher commitment to totality as manifested dialectically in situations. The problem, which appears grave at this point, is the relation of becoming to action. The notion of developmental becoming involves both continuity and directedness. Actions, on the other hand, are always specific, whether they are personal or social in nature. If neither the party nor the masses are the "superadministrators" of their immediate life, then who is? The reply is that the orderings of totality through dialectical strategy gives the developmental process both its continuity and directedness. Everything appears to be done in the service of totality even in the philosophy of situationalism. Whether the party is a "dictatorship of the proletariat" or "the dictatorship for the proletariat" is a distinction that pales to insignificance when one senses a threat from a greater ordering power like the system of totality and its dialectical orderings of situations discussed above.

For Sartre, social spontaneity is a consciousness of totality committed to its situational manifestations. This is dialectical totality at work in situations with varying degrees of immediacy or forms of direct experience. Terms like "serialization" and "massification" mean either an unconscious state of affairs or manipulation by the other. There is an interesting contrast here with Freud, whose perspective equates immediate experience with the unconscious. For Sartre, consciousness develops in the matrix of situations where the dynamism of struggle is most intense. For intensity of experience to take place, the notion of *place* is central. The question uppermost in my mind is not the role of the party, but the role of totality in the situationally located revolutionary struggle. Put differently, who or what is responsible for the attainment of consciousness or its development, or the development of revolutionary consciousness, if the party and the mass are both instrumental to the guidance of a historical dialectic?

What I am questioning here is not only a consciousness of a direct state of affairs. I am also criticizing the notion of a direct state of affairs that a situation discloses, that perhaps this already implicates totality at work in some of its immanent forms. In the light of my theory, both direct consciousness and direct experience are already abstract labels for experience. If this is the case with personal experience, the mixture of abstractions with direct forms of immediate experience is multiplied to no end in collective forms of immediacy. Unless collective immediacy is inextricably bound to a series of social mediations, it is a myth. It is an illusion because social encounter, while it epitomizes movement and vitality, does not supply its own sense of directedness but borrows it either from the human orderer (in the case of culture, the social self-orderer) or from the directives of totality. We have dismissed the middle ground of neutral and autonomous social encounter for reasons mentioned above. Thus situationism, unitive as it appears in situations, shares in that larger principle of comprehension I have earlier called the system of totality. One may call it functional holism, a form of situational participation in existence of an immediate variety. This is more of a concern to us than the conflict between spontaneity and institutionalism, as between the mass and the party, or the conflict of a similar nature in the party itself, as Sartre conceives it. We are concerned with it because man's claims on responsibility cannot be established when its source has already been placed in a system of totality. Man is responsible for response-relations only because he is more than a responding creature in some system of totality. He is, in fact, responsible for such systems of responsibility.

Universal Dimensions of Social Spontaneity

If Sartre dealt with the notion of spontaneity situationally, he did so only to escape the notion of mass or class spontaneity. He preferred smaller groups to be the bearers of unitive experience. The case is otherwise with the universal pattern of social immediacy. Murray Bookchin, the anarcho-communist, would apply spontaneity universally to man's everyday life, beyond party, mass, and class. Universal spontaneity thus takes a more practical turn and is less pluralistic. However, its social equivalent is mass immediacy. It also takes a more unconscious turn in order to make more room for another pattern of dialectics to operate in experience. We have already mentioned Sartre's antipathy toward relating spontaneity to the unconscious. This is not a face-to-face relationship for Sartre. He does not want to make the unconscious responsible for things that consciousness ought to be responsible for. The psychoanalytic dialogue considers man as object, patient, as one not responsible. Man in this context is no longer a subject of being. Sartre, therefore, regards this view of man as being too passive and dependent. Spontaneity, for Sartre, is a confrontation, face to face, a joint enterprise with risks and choices made. Otherwise it is not an encounter-experience of an immediate variety.[15] We mention this in passing because the universal spontaneity of the anarchists takes a more unconscious turn, and it presents us with a challenge of a new and more naturalistic dialectic.

We have seen that dialectical spontaneity, or unity of experience, does for man what he cannot do for himself. It gives continuity and directionality to his becoming. Man can only react to its directed movement, however indirect and devious its course of development in history. This is the case because living dialectics is part of the elemental upsurge of history in its march through institutions and social forms. The dialectical method, feeding as it does on inherent conflicts in neocapitalist society, moves by its own pace to achieve a state of positive anarchy. It has control not only of modes of production, but also over man's everyday life. It has a holistic sweep.

Murray Bookchin, the editor of *Anarchos*, regards the Marxian vision of dialectical materialism (now outdated) as having been of service to its own era, as having supplied only the *preconditions* of the revolution of totality that Bookchin envisions. This necessitates placing the dialectical method in nature itself, which has its own ecological balance, movement, and directionality. His method does not absorb nature into history and economics, as did the Marxian view. What assures man of spontaneous living now is nature's mysterious balance and its goal-directedness. The choice facing modern man is between anarchy and annihilation, which, to

[15] Jean-Paul Sartre, "A Psychoanalytic Dialogue . . . ," *Ramparts* (October, 1969), 43–49.

Bookchin, is congruent with the "problems of freedom and life." These problems, the author contends, are reducible "to practical tasks that can be solved spontaneously by self-liberatory acts of society."[16]

I find similar problems on this social level of spontaneity to those above, and these can be summarized in the following way. How can society express the notions of self-management, self-activity, or *gestation*, if it is implicated in a system of dialectics set in the ecological balance of nature? If it is not its own, how can it practice self-management without being implicated in a wider system of naturalistic totality operating by dialectics of its own? All that Bookchin manages to be rid of is the notion of the human orderer, individually and socially. The concept of social encounter, or self-activity on the social plane, is either derived from the concept of social self-direction, from the human orderer, or from a scheme of naturalistic totality. Bookchin fuses the last two notions to make out a case for self-management. On the other hand, I believe that such self-action or self-performance, conceived either socially or personally, is an abstraction from the human orderer, individually or socially conceived. Self-action makes no sense unless it is postulated in some context of self-direction. The reason why there is so much confusion about the notion of subjective social encounter is that the theme of coresponsibility which it suggests implicates a larger system of totality or the orderings by totality.

Bookchin regards the revolutionary dialectic as "redemptive," and he believes it will usher in a healthy society through the work of the masses in combination with ecological cooperation of community, assemblage, and spontaneity. Authenticity will be achieved in and by affinity groups, which are "ecologically balanced communes." The driving force that will bring about such fulfillment is the unconscious Eros-derived impulse(s) in man and society. Man has an instinct, stiffled by society, for life, love, and freedom. The most naïve aspect of this theory is that individual self-seeking, social self-seeking, and nature's self-seeking are all on the same wavelength. This is the optimism which all anarchists share: that need will be transferred into desire, but that the sensuous life will be authenticating and the "lure of the marvelous" will be within reach of the new society. Primitivism is the answer to the complexity of the modern world. It is precisely this primitivism that is implicated in a system of ecological totality, which is a new way of talking about final purpose in nature on the part of social scientists.

[16] Lothstein, *op. cit.*, 350.

However, the miracle will take place only if the lines of communication are kept open on the level of direct experience tied to the practicality of everyday life. When this condition is achieved, man will reach a condition of spontaneous harmony based on the ecological balance present in nature itself. The goal of man is to be directed dialectically to nature itself, not only for sustenance but for directedness and authentication. Once the goal-direction to nature is established, the next move becomes rather obvious, namely, its implication in a system of totality. Schemes of holism are merely extreme manifestations, or ultimate goals, in a goal-directed life, whether it is individual or social. It is not the case that totality serves as the domain or base for goals, as the totalists in the history of thought have instructed us, and as Bookchin will try to convince us in terms of the new concept of ecology.

Just what is man's role in the ecosystem? According to Bookchin, man finds harmony with such a system when he tunes his emotional life into the equilibrium that makes up the structure of such a system. The first task of man is to rediscover his immediate being. The second is to view this discovery as a "rediscovery nourished by ecology" and supported by the revolutionary process in society. When Bookchin appeals to ecology, he is in essence pleading for an organismic situationism which implicates totality: "What ecology has shown is that in nature, balance is achieved by organic differentiation and complexity, not by homogeneity and simplification."[17] But such differentiation works only because it is on the plane of unitive and immediate experience. The differentiation thus has a base in unitive nature. In this system of totality, directedness by spontaneity is like that of "steering a boat." But the problem still remains: the boat does not steer itself, regardless of whether it is the human orderer or the orderings of totality that produces the healthy community of free and spontaneous persons. This is essentially a form of "freedom in community," held together by the dialectic of freedom and necessity, which are two sides of the coin of human experience. Bookchin does not suspect that this is only one model of human participation, and that the phrase "freedom in community" can be conceived in terms of other models. Once man is goal-directed toward nature to achieve freedom and meaning in life, there is no significant way of reclaiming the human orderer as the source of responsibility.

17 *Ibid.*, 351.

26

For Bookchin, the perspective of a spontaneous community based on nature's balance and steering provides an ebullient vision of society.

The community becomes a beautifully molded arena of life, a vitalized source of culture and a deeply personal, ever-nourishing source of human solidarity. From this point onward, the community ceases to be a structural concept and becomes a deeply human *process*—a process of communizing.[18]

However, what is important to any process philosophy is the relation of the part to the whole and not necessarily the reconstruction of the human orderer. An immediate relation to the whole is a way of submitting to the directives of totality in one way or another. Such piety exhibited toward the source of one's being, or of the community's being, is admirable. But Bookchin forgets to reflect on the issue that all questions of origin arise in man's purposive nature and presupposes a self-directing creature who is interested in origins and sources. Neither is he cognizant of the fact that cultural evolutionism, as a movement in anthropology, failed to establish a parallel relationship of lawfulness between nature and culture.

Bookchin is not content to leave it to nature to perform its wondrous works. He advocates the revolution of totality to help nature accomplish its goals on the societal level, to transform daily life into liberated activities. But what is the evidence that the revolution in all its totality is the same totality that nature exhibits in her balanced activities? Man is advised to "live" the revolution of totality, not merely to "participate" in it. This would indicate that the goal of every totalist is to make totalitarian claims on life because it is believed that the comprehensive world-view is not a model of existence but the real thing. Other than simply participating in existence, Bookchin never makes clear what that deeper kind of living means, unless he means to imply that making an identification between a model of existence and existence as existence is prior to human participation in existence.

What is the relationship of social spontaneity to the revolution? Social encounter, in terms of self-activity and self-management, provides not only the wind for the sails, the steam for the locomotive, but steering (implicating totality) to the revolution of totality. Moreover, social encounter of an immediate variety provides a decentralization of structure in community and provides a free assemblage of the masses to live a life of "indiscipline, spontaneity, radicalism, and freedom." In this kind of "freedom in com-

---

[18] *Ibid.*, 355.

munity," there is spontaneous shift in experience from the private to the social, a shift in experience from abstract institutionalism (as well as from the abstractions of social revolt) to everyday life. The practical is the domain of the immediate for this philosophy of universal social encounter. At the base of all these transformations is the belief in the autonomy and neutrality of action—the "work of spontaneous direct action" of the masses.

The Real Paradox

I have given a detailed account of three models of social subjectivity. They represent varying degrees of participation in the field of social encounter by social immediacy. The authors discussed held the common position that social encounter is free of mediation, abstraction, and model-making on the level of primitive experience. We criticized the perspective of social encounter through spontaneity as being incapable of giving us the source of shared responsibility because it was itself a form of derived directionality. To me, these are simply three models of social spontaneity. In the next chapter I shall mention the subjective model of participation which will have fewer references to the collective. We may view personal subjectivity and social subjectivity as two different models of participation in existence.

While the various authors agree on the nature of a model-free social spontaneity, such a direct form of immediate experience is not as unitive as they presupposed it to be. For Sartre, spontaneity is operative in small groups. For Marx, it is operative in classes. For Bookchin, it is operative in the masses and in nature. What is an experience of affinity and fusing for one writer is an experience of serialization and massification for another. This is tantamount to saying that the New Left has no common agreement as to the significance of spontaneity for the revolution of totality. Sartre questions its efficacy without party guidance. André Gorz believes that such immediacy is not enough either to sustain or guide a revolution. He refers to it as a "quasi-instantaneous act." He favors, along with Sartre, more theoretical steering by the party of the masses. His main point of criticism is that such immediate situations cannot be produced or repeated at will. Therefore, one cannot control the upsurge of revolutionary activity.[19]

What has the New Left disclosed about the linkage of spontaneity to

19 *Ibid.*, 340–42. (Gorz's article on "The Way Forward")

responsibility? One, that they are capable of responding to immediate experience, but they will not share responsibility for its directionality. Two, they exhibit a firm belief in social encounter free of abstractions and mediations. Three, they also assume that participation by social subjectivity is the same as the individual's subjective participation in experience, and that this analogy does not rest on abstractions and model-making.

In the light of my thesis, the real paradox of social spontaneity is that if the human orderer does not have claims on the source of shared responsibility, or if there is no significant social self-direction prior to social encounter in such immediate situations, then the controls for directing life pass over to some system of totality and its dialectical intentions. When this transfer of responsibility takes place (from the human orderer to some system of totality), man can only show *responsibility to* and not *responsibility for* human participation in existence. The paradox is not between spontaneity and outer institutional order, or between immediacy and the institutionalization of the party, but rather it resides in the fact that the more we emphasize self-expression the less control we have over life and its directives. The New Left has blended man with community to such an extent that even the notion of social self-expression does not extricate it from the problem, unless there is some meaningful notion of individual and social self-direction as a prior purposive commitment to life. If the living of life does not suffice as human participation in existence, spontaneous living will not improve upon it. What the New Left has experienced is the rejection of some external order for the orderings of totality inwardly conceived. But if such a totality is beyond human participation, even though inwardly conceived, we have a right to call it another external ordering of life rather than the misguided notion that somehow self-expression as the source of responsibility is the magic talisman for living.

R. Aronson and J. C. Cowley have other fears about the nature of spontaneity, which they conceive as the "process of self-creation," namely, how to develop a "socialist consciousness capable of directly challenging the existing intellectual and moral supremacy of liberalism. . . ."[20] Their fear is that immediate experience will blend in too much with the rationalism of the liberals and produce "ideological unanimity." The liberals have the directives of practical reason which may well absorb social spontaneity.

[20] *Ibid.*, 44.

This fear may be well based. But in the notion of "organic self-creation," the self-activity has little meaning because spontaneity itself is of a paradoxical nature. They fail to see that the model of the organism, like the model of a machine, is only man's way of understanding himself, rather than the way life sees itself through immediate experience. The machine model is a way of understanding ourselves externally. The organismic model is a way of understanding ourselves in terms of nature "from below" through the creativity of nature in us. The New Left presupposes that there are prior purposive commitments mediating such alleged organic immediacy.

The paradox of spontaneity cannot be solved in terms of theories of totality. We can only begin to fathom the problem concerning spontaneity if we postulate the prior status of purposive being and then read off spontaneity as a model of direct experience, which is a technique that man has developed in relating himself to nature by models of participation in existence. Spontaneity is too receptive a category to be used by aggressive radicals for assertive social encounters. In short, in itself it does not yield shared responsibility or the new norms for society. While it is expressive of vitality, it is itself in need of directionality.

It appears to be one of the ironies of history that at a time when a highly advanced technological society has rejected the importance of the subjective model of participation, the reactive New Left should hit upon social subjectivity to counteract the institutionalism of that society. If the subjective model of participation on the personal level has failed modern culture in being an adequate human orderer of life, what guarantee is there that social subjectivity will take its place and do a better job? Social subjectivity in the guise of a sociohuman orderer is thus a dubious notion if it is taken as the source of human responsibility. Moreover, if we add to this complication its commerce with totality(s), then it has replaced one form of order with another scheme of order even more mystifying than the one rejected. The radicals have rejected intellectual alienation from lived experience (of which our culture is guilty) and substituted for it emotional alienation not only from that society, but, more importantly, from the human orderer in existence. Hence the New Left is incapable of being responsible for the new way of life, but instead is responsible to it. That is to say, "autogestion" is a myth or a new form of hidden alienation.

In summary, it can be said that whereas some members of the New Left have questioned the efficacy of spontaneity as a guide to the revolution of totality, we have questioned it as a guide to life and, therefore, as the source of human responsibility. Perhaps the impotence experienced among the young comes directly from having placed such great reliance on the directives of immediacy. Social spontaneity may serve as a reservoir of energy but not as a guide to life. Such a flow of energy or élan is merely the raw material out of which man can build a sense of directionality that will give meaning to shared responsibility. People are not born into totality; neither are they born into immediate experience. This or that model of existence may make such demands upon man, but this perspective already assumes the work of purposive being and its participation in existence. Both spontaneous forms of immediate experience and systems of totality are ways of seeing ourselves in relation to life. Thus man is self-directing in personal and social encounters.

If it is the case that spontaneity cannot be the source of responsibility, then the call to "do one's own thing" is devoid of meaning because there is no ownership of directionality. The expression is more fitting for the language of things and objects. Social immediacy already points to the loss of ownership in directionality. Here one belongs to the medium of social encounter. As we have seen, even on the level of such social encounter the group is not its own unless it takes on the posture of a purpose-bearing (not only immediacy-bearing) role. Without either individual or social self-direction, the philosophy of social encounter, in the form of collective immediacy, becomes a spawning ground for an old breed of salmon—that of self-created systems of totality which usurp man's prerogatives for directionality in order to make totalitarian claims on life.

Youth is not the first group to be duped by the tyranny of totality(s) and its barrage of dialectics. Nor will they be the last, unless man finds a way to reclaim the human orderer in existence and thereby establishes his claims on responsibility. When spontaneity is not related to purposive being, human vitality is released without a sense of directionality and is ready for exploitation by totalists. Unless man takes responsibility for anthropologizing immediate experience in all its appearances, there is no way we can have a world that makes sense. "Doing one's own thing," admirable as it seems, makes no sense unless one takes the responsibility for the doing of it.

2. Some Popular Dimensions of Human Participation

Of central concern to us in this chapter is the problem of the *subject-object split* and the various attempts to resolve the problem. Each of the three models of participation discussed herein tries its hand at it, but the problem, nonetheless, seems insurmountable. However, the three models have something in common in their effort to solve the problem. First, all the models presuppose that a resolution of the split is both highly desirable and possible, and that it must be overcome because it is an intruding and uncomfortable bifurcation of man and the world. Second, they have in common the belief that the proper way to solve the problem will eventually lead one to reality or the whole of existence and thus to a better rapport with the world-totality because man as subject will have been more properly fitted into the whole of reality. Third, they also share a common belief that the split between the subject and object somehow concerns the issue of man's relation to the world, and that once this relationship is smoothed out man will be at peace with himself and also have an authentic existence in the world of totality. Thus all three models expend much effort in "going beyond" or "overcoming" the subject-object split.

Admirable as this ideal is, I am in strong disagreement with it. The basic reason for my disagreement is perhaps the realization that going beyond the split will lead to some undesirable system of totality which will prematurely restrict man's participation in existence, that man's search for wholeness and the world-totality itself will be confused by a limiting identification of the two in some scheme of totality. A better way to say it is that epistemological solutions to the split in terms of "overcoming" will lead man to some undesirable ontological commitment(s) to some system of totality(s). I think it is more desirable to proceed in the reverse direction. If man does not overcome the split in life, why should he bother to do so in his philosophies, especially if the effort at enlightenment leads away from the human orderer toward a system of totality? When the philosophers appreciate their mosaics more than life, the effort seems misguided.

The fact of the matter is that this effort may simply be the requirement of one's model of existence rather than of life itself. What I am suggesting is that the problem of the subject-object split is, first, man's problem before it becomes the problem of man's relation to the world. The relation of thought to experience is similarly man's problem first before it becomes that in his relation to the world.

Some reference to this problem and its possible solution was made in my book *The Promise and Peril of Human Purpose*,[1] on which I wish to elaborate more in this volume. Perhaps a new interaction with the three models of participation given below will help to make more explicit my new orientation of the reconsideration of the subject-object split. In the volume mentioned above, I defined man as the subject-object dialogue mediated by his purposive nature. This ontological interactionism is not meant as a unitive theory of man. It is meant more as a dialogical theory of man which depicts the human orderer as being self-directing in the matrix of participation in existence. As a human orderer, it is in fact true that man has a quest for wholeness, but he has this search for wholeness only because he is a creature of self-direction. Ontological self-direction is prior to man's drive for totalization or unitive experience. My criticism of totalists is that they sever their schemes of totality from man's search for wholeness.

Moreover, the above theory of man postulates that man is responsible for systems of responsibility and totality, that he is responsible even for those systems of totality which lead him beyond the subject-object split, as when they relate man to the world. By reconstructing man in a system of totality, totalists refuse to take responsibility for the wholes which they design; they wish only to make man obligated or responsible to such systems. In short, they refuse to take responsibility for the total relationship between man and the world which their philosophies postulate or project. In the remainder of this chapter I wish to consider three separate models of human participation which implicate the kind of totalism I am critical of. They are, respectively, the subjective model of participation, the objective, and the confluent models.

[1] William Horosz, *The Promise and Peril of Human Purpose* (St. Louis, Warren H. Green, 1970), 55–61.

THE SUBJECTIVE MODEL OF PARTICIPATION

This is a separate dimension of personal participation in existence from the model of social subjectivity which was considered in Chapter 1. I believe that they represent two levels of immediacy or, rather, models of direct experience. Both the phenomenology of existence and Marxism, as well as the New Left, disregard the distinction I am making between the two modes of participation. The subjective model of personal participation is replete with personal commitments, language of self-reference, and the freedom of self-possession, self-activity. It is assumed in this model of participation that the subject self has ontological priority to the object self and to the principle of objectification. This basic tenet prepares the thinker to derive objectivity from some center of subjectivity. But this involves the thinker in a rather curious procedure. In order to make the objectivity a parenthesis in the life of subjectivity, the thinker must first subjectivize objective phenomena and then reconstitute its objectivity subjectively. Michael Polanyi's system of subjective participation in personal knowledge is a good paradigm of such procedure. We shall examine some of the pivotal beliefs which are important to such a subjective model of human participation, which, according to the author, even the world of science cannot live without.

In order to solve the subject-object split, Polanyi first relates the world of objective science to the human dimension that is deeply personal and subjective and then absorbs both in a system of subjective totality. Polanyi says that human participation is "a personal component, inarticulate and passionate, which declares our standards of values, drives us to fulfill them and judges our performance by these self-set standards."[2] The author calls this "unformulated knowledge," where we know things "tacitly" and where we are conscious of ourselves as upholding explicit objective knowledge. This is obviously an affinity that Polanyi shares both with William James and Husserl as to the importance of vague and marginal knowledge, both for living and as a foundation for theoretical activities and accomplishments. Polanyi considers the subjective participation of the knower in shaping objective knowledge as a positive asset to science and to other kinds of explicit knowledge, even though he admits the possibility that it may possibly impair the notion of objectivity.[3]

[2] Michael Polanyi, *Personal Knowledge* (Chicago, Chicago University Press, 1958), 195.

What is important to note is that subjectivity, even in this vague feeling for participation in understanding, is nonetheless the standard for participation and the standard for knowledge. However, in order to give some credence to this position, the author hastens to make a distinction between the *subjective* and *personal*. This distinction prepares the way for a consideration of the objective in the domain of subjectivity, as Polanyi conceives of the problem:

> This view entails a decisive change in our ideal of knowledge. The participation of the knower in shaping his knowledge, which had hitherto been tolerated only as a flaw—a shortcoming to be eliminated from perfect knowledge—is now recognized as the true guide and master of our cognitive powers. We acknowledge now that our powers of knowing operate widely without causing us to utter any explicit statements; and that even when they do issue in an utterance, this is used merely as an instrument for enlarging the range of the tacit powers that originated it. The ideal of a knowledge embodied in strictly impersonal statements now appears self-contradictory, meaningless, a fit subject for ridicule. We must learn to accept as our ideal a knowledge that is manifestly personal.
>
> Such a position is obviously difficult; for we seem to define here as knowledge something that we could determine at will, as we think fit. I have wrestled with this objection in a volume entitled *Personal Knowledge*. There I have argued that personal knowledge is fully determined, provided that it is pursued with unwavering universal intent. I have expounded the belief that the capacity of our minds to make contact with reality and the intellectual passion which impels us towards this contact will always suffice so to guide our personal judgment that it will achieve the full measure of truth that lies within the scope of our particular calling.[4]

The personal, then, is to be correlated with reason's capacity to universalize within the commitment situation. The *personal*, Polanyi tells us, intends the universal, whereas the subjective is merely a matter of private conviction. Such a personal commitment is more than the "subjective choice of values" that Carl Rogers alludes to before the use of scientific method is operative, for the commitment establishes the very validity of impersonal, universal, and objective standard in science.[5] What Polanyi appears to be saying is that the psychology of the scientist is essential for establishing the validity of objectivity in science. Most scientists would

[3] Michael Polanyi, *The Study of Man* (Chicago, Chicago University Press, 1965), 12–13.

[4] *Ibid.*, 26–27.

[5] Polanyi, *Personal Knowledge*, 302.

35

object to this, saying that objectivity is established by social rules, by the rules of the game scientists play. In short, they would refuse to derive objectivity and its validity from the domain of subjectivity because science, at its ideal best, has the goal of achieving presubjective knowledge. However, what is central to Polanyi's perspective is the notion of a situational commitment and the pursuit "with unwavering universal intent" of that commitment.

What is Polanyi's notion of the human orderer who participates in existence through the acts and the medium of the understanding? Michael Novak has coined the phrase "intelligent subjectivity" for this subjective knower who participates in existence. To answer the question we must make reference to Polanyi's "ontology of commitment." It begins with the notion of "selfless subjectivity," which in turn splits up into the lower self, or the subject of private convictions, and the higher self with its outreach of universal intent. The knower as a participating person is motivated by beliefs, by self-compulsion, by commitment, and also directed by self-set ideals. There is a certain burden of responsibility placed upon the subject of understanding in the act of understanding in the framework of commitment that is difficult to decipher in Polanyi's writings. But such is the source of human participation and its yield of responsibility. Moreover, since the personal and the universal are correlative terms of unitive experience arising simultaneously from an "antecedent state of selfless subjectivity," it is difficult to decide whether it is subjectivity that has universal intent or the mind that possesses it. Nonetheless, such participation is self-transcending and universal in intent. It provides the framework for more abstract and objective systems of knowledge. There is a self-seeking on the part of the subject of the acts of understanding (*Verstehen*) that is somehow prior to man's ontological capacity for self-direction. It is that self-seeker, in self-possession of its mind, that participates in existence and contributes to the meaning of scientific knowledge.

To see the contributions of the human orderer through the matrix of participation in existence simply in terms of the focus of "personal knowledge" is a rather restricting view of the human orderer and his role in life. That it functions by self-set ideals, and is driven in this by self-compulsion in a structured framework of an ontology of commitment, does not speak highly of the human orderer. Such a passionate ordering of life or of science by the person knowing what is being known simply gives us the image of a human orderer passionately goal-directed toward truth and the achievements of knowledge in a framework of commitment, compulsion, and emotion. One can only be responsible to such participation, but not responsible for it. The source of human responsibility can only be the process of evolution and historical development. For the subject self is not his own even as a passionate knower of things known. The subject self is goal-directed toward nature and exercises its passion for understanding in varying stages of commitment. Is personal commitment with an aura of self-compulsion a satisfactory model of the human orderer?

Polanyi gives an extended treatment of subjective participation by personal knowledge in the perspective of commitment. The gist of these theories of commitment appears to be the self-assertion of universal intent by intelligent subjectivity, and "the universal is constituted by being accepted as the impersonal term of this personal commitment."[6] Is this a way of talking about objectivity in the domain of subjectivity? Is it the acceptable standard for judging objectivity? Most scientists would object to this and say that private conviction, however universal in its intent, cannot be the standard of public scientific truth. Polanyi, however, believes that he has come up with the proper balance of freedom and necessity in the person who feels the responsibility "to act as he must."[7] We act as we believe we must, the author contends. Yet he has no satisfactory theory of responsibility in accounting for such a "responsible person" who views truth as a matter of self-compulsion.

Several critical remarks are in order. One, the concept of self-compulsion is still compulsion, the compulsion of a feelingful subject. And the whole point about feelings is that we are not responsible for them. Is intelligent subjectivity responsible for its goal-directions, for its commitments? Obviously not. The understanding owes its vitality to the subject self and the latter is emergent from nature and history. The sense of responsibility that a subjective participant knower has in his activities is thus a derived kind of responsibility. He is responsible to, but not responsible for, the truth and for a sense of direction. In the light of our perspective, terms like "self-compulsion" and "self-seeking" are abstractions from man's ontological capacity to be self-directing in existence. Purposes are not the end results of intelligent subjectivity. Man's purposive nature is what makes intelligent subjectivity operative in life.

Two, Polanyi's ontological structure of commitment is a way of holding

[6] *Ibid.*, 308.
[7] *Ibid.*, 309.

on tenaciously to the goals of the subject self in situations of knowledge. It presupposes a meaningful human orderer and is the end result of onto-logical self-direction in existence, just as our beliefs and actions presuppose it. The author's own procedure in attempting to justify explicit knowledge and scientific knowledge in the domain of subjectivity, by tacit personal knowledge, exhibits the kind of purposiveness that I have been emphasiz-ing and for which his theory cannot account. Commitment cannot be placed prior to purposive being that is self-directing in life because it is a form of fixed goal-direction with overtones of tenacity. Commitment is posterior to purposive being as self-directing even in its dogmatic versions. It presupposes man's moves in self-direction.

Three, it is of interest to note that the same starting point in the sub-jective *ratio* leads Edmund Husserl to the transcendental realm of detach-ment from life where the disinterested spectator plays a prime role in the attainment of universal knowledge through universal self-responsibility; it leads him to another world of totality. The same subjective *ratio* leads Polanyi to situational commitment in the attainment of universal knowl-edge, also by self-set ideals and universal intent. Both finally disregard the human orderer for a system of totality that orders man. What legitimate standard do we have for these two different points of departure from the domain of intelligent subjectivity with its fuzzy personal knowledge? It is a well-known fact that Husserl was very much dissatisfied with Dilthey's *Lebensphilosophie*, which Polanyi had a high regard for. Husserl is proud of the fact that he dismissed the human person for the transcendental spectator, and Polanyi is still looking for "the missing human person." The "science of understanding," however great, does not yield the human orderer as a real participant in existence.

Four, Polanyi believes that if science cannot produce an adequate notion of the human orderer by its objectivating methods, because of its detach-ment from life and its disinterestedness in personal knowledge, the sub-jective knower as a participant in existence can produce an adequate view of man in the pursuit of knowledge. One of the assumptions is that the object self is abstract and artificial when severed from personal knowledge and intelligent subjectivity. This is not the case, however, of the partici-pant as subjective knower. He is the real human orderer in existence be-cause of his level of emergence in evolutionary development. The very fact that Polanyi reduces objectivity to the personal domain indicates that he regards the subjective model of participation as "real participation" and scientific participation as something abstract. This position leaves the subject-object split at a stage of conflict which very few practicing scientists would accept. One need not reduce the ideal of objectivity to its proper subjective size in personal knowledge in order to make peace with science or to broaden the scientist's perspective of his own work. This is still a form of apologetics which favors the subjective domain of personal experience and personal knowledge to that of science. Moreover, Polanyi never makes clear how he goes from personal "universal intent" to objective reality without simply winding up with a reality constituted by subjectivity.

Five, perhaps if Polanyi had made the distinction between the "makings of science" and the "uses of science" he could have saved himself needless trouble. Part of what he has to say about science in the context of the "appreciative consciousness" has more to do with the uses of science than with the makings of it. But making such a distinction was not his intention, which was to reduce the domain of objectivity to an abstract model of participation and then to incorporate it into the real domain of the subjective. Personal knowledge is the use we make of scientific knowledge, rather than a concern with the makings of science.

Six, my main objection to the subjective model of participation is that Polanyi does not regard it as a model. He thinks it is the real domain of personhood interacting with existence. However, if it is assumed that man is a subject-object dialogue mediated by his purposive nature, as this volume presupposes, then subjectivity is as much a way of looking at ourselves, even through our feelings and our participations, than is objectivity as a model. Both require the mediation of purposive being through its capacity for self-direction respectively through acts of self-subjectification and through acts of self-objectification. The whole point of the history of thought is that thinkers have spent as much time on constructing and reconstructing selfhood in terms of subjectivity and personal knowledge as they have constructing and reconstructing the object self into selfhood. Neither is less human than the other, nor is one more real than the other. They are both models of human participation in existence. Polanyi believes that it is only the subject self and its inner direct access to personal knowledge that is privileged to know the "firmament of universal obligation," from which the object self is barred. The fact is that each has a perspectival view of this "firmament of universal obligation." But this requires another theory of the human orderer utilizing both modes of participation, which we shall develop in Part Two.

Seven, if the subject self is a model of the human orderer, how adequate is it as a model to guide man in his understanding of himself and the world? Polanyi believes that the subject self is adequate to be the master of human participation, that through its inner access to personal knowledge it is adequate to master more explicit and objective kinds of knowledge. I have my reservations about this belief for various reasons—principally, that it cannot function as a gathering focus for all its elemental modes of response to existence. It has failed our highly technological society by being too inward and retiring in its actions of self-determination. Now I am suggesting it has also failed us inwardly by not being able to function as the gathering focus for all its elemental modes of response to experience. Such responses as will, self-determination, appreciation, commitment, faith, imagination, spontaneity, spirit, and self-transcendence have no adequate orderer on the level of subjectivity. Such an ordering self is as weak on the inside as it is on the outside. If that is the case, then any attempt to "anthropologize" the sciences will turn out to be ineffectual.

Now, for the main elemental response that has been the aspirant to the throne of being the human orderer, man's quest for identity, wholeness, unitive experience, totalization—what are we to say of this response in subjectivity in terms of the human orderer? The reply is that it is only one elemental mode of response among others, that it has been hypostatized, and this abstraction has served as man's greatest guide in personal and social living. But one cannot identify the unitive self with all its elemental modes of response. It can only function as their orderer or director. The whole self is still too emotional to be an adequate guide of man in the quest for unitive experience. What is more, the whole self is not its own in such unitive experience; it is a partial-totality in a larger totality in which the logic of relatedness dominates the subject self.

What is at stake here is whether the whole self or the self-directing self should be given primacy in guiding man. Which is master of the self? Which is the proper gathering focus for all the elemental modes of response, not counting simple motions and physiological reactions as part of the theme? Who or what transforms, transfigures, or orders man's elemental modes of response into meaningful structures and provides the guidance for his being, acts, and thoughts? The model of the subject self has suggested unitive participation or wholeness as the answer. But the subject self is not its own. It needs a larger self to be a partial-whole itself. It is my contention that man's ontological capacity for self-direction (purposive being) is a more vigorous guide than the quest for identity. The choice is rather limited here. Either we absorb man in a system of totality through the quest for identity, or we make of man a human orderer in the matrix of participation where personal being and world meet.

In defining man as the subject-object dialogue mediated by his purposive nature, and regarding both the subject and object selves as models of unified selfhood, I wish to point out the same deficiency in the subject self as Polanyi pointed to in the object self. How does one conceive of man as a human orderer? Answers to this question have always turned out to be models or images of man in the history of thought. Then why persist in fighting the battle, whether my model or someone else's is real or abstract? The very quest is a process of model-making. One cannot go from one's model or from model-making to lived experience unless one has hypostatized his model of man and identified it with man *qua* man. The purposive model of the human orderer remains a model that is the source of such model-making. It is not to be identified with human nature itself. We move next to the objective model of human participation. Here we hope to find the same thing: how man is a model-maker in the matrix of participation when he takes a look at human nature through more objectivating procedures. This image of man likewise has the imprint on it of having been anthropologized by the very process of human participation in existence.

The Objective Model of Human Participation

The objective model of man is as much a matter of participation in existence as is its correlate discussed above. Thus to say that it is a totally nonparticipatory view of life, the attitude of detachment and disinterestedness, is only true with respect to the subjective model of participation because the goal of objectivating science is presubjective knowledge. To distort this ideal of scientific objectivity by making the subject self and its personal knowledge master of objectivating procedures in science is, I believe, to miss the point. In his own way, through acts of self-objectifications, man has tapped another dimension of human participation yielding important objective knowledge about this side of human life. The movement of participation, in one sense, is similar; it is an act of self-objectification, just as in the subjective model it is an act of self-subjectification. But the parallel between the two models ends precisely at the starting point, namely, that the human orderer practices both kinds of creativity in the attainment of knowledge and of participation in existence. The movement of participation appears to be in the reverse situation from the subjective model. It goes from the phenomena toward the human orderer, once the process of self-objectification is started and scientific procedures are used. The objectivists deliberately decides to be detached in such a situation, to learn something both from the method of obtaining knowledge and from the phenomena itself. There are parallels to such objectivating procedures even in phenomenology, where there is new respect for the thing itself as revealed in the undistorted phenomena.

But the detachment of the object self is only detachment from the subject self for certain deliberate reasons. This does not give supremacy to the subject self in its personal knowledge over the more explicit objectivating knowledge. I have called it "positive, deliberate, or purposive alienation" in *The Promise and Peril of Human Purpose*. This is a scientific use of the human orderer rather than a subjective use of the human orderer, as Polanyi believes. The vital issue between methodology and subject matter in empirical knowledge, important as it is, is more of a family quarrel and does not concern us at the moment. Moreover, I have touched on this matter in an article, "Is There a Third Alternative to Knowledge?"[8]

George Herbert Mead is the paradigm we shall use in this case because he represents "social behaviorism" representing a form of "connective realism" that utilizes objectivating procedures in a maximal way. While these models of participation, like Mead's view of social objectivism, are merely samples taken at random, the reason for choosing Mead was to have a contrast to Chapter 1 and the model of participation called social subjectivity. Mead could as easily be used as an example of the confluent model of participation which is our next consideration. I choose to treat him in this context only to have a contrast with Chapter 1. He is as good an objectivist as any other in the field.

The reverse case takes place in Mead's philosophy of social behaviorism concerning the subject-object split. Here it is the subject self that is absorbed by the objective domain and is given a parenthetical life therein. Since the goal is to avoid subjectivity and personal knowledge by rooting these in the domain of social behaviorism, it is almost impossible to separate subjectivity from its ground in social objectivism. Such a result is a deliberate

[8] William Horosz, "Is There a Third Alternative To Knowledge?" *Philosophy and Phenomenological Research* (December, 1970), 273–81.

calculation, or positive alienation, on the part of Mead or any other objectivist. By the time Mead explicates something that resembles subjectivity—the concepts of internalization and reflexiveness—one begins to wonder what the line is between the subjective figure and its ground in such a philosophy of transactionalism, which we shall treat more extensively when we consider the theme of the confluent model.

As any empirical thinker would be, Mead had a great interest in the whole of nature as accounting for matter and spirit, object and subject. He was fascinated with the evolving aspects of nature culminating in society. He viewed the relation of society to nature as being objective, as having cosmic dimensions, and as a social emergent that was prior to the self. The self was merely a responding phenomenon to social behaviorism through a process of interaction. What counts in this relationship of participation is man's "response" to the objective conditions of nature and society and not the fact that man is a human orderer by his participation in it. As Mead himself remarks:

The intelligence that is involved in perception [a form of participation] is elaborated enormously in what we call "thought." One perceives an object in terms of his response to it. . . . It is true of all of our experience that it is the response that interprets to us what comes to us in the stimulus, and it is such attention which makes the percept out of what we call "sensation." The interpretation of the response is what gives the content to it.[9]

Such a response is a joint product of an interaction between man and his environment and not specifically the work of the human orderer in the social encounter with its structures of objective conditions. The response is literally the instructor of the human orderer in the matrix of social objectivism. It is fair to ask, who or what is the ordering factor of such a response? The reply that it is a product of joint interaction is rather insignificant if it is the case that such situational interactionism implicates a system of naturalistic totality. If the latter is taken seriously, then it is nature as a totality that discloses its directives socially to man, and the human orderer is left in the cold because he can only interpret the response. This means he can only be responsible to it, not for it, and we have our schizoid responsible self all over again. The notion of the "responder" is not yet the human orderer. It is not clear in Mead's writings how nature or society as an emergent from nature is responsible for human response-

[9] Floyd W. Matson, *The Broken Image* (Garden City, N.Y., Doubleday, 1966), 310.

relations. Mead simply says that the relational activities in social behavior-ism are in fact the readjustments of the process of emergence socially disclosed.

Human participation in existence is either reduced to such primal inter-actions, or it is the highest level of interaction, as in Dewey's writings. Social behavioral participation is first activated by the nature-society totality and then sustained by their relations and interchanges of experience. This would give the priority to social objectivism even in the context of human participation. In this context, subjective experiences are absorbed and held to a minimal confrontation. Mead tells us that even the subject-object distinction derives from that natural-social complex:

There are, then, two assumptions involved in such intelligibility: (1) that events in their passage are determined, although the degree of this determination is not fixed by this assumption; and (2) that in so far as the determining conditions are given, the character of later events is also given. . . . But while there is in all passage determination—in abstract phraseology the carrying on of relations— there is also the indeterminateness of what occurs. There is always qualitative difference in passage, as well as identity of relation extending through passage. The "what" that is occurring is given in this relational aspect only. In this lies the rationality of all experience, and the source of symbolism. It is here also that we find the fundamental distinction between the objective and subjective phases of experience. The carrying on of relations is objective. The anticipated quali-tative "what" that will occur is subjective. Its locus is mind. Here we find the second sort of giveness—that which belongs to later events. In so far as the relations in the passage are there in experience they pass in their identity into further events, but the "what" that will occur is only symbolically present. And the indeterminate "what" involves always a possible new situation with a new complex of relationships. The givenness of later events is then the extension of the structure of relations found in experience. . . .[10]

In going beyond the subject-object split to a system of socionatural to-tality to resolve the problem, Mead is more concerned to show a solution to the problem in man's relation to the world. It is only secondarily that the subject-object split is a problem for man himself (as I remarked at the beginning of this chapter). Mead is thus willing to naturalize and socialize human participation in existence, but as a social objectivist (with a built-in grudge against personal knowledge), Mead refuses to anthropologize hu-man participation. There is a remarkable paradox to this procedure among the behaviorists, as Floyd W. Matson reminds us:

[10] George H. Mead, *The Philosophy of the Present*, ed. by A. E. Murphy (Chicago, Open Court, 1932), 96–97.

44

On the one hand they are seldom reluctant to attribute to human behavior the mechanisms and automatisms found in the study of nonhuman subjects, whether rodents or robots; on the other hand they are almost obsessively concerned over the error of imputing "anthropomorphic" tendencies to any organisms whatsoever—including human organisms.[11]

If man remains only an interpreter of his responses to the directives of a socionatural totality situationally and behavioristically manifest in the world, we are far from the human orderer that we wish to recover from its submerged status in systems of totality. The fact is that we antropologize both subjective and objective modes of human participation; otherwise, they would not be human. My whole concern with the "crisis of responsibility" is to show that if it is to be operative at all, it needs some minimal notion of a human orderer; otherwise, there is neither questioner nor questionings, neither an answerer nor answerings.

Mead seems unaware of the fact that any philosophy of social encounter, whether it is by the New Left or social behaviorism, presupposes, on the social level of encounter, social self-direction by some purpose-bearing groups. Mead simply ignores this creative element in society, which is a prior socially purposive function of society to given patterns of roles, rules, and relations. While the latter is more amenable to scientific inquiry, the former is also real and operative in society. If there is no social self-direction to social behavior, then social behavior is directed by a system of totality, which appears to be the case in Mead's writings. The same applies to the individual in confronting his roles in society, for he is more than a function of his roles. In that case we make reference to man's purposive being that is present in self-direction before internalization and reflexivity can be operative in the interaction between the organism and its environment. But Mead is not concerned with this problem in his design of the objective model of participation. He shows how man is responsible to his own and social encounter, but he has no way of demonstrating how man can be responsible, either individually or socially, for such encounters. Before society can behaviorally manipulate, exploit, or genuinely move man as an individual, it must itself be socially self-directing in such designs of controlling man and his community. Otherwise, we have on our hands the control of human behavior, the planned society of Burrhus F. Skinner, who has not only discarded purpose, as Watson's behaviorism had done, but is now prepared to discard the notion of human responsibility along with

[11] Matson, *op. cit.*, 55.

purpose.[12] To be sure, Mead's system is some improvement over classical behaviorism because he at least provides for external purposes and responsibilities that somehow can be legitimately internalized and used by the individual. However, Mead cannot show positive concern for human responsibility because he has placed the solution for the subject-object split into a socionatural totality. Because of his basic orientation his primal concern is to derive from the domain of objectivity whatever remains there are of subjectivity in his social behaviorism. This apparent need may simply be the requirement of the objective model of participation and not the demand of life.

Perhaps the best way to state the case for "participation" in such a philosophy of social encounter as Mead's is to discuss the theme of the "participant observer" in the dimension of the present. Objective participation is accomplished through the role of the participant observer. Many claim, and I agree with their perspective, that Mead's behaviorism is a perspective that goes beyond strict behaviorism of the simple stimulus-response variety, and some, like Maurice Natanson, believe that it even transcends such behaviorism. Nonetheless, it is insufficient to account for the human orderer and his capacity to anthropologize the process of participation. While I sympathize with this more dynamic kind of inter-relatedness in the context of the part-to-whole relationship, I am dissatisfied in stating the case of the human orderer and his participation in existence in the logic of the part-to-the whole. Such functionalism is adequate to define the role of the part, but not that of the human orderer.

Mead assigns to man the role of actor or agent. The part plays its role magnanimously, for it is creative, active, and selective in such interchange with the whole. But it remains a "part" in the present, where all reality is to be found. Mead's thesis that "reality exists in a present" signifies that man remains a "part" in the present, and that is his sole reality in the matrix of transactional totality. I agree, then, that Mead is an improvement over early statements of strict behaviorism, but this is not enough. His problem in defining participation is to provide a significant difference between reaction and response. The problem I am attempting to define in

[12] "A Symposium," *Science*, Vol. CXXIV (November 30, 1956). In the debate on the control of human behavior with Carl R. Rogers, Skinner indicated that human responsibility was an obsolete human experience to be superceded by the notion of "control," and indicated that it was no longer a meaningful term in our government's dealings with its citizens.

this volume is to state the significant difference between man as responder and man as ontologically self-directing in existence (my definition of the human orderer).

Polanyi and Floyd Matson are certain that Mead's "participant observer" is out to vindicate the cause of the subject self and his personal knowledge. But this is a mistaken interpretation of Mead. He uses the subject self as a contribution to the whole of experience, which is synonymous with objectivity or its transactional ground. Once an experience is established as truly interactive, it is believed to be objective. Mead's interest in the self is to define his "part-participation" in the matrix of social behaviorism. The goal is to achieve unitive experience that is objective in nature. The attempt to understand the "behaver" is not to understand him on his own terms, as Matson believes, but to appraise his part-contribution to the wholeness of experience.[13] Creativity does not come from the human orderer in the present; it comes from the interaction. I shall discuss this point in more detail when I touch upon the confluent model of participation.

The present, for Mead, is the moving stream of social reality. Society, then, is nature's emergent field of interaction in the present. As Natason remarks, "Sociality in Mead means both the objective existence of multiple perspectives in which organisms have simultaneous membership and the emergent character of the present, understood as the locus of reality."[14] The individual as the part-participant in the present social milieu is merely "an eddy in the social current and so still a part of the current." The I-process is merely a reactive phenomenon to the stream of social life and knows itself only as it reflects itself in the social "me." If it has any real contributions to make to the situation, it is on the level of immediate experience, where the "me" operates and where the mystery of time in the present reveals its living current of directionality.

On the level of the social act, subjectivity is seen in terms of the "generalized other." It can only exist in terms of other selves in an objective matrix. The social is the bearer of the directives of totality in the present. The self can find authentication for itself only by immersing itself in that objective stream. What this amounts to is that Mead prefers the directives of totality, to which the part-participant is adapted, rather than a strong sense of the human orderer, both individual and social, that anthropolo-

[13] Matson, *op. cit.*, 171–75.
[14] Maurice Natanson, "George H. Mead's Metaphysic of Time," *The Journal of Philosophy* (December 3, 1953), 776.

gizes the stream of participation. However, since many of these problems of the objective model of participation shade off into the confluent, we shall turn to this perspective in the writings of John Dewey and touch on some of the issues raised here in the pages that follow.

THE CONFLUENT MODEL OF PARTICIPATION

There is one passage in John Dewey's *Art As Experience* that maps out both man's dependence and possibilities in the context of interactional participation. The passage appears at the beginning of the book:

Experience is the result, the sign, and the reward of that interaction of organism and environment which, when it is carried to the full, is a transformation of interaction into participation and communication.[15]

The word which best describes such participation in interaction, which Dewey views as "a ground-plan," is the term "confluence." He admired William James, as much as he admired his term, because both introduced him to the experience of "joint participation," to the theory of the "mutual determination of form or organism and the environment," which I shall call the principle of "coresponsibility," having its base in "coparticipation." What is the bearer of directionality or life's meaning is the wholeness of such experiences, and not the human orderer.

Dewey's favorite term for the human orderer, if there be such a one, is the "live creature." The live creature shares with other living creatures the signal honor of being a vital part of the ongoingness of life with its search for unitive experience. The intellectual and purposive achievements of man are of secondary importance to the perceptual unitive experiences of the live creature enmeshed in the stream of experience. The passage cited above indicates the fact that human participation, while it may be the highest level of action and reaction, is nonetheless still within the confines of immediate interactions between the organism and the environment. Man simply makes better adjustments in transactionalism than do other animals, and thus he makes a greater contribution to such interaction in its search for unitive experience.

What is at stake here is Dewey's insistence on relating the live creature to a system of socionatural totality, rather than relating him to the human orderer whose purposes lead man to find the fulfillment of his life in the realm of immediate experience. The gateway and directionality to such

[15] John Dewey, *Art As Experience* (New York, Minton, Balch, 1934), 22.

interactive experience is sensation, not human purposes. In solving other dualisms, Dewey created other forms of dualisms, like the competition between sensory and purposive directives. But Dewey has no concern for this problem because he is totally preoccupied with the problem of relating sensation to reason:

The senses are the organs through which the live creature participates directly in the ongoings of the world about him. In this participation the varied wonder and splendor of this world are made actual for him in the qualities he experiences. This material cannot be opposed to action, for motor apparatus and "will" itself are the means by which this participation is carried on and directed. It cannot be opposed to "intellect," for mind is the means by which participation is rendered fruitful through sense; by which meanings and values are extracted, retained, and put to further service in the intercourse of the live creature with his surroundings.[16]

Dewey is obviously contending with the view of the human orderer where reason is the master of the self and rules the live creature from above. His great dissatisfaction with past views of the human orderer have led him to deny the possibility of reconstructing another model of the human orderer. Having despaired of such, he decided to immerse man in a stream of real immediate experience, to enable him to function in a system of socionatural totality as part of unitive experience that bears the directives of totality.

Life goes on, true, but it may not move because of Dewey's theory about life. That such movement on the part of the live creature has a certain directionality is only a theory about life's ongoing process. In short, a processive reading of life is itself a model of existence, not to be identified with life as life. Once the problem is put this way, it is necessary to make a distinction between a model about the ongoingness of life and the ongoingness itself. Dewey makes no such distinction. He offers us another totalistic scheme of life which he identifies with the ongoingness of life itself and gives its interactional content. The fact that he blends or identifies the two, the model and life, on the plane of immediate experience, where all sorts of hidden mediations are allowed on the plane of unmediated experience, is not surprising. Every totalist in history has played the same game. Because immediate experience is unjustified experience, such mediations are permitted. But if all totalists play the same game, then all mediations are indiscriminately permitted.

---

[16] *Ibid.*, 22.

Because Dewey is unmindful of the distinction between a model of existence and existence *qua* existence, it is necessary to examine the claims of transactionalism which serves as a foundation for human participation. Absorbing the human orderer in a system of totality where man is goal-directed to nature is bad enough, but to claim then that this is not a model of existence, but rather the way the universe of cosmic reality itself works, is rather presumptuous. My efforts in this section are to show how transactionalism and its principle of coresponsibility or mutual determination by joint participation is, in effect, a model of existence. The best way to introduce the issue is with Dewey's article, "The Reflex Arc Concept of Psychology" (1896), which is a dominant perspective in his philosophy.

Dewey's main concern in this article is to point out the continuity on the level of immediate experience between stimulus and response, suggesting perhaps that the two terms have meaning only in terms of unitive immediate experience. He prefers the term "circuit," which suggests an organic connection rather than a simple "reflex." Obviously, his plan is to treat these notions as functional terms in a unitive transaction. For one to talk about responses, one does not have to assume a responder or a human orderer outside the unitive and streamish experience. Moreover, the two terms are flexible and interchangeable in the dynamics of immediacy. Thus they are "distinctions of flexible function only, not of fixed existence. . . ."[17] In fact, one need not even postulate the notion of a human agent for such immediate action and reaction. The functions reveal all there is about the human situation in such contexts, for Dewey's interest in man is that of a part-contributor to unitive experience with its structure of objective inter-actionism:

To sum up: the distinction of sensation and movement as stimulus and response respectively is not a distinction which can be regarded as descriptive of anything which holds of psychical events or existences as such. . . . The circle is a co-ordination, some of whose members have come into conflict with each other. It is the temporary disintegration and need of reconstitution which occasions, which affords the genesis of, the conscious distinction into sensory stimulus on one side and motor response on the other. The stimulus is that phase of the forming co-ordination which represents the conditions which have to be met in bringing it to a successful issue; the response is that phase of one and the same forming co-ordination which gives the key to meeting these conditions, which serves as instrument in effecting the successful co-ordination. They are therefore strictly correlative and contemporaneous. . . . It is the circuit within

[17] Joseph Ratner (ed.), *John Dewey* (New York, Capricorn Books, 1965), 259.

which fall distinctions of stimulus and response as functional phases of its own mediation or completion.[18]

Dewey continues to expand this theory in chapter four of *Reconstruction in Philosophy*, where his prime concern is to show how such primal experience is both a "sure ground of belief and a safe guide of conduct," where "experience is aligned with the life-process and sensations are seen to be points of readjustment. . . ."[19] But the message is the same, namely, that the "union of doing and undergoing" constitutes the dialectic of unitive experience which is regarded as a model-free process. The upshot of this definition of experience, in terms of its own movement and self-regulation (in terms of its own directedness), is that it provides a substitute directionality for the human orderer and his self-directives in existence. It is the stream, or the field, or the whole of experience which instructs man and advises his directionality, not the human orderer. He plays a part-function in the philosophy of total interactionism. This is Hegelianism naturalized, as I shall indicate below.

There is a dialectical self-sufficiency about unitive experience which man as a human orderer does not possess. For experience is that process by which life sustains itself, by certain mediations, manipulations, and accumulations, in the stream of experience as a given field of interaction. Dewey calls this gross experience. *Art As Experience* reveals this unitive nature of "an experience" in a more revealing and consummating way. Such unitive experience is the bearer of nature's totality, which it merely appropriates dialectically, immediately, in the ongoing process of life itself. Nature is not only the subject matter for this kind of experience. It is also its total guide, as I shall indicate later. Life not only sustains itself, but it sustains itself in directionality and meaning, which unitive experience measures in terms of progress.

We have indicated that this is a form of Hegelian dialectic naturalized. Hegel's Absolute is transformed into situational absolutes that are the bearers of unitive experience and directionality. In terms of my theory, whether it is the unity of opposites, the unity of doing and undergoing, or the unity of stimulus and response, it is a dialectical ordering of life, which I regard as a substitute form of directionality and hence posterior to purposive being. That Dewey thinks otherwise is only too obvious in his writ-

<hr>

[18] *Ibid.*, 265–66.

[19] W. Barrett and H. D. Aiken (eds.), *Philosophy in the Twentieth Century* (New York, Random House, 1962), I, 315.

ings. He thinks he has found a part-to-whole logic that is imprinted on the nature of things, that is not a model of existence. As Rollo Handy reminds us, Dewey and Bentley are anxious to avoid "any form of hypostatized underpinning" for transactionalism. This is an accurate appraisal of Dewey's position, for transaction is defined in the following manner:

Where systems of description and naming are employed to deal with aspects and phases of action, without final attribution to "elements" or other presumptively detachable or independent "entities," "essences," or "realities," and without isolation of presumptively detachable "relations" from such detachable "elements."[20]

It is necessary to criticize Dewey's neglect of the distinction between the model of totality and the totality of natural existence. He believes that direct experience is a by-product of the interaction between nature and man, that such immediate experience has its own flow, rhythm, and directionality, which is occasionally dammed up, frustrated, or problematic. Dewey feels that if he is giving a model of existence as a whole, it is only a descriptive one, describing and naming the ongoingness of life itself without distortion. But to make this claim, he already presupposes a mistaken identification between his model of existence and existence as existence, which I think is posterior to man's participation in existence. The following criticisms are in order.

One, the part-to-whole logic is a mental distinction, a product of the mind. More specifically, it belongs to that part of the reasoning process we call analogical thinking. It is thus an analogy of the mind. Dewey imposes this abstraction upon the whole of existence and breathes life into it by explicating the interaction between the organisms and its environment. Man is not born into the part-to-whole logic. It is the invention of a human mind in a purposive being participating in existence. Transactionalism is thus not a neutral system of description and naming of phases of experience. It is that only secondarily, once it has its base in the part-to-whole logical relationship.

Two, any dialectical position, whether it is above experience, below it,

<hr>

[20] Rollo Handy, *Methodology of the Behavioral Sciences* (Springfield, Ill., Charles C. Thomas, 1964), 55–56, 59. Dewey even defines a "postulate" as a condition required for further operations, since he wants it to come from observations and from lived experience, "to increase efficiency of observation, never to restrain it." The very attempt to work out a description of a real and immediate totality through such postulations is a myth. Description is minimal interpretation, or interpretation by participation. It is not free of abstractions and model-making.

or in it, is always a servant of totality in that it orders man and assigns him the proper turning space in such a system of totality.

Three, there are many models of the part-to-whole logic, not only one perspective. Which of these do we select and by what standard in order to guarantee that the logic is born out of life itself? A preference for the Hegelian model of relatedness to totality does not necessarily guarantee the immediate relation of the part-to-whole logic in relationship to the ongoingness of life. Marx has come up with another system of totality in sociohistorical existence that is different from Dewey's, and he, too, also naturalized Hegel's logic of the part to the whole.

In Dewey's theory of experience, it is usually the category of "undergoing" that is the bearer of unitive experience, not so much the specificity of "doing." This, too, would imply that situational and dialectical unitive experience is the servant of a dialectic which, in turn, is the servant of totality. This experiential brand of dialectics, or processive dialectic, is one pattern among many others in history. The concept of "problematic" which sensation confronts in immediacy and which Dewey calls "shocks," is a version of Hegel's principle of contradiction that accounts for progress in history—only in Dewey this is naturalized.

Four, the human orderer, in Dewey's system, does not participate in existence. He is a part-participant in the logic of relatedness we have called the part-to-whole logic. Dewey does not even require the notion of human agency to have action going on. Action in itself, as a phase of the stream of experience, knows how to perform its part-functions. The human orderer is thus identified with or reduced to his functions in primal immediate experience and there invited to interact with the receptive category of undergoing, implicating the guidance of unitive experience. Dewey remarks:

For my own part, I wish by "causation" to mean nothing more nor less than the possibility of analyzing the vague undefined datum of a volition into a group of specific and concrete conditions, that is, factors. . . . In either case, the role of ego as separate efficient agent in causation seems to be excluded.[21]

The ego is only one object among other objects, one agent among other agents, in the interactive field of situational unitive experience. The ego is thus not self-sufficient, by its own magic creating the world.

It esteems the individual not as an exaggeratedly self-sufficient Ego which by

[21] Ratner, op. cit., 203, 208.

some magic creates the world, but as the agent who is responsible through initiative, inventiveness and intelligently directed labor for re-creating the world, transforming it into an instrument and possession of intelligence.[22]

This contradictory view of agency reveals Dewey's muddle. The fact of the matter is that Dewey cannot work out a human agent as the source of actions, as linguistic philosophy can in the study of intentional human behavior, because he has gone beyond the subject-object split, posited its solution in a socionatural totality of transactionalism which is itself a model of existence, as I am attempting to show. This is the problem of any serious functionalism. It has to posit an abstraction, or an abstract system of totality, to account for concrete actions. Dewey has to deny the principle of "self-action," defined as the place "where things are viewed as acting under their own powers," because of his belief in inter-action and trans-action. He has to settle for a human orderer that is part-participant in the part-to-whole logic. This is an abstraction of man as a human orderer participating in existence.

From our perspective, transactionalism is a model of existence because of the identification that is presupposed by it between the model of existence and existence *qua* existence. Man participates in existence as a human orderer, and such identifications as Dewey feels free to make are secondary to such real participation. It is model-making by participation in existence. The postulate of totality is not a matter of observation. One does not even see it in unitive experience. It is a commitment to the immanence of totality at work in such situational unitive experience. A parallel may be drawn to the Protestant commitment to divine immanence during the liberal period of theology, which claimed another totality at work in the world providing integration and unity to experience. I have worked this theme out in *Religion and Human Purpose*,[23] where additional evidence is brought to bear on the false identification between a model of existence and existence *qua* existence in order to emphasize the immanent workings of totality in the world, as the source of integration and unification of experience. The liberal thinkers I discussed there were empirically oriented, like Dewey. This seems like an odd association, to relate Dewey to Protestant liberalism, but they were essentially playing the same game of totality with two different ultimate goals in mind.

[22] Barrett and Aiken, *op. cit.*, 298.
[23] William Horosz and Tad Clements (eds.), *Religion and Human Purpose* (St. Louis, Warren H. Green, in process of publication).

Five, perhaps all the above criticisms can be caught up in this last critique, namely, that man, in Dewey's perspective, is goal-directed toward nature, and direct experience, which is a joint product of the interaction between the live creature and its environment, sustains and directs that goal-direction to nature. Hence the emphasis on unitive experience is a way of keeping man vitally bound to nature as a totality. Even unitive experience, in spite of its pragmatic self-sufficiency in the act of consummation, is not its own; it implicates totality or the whole of nature, of which human experience is an appropriation. The same pattern may be found in Martin Heidegger's *Dasein*, who guards man's goal-direction to Being; only this merging of self with "the Being of beings" is done on the subjective and intersubjective level. Both go beyond the subject-object split to immerse man in a system of totality(s). The basic difference is that to achieve the merger. Dewey uses a processive dialectic and Heidegger an ontological one. And here we have two models of direct exprience, each governed by a system of totality, yet each claiming a model-free presentation of the part-to-whole logic of relatedness about the ongoingness of life. It is necessary next to examine the *unitive moment*, or what Dewey calls "an experience," and the process by which the unification of the self is achieved in Dewey's writings.

Since unitive experience takes over the guidance function of man and the individual's direction of becoming, it is necessary to examine what Dewey means by such unitive experience—"an experience." Dewey regards "art as experience" as exhibit A of this qualitative experience and hopes that philosophy as a discipline will follow it. Artistic experience places the emphasis on processive participation in existence, since "art is a process of creation" which is model-free. What kind of unity does art exhibit in an experience? Irwin Edman suggests, in his usual perceptive manner, that unitive experience is one of Dewey's absolutes:

There is an aesthetic Absolute in Dewey too: experience in its integrity. But mostly in art do we find instances of such integrity, means fused with ends, medium with meaning, part with whole. . . . It serves as a model of what society and life might approximate, ordered vitality, patterned energy and immediate delight.[24]

Edman, however, does not suspect how absolute such an experience can be when qualitative unity decides the directional becoming of individuality.

[24] Sidney Hook (ed.), *John Dewey* (New York, Dial Press, 1950), 65.

Dewey prepares the reader quite adequately with the new language of transactionalism to accomplish the unity of stream and field that takes over human directionality. In art it happens to be "form" that orders unitive experience. Since form is connected with the energies of life, it has overtones of wholeness to its organizing capacity. Such phrases as "the total organism," "total response," and "total organic resonance" share in the overtones of wholeness in unitive experience. Dewey is intent on showing how alive and empowering such unitive experience can be in taking over the directional becoming of man. It is literately the pedagogue of the human orderer. There are many passages in *Art As Experience* that bear this out:

In short, art, in its form, unites the very same relation of doing and undergoing, outgoing and incoming energy, that makes an experience to be an experience. . . . In every integral experience there is form because there is dynamic organization. I call the organization dynamic because it takes time to complete it, because it is a growth. . . . Each resting place in experience is an undergoing in which is absorbed and taken home the consequences of prior doing, and, unless the doing is that of utter caprice or sheer routine, each doing carries in itself meaning that has been extracted and conserved.[25]

The *form* of the whole is therefore present in every member. . . . The series of doings in the rhythm of experience give variety and movement; they save the work from monotony and useless repetitions. The undergoings are the corresponding elements in the rhythm, and they supply unity; they save the work from the aimlessness of a mere succession of excitations.[26]

There is obviously an attempt on the part of Dewey to talk about man's contribution to unitive experience and to talk about the guidance of man by unitive experience as though it were simply a matter of organic maturation or growth, to free his view of the whole of natural existence from abstractions and model-making. The language is well calculated, but it misses the point. Dewey is led to the belief that both aesthetic and religious experiences provide unification for selfhood, and this means they provide directionality for its becoming. According to his schema, Dewey would have us believe that because growth takes place in life, continuity comes out of growth, and totality (open-ended as it is) grows out of continuity or out of contextual unitive experience. The whole effort of Dewey is to show how his model of existence has achieved reality status.

[25] Dewey, *op. cit.*, 48, 55, 56.
[26] *Ibid.*, 56–57.

Nothing could be farther from the truth. Such an identification of the two, the model and existence, remains model-making, nonetheless, because it does not lead to lived experience; it leads to another model about the totality of existence. I am suggesting that Dewey is a totalist first, situationalist second, and through these two abstractions (totalistic contextualism) he reads off the meaning of growth in the ongoing processes of life. Man is merely *a function of* unitive experience and *a function for* totality (a child on his way home to nature). Thus "confluence" is a model of human participation and not real participation. The latter precedes the identification that the part-to-whole logic of relatedness that Dewey has initially posited in his transactionalism. What I want to establish in this volume is that man is creative not only in the part-to-whole logic-situation, but that he is creative as a purposive being in existence, and through participation, of such systems of totality. They appear to be "a dime a dozen" in the history of thought, and they survive only by such claims to ultimacy that Dewey and others make for their respective models of existence. The epistemological niceties that Dewey believes are harmless ontologically, do, in effect, impose ontological commitments upon the human orderer from which he never recovers in the stream of experience.

Just to show to what lengths Dewey goes in his functional epistemology, let me take the example of his processive dialectic of the "union of doing and undergoing." By pushing the category of doing or acting to its extreme function, the term "doing" takes on a receptive function. Similarly, by pushing the category of "undergoing" or receptivity to its extreme dynamic function, "undergoing" takes on the character of the category of doing. The epistemological juggling is done for a simple reason, namely, to establish the notion of a transactional field or stream as the bedrock of unitive experience that would guide man. The point is that no matter how dynamic we wish to make either the category of doing or undergoing, we simply deepen each respective category. It is meaningful to talk about dynamic passivity as receptivity and dynamic activity as a doing. That is what they are with respect to the human orderer. But once these categories are functionalized and transposed to a stream or field of experience, they are transmolded in order to establish the case for unitive experience. This is an epistemological nicety that commits man to an ontological position.

I have no space in which to develop the notion of how aesthetic and religious experiences contribute to the unification of the self. I want only to show that it is not the human orderer that unifies these experiences.

These experiences unify man and define his directional becoming. Dewey would probably reply that he is merely trying to tone down our sense of egocentricity, but that he is not trying to get rid of the human orderer. My point is that there is no way to establish a case for a human orderer once he is gripped by the part-to-whole logic. We can feel at home in the universe by means other than the strictures of the part-to-whole logic. In trying to avoid subjective at-homeness, Dewey posits in its place "the unity of practical modes of activity" in the stream or field of experience. These remain part-functions, and the human orderer is never reclaimed either inside or outside the stream of experience. The reason for this is that direct experience guards the relationship of man to nature, to which Dewey has directed the human orderer by encounter experiences in the field of inter-action.

If Dewey is attempting to rescue man from a narrow behaviorism, I would agree with him. But if he is attempting to establish the uniqueness of individuality by man's goal-direction to nature, by emphasizing his "unique connections and position in the whole" as a living transactional field, I am in profound disagreement with him. For man does not "belong" to the whole. The whole is the product of man's participation in existence, a postulate of the analogical reasoning powers of his mind, an abstraction that must be given life by situational experience.

Milton Mayeroff, in an excellent article, "Concept of the Unification of the Self," indicated the contribution of religious experience to man's directional becoming. He is in agreement with Dewey about the peace and harmony that such relatedness to nature gives to man. Mayeroff remarks:

Dewey states that *what* we experience is a function of *how* we experience. The profundity of what we are aware of is a function of the development of our being, of the depth of our living. Since with unification there is a pervasive and enduring modification of our being in its entirety, there is necessarily a profound change in what the world has become for us. With unification, in the plenitude of our being, the world takes on a unity, it becomes a universe. If we contrast the world of the impious man with that of Dewey's pious man, we can speak of the former as Appearance and the latter as Reality. Since awareness of Reality presupposes unification, the unified self is at home in Reality. And, therefore, in terms of the preceding discussion, it may be said to know Reality.[27]

Mayeroff is not aware of the fact that religion has postulated similar

[27] Milton Mayeroff, "Concept of the Unification of the Self," *The Personalist* (Winter, 1964), 21.

totalities on the grounds of such feelingful awareness. One writer (Clyde Macintosh, who made attempts to deal with religious experience on an objective scientific level) has even called it, quite properly in its own context, a "reality-feeling." But these two authors had two totally different models of totality. Unless man is first given his birthright, namely, the capacity on the part of his being to be self-directing in awareness about himself or about reality, as the precondition for thoughts about totality, we have nothing but claims of ultimacy to go on to legislate among the systems of totality. There is no such thing as a real totality contending with an abstract one. They are all models of existence postulated by purposive being in its participation in existence. This requires the priority of self-direction.

We may summarize Dewey's theory of totality and man's participation in it, as well as the contents of this chapter, by the distinction of an open and a closed totality. In a sense, all the writers considered in this chapter reject a closed system of totality that is highly structured. They prefer more open-ended, functional systems of totality. In Dewey's case, the world of totality is certainly unfinished and wide open to the infinite possibilities of growth from one unitive experience to another in the matrix of the continuousness of experience. Though I consider this an improvement over some past systems of totality, the difference is really not that great. The reason for it is that even a functional, open system of totality can make totalitarian claims on human life, as we noted by pointing to the fact that Dewey's epistemological niceties make ontological commitments upon the human orderer.

Robert C. Pollack has done a fine exposition of the notion of Dewey's "incomplete universe" in "Process and Experience," where he endeavors to show that the unitive experiences in life find their place in an ongoing process. He, too, sympathizes with Dewey's perspective of equating process with experience which, in turn, yields the "universe of experience."[28] However, I have given ample evidence in this chapter to show that one cannot go from one's search for wholeness to the ultimate (though unfinished) universe of experience without making certain mistakes of identification that involve abstractions both mentally and experientially. If such an identification is taken for real, this is simply a commitment to the immanent workings of an unfinished totality through unitive and continuous experiences. It is at this point that claims to ultimacy arise that even an open

---

[28] R. C. Pollock, "Process and Experience," *John Dewey*, J. Blewett (ed.) (New York, Fordham University Press, 1960), 161–97.

totality cannot ignore. While trees grow, continuity does not grow on trees, and totality does not grow out of unitive experiences unless we have first modeled or formed such a philosophy of organic relatedness in which process is identified with experience and the category of unity has been hypostatized into some form of growth.

In the next chapter I hope to cover the inner dynamics of what it means to participate in the whole of reality and point out some of its shortcomings.

3. The Self and the Drama of Totalities

Each totalist who has ever plowed up the universe with the blade of his mind has charged an exorbitant price. The exacting price for such work is his own mistaken identity between the total work of plowing and the universe of experience as a whole. He does not say, for example, now follow my comprehensive vision of life, but rather he insists on saying, follow the unitive totality of cosmic reality (follow it). In each such instance there is a forgetfulness about the distinction between one's model of life and life itself. The strange fact is that everyone appears to be content with this exorbitant price for the work. We have recognized such totalism as authoritarianism in religion and the field of politics, but we have not yet learned to recognize such totalistic claims by philosophers. Perhaps this is the reason (this complacent inattention) why the totalists have had a field day of it in history and continue to play the game of totalism on the contemporary scene.

Such a claim to universality, which is really the philosopher's search for wholeness, cannot be identified with cosmic reality for two reasons: (1) that such a pretentious claim to ultimacy is too high a price to pay for having commerce with totality; and (2) that it rests on a mistaken identification between the work of plowing and the universe of cosmic experience. They are two different realms of discourse artificially brought together by the part-to-whole logic. This analogy is hypostatized and then given life by dialectical schemes about unitive experience. My concern in this chapter is to examine the totalistic model of human participation which the models in the previous chapters implicated in their schemes of participation. This is an important consideration because of my interest in pinning down the source of human responsibility, which always rests in some philosophy of participation.

Participation in the Whole

This may or may not be a distinct model of human participation, since the other models of participation involved totalistic notions. I am, however, treating it as a distinctive model of human participation because there are philosophies which consider the subject-object split not as an inherent problem of man himself, but as a bifurcation in the heart of a universe of totality. Howard Press gives such an example in the systems of Marx and Freud:

The root of radicalism, as Marx said, is the living man, rooted in the material world, a sensuous subject among sensuous objects. It is this relationship of subject and object, of subject separated from its object, and object opposed to subject, this concrete material relationship—this *alienated* relationship, as we have learned to say—that first of all defines for Marx the human situation. And so is it also for Freud.[1]

I shall use Mikel Dufrenne and Herbert Marcuse as examples of totalistic participation. The common theme in all these examples is that man is neither responsible for, nor responsible to, such a subject-object bifurcation in totality. But nonetheless he is still responsible for overcoming that split. Why and how man feels obligated to the principle of overcoming the dichotomy is a mystery. Even Herbert Marcuse does not admit clarity at this point. He merely asserts that man can be determined negatively by society, which is to say that he can become alienated and then become a rebel, determined to fight the society that formed him. He has no answer either why man should be responsible for such a principle of overcoming. He only advocates being responsible to the revolution through political commitment. In probing the source of human responsibility, we are interested in knowing why he feels such an obligation in and through political commitments.

Systems of totality have had an unusually lucrative career in the history of thought on the issue of being the alleged source of human responsibility. That is precisely the focal point of my attack in this volume. It is my contention that this leads to a pluralism and a relativism in the sources of responsibility. This creates an impasse in communication with varying claims to ultimacy and obedience to one's chosen system of totality. A viable

---

[1] Howard Press, "Marx, Freud, and the Pleasure Principle," *The Philosophical Forum* (Fall, 1970), 36.

alternative has to be found to prevent a further breakdown in human responsibility. The course I have chosen is to construct a new model of the human orderer that will give us both a strong sense of human participation in existence and prevent the absorption of man in some system of totality. If this program is successful, man can overcome the schizoid attitude toward responsibility, toward the split I mentioned earlier, between responsibility to something and responsibility for it. Unless man finds a way to stand behind such systems of responsibility as a human orderer, the split between these two obligatory dimensions of responsibility will be hard to overcome. As long as the condition prevails in modern society, there will be a crisis of responsibility. What I am suggesting is that the tyranny of philosophical totalities has contributed to the breakdown of human responsibility. Its solution, too, should be philosophical in nature.

"Participating in the whole," it is my contention, is an abstraction from "participating in existence." I have made the earlier claim that if the human orderer is given credit for participating in existence, we find him practicing model-making to make up for the perspectival nature of human participation. Schemes of totality are designed both in terms of immediate experience and in terms of reflection. My theory of the human orderer, as being capable of ontological self-direction in participation, enables us to claim model-making by participation. This means that we cannot talk about human sensibilities and elemental modes of response from a neutral posture. Either man is the gathering focus for them and anthropologizes these immediate sensibilities or modes of response, or a system of totality does by placing the imprint of totalization upon human participation. Man cannot be neutral either in his intellectual endeavors or in his participation in existence. When man does choose to play such a game of neutrality, he has already abdicated the ordering of human life to some totality.

"Participation in the whole" carries with it the limitation of vision either of the human orderer or of a system of totality(s). It is a temporal expression of a structure of meaning designed by human participation in existence or by man's intellect to aid him in the search for further meaning. Thus it is necessary to relate such participation in the whole of existence to man's search for wholeness first before it is related to a given universe of cosmic reality. This is what I meant earlier when I said that this is man's problem first, and only secondly the problem of man's relatedness to the world-totality. The totalist, obviously, feels differently about it because he postulates the subject-object rift as part of a cleavage in the heart of totality itself,

63

and then some of them feel the need to overcome it by a revolution of totality.

The thesis of this chapter can now be summarized. It is two-fold: (1) that "participation in the whole" involves abstractions, both mental and participatory, because it is designed by a participant in existence that we recognize as a purposive being of a human orderer; and (2) that such totalistic models of participation are merely the apologetic claims of man, in which man makes certain claims of ultimacy about his search for wholeness and its ultimate results. If we put these two points together, it can be said that when such claims to ultimacy are made for one's system of totality, one is well on his way to claiming absolute participation. A totalist is not interested in giving us a "sign" of "participating in the whole"; he is beckoning us to follow the very pattern of the universe of totality (existence *qua* existence). Moreover, he would have us believe that it is the wholeness of existence itself which invites man's search for wholeness. If such is the case, man needs only to be assigned a position in totality, a turning space in which to squirm. For man is no longer a human orderer and responsibility is no longer the confrontation of man as a human orderer, both individually and socially. When these events take place, we not only have a language of closure, but a closed system of the universe that is oppressive to man.

Take Mikel Dufrenne's notion of totality as a case in point:

How is one to situate the thought of the One within the One? . . . We still have not escaped the dualism of man and the world. To think totality, it is still necessary to conceive a genesis of man. . . . Does not that Night impose silence upon philosophy? Certainly, the idea of totality is in the end unthinkable; we have said it often enough. . . . But it (totality) is always attested to by the way the real exceeds the thinkable, it is always at the horizon of the gaze or of the system, it is that very horizon.[2]

Is this an attempt to state the claim of ultimacy for one's vision of totality? While it is the very horizon of the system of totality, even though unthinkable, such a system draws all things to itself and directs man's becoming. It even unifies the powers of the human intellect which fails in the task of totalization or in its search for wholeness. Such mystification leads the author to a preference of totality over reality in order to show how man lives his being *sub specie totalitatis*.

[2] Mikel Dufrenne, "Introduction to Jalons: My Intellectual Autobiography," *Philosophy Today* (Fall, 1970), 174, 184, 186.

This is "participation in the whole" par excellence. It represents a plea for absolute participation in the midst of human frailty. The thought seldom occurs to Dufrenne that every question of genesis and every manifestation of piety toward the source of our origins arises in man's purposive nature. While it may certainly originate during the *night*, the question cannot be raised unless it is raised by a purposive being who is concerned about his whereabouts. Nor does it occur to Dufrenne that the origin of such schemes of holism arise on the phenomenal level of goal-direction (totalities being ultimate goal-directions), which presuppose purposive being and self-directive participation in existence. If totality is the Unthinkable, Dufrenne reaches it by participatory model-making, a product of purposive nature and its capacity to immediatize experience, that is to say, to give us models or close-ups of direct experience. The point is that "participation in the whole" is both a form of perspectival participation and perspectival holism accompanied by the designing powers of purposive being. Though Dufrenne would be the first to admit the perspectival nature of the intellect (for which totality is incomprehensible), as an encounter philosopher he would be the last to admit (if he admitted it at all) the fact that we are just as perspectival in our participation in existence, either when we participate in the whole of existence, as in our mental processes.

How does one distinguish between man's search for totality and the experience of the "presence of totality" except by the designs of purposive being? The failure to make such a distinction, so as not to despoil the presence of totality, opens the door for mystic commerce with the universe of wholeness. Mysticism usually starts in such dark recessive corners of immediate experience where there is no distinction between light and darkness. The thing which fascinates me about such enterprises is the fact that most totalists set up their claims for ultimacy by an appeal to model-free immediate experience. But can a direct form of primary experience, exalting as some think it is, give man the feeling of absolute participation by "participating in the whole"? Even when totality is construed as the Unthinkable, it does not yield the experience of absolute participation by its presence. This is merely a claim to ultimacy for one's experience or experiences in one's search for wholeness.

It is ironic that we should have given up the claim of "absolute knowledge" in the field of thought before we gave up the notion of "absolute participation" in the field of experience. For we have always recognized the universal intent of reason but scoffed at such universal intent in sensory experience. It is only with radical empiricism that the universality of sensory experience became a reality through real relations in experience. In terms of our beliefs about both, it stands to reason that we should have given up the claim to "absolute participation" first because of its perspectival nature.

However, this ironic situation does not deter Mikel Dufrenne. The more he sees totality as the Unthinkable, the more he asserts its reality or presence, as in the passage that follows: "Light identifies itself with what it illuminates, thought identifies itself with being in order to think the totality of being . . . so philosophy begins with totality."[3] One may add that, according to this logic, man's search for wholeness identifies itself with the wholeness of reality itself. That is precisely the point of my main objection to every totalist.

The "totality of being" or "totality itself" is a model of existence. For Aristotle, "being in general" represented such totality. For Heidegger, it meant "being in time." For Kant, it was conceived as "being in imagination." For Plato, it meant "being in thought." For Husserl, it was "being in essence." For Hegel, it was "being in self-consciousness." For Tillich, such a grasp of being was "being in courage." While for Max Scheler, it was "being in loving." With such an array of perspectives before us we have only few alternatives to face concerning the universe of totality. One is to postulate "the totality of the universe" behind all these expressions or manifestations of it. Or we can view them as models of existence that presuppose a human orderer and his self-directing participation in existence. I have chosen the second alternative for the simple reason that the first view is more open to claims to ultimacy than my perspective. The totalist is always tempted to say, after he has pointed to the universe of totality itself, that it is precisely his perspective, or else his perspective points to it. Such a referential pointing, however, is also goal-directedness, makes certain authoritarian claims on man, and places the burden of ontological commitments upon him. The first alternative is nothing but a plea for the possibility of "absolute participation" in existence. The term "ground" is an inoffensive word that points to a rather offensive situation—topic of absolute participation in the midst of human perspectival participation.

But, it may be objected, how does one state the case for the ground of being if not through some account of totality? I am raising a prior ques-

[3] *Ibid.,* 174.

tion: Where does such a question originate in man? The reply is: In man's purposive being. If the latter is the case, claims of ultimacy will not save us embarrassment. The attempt to prove the case for totality by an appeal to direct experience is just a way of avoiding an embarrassment and the confusion about such totality. For direct experience is the unjustified and the unjustifiable. A model-free immediate form of experience is even a bigger problem than the problem of totality. Compounding both in the notion of "real and immediate totality" merely sets up the problem which concerns us. The answer of the totalist becomes a new question for philosophers. Perhaps immediate experience that is free of abstractions and mediations is also a claim to "absolute participation." I believe that when a thinker transfigures his search for wholeness to the wholeness of the universe, this can only result in a claim to ultimacy for one's quest for perfection.

The claims of ultimacy for totality derive from man's fear of himself, from the impotence of his search for wholeness and the fear of himself as a human orderer in existence. This is the fear of taking on the responsibility for systems of responsibility. One would rather follow the leads of totality, by being responsible to its intentions and directives, and avoid the burdensome task of being responsible for informing it, either by reflection or by participation—or by both. Why does man continue to take an irresponsible position for systems of responsibility? Perhaps we shall find an answer to some of these questions in giving a more extended treatment of Herbert Marcuse's system of totality.

Marcuse is obsessed with the notion of an "ideology-free totality." Reason points to cosmic reality because it is at the service of life. Man's sensuous experience points to reality because it is the closest to life. Together, on the field of historical becoming (immediacy), they are aided by a dialectic which gives direction to the process of becoming, which is the nearest to life. While Marcuse can point to many influences on his thinking (Max Horkheimer, T. W. Adorno, Hegel, Marx, Freud, etc.), the common influential factor is to be found in the "sense of totality" these men impart to him. This is not to discredit more special influences, like deriving Eros from Freud, reason from Hegel, and radicalism from Marx, Horkheimer, and Adorno. I know of no other writer in the twentieth century who makes as excessive a claim to absolute participation that is ideology-free as Marcuse. Perhaps this is the reason why he regards some of the work that social scientists are doing as inadequate to the study of the dynamic social forms in history. They are not revolutionary enough and do not lead to his dream of absolute participation in history. Neither was he satisfied with the work of Edmund Husserl, whose concept of the lifeworld excited him some because it fell short of the political realities of history. We shall examine first Marcuse's relation to the lifeworld.

HUSSERL AND MARCUSE

As early as 1936, Marcuse was criticizing the shortcomings of Husserl's system of totality, which the author called the *Lebenswelt*, or lifeworld. It fell short of a revolutionary concept because it truncated human sensibility by concentrating only on the essential structures in phenomena. The lifeworld, he had hoped, would give him access to the political realities of history and its dynamic social forms, but Husserl had no interest in this area. At that time he viewed the lifeworld as being too quietistic to help him with the radical cultural critique of society that he himself and the Frankfurt School were interested in promulgating. In short, he was reading Husserl through Marx, and in the context of this second totality he found grave difficulties with Husserl's approach. The main shortcoming of Husserl, he thought, was his lack of interest in changing the world. Commenting on the relation of Marcuse to Husserl, Theodore Kisiel states:

The overtly critical move of the *epoché* does not abolish or change the world that it brackets, but only understands it. Moreover, the receptivity of the intuition of essence replaces the spontaneity of the kind of understanding that is inseparable from critical reason. The phenomenological reduction subjects itself to the powers that be under the guise of the "given," which promotes the resignation of quietistic indifference and paves the way for further ideologies.[4]

The root of radicalism was what separated Marcuse from Husserl. This interest in revolution, which came from Marx's system of totality, showed up the difference between the two totalities. Yet Marcuse was impressed with the way Husserl exposed the ideological nature of the scientific world-view. This gave him the idea to transform Husserl's lifeworld into more revolutionary channels, as Kisiel once more informs us:

Marcuse now proceeds to extend the ontological conservatism (of science) to the political life of the lifeworld. . . . This strategy of shifting from ontological to political structures, or in other instances, of shifting epistemological structures

[4] Theodore Kisiel, "Ideology Critique and Phenomenology," *Philosophy Today* (Fall, 1970), 152.

into social structures, in effect defines the basic rift between phenomenology and ideology critique.[5]

They differ greatly not only in terms of the notion of "critique," which for Husserl means the clarification of meaning through *Be-Sinnung* and for Marcuse means liberation from ideology encased in traditionalism, but also in their models of existence. Both regard science as an artificial world-view, an abstraction from the *Lebenswelt*. For Marcuse, the world-view of science also reflects the culture of neocapitalism, which is also an abstract form of totality. Marcuse thus relies on Marx's model of existence, which he regards as being more immediate and real than Husserl's to combat certain limitations inherent in Husserl's *Lebenswelt*.

In the case of Husserl's lifeworld, the concern is with a world-horizon that is more than "an entity," that exists with such "uniqueness" that only the singular applies to it. Yet Marcuse questions this totality and eventually departs from its intentions and directives. His first concern, however, is merely to radicalize the lifeworld to include in it the political realm and the process of history. At this early stage, Marcuse thought Husserl was too quietistic, too much interested in the transcendental spectator, in the transcendental realm, in pure essential structures. Marcuse's concern was to become a participant in the lifeworld, to share in the revolution of totality in which the species-being (man) was to realize his authenticity. The pre-given lifeworld was to have another ultimate goal and another dialectical pattern of realization from Husserl's world-reality. Marcuse's criticism of Husserl is obviously an effort to formulate a new model of existence patterned more after Hegel and Marx. But he must make certain reality claims for it so that he must deny this forming of the lifeworld; he must regard it as a "discovery," as something pregiven and free of ideology and model-making. Obviously the pregiven lifeworld in both thinkers is not prior to purposive being. Each model of totality is fashioned by the author's purposive nature but denied in theory, enabling each to make claims of ultimacy for his respective model of existence. They are two different models of existence, but Marcuse, in this early questioning of Husserl's lifeworld, chooses only to transform the lifeworld for political reasons. This is one reading of Marcuse's attitude toward Husserl's totality.

The other reading of the lifeworld is that it, too, is a life of abstraction. He calls Husserl a positivist, an ideologist who has failed to root totality

[5] *Ibid.*, 153.

in the sociohistoric world. If this is the case, Marcuse has a definite preference for the Marxian model, which is free of such ideology. But the question I am raising in this volume is, why does there have to be always one
real totality and all the others abstract ones? Is this merely a claim to
ultimacy, as I suggested?

IDEOLOGY CRITIQUE AND TOTALITY

The fall of totalities is almost like the fall of empires. There is no reality-
continuity among the totalities in history. There is only the downfall of
the one (the target of an abstract totality) and the establishment of the
other (of a real totality). In his "ideology critique," Marcuse would have
us believe that there is a totality running throughout history and that the
real totality remains in the ascendency as the abstract ones fall by the way-
side. This is the reason why Marcuse regards ideology as an unwelcome
theme in social theorizing. "Participation in the whole" must be ideology-
free even when philosophizing about it. Such social inquiry requires "negative thinking" that critically exposes the inner contradictions of an abstract
society. There is a problem that Marcuse never raises, namely, how can an
abstract totality, like neocapitalism, give rise to real contradictions that
negative thinking reads off critically to aid the cause of revolution? The
other problem is, how does Marcuse avoid the confusion in such ideology-
free criticism of running together the ephemeral present with more permanent trends that somehow represent the developmental bent of totality
at work in history?

Whose demand is it that a social critique of social forms be carried on
without abstractions and models? Is it the requirement of one's model of
existence? Or is it the demand of life itself? Marcuse would have us believe that it is the latter. This means that such an "end to ideology," as
sociocritical evaluation (negative thinking), is to be viewed as part of the
larger project Marcuse has in mind of going beyond the subject-object split.
The part-to-whole logic controls the social critique also and does not allow
it to get out of hand. Is this merely an awkward language that plays into
the hands of the notion of absolute participation? Is this a way of talking
about social universal immediacy? Once the subject-object dichotomy is
posited in a real totality, man's method of interpretation must follow suit.
Man is denied the capacity to understand human participation on his own.
He can be trusted to know what is going on only as a "participant in the
whole." This appears to be the rationale behind "the end of ideology."

If Edmund Husserl missed the mark of reality in his concept of the lifeworld, Karl Marx did not. Marcuse believes that he had an inside lead to total historical development. In contrast to Feuerbach, who advocated "perceptual materialism," Marx emphasized "dialectic materialism" as the base for sociohistorical critique. Marcuse believes this is a more dynamic materialistic interpretation of ideas:

Marx focused his theory on the labor process and by so doing held to and consummated the principle of the Hegelian dialectic that the structure of the content (reality) determines the structure of the theory. He made the foundations of civil society the foundations of the theory of civil society.[6]

The phenomenon of universal labor, the most decisive factor in human development, thus plays a central role in dialectical materialism. It represents historical facts on the level of social immediacy and determines man's thinking on these facts in a holistic context. The root of radicalism in such an ideology critique is guided by the materialistic quality of the society that one is analyzing. The social sciences miss this holistic concept of inquiry and thus miss the significance of history as a revolutionary tool. Political economy lacks something because it is not such a "participation in the whole." Its primary concern is with "an isolated objective cluster of facts."

What this amounts to is that totality requires total human participation from man in the whole. This is the primary requirement. Social theorizing must follow the same bent. It cannot afford to have commerce with abstractions because such model-making leads man away from participation in the whole. Let me suggest some critical remarks about the alleged reality of the Marcusean-Marxian theory of totality.

One, the notion that the part-to-whole logic, or the whole of historical reality, because it is materialistically interpreted and, therefore, free of abstractions or ideology, is in fact a new ideology and not the "end of ideology" or "the end of utopia." When a thinker rejects one model of totality, he is bound to replace it with another. No author has the right to identify his model of existence with existence *qua* existence. One cannot go from model-making, or from the rejection of model-making, to lived historical existence as existence without playing God.

Two, dialectical materialism, as a theory of materialism (as compared with Greek atomism or evolutionary materialism), is a theory competing with other models of material existence. Thus the belief that modes of

[6] Marcuse, *Reason and Revolution*, 272.

economic production determine man's whole existence through the principle of universal labor is merely a way of claiming ultimacy by asserting that one's model of the universe of totality is in fact cosmic reality itself. Marcuse does not realize that even a materialism is not free of model-making, that it is one materialistic model, among others, competing for an understanding of man's social life.

Three, such claims to ultimacy on the part of totalists are postulated by one's desire for "absolute participation," which we read as being synonymous with "participation in the whole." Perhaps this is the greatest ideology of all. It will reign supreme in history until another model of totality is postulated as the real which will challenge the ideological taint of the Marxian view of the universe. There is no scheme of totality that is free of man's attempts to anthropologize human participation, even the scheme that man is a "participant in the whole."

Four, the illusion that man has gone beyond the subject-object split is supported by another, namely, that one has left behind the individual's efforts to anthropologize experience and come to grips with "real participation." But any attempt to go beyond the subject-object bifurcation results in what I have called more model-making by participation. The old saying, that in moving to another place (to have a new start in life) we take the old self along, is applicable here. In going beyond the subject-object split, the human orderer accompanies the project and helps to create more models of participation, like the participation in the whole. It is rather odd to hold the belief that one makes abstractions only by reflection but not by participation. Such restructuring of human life as goes on beyond the subject-object split has the consent and the understanding of the human orderer himself. He accompanies all such projects as a purposive being in history. The very fact that the game of real "social encounter" can be played by existentialism, phenomenology, naturalism, and dialectic materialism should signal the fact that such a program of "participation in the whole" is in fact the game of our models of existence. While each school of thought can legitimately claim a social encounter that is prior to conceptualization, it cannot legitimately claim that it is free of the human orderer as self-directing in such encounters, both individually and socially.

Five, most theories which adhere to the belief in real and immediate totality(s) deny a forming capability to purposive being in such ventures beyond the subject-object split. The program of ideology critique is a way of upholding the integrity of this belief to make the claim to ultimacy more justifiable. It is my position that all such schemes utilize purpose in its holistic tendencies but refuse to use the prior function in man's purposive nature (its capacity of ontological self-direction in participation). I shall point up this difficulty later by pointing out the birth of totalities in man's purposive nature.

MARCUSE'S CONSTRUCT OF MAN IN THE CONTEXT OF TOTALITY

The essence of man is the discovery of his universal nature, the fact that he is a social whole. Such universals are real; they denote totality. Marcuse is a firm believer in the social being that Marx brought to light under the label of "species-being."

Man's very nature lies in his universality. His intellectual and physical faculties can be fulfilled only if all men exist as men, in the developed wealth of their human resources. Man is free only if all men are free and exist as "universal beings." When this condition is attained, life will be shaped by the potentialities of the genus, Man, which embraces the potentialities of all the individuals that comprise it. The emphasis on this universality brings nature as well into the self-development of mankind.[7]

Marcuse had a similar revelation from Freud about the reality of such universals, similarly denoting or implicating totality. In *Eros and Civilization* he accepts Freud's theory of the power of the universal in and over the individual as somehow sharing "in the archaic identity with the species." The individual is not the master of his own house, but he lives "the universal fate of mankind."[8] Is such "genus-formation" of human life the demand of existence? Or is it the requirement of a prepurposive model of social encounter? Is it the requirement of the belief that to solve the problems of man's alienation one must go beyond the subject-object split? It is necessary to raise these questions because all such moves, demanding the restructuring of man and his distribution in a system of totality, presupposes the human orderer as a purposive being in such participation. Man first must confront the human orderer in himself before he can be called upon to restructure relationships beyond himself. This view necessitates the rejection of an ideology-free whole man. I shall deal with this issue more extensively in the next chapter, where I plan to summarize the consequences of going beyond the subject-object split and describe the dynamics of the purposive model of human participation.

[7] *Ibid.*, 275.
[8] Herbert Marcuse, *Eros and Civilization* (Boston, Beacon Press, 1955), 58.

Once the human orderer is reduced to a social universal being, participation in the whole can only mean being guided by social encounter that is dialectically instructed. Man is thus alienated from the human orderer in order to be receptive to the orderings of totality by the dialectics of social forms and class struggle. There is a sense, then, that totality, defined in terms of class and social forms, is beyond human participation, even when it is called "participation in the whole." One is responsible to it, but not responsible for its directions. Is this a way of totally externalizing human purpose? The theme of goal-direction—and man is goal-directed to a system of historical totality and historically created possibilities, to the historical process itself—is nothing but ultimate goal-directedness when conceived in the part-to-whole relationship. Totality knows its achievements in self-consciousness, social forms are aware of their dialectical doings, and man as a social or species-being knows, too, what it is all about—all do, except the human orderer. His work of anthropologizing the process of participation is forbidden. Man's goals in history have been severed both from the human orderer and from society's capacity to be socially self-directing. Human purpose has been socialized, naturalized, historicized, as a form of external goal-direction. Once this meaning of purpose is placed in a part-to-whole logic, the totality can only have an external guidance value for man. The only way man can play this game is to identify with such participation in the whole, call it his own, and seek fulfillment as a social being. Marcuse's ideology critique defends such a truncated view of man in history. It is designed to nurture the directives of dialectical totality.

Ideological analysis is revolutionary analysis. It is the practice of socio-historic analysis, practice rather than theory oriented. This is what the pre-purposive model of man requires, once it is established that there is a real solution of the subject-object dichotomy in a real and immediate socio-historic totality. Man's social theorizing must follow pace. But just because the realm of the practical is pretheoretical, it does not necessarily follow that it is also prepurposive in orientation. But the question is, whose purposes order the social or species-being? Marcuse prefers the orderings of dialectical totality to those of the human orderer. Ideology critique is thus neutral only with respect to the human orderer but not with respect to the dialectical orderings of totality. Such totalistic participation, for Marcuse, means that the individual as an autonomous being be discarded and that he be declared a social entity if man is to accomplish his destiny. Thus

74

"participation in the whole" means that man should be regarded as a social universal and undergo the transformation of the interplay of revolutionary social forms. Such totalistic participation is prior to human participation in existence. In fact, the individual is only a function of such absolute participation in history. Society, too, is only a functionary of the total revolutionary and dialectical movement of history. The belief that the "individual is the social entity," and to identify this claim with man *qua* man, is perhaps the greatest ideology of all. Every totalist in the history of thought has played this game.

The upshot of the belief in "the end of ideology" is the ruthless violation of man as a human orderer in existence, not the ruthless violation of nature and the ecosystem, as Marcuse would have us believe. Man is deprived from understanding what he creates. He is deprived of his participatory privileges in history both as an individual and as a social orderer. If man is only a social entity, caught up in the revolution of totality, he owes primary responsibility to the system of totality, not to himself and/or to society. Expressions of violence may simply be claims of ultimacy for such a system of totality because it is only a model of existence in search of reality. In the context of absolute participation, the laws appear to be different than in perspectival human participation. Violence is an accredited procedure in making claims to ultimacy for one's model of existence. Violence is endorsed as an instrument of empowerment, for everything is legitimate that would immerse man in a system of sociohistoric totality. Its techniques are designed to make the construct of man, as social or species-being, into the real living man, man *qua* man. Is this a model in search of identity, a theory of man in search of its reality?

Marcuse's distinction between aggressive violence and defensive counter-violence, as being different in their goals and in their instinctual structures, has to do with man's relation to society and its institutional life. Aggressive violence subdues the erotic element in life. In defensive violence there is positive self-expression of the erotic in life. The only trouble with this theory is that defensive violence is given a prestige in the revolutionary system of totality which it does not have in the capitalist system of totality. But, on the other hand, offensive violence has the prestigious position in the capitalist society. Both models of totality define violence to suit the inner content and form of direction of the system of totality. Each system of totality is in search of identity and reality and approves of one kind of violence or the other in order to achieve totalization. Violence is the servant of totalization in one form or another, and it is usually an accredited procedure in moving the system of totality from its abstract status to that of real and immediate totality. Man is a tool of totality in such contexts. The cost of full absorption in any system of totality is high indeed. "Participation in the whole" is thus a mediated process. The main problem of any revolutionary program is how to make such a part-to-whole logical abstraction conform to cosmic reality. Violence thus plays its role well as an instrument of hypostatization. The meaning of such hypostatization is that it can be practiced in participation as well as in reflection. Philosophers have limited its use to illegitimate reflections.

Marcuse, as a totalist, believes there can be a beautiful blending of the individual with totality in terms of an "interest of the whole." He makes the following remark to this effect:

The true history of mankind will be, in the strict sense, the history of free individuals, so that the interest of the whole will be woven into the individual existence of each. In all prior forms of society, the interest of the whole lay in separate social and political institutions, which represented the right of society as against the right of the individual.[9]

He is personally convinced that such an arrangement of fusing immediacy is the most wholesome kind of freedom that man is capable of. Thus he advocates a freedom-loving socialism with an emphasis on the "aesthetic-erotic dimension," in which play and dis-play have their part, and work is creatively transformed into play. But to bring about such a state of affairs, one has to revolutionize the existing institutions of society and provide an ideally structured one in its place.

There are many problems with such a utopian plan for human well-being. Whose "interest of the whole" is it? Is it an interest created by cosmic reality itself? Is it an interest created by one's model of existence? Or is it an interest created by one's immersion in nature mysticism? The fact of the matter is that such a free individual is not his own; he belongs either to the human orderer or to a system of totality. Blending freedom with necessity is an old trick in philosophy, but in such a mixture it is necessity or the part-to-whole logic which always wins out. Is this to be equated with the new qualitative life and with the new birth in history of the Subject? If man is not the gathering focus for free self-expression, and if one's interest in the whole is not an integral part of one's search for wholeness, the

[9] Marcuse, *Reason and Revolution*, 283.

distance to Marcuse's utopia is greater than hitherto conceived. Also there appears to be a new oppressiveness detected in such a scheme of absolute participation in the whole. If man is reduced to a social entity, what point is there in talking about freedom, the qualitative life, interest in the whole? These appear to be terms borrowed uncritically from another system of totality and from subjective participation in life.

The role of universals, significant not only for theorizing about man, is enhanced in Marcuse's totalism. We already cited some passages to this effect from *Eros and Civilization*. However, his *One-Dimensional Man* is more explicit on the issue. Such universals "denote" totality; they are the bearers of totality's intentions. Marcuse remarks:

> To be sure, such universals cannot be validated by the assertion that they denote a whole which is more and other than its parts. They apparently do, but this "whole" requires an analysis of the unmutilated experiential context. . . . Universals are primary elements of experience—universals not as philosophic concepts but as the very qualities of the world with which one is daily confronted. . . . In this sense, universals seem to designate the "stuff" of the world.[10]

What is of interest in the above passage is the disconnection of universals from the human orderer. The universal is above the individual. But the appeal to direct experience is a way of relating universals to totality. They appear to function as unitive-experience guides of human life, dialectically ordered to serve the interests of the whole. His attempt to go beyond the subject-object split gives such universals the quality of a directive agency in the service of totality. The fact that it is man's mind that has the capacity for a universal outreach (in man's search for wholeness) has little significance for Marcuse. Universals have a way of walking through history over the heads of particulars, including the particularity of man (who has been reduced to a social entity), as in the following passage: "The substantive universal intends qualities which surpass all particular experience, but persist in the mind, not as a figment of the imagination nor as more logical possibilities but as the 'stuff' of which our world consists."[11]

Such universals have a prescriptive role to play as servants of totality on the field of primal experience. They have what Marcuse calls "an internal historical character" that is free of ideology. As such, their function is to liberate, transform, and even subvert immediate experience in terms of

[10] Herbert Marcuse, *One-Dimensional Man* (Boston, Beacon Press, 1964), 203–204, 211.

[11] *Ibid.*, 213.

the "interest of the whole." What this means is that such universals are dialectically arranged, ordered, and reordered to suit the intentions of totality. It is a living dialectic which has historical content in it. Its function is to relate experience to totality and thought to reality. Universals are thus forms of unitive experience that usurp man's burden of self-direction in existence.

UNITIVE EXPERIENCE AS A GUIDE TO LIFE

Unitive experience is composed of Eros and Logos dialectically blended as the effective guides of human life. The inspiration for such a formulation of immediate unitive experience came from Schiller, who discussed the possibility of their union, "in which reason is sensuous and sensuousness is rational."[12] Each of these universal drives in man (one borrowed from Freud, or from a modification of Freud, and the other from Hegel, modified by Marx), serves the cause of totality by its immanent workings in unitive experience. Man is not his own either in Eros or in Logos or in their blend of unitive experience. He is responsible to these three blind guides, but not responsible for their directives. They are dialectically ordered by totality to serve the "interest of the whole." Such unitive experience has already replaced the human orderer in his "participation in the whole." The only difficulty with such a pedagogy is that it needs an ideal classroom of society in which to teach mankind this new way of life.

At this juncture of thought Marcuse faces insurmountable problems in relating the concept of revolution to such basic human sensibilities disclosed by primal experience. In an exciting interview with Sam Keen and John Raser in *Psychology Today*, Marcuse is asked to face up to the issue of who transforms what in the revolution of totality. Marcuse admits that he wants a revolutionary concept of human needs (not only biological, but with historical modifications) and sensibilities. Yet these are not his own; they belong to a sociohistoric totality for which he is not responsible. The dialogue takes the following focus:

Marcuse: That's right. The eroticized body would rebel against exploitation, competition, false virility, conquest of space and violation of nature—all the established conditions. In this context we can say that the seeds of revolution lie in the emancipation of the senses (Marx)—but only when the senses become practical, productive forces in changing reality.

[12] Marcuse, *Eros and Civilization*, 180.

Keen: Then the real limitations to the development of sensibility are first in the community and only then in the psyche?

Marcuse: No. I would have to say it the other way around. You will be able to establish an authentic community only if it consists of human beings who have this new sensibility.

Raser: It seems like a closed circle to me.

Marcuse: Why?

Raser: If the structure of our psyche, that form of our consciousness, is so determined by the nature of the society in which we live, I can't understand how you can have transformation of the individual without the transformation of society and vice versa.

Marcuse: I can't see it clearly either. But as we discussed before, you can be determined by your community and the determination can be a negative one.

Keen: So you may be determined to fight that which is determining you.

Marcuse: Yes.[13]

That precisely is the problem of being guided by dialectical unitive experience: the creature determined by society is determined to fight the ills of that society. The organized man is organizing; he is a destiny that destines; he is the one who is condemned to be free. The problem is lack of ontological self-direction on the part of the human orderer in his participation in existence and lack of social self-direction on the part of society. Both are in fact functions of a totalization and responsible to its intentions in unitive experience. It is little wonder that Marcuse admits to not seeing the issue clearly.

The "unitive moment of experience" is not new in the history of thought. John Dewey emphasized it in terms of the "union of doing and undergoing." Marcuse places the emphasis on the new relations between instincts and reason. There are many models of "unitive experience." If we consider the notion of "moment," it has been identified as an experience of crisis by Kierkegaard (which is not a section in time, but eternity breaking into time). Nietzsche thought of the moment in terms of the eternal Now. I do not object to unitive moments of experience as models of experience, but the claim that such momentary experience is real and immediate, free of abstractions and ideology, defies my imagination.

Moreover, Marcuse takes great liberties in modifying the Freudian theory of instincts. He prefers the later, more philosophical notion of instincts, which Marcuse reads off as the new phenomenon of "historical needs."

[13] Sam Keen and John Raser, "Interview with Herbert Marcuse," *Psychology Today* (February, 1971), 64.

This idea implies that human needs have a historical character. All human needs, including sexuality, lie beyond the animal world. They are historically determined and historically mutable. And the break with the continuity of those needs that already carry repression within them, the leap into qualitative difference, is not a mere invention but inheres in the development of the productive forces themselves. The development has reached a level where it actually demands new vital needs in order to do justice to its own potentialities.[14]

These vital new historical needs will be more amenable to universal gratification and provide new standards for the conception of the good society. They are, in fact, the drives which compete with the directives of the human orderer in participation.

The trust which Marcuse places in the unitive combination of Eros and Logos is rather excessive; it will produce the "new historical Subject." Herbert Read is disturbed by the construct of unitive experience as a guide of man for many reasons. But the one which troubles him the most is the irreconcilability of the two. He raises a rather profound question:

But can the senses be liberated to create their own order in a society that has achieved "the pacification of the struggle for existence"? Is there not some final contradiction between an irrational art and a rational society, between the paradoxical man who insists on going "infinitely beyond man" and the technological man who plans "the utilization of resources for the satisfaction of vital needs with a minimum of toil"? If pacification and sublimation are contradictory processes, what then is the difference between the new Subject and the old Myth?[15]

The problem, I believe, is greater even than that: how such a principle of coresponsiveness between Eros and Logos becomes the bearer of a more oppressive totality by functioning as cosponsors of the dialectics of totality. The passage beyond the subject-object split is strewn with insurmountable difficulties, some of which implicate man in a system of totality that gets rid of the human orderer and the anthropologization of participation in existence. I will elaborate on this issue in some detail at the beginning of the next chapter.

Perhaps Marcuse's basic problem is the same as that of the New Left: how does one derive the notion of shared responsibility from anarchically unorganized spontaneous feelings? My reply is that human vitality, energetic and revolutionary as it may appear to be, does not even touch the

---

14 Herbert Marcuse, "The End of Utopia," *Ramparts* (April, 1970), 30.

15 K. H. Wolff and B. Moore (eds.), *The Critical Spirit* (Boston, Beacon Press, 1967), 215.

problem of the sources of human responsibility. For that we need a human sense of direction.

When the "unifying moment of experience" is not the identifying synthesis of a purposive being, it is a method of totalization, a way of totalizing human experience without human consent. Totalization has priority to the humanization of life. The dialectic of Eros and Logos is such a servant of totality, in the case of Marcuse, of "eroticized reality." The identifying synthesis escapes man's control or the directionality of a purposive being. Man's life is centered in a totality and the dialectics is a method of totalizing life without human consent. The dialectics is, in fact, a *human* reality claim for a method of philosophizing. Cohen sees through it when he writes:

This style [of Marcuse's prose] is dictated by an affection for Hegelian reason (*Vernunft*), a thought-process in which the concept embraces and devours concept after concept in a perpetual and breathtaking synthesis. When we catch our breath we realize that *Vernunft* is only analysis (*Verstand*) in disguise. This disguise is dramatic, so the prose it clothes has power, but it is a serious mistake to conclude that thinking carries special insight because it is manifested in this way. Generally speaking, *Verstand* is the truth of *Vernunft*.[16]

My way of saying it, *Vernunft* is a *human* reality claim for *Verstand*; thus it belongs to the claims department of philosophy and has nothing to do with the truth or falsity of something. It belongs to human pretention and power rather than to analysis itself. The point is that dialectics, which slip past man's control, is the servant of Marcuse's totality, which is *the Lebenswelt of Art*, of eroticized reality itself.

If it was the intention of Marcuse to merge Hegel, Marx, and Freud in a new totality, he has merely multiplied the totalities and thus contributed to the problem of relativism of totalities. If the goal was to obtain a common structure among the three mutually exclusive totalities (Hegel, Marx, Freud), he has failed to reveal this. In my view, he has merely multiplied the totalities by adding Art as a new lifeworld. Cohen writes that Marcuse endorses Hegel's dictum, "the truth is the whole," but then he is "careful to add that the Whole is composed of discriminable parts. But sometimes the principle weighs more with him than the qualifications."[17] From my perspective, the "participation in the whole" is paramount and always domi-

---

[16] Jerry Cohen, "Critical Theory: The Philosophy of Marcuse," *New Left Review*, No. 57 (September/October, 1969), 50.

[17] *Ibid.*, 50.

nates, and the method of totalization, the dialectic of Eros and Logos, is the servant of that Whole.

Cohen, however, is essentially correct in saying:

A vision dominates Marcuse's career, explaining both his hope and his despair. It derives from German Philosophy of History, from which he appropriated the conviction that the history of humanity can be read as the result of a great project, drafted and executed by a single agency, mankind. . . . Marcuse has felt the gales of our world-historical season.[18]

However, it never occurs to Marcuse that this drive for totalisms may have a human genesis and meaning, that such totalities come from man's search for wholeness, as human projections and productions, as in the case of Karl Marx. If the latter is the case, then the phrase "participation in the whole," as one model of human participation, does not have the priority of a lifeworld, whether that *Lebenswelt* is eroticized or proletarianized. Marcuse's confusion rests on the fact that he relates totality to reality instead of to a theory of man. But this again requires separate argumentation. The present task is to shed some light on the possible sources of human responsibility. This much is clear, however, that if man's primary obligation is to a totality that is integrated with reality itself, however it is read out of reality, man must fail in establishing his *human claims* upon responsibility. The most he can achieve by "participating in the whole" is to show "responsibility to" it and its methods of totalization. In the following chapter the task will be to formulate an alternative to Marcuse's model of human participation.

[18] *Ibid.*, 35, 46.

4. The Purposive Model of Participation

In this chapter I wish to develop two themes: (1) to give a summary of the consequences that are entailed in going beyond the subject-object split, thus giving an evaluation of the five models of participation discussed in the previous chapters; and (2) to develop the ontological model of participation in which man's purposive being significantly anthropologizes the matrix of participation and provides a new solution to the subject-object split without going beyond it. In Part Two the various theories resulting from these six models of human participation will be examined and a new perspective of the sources and dimensions of human responsibility will be discussed in earnest.

Some Consequences of Going Beyond the Subject-object Split

There is an implicit rationale in all the models of participation that we have examined thus far which emphasize going beyond the subject-object split. This is a firm belief in the desirability of such a venture. There is a certain common pattern in all the models of participation that implicate totality in one form or another.

One, the human orderer, having been blended with the field of unitive experience, is replaced in his directive function in participation by the guidance of unitive experience. In process philosophy, such as Mead's and Dewey's, "qualitative thought" and "qualitative purpose" are always symbolic of such "qualitative situations" or unitive experience. The situation, which is the joint product of the organism interacting with its environment, is unitive, self-regulative, to the point where it is no longer meaningful to talk about the subject-object dichotomy in such a field or stream of experience that the situation exhibits. Events, relations, and qualities in their natural occurrence are neither subjective nor objective. The situation already speaks the language of coresponsiveness or mutual determination. It needs only a "problematic situation" to move it into action, without having need of the notion of the human orderer. It is like the situation of a swimmer in the water who remains in the current even while taking a breath out of the water. Man is a phase of the interactive stream and receives proper guidance therefrom. Dewey even improves on William James's "dumb responses" made within the stream of immediate experience by giving them an honorific label, "qualitative experience." The upshot of this perspective is that unitive experiences literally retrace the steps of the creative process itself—free of abstractions and ideology.[1]

But Marcuse offers a fascinating contrast to this model of unitive experience, with the touch of dialectical materialism, by offering another construct of unitive experience in terms of Eros and Logos. In this case, human sensibility has historical revolution on its mind, not piecemeal liberal reformism as in Dewey, where it reflects an evolutionary perspective of history. Thus to say that both men are talking about unitive experience that is free of abstractions and ideology is somewhat foolhardy. The name of the game is constructionism. Direct experience, in its first reading or in its virgin consciousness, is already a model of experience. The holistic tendency of human purpose has had a hand in forming and shaping the stream of experience in which man looses his directive agency.

In chapter 1 we noted three models of social immediacy, each of them claiming the essence of unitive experience: the whole man theme, situational spontaneity, and universal social immediacy. This is evidence of more constructionism, or of covert forms of mediation on the level of the unmediated.

Two, it was also noted that such unitive experience is the servant of different dialectical procedures also embedded in direct experience. This involves the notion of the hypostatization of dialectics. First of all, dialectics is a product of the human mind. It is that speculative part of the mind where reason operates without the strictures of logical laws. This is the primal meaning of dialectical method. When it is given other functions to perform by a system of totality, like the function of controlling unitive experience, this is already a derivative use of dialectics. It is a hypostatization of a reflected methodology. When it is placed prior to purposive being,

[1] R. J. Bernstein, *On Experience, Nature, And Freedom* (New York, Bobbs-Merrill, 1960), 176–98.

84

it signals the end of the human orderer and his capacity for ontological self-direction in participation.

Three, both unitive experience and dialectical method are servants of totality because they are substitute forms of directionality in the place of the human orderer. There is an inexorable logic to all this, a kind of inevitability to all these movements, which attempts to solve the problem of man by going beyond the subject-object split. They all signalize man's immersion or total absorption in some system of totality. This point should influence us to take a second look at the attempts to go beyond the subject-object dichotomy because such epistemological niceties grip human nature in certain ontological commitments. This is not an understanding but a restructuring of human nature and the human condition.

No matter how such a system of totality is constructed (and even its alleged discovery or disclosure is construction by participation, in terms of my theory), man always finds himself a "functionary of" in such a totalistic scheme. If this is the case, why are such systems of total comprehensiveness so appealing to mankind? Is it man's fear or reticence in taking on "responsibility for" it? Let me hazard a guess why such systems of totalization have an enduring charm for mankind.

One, man's search for wholeness is such a significant part of his search for meaning that, more often than not, he mistakes the search for wholeness for the universe of totality. He justifies this venture in terms of his intention or conviction by saying to himself, if there is in man such a drive for wholeness, there must be a totality waiting at the other end of the line in such an open communication.

Two, this mistaken identification between the search for wholeness, on the part of man, and the universe of totality, on the other, is, I think, due to man's fear of the burden of responsibility for such systems of responsibility. Thus while man partakes of the search for wholeness, he wants to be relieved of the burden of sharing the responsibility for the system of totality. For man, the search is fraught with perils for him to feel too secure in the quest.

Three, because man lives out his life in community, in interchanges with others, and has commerce with persons, objects, things, causes, agencies, etc., he comes to believe that such a context of interchanges, to be successful or operative, needs a total context that involves transcendence to the Completely Other—that is to say, that such interchanges with things and others involves or points to a totality that is beyond human participation (even though man is a part-participant in such a totality).

What does it mean to say that man has become a "functionary of" a system of totality(s)? In terms of my theory, man has become his own tyrant by establishing the tyranny of totality(s) over his existence. What kind of creature must he be to desire going beyond the subject-object split? Since man confronts others in human participation, he feels he must confront the Completely Other beyond human participation. How justified is this mode of response to life? Does man deny his purposive being when he denies the directives of his purposive actions or purposive thoughts? Or is his purposive being asserted or implied even in such denials, as in the giving over a goal-directedness to some other power like a system of totality(s)? I have called this elsewhere "purposive or positive alienation." Just because man in his plans gives over the directives to another, or to the Completely Other, does not mean he denies his purposive being, for the denial takes place only on the level of action or thought. The mistaken belief—that when certain purposes (as goals) are denied, man's purposive being is also denied—has brought us to believe that systems of totality are the source of human responsibility, rather than man, as a human orderer or purposive being, in existence. Through this mistake man has become his own tyrant by swearing allegiance to systems of totality. The appeal of transferring allegiance from man to a system of totality(s) thus rests on certain fuzzy notions about human purpose and its ultimate capabilities. This confusion about purpose has brought about the artificial need to transform man's search for wholeness into a system of absolute participation— "participation in the whole." The commitment of purposes (goals) to others and to the Completely Other has completely externalized man. It has led man to the denial of his purposive being as the source of responsibility.

What I am suggesting is that man's confusion about the nature of his purposive life has led him to an uncritical acceptance of the orderings by a system of totality(s). The need to go beyond the subject-object split may thus be a methodogenic artificial problem and not the requirement of life, as totalists believe. More specifically, because man has never conceived of the human orderer in terms of purposive being (as having an ontological capacity for self-direction), he has been more than willing to accept the directives and responsibilities assigned to him by a system of totality(s), even if it was one of his own making. He has been willing to give his life over to models of existence in exchange for guidance and directionality. Thus man's complacent inattention to his own purposive being has brought about the tyranny of totality(s).

I have not been describing the psychoanalysis of systems of totality. The critique derives from a new theory of purposive being which has new relevance for human participation and responsibility. In fact, it requires the rethinking of man's relationships to systems of totality(s). Thus the crisis of responsibility is more than a "crisis in values," as some have suggested, because a decision has to be made about the claims of responsibility, as to whether it takes a human or a totalistic form (as in the past). There is no point in discussing the niceties of human responsibility when we are confused about the nature of its source.

Four, going beyond the subject-object dichotomy produces another model of existence. It does not enable one to touch the hem of the universe of totality. What has inspired the totalist to believe that he has touched the real system of totality is his appeal to direct experience which he thinks is model-free. But if the postulate of an ontological human orderer is assumed, as my theory enables us to do, then direct experience cannot be disassociated from the immediatizing capacity of man's purposive nature. Man goes on all the trips taken by direct experience, even on the trip of universal immediacy. The human orderer may be left behind in his plans of action or thought, but he goes along as a purposive being in the capacity of ontological self-direction. He anthropologizes direct experience. This means that even direct experience, as a model of experience by participation, is a manner of relating oneself to the world, however immersive such an experience may be. It can only be a close-up of experience for the human orderer. Thus one never escapes model-making in claims of participation in existence. Even the posture of an ideology critique, as in Marcuse, involves man on a trip in direct experience. In short, the trouble with such excursions beyond the subject-object split is precisely the fact that the human orderer as a purposive being goes on all such trips and does so deliberately. This manner of relating oneself to the world, through a direct form of immediate experience, does not escape the attention of man. In fact, it has the endorsement of the human orderer on the phenomenal level of action and analysis. The fact that the part-to-whole logic cannot be stated apart from him shows his indispensability both to participation and to the process of reflection. Whether one is thrown into such situations "in der Welt sein," or found to be interacting with it, makes little difference. The

87

human orderer is there managing the manner of one's relatedness to the world.

Such solutions to the subject-object split in terms of totality imply some residue of totality that is beyond human participation. This aspect of the problem suggests that all such schemes of totality, to the extent they are beyond human participation, are models of existence. In the previous chapters I noted that a scheme of subjective totality absorbs the function of objectivity, in both the personal and social versions of subjectivity, as one way of resolving the subject-object split. I also noted that the scheme of objective totality similarly absorbed the function of subjectivity (private experiences) to resolve the subject-object dichotomy. Next it was noted how nature absorbed both and sustained their emergence (in Mead and Dewey). Whether the solution to the dichotomy is sought within or outside the context of human participation, the question first arises in man's purposive being and requires a solution in terms of a theory of man as a human orderer before the problem is projected on man's relationship to the world. The effort to transcend man by solving the subject-object split in some reality beyond man merely provides new models about man's relatedness to the world and not a living and breathing totality.

Five, the claim is usually made that going beyond the subject-object split provides man with a new sense of participation and responsibility in terms of some principle of coresponsiveness, coresponsibility, mutual participation, or coexperience. This principle is read off as something real and inherent in direct experience itself. Peter Bertocci, for example, discusses such a "co-responsive community" in terms of the Christian scheme of totality. He means to encourage a strong belief in a real "freedom in community" through such coresponsiveness. Bertocci states:

In short, in what I would call the inner voice of Judeo-Christian perspective, the authentic individual is he who proves his faith in individuality, not by asking to be understood and approved, but by understanding the nature of the needs of others within a community of mutual concern. . . . The individual and the social can enrich each other when the ideal of community supplants the contrast of individual and common.[2]

The problem with the principle of coresponsiveness is that it is not merely the summation of individual and communal responsibilities, that it is more than the sum of these. It would seem to indicate a reference to

[2] P. A. Bertocci, "The Co-responsive Community," in *The Knowledge Explosion*, ed. by F. Sweeney (New York, Farrar, Straus, Giroux, 1966), 57.

totality beyond or below man, and thus it involves a principle of comprehension from beyond itself. We noted similar implications to totality in Sartre, Mead, and Dewey's notions of codetermination. Thus the trip beyond the subject-object split yields a principle which is rather problematic. In one way or another, coresponsibility favors the orderings of totality to the neglect of the human orderer, even though he is functionally subsummed in the dynamics of coresponsiveness. If one asks the question, why is such a principle more than the sum total of the two contributing factors involved in it, then the reply is that some other ordering power has been invoked to make the principle transcendent to the two terms in its dynamic make-up.

Six, we noted also that this may simply be a way of claiming a mode of absolute participation by "participation in the whole." Since this can never be demonstrated in perspectival human participation, even in perspectival holism, it can be established only by certain claims to ultimacy, by forms of apologetics. Thus there is introduced in the midst of arbitrary experiences a standard of reference that is foreign to human experience. This is established by subsumming the human factor in the class of totality. Because immediate experience is the realm of the unjustified, it is open to such exploitation by the totalists.

I suppose that all six criticisms hinge on one central factor: how a system of totality becomes the source of human directionality and responsibility in the place of the human orderer (whom we respect as a purposive being in existence). Two dominant methods have been used to create such systems of totality that usurp man's prerogatives in directionality: (1) self-transcendence, and (2) interactionism, or discontinuity and continuity, respectively. Both these modes of human directionality, the first rising above immediate experience and achieving its goals, and the other staying within experience in a spirit of progressive expansionism, are methods for totalizing human experience. I regard both these forms of human directionality as being goal-directed toward some system of totality and as abstractions from man's capacity for ontological self-direction in participation. Unless man as a human orderer in participation can stand behind such ultimately planned and deliberate goal-directedness (as in a system of totality) and make his presence count in self-direction even in such "participation in the whole," there is little meaning in such choices and goals. In what follows I shall endeavor to point out that systems of totality are the by-products of phenomenal goals, that such totalities do not function as the domain of goals. Such goal-directedness requires ontological self-direction to be operative on the phenomenal level of existence. Otherwise they become dictatorial claims.

THE PURPOSIVE MODEL OF PARTICIPATION

In this section I hope to show there is no need to go beyond the subject-object split, beyond an adequate theory of man, to solve the problem in some systems of totality which absorbs and restructures man. This will involve a statement of the human orderer and of his capacity for ontological participation in existence. It will also involve bypassing the issue of freedom and determinism in stating the new theory of the human orderer in terms of purposive being.

The Liberation of the Human Orderer

The liberation of the human orderer in the matrix of participation involves bypassing the issue of freedom and determinism and of solving the subject-object split in relation to man's purposive being. We have often used the term where man "anthropologizes" or humanizes participation. This involves the "radicalization" of participation. Bypassing the issue of freedom and determinism may seem like an odd requirement for a philosophy of participation, of relating purpose to the thickness of human participation. For my theory, however, purpose is a primitive, not freedom or determinism. Purpose is far more than a function of subjectivity. So is human participation more than a function of subjectivity or of self-possession. Participation, in terms of my theory, is the human orderer manifesting his being in self-direction in the confrontation with existence. Man is self-directing in such encounter experiences. In such a perspective, which defines man as the subject-object dialogue mediated by his purposive nature, the freedom of the subject self is no more privileged than the object self. They are both models of existence mediated by man's purposive nature. The free subject is mediated by man's purposive nature in acts of self-subjectification. The object self is similarly mediated by purposive being in acts of self-objectification. Both require the model-making capacity of man's purposive being in participation. Consequently, this theory requires another order of priorities than the old dichotomy of freedom and determinism which, while it has had an impressive historical career, has largely remained a problem rather than a resolution of the subject-object split. It

90

has encouraged camp followers and led to new models of totality under false pretenses.

As a problematic dichotomy, it has played a vital role and given man some new images of himself and of totality. But such images or models are to be used further in man's search for meaning in understanding himself and the world about him. The freedom-determinism split has, as noted above, contributed greatly to the upsurge of systems of totality, as was noted in the subject-object split and the many attempts to go beyond it. Historically, the subject of being has been identified as the bearer of responsibility and the object self was disassociated from it. There have been some modern attempts to relate responsibility to the object self and the determinists' view of man. There are current linguistic attempts to reexamine this issue in order to show that responsibility is reconcilable with the "incompatibility principle" in the deterministic theory of man.[3] These issues have never been satisfactorily resolved. Where solutions have been offered that have led beyond the subject-object split, they have moved in the direction of totalization. The impasse is as new as science and as old as philosophy and religion. Perhaps it is better to begin anew, to put down new stakes in defining the perimeter of human participation, to see if we can liberate the human orderer in the matrix of participation without immersing him in some system of totality. At least this is the course I have taken in this volume.

Three elite terms are essential to the theory advocated in this book: purpose, participation, and responsibility (in respective order of importance). I am using the human orderer, as a purposive being in existence, to define human participation, as over against totalistic or absolute participation in the whole. This philosophy of participation serves as a new foundation for the theory of responsibility. Both freedom and determinism are functions or operations of man's purposive being in the matrix of participation. Their relevance to existence is functional on the level of the phenomenal, where choices and goals are found to operate. Let me form some of these ideas into definitions.

Freedom means, in this new model of participation, the use we make of our purposive directives to contribute to our development in existence. It is what we do (in our capacity for self-direction) with our acts of self-subjectification in the process of becoming. Freedom here is a functional

<hr>

[3] G. H. Paske, "Responsibility and the Incompatibility Principle," *The Personalist* (Autumn, 1970), 477–85.

term appearing for the first time on the phenomenal level of experience, where we are concerned with choice-making and goal-seeking possibilities. Although we do not give it primitive status in primordial experience, it makes more sense than the mindless encounters of existentialism, where it is accepted as a primitive term. Thus we are most free when we contribute to our development through the directives of our purposive nature in acts of self-subjectification. Man's purposive nature is here a requirement for the subject self to be operative in its enterprises of participation in existence. Man's directive being-agency is a mediative phenomenon on the level of ontological interaction. This prior meaning of purposiveness in its role of mediation comes before the recognition of the wholeness of experience. Such a scheme of totality, as part of the subject self's desires, is a project first of human self-direction. For the centeredness that is at the core of the human orderer in the matrix of participation is that of self-direction and not a scheme of totality as a measure of some final scheme of coherence that makes life move.

Similarly, determinism is also the use we make of the directives of our purposive nature in contributing to our development. Only here we use these directives in acts of self-objectification. Both freedom and determinism are models of man. Freedom is the undifferentiated model of the subject self; determinism is the highly structured model of the object self. Both models presuppose the mediative capacity of man's purposive nature. This brings us to our definition of man, stated elsewhere first, that man is a subject-object dialogue mediated by his purposive nature. Thus it is presupposed even when we picture man as a determined creature and causally determined.

Both the subject and object selves are images of man, models of human nature. When each is taken to be something more than that it is usually goal-directed to some system of totality. When each is taken as immediately real, it turns out, paradoxically, that it is not its own but belongs to some system of totality. The case for the human orderer cannot be stated in terms of goal-directedness alone, for it leads to pluralism and relativism and to further claims of ultimacy to get out of both. If neither the subject nor object self is its own, apart from a system of totality, each is capable only of *responsibility to* but not *responsibility for*, for its actions. If there is no purposive being standing behind such acts and present in such self-directing acts of self-subjectification or self-objectification, there is no way to account for the *responsibility for* something. One may be able to show *action to* something or *reaction* toward it, but not responsibility for such actions. Unless purposive being backs and is present in actions, actions cannot produce being accumulatively by choices and goals. Jean-Paul Sartre's predicament—the reduction of being to action and the derivation of being, through active choices, from such action—is a magic talisman that just does not work in reality. This accounts for the unavailability of an ethic from Sartre's perspective, in spite of all the emphasis on how the lone individual is responsible to his loneliness. The subject of being owes its life to dialectical totality. It is *responsible to* something, but not *responsible for* it.

The same predicament shows up when attempts are made to derive responsibility from the object self. Gerald Paske, for example, argues that even if the world is deterministic, it still does not follow that no one would be responsible for his actions. He dismisses the problem of what constitutes human rationality. It can be bypassed since one needs only to assume that there is such a thing as rationality to have responsible actions. The concept of responsibility does not require that a person "had to be able to do other than he did in order to do other than he did," which would be irrational. Thus the placing of responsibility in the deterministic or causal sequence does not preclude responsible behavior. He gives the analogy of a puppeteer and a puppet which applies to many situations but not to normal human behavior. Paske remarks:

But when we turn to the normal individual the analogy fails, for in this case both the puppeteer and the puppet represent the rational self. Thus, abandoning the analogy, to say that a man is controlled by his reason is to say that he is not controlled at all, or, more accurately, it is to say that he is self-controlled. True, it is no credit to him that he has become self-controlled, but he is self-controlled nonetheless.[4]

One is thus not forced in one's intellectual processes and can be responsible in his actions even in terms of the deterministic image of man. The intellect cannot be so coerced or it would not be rationality. The relevant self, as the rational self, is thus free to be responsible in behavior even in a determinist view of man. Paske continues: "If this is correct, then determinism is perfectly compatible with responsibility, for it is not whether one's behavior is caused or uncaused that is important, it is rather the nature of the causes that is crucial."[5]

[4] *Ibid.*, 485.
[5] *Ibid.*

Such a view of responsibility is a "functionary of" a system of totality. It can only show, in its actions, responsibility to them, not responsibility for them. The victory of a determinist is thus empty. One does not speak well of the human mind to equate it with the puppeteer and the puppet analogy, for the puppeteer is as much a functionary as the puppet. Paske is incorrect to say that the analogy does not apply to man. He does not progress too far with the notion of responsible actions. One does not derive responsible being out of such responsible actions. It adds nothing to the concept of selfhood. All it says is that actions are *responsible to* something or someone.

Is this a way of dismissing a problem for epistemological niceties? But such niceties commit one to an ontological perspective of man. The human orderer is somehow less than his autonomous intellect, which is odd and hardly acceptable in this somewhat anti-intellectual age. Is the mind that much a master either of its acts or its thoughts, as Paske supposes? He does not face up to these questions. Just because the mind is already here does not make it less a functionary of its thoughts and actions or of its alleged genius for shared responsibility. This issue needs to be reexamined anew. What is the relation of mind to purposive being? Only when we have answers to this question can we relate the goals of the mind to actions and responsibility. Yet I do not propose to examine this issue in the sequel. It should be another writing project. The goals of the mind may turn out to have little significance if the mind is separated from the human orderer and yet has the capacity to legislate shared responsibility in programs of action. If the mind is part of the part-to-whole logic, which a deterministic view of man adheres to, then it is really a meaningless act to say that the mind is both puppeteer and a puppet. What is at issue is not only the genesis of the mind, but its current positionality in the part-to-whole logic. If the object self is not a model of man in a model of totality, it is a hypostatized entity.

The more representative view of the relation of man-the-object to responsibility is indicated by Elton Trueblood, citing Kant's theory that the "ought" is operative only where there is "possibility." People are not held accountable for their failure to do what they cannot do. Thus if one is necessitated in his behavior and there is no freedom (in terms of autonomy), one is not responsible for his actions. Trueblood is especially pleased with Karl Jaspers' solution to the problem, which says, in effect, that because man is a subject, he falls outside the system of any objective totality.

This opens the gate to another kind of order in existence, other than the order of natural necessity. The upshot of Trueblood's view is that it is useless to search for responsibility in man-the-object, but that such notions of responsibility are to be found in man-the-subject and the possibility of a new order that comes from such existential insights. While this is not a solution to the objectivist, it is a popular theory of the subjectivist, who thinks that responsibility is on the side of the real subject self against an artificial object self.[6]

I believe the task of liberating the human orderer must be different from the problems that cluster around man-the-subject, man-the-object, and the respective problems that have to do with the freedom-determinism controversy and its relation to the theme of responsibility. As I envision the task of liberating the human orderer by bypassing the freedom-determinism issue, it may sound like a paradox. But if the reader keeps in mind that such controversies have led man out of himself to systems of totality, then the task does not appear so paradoxical. Freedom and determinism, just as subjectivity and objectivity, need to be related first to a theory of man in terms of the human orderer before the issue is applied to man's relationship to the world. If freedom and determinism are viewed as functions of certain images of man, they can be of greater service to us—as functions of the human orderer in participation—rather than as primitives. The issue of freedom and determinism was kept alive, and is still kept alive, only by viewing one or the other, as the case may be, as the work of the living man-as-subject or as the living man-as-object. We consider both images of man, with freedom or determinism as functions of these models of man. To hide this crucial issue behind some form of "unique immediacy" is to invite more controversy, which has already the stigma of having been too barren in the history of thought.

Take the example of James Bugental, who makes a plea for the model-free subject self, as a humanistic psychologist opposing the scientific model of man as object:

To the psychotherapist is offered the opportunity to participate with unique immediacy in the business of life itself. In psychotherapeutic practice one deals daily with the life and death of human personality and potential. I mean no

[6] D. E. Trueblood, "Contemporary Psychiatry and the Concept of Responsibility," *Psychiatry and Responsibility*, ed. by H. Schoeck and J. Wiggins (New York, Van Nostrand, 1962), 19–37.

play on words, and the melodrama implicit in this characterization is that of the human experience itself.[7]

Without meaning to disparage Dr. Bugental as a practicing psychiatrist, or for the mystery of such first-hand experience and interrelationship, I believe that the deepest meaning of living is by participating as a human orderer in existence. The phrase "the human experience itself" suggests some other alternative to man's participation in experience, perhaps the alternative where man is already absorbed "with unique immediacy in the business of life itself." Such "conformity to Being" in the part-to-whole logic is already a sell-out of the participant in experience as a human orderer. If this is the case, such "unique immediacy" is merely a claim to ultimacy for one's model of participation—in the case of Bugental, the model of doctor-patient participation—unless one assumes this is the universal standard for human participation in the business of life itself. The point is, there is no universal immediacy, just as there is no universal toothpaste. It is significant that both products of human participation come out in the form of brands with their respective labels. The melodrama is not to be found in the business of life itself, as Bugental suggests, but in the drama of totalities, which are models of existence parading as the real thing. What permits him to take such liberties is the mistaken identification of model with existence. Once this move is made, the rest follows. Why should model-making not apply to primal experience if the human orderer is a part of it? If he is not a part of primal experience, it makes no difference whether experience is immediate or mediate, crude or ineffable. Man is not responsible for it anyway. Thus the effort to absorb man in some form of unitive experience like "unique immediacy" is a way of relating man to a system of totality which is below or above him but which does not issue from him as a human orderer. This is to no avail, however, because the human orderer is self-directing in and through such involvements and goes along on each trip that would absorb him in a system of totality. The other alternative is that if man is so lost in a system of totality, what is the point of responsibility even to that system of totality?

In the light of my theory, the subject self does not drool before reality in unique immediacy. Man confronts reality as a human orderer. The subject self is mediated by man's purposive nature in acts of self-subjectifica-

---

[7] James F. T. Bugental, *The Search For Authenticity* (New York, Holt, Rinehart, Winston, 1965), 367.

tion. This means that the subject self is as much a construct as the object self and so is its participation in the business of life itself. This means that human participation is creative participation, which radicalizes or anthropologizes the very process of human participation in existence. This necessitates the distinction between models of participation and real participation, with no attempt to run the two together by some spurious claims to ultimacy for one's model about such participation. One may call this model-making by experience. This is just as commonly practiced as model-making by the mind. In terms of this theory, it is possible to have a responsible view of systems of responsibility where man shows *responsibility for* them. This is also the meaning of responsibility in the human sense: responsibility is man confronting the human orderer in himself and in society. This is the reason why man can have a sense of responsibility and participation instead of being absorbed by unitive experience that follows the directives of totality. This also means that man's freedom and determinism are both molded by self-directive being. Between man and responsibility is the human orderer participating in existence.

The human orderer is mediative both of freedom and determinism and permiates the man as subject and the man as object. Unitive experience is possible only because of this ontological capacity of self-direction. Even when the case for unitive totality is stated, it requires the holistic use of man's purposive nature to get the postulate off the ground. The whole point of the purposive model of participation is to strengthen the cause of participation by strengthening the work of the human orderer as purposive being in existence. Twentieth-century philosophy has moved in the opposite direction; to strengthen the cause of participation it felt constrained to weaken the human orderer by accepting only some of his functions as contributions to some phases of unitive experience. This practice was also popular in Europe along subjective and intersubjective lines. Unless man can claim the ownership of himself as a human orderer in the sense of ontological self-direction, we have no way of coming up with a strong philosophy of participation. I do not consider "participation in the whole" a strong view of human participation, as I indicated in the last chapter. The whole point of this book is how to rescue the human orderer from the uniqueness of immediate experience that is free of model-making. The path I have chosen is to disregard the uniqueness of immediate experience and by looking at it from the standpoint of model-making by participation. If there is any uniqueness in given immediate experience, it derives from the human orderer and his capacity to immediatize or anthropologize the process of participation.

It is imperative for our theory of responsibility that we include the human orderer in his full strength in the matrix of participation to account for response-relations. He must be inclusive of primal experience. This necessitates a new perspective of given immediate experience as something that is part of the process of participation. The "given" is the name we give to the terminus of participation; it is the object of participation and not something beyond human participation. In Dewey's perspective, the "given" is the quality of experience produced by the interaction of organism with its environment. It is undetermined until it has correlative determination by the interaction. This means that direct unitive experience is the given and man as part of the field of experience contributes some phase or function to it but is not a guiding factor of the unitive experience. Dewey says: "In truth 'given' in this connection signifies only that the quality immediately exists, or it is brutely there. . . . The only thing that is unqualifiedly given is the total pervasive quality. . . ."[8] A given is thus a quality of unitive experience produced by the interaction, of which man is a factor. It is situationally contained and it is there that the given appears. It should be noted here that the given in the form of unitive experience is more than the joint participation of organism interacting with its environment. It implicates totality and its directives and is prior to the human orderer as we have defined him. To say that the given is the object of participation (or its terminus) enables the human orderer to anthropologize the process of participation. In a certain sense, even though man participates in unitive experience, the unitive experience in its guidance function, for Dewey, is beyond human participation. For such immediate situations are closer to the system of natural totality than they are to the human orderer, as the principle of mutual determination has revealed in terms of our analysis.

In terms of my theory, freedom foreshadows the human orderer in participation when participation is underscored by acts of self-subjectification. Determinism is foreshadowed in participation when the human orderer is participating in acts of self-objectification. The full impact of the human orderer is felt in the matrix of participation when its capacity for model-making is recognized as the human way of participating in experience. Such choice-making and goal-seeking that goes on in the milieu of human participation in existence is the acknowledged operational aspect of man's

[8] R. J. Bernstein, *op. cit.*, 189–90.

potentiality to be self-directing in participation and responsibility in the matrix of existence. Should human purpose become coexperiential with the principle of objectification in seeking its own kind of participation, the function of determinism will be manifest as an aspect of participation. But the potentiality for model-making is prior to the distinction of freedom and determinism and is mediative even of the subject-object distinction. Although the issue of freedom and determinism is bypassed on the primitive level of interchange, it reappears liberated to function legitimately in the process of human creativity under the guidance of purposive being. The question of freedom and determinism arises first in man's purposive being. It would have no meaning to a creature devoid of purposiveness. If we bypass freedom and determinism as primitives, we do so only to accept them functionally because of our belief that man's purposive nature is mediative both of subject and object selves as well as of the dialogue between them. The existentialist's attempt to state the case for ontological freedom of the subject of being is an attempt to construct an encounter philosophy by excluding purposive being from primal experience. Ontological freedom is the primitive and purpose is its by-product or a reactive phenomenon to it. The same issue reappears in empirical philosophy, bent on encounter experiences, where causality and necessity are viewed as part of the matrix of primal experience and purpose is either a by-product of it or a reaction to it.

Both attempts to construct a model-free subjectivity or objectivity have either limited the human orderer to peripheral nondirective functions, separating man's elemental modes of response from the human orderer, or they have excised him from primal situations altogether and made him an onlooker of the scene of primal experience. It is our wish to avoid both these mistakes by (1) utilizing a theory of purposive being recently developed in a philosophy of participation and responsibility, and (2) by showing the relevance of the new theory of responsibility to experience, which would hopefully show sufficient contrast with theories of responsibility in other schools of thought which have commerce with totalities. It is our wish to establish a model of participation that will serve as a base for responsibility and give the human responder a rootedness in purposive being, rather than in some system of totality. What makes possible a responsible theory of participation and a participatory theory of responsibility is the new model of the human orderer that we have proposed for the matrix of participation.

99

Encounter by Self-direction

Philosophies of encounter-experiences are tuned in on immediate experience more than others. In existentialism, for example, the placing of existence before essence, being before the thought of being, enables the thinkers to claim immediate experience in individual and social encounters. Such encounters are alleged to be free of abstraction and ideology. It is believed that somehow actions themselves flow on in the stream of life from particular to particular in the involvement of life's situations, that somehow life is speaking for itself and on its own in such encounters. This point of view I have labeled elsewhere as "instant being." Like "instant coffee," it affords some thinkers momentary pleasure in theorizing about life in this fashion.

In empiricism, pragmatism has similarly placed action before thought and assumed its immediacy, that it was free of abstraction and ideology, but it should be noted that this is a competing model of existence that requires a strong distinction between the existential and the natural. They are, in fact, two models of encounter experiences.

Such model-making is not eliminated in encounter experience because the human orderer goes along on all such trips. Man is self-directing in encounter, individual and social. Therefore, he cannot take second place to unitive experience felt in such encounters. This does not mean that man creates these encounters of being, but that he is self-directing in such encounter experiences. We are what we do only if we are self-directing in our doing. Thus when we use the caption above "encounter as self-direction," we are attempting to underscore the anthropologization of immediate experience and not simply leave it to given immediate forms of experience to guide us. In terms of our either/or logic, encounter experiences are directed either by totality or the human orderer. Encounters do not direct themselves. Dynamic as they are, they are not their own; neither are they simply the products of mutual determination. The principle of corresponsiveness appeals to a principle above itself for guidance.

In this section I am trying to state the overall human condition of purposive participation in existence: what it means to participate in existence, what it means to be responsible in a human sense. Such an issue is prior to more specific areas of concern, like moral responsibility and participation. For example, the moral distinction between what man is, what man ought to be, and what man ought to do, is a secondary problem in terms of my thesis. They are really three models or images of man in terms of the moral theme. I am concerned with the issue of the kind of participation that it takes to produce such models in specific dimensions of experience. From my standpoint, "what man is," is as much a model of man as are the other two. The appeal to direct experience, or a description of it, will not give us the "real man" unless the human orderer has some interest in seeking this image of himself for purposes of knowledge or for something else. Participation is thus a human problem before it is a moral or religious problem.

The problem with the purposive model of participation is how to stay on the model-making level. As W. Scott Morton, quoting Confucius, said: "He sets up an ideal and keeps it as an ideal." So long as the human orderer is an anthropologizing factor in the matrix of participation, one can never discount model-making by participation. This is an important point to grasp if one is to refrain from identifying his model of existence with existence as existence, if one is to refrain from hypostatizing one's model of existence. Encounter philosophies, whatever school of thought, neglect this truth and give us mindless and purposeless encounters as the true guides of life. "Encounter as self-directing" is a way of introducing the human orderer into the matrix of participation where his humanizing tendency is felt and understood. That is, in part, what I meant by the need for a functional ontology when I defined man as a subject-object dialogue mediated by his purposive nature.

With such a definition of man we can bypass the need for going beyond the subject-object split and create a new level of participation by a functional ontology. The subject-object split is no longer a conflict; it is rather a dialogue in which each has a limited but legitimate and creative function to perform. Both the subjective and objective models have legitimate functions of reconstruction to perform in the midst of participation, and they require the mediation of man's purposive being. The purposive model of participation is also a model of experience, like the others. But it provides better correlations with existence and accounts better for the process of model-making in experience. Moreover, it has a better way of coping with systems of totality and does not itself succumb to the problem of relativism. Purposive being is always there to order its goals and to reorder the schemes of totality.

Subjectivity and objectivity, as images of man or as principles of his self-understanding, originate in man's purposive being, the source of model-making, of goals, and of totalities. This means that man is a creature of ontological interaction even as a participant in experience when he relates to life in elemental modes of response. It also means that participation in experience has ontological relevance to existence through the mediation of a human orderer.

How is the subject-object distinction derived in the purposive model of participation? It derives from the process of ontological interaction, from the mediation of purposive being in the matrix of participation. Man's purposive nature is already coexperiential with acts of self-subjectification and acts of self-objectification. As models of directive participation, both subjectivity and objectivity require the mediation of ontological self-direction or the coexperience with purposive being. Consequently, in terms of my theory, the attempts to go back, to solve the subject-object dichotomy by going beyond it to some reality beyond self-directive being, have been misguided. We need only to find their support in a theory of man. I noted earlier how Mead derived the split from the inner and outer aspects of nature, where the freedom of subjectivity was related to the indeterminate experiences of nature and objective necessity was derived from the determinate aspects of nature. It was also noted how some attempts were made to derive subjectivity out of objectivity and, vice versa, to read objectivity out of the domain of subjectivity, or both principles out of unitive immediate experience, or both out of some scheme of totality. Yet there is a simple explanation for all this.

Acts of self-subjectification are goal-directed activities. They require the mediation of purposive being as self-directing in the matrix of participation. Acts of self-objectification are also goal-directed activities requiring self-direction of a human orderer as a purposive being in the matrix of participation. Without such mediative being (my concept of the human orderer), and without such model-making in existence, one is left with the primacy of goal direction for which totality functions as the "domain of goals." What this means as a counterthesis is that basically some form of totality(s) is the source of and the solution of the subject-object split. Such a solution would be highly desirable if it could be shown that somewhere up there in the blue horizon there is the real ultimate totality that serves as a standard for all models of totality. Since this would be a utopian claim— and the totalists know this when they identify the real totality with their models of totality—I have chosen an alternate course. It is more feasible to relate the models of subjectivity and objectivity to purposive being (to the self-directive human orderer in existence) to account for their participation and their dialogue than to get lost in one system of totality after another and one spurious claim after another. At least this is what I mean by the phrase "encounter by self-direction." This is also what I meant by solving the problem first in a theory of man before considering it as a problem of man's relation to the world-totality. Man's purposive being is thus the source of the subject-object polarity, as modes of participation in existence requiring the mediative and model-making capacity of purposive being. This is what we call creative participation, underscored by the functional ontology of man's purposive nature.

It is my contention that it is possible to get around the totalitarian thought symbolized by systems of totality by a model of ontological participation which breaks with the intentions of these totalities. Moreover, it is not necessary to claim the reality of such ontological participation. It is enough to keep it as a model of participation, calling it a functional ontology that allows for the possibility of this human modeling power or forming process in participation. The claim that man's purposive nature has a relevance to existence, that it relates to encounter experiences, is a saner program than the attempt to make claims of ultimacy for one's model of existence by claiming real and immediate "participation in the whole." I believe this is the real choice we face at this time. If we view purposive being as the human orderer in experience, as having a triadic relationship on the level of ontological interaction, it is possible to relate being to participation through subjectivity and objectivity. Purposive being, in the ontological model of participation, has the function of immediatizing elemental modes of response in experience, just as it has the function of mediatizing such experience by reflective thought. Through such capacities, it becomes the source of model-making in participation by being the source and sustenance of goals, choices, ideals, and systems of totality. Without this capacity, man could not even have images or models of human nature, let alone have images of totality. That such images have been constructed by an appeal to immediate experience, to the exclusion of human purpose, has given us the fierce competitive systems of totality with immediate claims to ultimacy. In short, it has given us totalitarian thought at its worst because such totalitarianism has taken possession of the human understanding. Once the human orderer is seen as a significant part of primal experience, his model-making by experience or by participation makes possible the exposure of alleged real totalities as models of existence.

The contribution of the ontological model is in "purposive" participation or encounter. It provides the possibility of a designing quality in experience not because of the unitive nature of experience, but because the designer is included as part of primal experience. Participation is thus a creative venture of a creative purposive being in existence who provides models of interaction and models of existential encounter in the matrix of participation. It is man's closeness to or distance from experience that enables the human orderer to label experience as immediate or mediate. Without his participation in existence on this purposive level of encounter, systems of totality would not even arise to man as a possibility. Nor would it be possible to talk about the notion of the "ground" of experience or the "given" in experience. Such questions arise within purposive being. They are also formed and sustained by man's ontological capacity for self-direction in experience. If this appears like a utopian dream, it is not so far-fetched as one would believe when compared with man's immersion in systems of totality that have nowhere else to go than to claim their self-sufficiency in reality. Such totalitarian models of existence, however they absorb man's functions in the service of totality or in the service of unitive experience establishing links of continuity for totality, always deny man's purposive posture in primal experience. It is too much of a threat to its own directives to have it play a vital role in the matrix of participation.

Rather than showing the relevance of totality(s) to existence, the ontological model of participation would show the relevance of the human orderer to existence through the ontological function of man's purposive nature. Freedom and determinism find their way into human participation through the subjective and objective models of participation. They are not functions of totality or its servants.

The Janus face of purpose, its capacity to deny itself (like the phenomenon of the split will mentioned earlier), has been read off as the denial of the relevance of purpose to participation and existence. It has been read off as the denial of the human orderer's contributions to participation in the system of totality(s). But this has been a gross mistake. When purposive being gives up its ordering power to a system of totality, as when it denies its capacity for self-direction, it does not stop functioning ontologically. This is only a phenomenal denial of its plans or goals. But even such denials require the continued functioning of purposive being in existence. I have called this elsewhere the phenomenon of positive alienation. It means that the human orderer goes along on all the trips that man takes beyond the subject-object split to mediate the holistic use of systems of totality. Purposive being is needed in its holistic function to establish the unity in systems of totality. While purpose denies some of its goals to establish others, ultimate ones, such as systems of totality, it does not mean that man's purposive nature is canceled by such participation. Ontological self-direction is needed as a prior purposiveness to establish such systems of totality. Purposive participation is thus prior to "participation in the whole," which is an abstraction, a temporary scheme of meaning on the part of the human orderer participating in existence. Man is not programmed by systems of totality(s) unless he, as a purposive being, has had a share in that programming on the primal level of experience. The appeal to immediate experience, the "back to experience" movement in modern thought, to disprove the claims of the human orderer in participation and in the matrix of existence, is an ingenious piece of work by the human orderer himself. That he is capable of such is certainly true, but this is only a denial of some of its own tactics rather than a denial of purposive being itself. This Janus face already shows itself on the ontological level of interaction, where man is defined as the subject-object dialogue mediated by his purposive nature. It is a function of its existence and not its existence itself. In its support of goals and plans, it is consistent. But in its choice of such, it is infinite. The eclipse of purpose is a functional phenomenon, not a substantive one. It is there ready to build other systems of totality, to glimpse other meanings of existence as system after system fails man in his correlations with existence.

From the liberation of the human orderer in the matrix of participation we move next to a participatory theory of responsibility in Part Two. The purposive model of participation provides new clues about the source of responsibility.

PART TWO: The Roots of Responsibility

5. Man's Claims on Responsibility

In this chapter we face a double task: (1) the liberation of the human orderer for responsible participation in existence, and (2) the radicalization of responsibility that will point to such a human orderer of response-relations beyond the image of him as a "responder." This involves emancipation from some of our attitudes toward ourselves and from cargoes of meaning we have picked up about ourselves in culture, as well as liberation from certain views we have attributed to immediate forms of experience and its alleged claims on man. The issue is, in part, an attitudinal one. But such a transformation of attitudes is required if man is to reclaim his claims on responsibility.

A Hidden Reference in Responsibility

The term "responsibility" has had many meanings in the history of thought and it will undoubtedly continue to disclose new meanings on the phenomenal field of action. However, it has consistently been viewed as having the central meaning of "response" and has been used in the context of "response-relations." It is my contention that we have to go under this phenomenal meaning of responsibility to understand its sources, that we even have to define "the responsible self" in a manner that suggests something deeper than the phenomenal understanding of man. In short, what is called for is a definition of the source of responsibility in terms of man's purposive being in the matrix of participation.

Let us take the concept of the "responsible person" first. This is a problematic notion. If by a responsible person we mean simply the responder or the answerer, as though he were always aim-directed, then this is not what we mean by the responsible person. The only responsible self my theory recognizes is where the human orderer takes on ontological self-directional responsibility for all his goal directions, choices, in response-relations. In his responses, man is not simply guided by unitive experience or by totalistic experience. The problem, then, is how to recover the human orderer from such unitive experience which implicate systems of totality. When the human orderer is thus liberated for responsibility (by remaining the human orderer even when he participates in the whole of experience), it can be properly said that he is responsible for such systems of total responsibility, however conflicting such comprehensive schemes are among themselves. When he takes his stand in participation and in shared responsibility as a human orderer, man is rightfully said to be responsible for systems of total responsibility. He is the author of systems of accountability or liability in every such system of totality. Accountability is not only culturally influenced and relativized; it is also anthropologized by the human orderer in each system of totality. Thus we shall not take the concept of "responsible person" at face value. We have yet to find out who and what the responsible person is by attending to the source of responsibility. If it can be shown that responsibility is man confronting the human orderer in himself individually and socially, then it can be said that man wears the colors of a "responsible self."

H. Richard Niebuhr's analysis is a good case in point. The analysis discloses four elements in responsibility: the response, the meaning interpretation of the response, the element of accountability, and the issue of social solidarity. The definition of responsibility follows this analysis: "The idea or pattern of responsibility, then, may summarily and abstractly be defined as the idea of an agent's action as response to an action upon him in accordance with his interpretation of the latter action and with his expectation of response to his response; and all of this is in a continuing community of agents."[1] The starting point, then, is responsibility, and man is interpreted in terms of the symbol of responsibility. Man comes out of this analysis as the "responsible self," in the "image of man-the-answerer, man engaged in dialogue, man acting in response to action upon him."[2]

George H. Mead has had a great influence on Niebuhr on the notion of social solidarity. But Richard Niebuhr does not stop with Mead's social behaviorism. He combines this cultural emphasis with the Christian sense of totality. This Protestant version of Mead may be attempting to har-

[1] J. M. Gustafson and J. T. Laney (eds.), *On Being Responsible* (New York, Harper, 1968), 35.
[2] *Ibid.*, 27.

monize two incompatible models of totality in an attempt to get at a theology of culture. We shall see. The attempt to define the whole man in terms of one of his activities, as through the symbol of responsibility, Niebuhr calls the method of "synecdochic analogy." The emphasis is on the relations we harbor in the present as we look to the future. The primary meaning of responsibility is still that of response, for man-the-answerer is still the responder, only now the responses take place in a more dynamic present. According to Niebuhr, the responsible self means man's ability to define and redefine himself in this matrix of dynamic social relationships, or to redefine himself in ongoing responsibilities, as "the self defines itself by the nature of its responses."[3] We have already seen this phenomenon at work in Mead's perspective. It enables man to show "responsibility to" but not "responsibility for." This schizoid reaction occurs because responsibility is disconnected from the human orderer and implicated in a system of totality. What guarantee does Niebuhr have that accountability is the same in the Christian scheme of totality as it is in Mead's social behaviorism? Or are they two different models of accountability in the matrix of participation? Richard Niebuhr never really faced up to this possibility in his writings.

That Niebuhr makes strenuous efforts to reduce man's claims on responsibility to account for the responsible self (odd as this may seem) is a deliberate move. Responsibility should be defined apart from the human orderer for the following reasons: (1) the meaning of suffering "cuts athwart our purposive movements"; (2) responsibility is the symbol that knows "what is going on" in the midst of suffering, while man's purposive nature (as goal-direction) is thwarted; (3) responsibility is more "fitting" in its responses to life and suffering than is human purpose in coping with life's problems; (4) such response-relations are thus geared to "fitting action" even in the midst of life that is permeated with obstacles, for it "fits into a total interaction as response and as anticipation of further response, is alone conducive to the good and alone is right."[4]

It is of interest to note that Niebuhr discards many images of man to define the notion of "human agency" in terms of responsibility, to arrive at the responsible self. The responsible self is socially responsible first before he has a glimpse of his own responsibility in self-action. Human agency is more than man-the-maker or man-the-citizen; he is man-the-answerer, or

[3] *Ibid.*, 30.
[4] *Ibid.*, 31.

the responder, I assume, to social questions. But man-the-answerer is not the human orderer in existence, either in society or in Protestant theology. The definition of human agency in terms of the meaning of one of its activities, that of responsibility (by synecdochic analogy), totally neglects the problem both of human agency as the source of concrete actions and the problem of the source of human responsibility. The human agent is capable of self-performance, or self-action, or of self-responses to life's problems. It knows what its responsibilities are in the midst of suffering, rather than in terms of ontological self-direction. Man is the kind of creature that is capable of the action of response. This is the equivalent of a responsible self. Let me give a list of criticisms suggesting the inadequacy of Niebuhr's notion of the responsible self.

First, the notion of human agency is an abstraction because it is not a concrete act; it is a source of such actions. If we take Mead and Dewey and combine the objective and confluent models of participation, which is the background of Niebuhr's thinking, we are even more at a loss to discover the concept of human agency. Somehow human agency is derived from a transactional situation in which the organism is interacting with its environment. This is a further abstraction to explain the abstraction of human agency. The most that Niebuhr could say for human agency, then, could be put hypothetically: if there were such a thing as human agency, it would function as a responsible person. The point is that human agency is more of a problem even than the term responsibility. Unless man is conceived as ontologically self-directing, even when he participates in the whole, it is difficult to conceive of a human agent and of a human responsible answerer. Unless this is established first (and Niebuhr has no desire to go in this direction), the human agent as a responsible answerer implicates being ordered by totality. But the question now arises, which totality: Mead and Dewey's, the Christian scheme of divine coherence (Niebuhr's model of it)?

Second, even on the phenomenal level of experience, Niebuhr's perspective offers difficulties just at the point where he disengages the goals of life from the human orderer and relates them to the social domain as the source of such goals and the domain of "fitting actions." But what is of interest to note is that he does not disengage goals from the directives of totality, both social and theological. His justification of their disengagement is interesting. Practical life has ignored teleological interpretations of life's problems. It has followed the leads of situations and their directives, like the situations of suffering and emergencies. These have called forth man's fitting responses rather than man's directives, or the directives of his purposive nature. The self truly defines itself by "the nature of its responses" rather than by its own directives. Of course, says Niebuhr, the purposes are there, but they don't really count. Thus something outside of our control calls forth our fitting responses, not human purpose. Niebuhr's objection to purposiveness is its definition in terms of wholes and preoccupation with totalities. It appears that situations call forth specific responses from man, whereas overall teleologies call forth too general a response that is not fitting for specific situations. Man's responses, then, are not self-directive; they are "functions of their interpretation of what is happening to them."[5] They are really responses to responses on an external track of meaning. Man is attracted by sources of concern outside himself and always comes up with fitting actions to cope with them.

Man does not learn by responding to images of himself. He learns his identity by the responses he makes to life's situations. But we have discovered that even situationalists appeal to totalities for guidance, and that such unitive experience implicates the intentions of systems of totality. When situations define man and his directives it is tantamount to saying that totality does in fact define him and his so-called "fitting actions." Niebuhr's approach to man's self-conduct, which "begins with neither purposes nor laws but with responses," with the answering self in response-relations, has externalized the issue of human responsibility. The external meaning of such responses is defined by the external meaning of purpose as external goal-directedness. This is a subtle form of goal direction on the level of experience. Man is at the mercy of that which evokes from him and defines for him fitting actions.

Third, despite the high sophistication of our age, despite the accumulation of knowledge, and despite the fact that man has been immersed in systems of totality (perhaps to better manage life's problems), there is a breakdown in human responsibility, just as there is an intensification of the conflict in human goals and ideals. Systems of totality, like Niebuhr's socio-theological perspective, have not been able to put Humpty Dumpty together again. Schemes of totality have not eased man's burdens in life. That social solidarity should call forth both the human agent and responsible fitting actions, when life there is already a chaos and where more and more persons are copping out, is looking for the responsible self in the wrong quarters. There is something hidden in responsibility. That something is

[5] *Ibid.*, 30.

the human orderer who is self-directing in his response-relations. Unless an explicit appeal is made to this factor, the appeals to totalitarian thought will continue. Such systems of totality keep obscuring the human orderer in and behind his response-relations to life. Niebuhr is simply making another plea of the same sort, only he wants the support of totalitarian cultures for his totalitarian thinking. The fact is that if we overplay human solidarity, we will miss the human orderer. If we make man too much a member of society, we will miss the human orderer. There is no way to define man as a human orderer on the action level of response-relations. Such attempts have always implicated man in some system of totality. The best responsible self, defined by each and every system of totality separately, can only be a person that is *responsible to* but not *responsible for*. For man as the answerer is not his own. At one end of the continuum he belongs to the totality of society, and at the other end he belongs to the solidarity of the theological community. He has to answer both ways to be fitting and proper in his actions and reactions.

Fourth, the problem of the "responsible self" is how to liberate the human to have self-possession of his responses. Unless he functions as the self-directing gathering focus for such response-relations, there is no way to establish man's claims on responsibility. The whole task must be envisioned as closing the gap between purposive participation and responsibility. This means placing the source of responsibility in purposive being. To be goal-directed in one's response-relations, as Niebuhr conceives it, where the "self defines itself by the nature of its responses," requiring an "agent's action as response to an action upon him," bypasses the problem completely. He is not interested in the source of responsibility or in the source of human agency. His prime interest is in typology, in patterns of responsibility and patterns of actions "in a continuing community of agents." But the problem cannot be so simply ignored. Response is an elemental mode of acting or reacting. This requires either a system of totality to order it or the human orderer. Richard Niebuhr prefers the directives of totality as the pedagogues of all such situational experience. The problem in any situational philosophy, which emphasizes response as a function, is how to preserve even the notion of a "responder" without losing him in the stream of unitive experience, in communal solidarity. If the responder is merely the result of situational interaction, the product of communal solidarity, merely read off from response-functions as phase-functions in the field of unitive experience, then it is hard to visualize the answerer as even a responder.

Fifth, the term "response" can be set on a continuum of existence with reaction at one end of the spectrum and self-direction on the other. Niebuhr's primary concern is to define response-relations in terms of sophisticated meanings, rather than as simple reactions to life. A person is given the initiative in interpreting response-situations. Along with F. S. C. Northrop of Yale and Pitrim Sorokin of Harvard, Niebuhr believes that man views facts and responses through logico-meanings, that is to say, they are not simple reactions. To be sure, this is already an advance over classical behaviorism. His agent is creative and meaning-giving in the matrix of stimulus-response. But the problem is more complicated than that, as noted above: how to define the answerer as a real responder. If man is merely the product of his responses interacting with other responses in a situation of communal solidarity, can a case be made out for man as responder?

Other thinkers have similarly distinguished between reaction and response, as in the perspective of Ernst Cassirer's *An Essay On Man*. Response is symbolic activity involving the realm of meaning. It has a shade of transcendence beyond direct and indirect reactions or signal behavior. In fact, "response," in the context of symbolic forms, for Cassirer has a "new dimension of reality." Niebuhr has much in common with the school of symbolic interactionism, and the life of symbols has a range of correlations with reality. The game has been played two ways in relating responses to reactions: (1) the symbolic has been reduced to signal behavior, and (2) the symbolic has been defined as a new dimension of meaning and reality. Cassirer distinguishes between sign and symbol, but such a distinction leads him to a new dimension of reality and the creation of being and ideal worlds rather than to the human orderer that is self-directing in such symbolization, even of the interactive variety.

But my concern is of another sort. To be sure, human responses are more complicated than animal reactions, but they are not sufficient to define either the human orderer, or even man as a responder, or as self-activating agent.

Niebuhr, on the other hand, would rather disengage both the responder and his response functions from a self-directing human orderer in order to fit him into a system of totality where he can perform "fitting actions" with its standards defined by totality. The kind of questions that would be important to Niebuhr are the following: What kind of reactor am I? How do

I fit into life's schemes when all purposes fail me? How do I fittingly respond to situations beyond me? How do I participate in a system of totality (Nature or God) that is, in fact, beyond human participation? How do I attribute the belief in truth to this totality and escape responsibility for that truth (for surely, God must have taught me that truth)? All these queries point to a kind of responsibility we have labeled "responsibility to" something and the most troublesome question of all is: How do I respond to responses of responses in the totalistic situation of communal solidarity? There is another way of saying this: How do I stay obedient to a system of totality that I have committed myself to? In the framework of totalitarian thought, it is impossible even to entertain the problem of the relation of the responder (and his response-functions) to a human orderer that is self-directing in the matrix of participation. The synecdochic analogy cuts out the debate between the two.

Sixth, in terms of my theory, before there can be symbolic interactionism or communal dialogue, the human orderer must be postulated in dialogical terms himself. This is, in part, what we mean by ontological interactionism, by the definition of man as a subject-object dialogue mediated by his purposive nature. This is where being talks with action, where there is presence of self-direction in choice-making, goal-making, symbolic form-making, totality(s)-making. Unless man is a conversational being, in which his purposive nature is a vital part of primal experience, there is no point in talking about man-the-answerer. Man must be self-directing before he is questioner or answerer, both on the private and public levels of human experience. Different questions arise in terms of this dialogical perspective of man (on the primal level of being). How can I postulate the human orderer that asks himself questions and gives himself answers? How am I the source of communal and religious dialogues, of myths, of responses, of symbols, in the matrix of participation? To such a human orderer, the concepts of self-conduct, self-action, self-intention, self-transcendence, self-definition, or the self-performer are really in essence abstractions from man's ontological capacity to be self-directing in the matrix of participation. So long as man remains a reactive, responding, or symbolic phenomenon, he still falls short of the human orderer. To the extent these do fall short of the human orderer, man cannot be a "responsible person." The reason for this is a simple one: phenomenal goal-directedness is the product of ontological self-directedness. To the extent the notion of responsibility shares this life of goal-directedness, it derives from man's purposive being, which is the true source of human responsibility even in the matrix of totalistic participation.

Seventh, there is thus a hidden reference in the notion of the responsible self. Such a goal-directed person faces the choice of whether to submit to the directives of totality or to his own directives. The hidden references are two: the human orderer and totality. We have rejected systems of totality as the source of the responsible person because they lead to totalitarian thought and are the breeding ground of pluralism and relativism. The latter mentioned charge is avoided in my theory because the human orderer is ready and present to reorder false plans and false totalities in making correlations (not identifications) with reality. As far as I am concerned, there is only one source for human responsibility—the human orderer. Even when he invents substitute forms of human directionality and responsibility, denying himself certain plans in experience, he is ready and present in terms of his capacity for self-direction to re-order such plans or schemes of totality to achieve better insights into reality.

One cannot reduce being to action and then produce being out of actions and choices, as does Sartre. The very phrase "*being* in action" indicates the hidden reference in action to being, in this case to purposive being, not to "instant being." The word responsibility also points beyond itself in the phrase "*being* responsible" to the hidden reference of purposive being. Just as social encounters point beyond themselves to social self-direction on the part of purpose-bearing groups. "Being in charge" of one's conduct on the action level in the midst of communal solidarity does not yet give us the responsible person as I have defined him. The term "being" is merely a loose term signifying a responsible actor that is not its own because it belongs to a system of totality. The responsible person fails to account for systems of responsibility, including his own, because it is in need of ontological self-direction to be operative in goal-directions and in response-relations. It is thus a phrase suggesting an abstraction from the human orderer. Human agency, even when responsible, is a model of behavior and a model of accountability. Man's purposive nature is the source of such model-creating and of such images of man. They are both products of the human modeling power that my model of man postulates. There is nothing wrong with having models either about human nature or the universe of existence. It is the hypostatization of such models of man and of such images of the whole of existence that is objectionable because it leads to totalitarian thinking and living.

Both agency and responsibility in the phrase "responsible agent" point beyond themselves to purposive being. These are the images in which purposive being is trying to understand human nature or the world. The alternative to this is functionalism, which has a highly undesirable quality about it (when its autonomy is taken for granted), that of derivativism (trying to stand on its own two feet), and also when it consciously or unconsciously leans on the intentions of a system of totality(s). The autonomy of such functional action philosophies, while I do not have time to spend on this theme, is just as illusory a game as that of totalitarian thought. Current trends in such philosophies are to relate such functional actions to systems of totality. Our objection to this strategy is not that such explanations do not yield proper knowledge, but that they neglect the human orderer who goes along on all such explanations of human life. Moreover, this is a way of talking about goal-directedness and response-relations that has about it the quality of abstraction and ideology. The choice we have postulated is a life that is totalized or humanized, with no middle ground in directionality and shared responsibility. In the light of my theory, even the first alternative can be dealt with justly in terms of the second if totalities are viewed as the product of human participation in existence rather than, as conceived by the totalists, in terms of "man's participation in the whole."

Eighth, when the responsible self is externally defined in terms of outbound responses in the milieu of communal or religious solidarity, he is goal-directed to social and religious totalities. Traditional directionality plays a greater part in both models of totality. If man is only goal-directed but not self-directing, the field is open for every totalist to play his totalitarian thought and culture. There is no way to stop this short of claiming ultimacy for one's system of totality as against another. When man responds to specific situations of suffering or an emergency of some sort (prior to purposive participation), he does so with the aid of totality. There is an irrational procedure in such encounter. If one asked Niebuhr, why should one be responsible in confronting suffering or some other extreme emergency, his reply would perhaps be because his God was first responsible in such situations and demands of him the same obedience. This satisfies well the religionist but not the philosopher.

Niebuhr is not aware of the fact that the Christian view of responsibility as accountability is a model of responsibility competing with systems of accountability set up by other totalities. If man is not self-directing in accountability, he is directed by social or religious totality. Responsibility as accountability, in Mead's system, comes "from below," from nature. In Niebuhr's Christian faith it comes "from above." These are two distinct models of responsibility which Niebuhr blends superficially to make out his case for the "responsible person." The whole point about responsibility in our pluralistic society is that accountability comes in all brands, like toothpaste. A transcendent standard for responsibility can only be made out by claims to ultimacy for one's system of accountability. Each system of totality requires either a responder or the responsive function to account for the definition of responsibility as the unifying system of each respective totality. Totalitarian thought and cultures have conditioned us to accept the reduced and truncated version of the human orderer in terms of the responder or his response-functions. It is not the requirement of life as life that we conceive the human orderer in this way. It is the requirement of our specific model of existence.

In the Christian scheme of totality, the Creator is concerned with the world because He made it. Because the world belongs to Him, there is concern, solicitude, care, and love for the things He has made. Such a theory of "accountability" in the context of creation is one model of totalistic responsibility. The believer is advised to show the same concern for God and His world. His first task is to regard responsibility as a unifying principle in that system of totality. Can this model of divine and human responsibility be passed off as the universal phenomenon of responsibility, and if so, by what means? It is only by identifying the Christian model of responsibility with the universal phenomenon of responsibility, and by making claims of ultimacy for such an identification, that it is possible to do this. But it is interesting that a philosopher like Heidegger uses the concept of "care" to bridge the gap between *Dasein* (man) and "the Being of beings" by introducing another model of responsibility where accountability comes "from below," not "from above." It is prepurposive rather than postpurposive in content and in the directionality of its response-relations. Here is an ontological theory of responsibility where creation is disregarded as a factor in accountability and "thrownness" or *Geworfenheit* becomes the occasion of responsibility for *Dasein* and its relation to "the Being of beings." It is obviously a competing model of responsibility defined as accountability. Yet man is a creature of *care* in both systems of totality. This would indicate that it is impossible to establish responsibility as a universal phenomenon, and accountability as a *sui generis* quality of life, by a totalistic approach to the problem. It always results in pluralism and relativism. The way out of the impasse is once more a reconstructed notion of the human orderer who is given the capacity to reorder the content and form of such all too human systems of totality or systems of total responsibility. It does not help much to define the source of responsibility by one of its components, like accountability.

Each system of totality has its own content of accountability and imputation (the attribution of fault or evil to someone), and these appear to be the oldest precursors to the word "responsibility." Richard McKeon has pointed to the development and enlargement of the meaning of these two terms in the history of thought. His interest was to show the enlarged meanings of these terms in terms of political development. The term "responsibility" was a latecomer in the development and originated in the context of a "responsible government," which is a significant way of talking about social totalities. McKeon remarks:

In a significant sense, the idea of *political* responsibility takes precedence in the evolution of the idea of responsibility. The idea of responsible government . . . had originally two ingredients: a government or a republic is responsible (1) if it operates within a framework of law in which official action and control are reasonably predictable, and (2) if its government reflects the attitude of its people through institutions which provide for the regular election of personnel and regular review of policy. These two aspects of the idea of responsibility are recognizable extensions of the older conceptions of accountability under the rule of law and the imputability of the actions of elected officials with limited terms of office.[6]

But there is no philosophic treatment of responsibility prior to 1859, according to McKeon, but the origin of the term "responsibility" preceded the philosophical analysis some seventy years.

The problem we are faced with in this volume is prior to the applicability of the term "responsibility" to either the "responsible person" or the "responsible government." My interest is to see responsibility first as a human dimension of the human condition, and we can know this only if we are certain about its source. The two most likely candidates for this are systems of totality and the human orderer, conceived individually and socially, in the matrix of participation. McKeon's view of a "responsible government" would not fit the Russian model of a "responsible government," for

[6] Richard McKeon, "The Development and the Significance of the Concept of Responsibility," *Revue Internationale de Philosophie*, Vol. II (1957), 23–24.

example. Constitutional and democratic governments are patterned after different models of responsibility—say, contractual theories of responsibility—whereas the Russian model would follow the organismic pattern of responsibility in which unity counts more than individuality. A developmental theory of responsibility, important as it is, does not allow us to get at the phenomenon of human responsibility in its most universal sense. It is not concerned with its source in the human orderer; it is concerned with responsibility in both individual and social practice. The phenomenal level of experience will not yield the source and origin of responsibility in human life. It merely reflects the goal-directed patterns of response-relations.

Incidentally, McKeon has a reference to Ben Jonson, who used the term "responsible" as the equivalent of "correspondent" (as answering to something), which is suggestive of Richard Niebuhr's solution to the problem of responsibility when he defines man as the answerer.[7]

The hidden reference of responsibility thus points to its use in practice, both with respect to individual and social practice. The phenomenal level of action will not yield the source or sources of responsibility in its "human" dimension, which is, of course, my primary concern here. Even though the term responsibility relates agents to actions, or actions to agents, in terms of causality or by care, solicitude, and concern, there is a breakdown of the sources of responsibility on the phenomenal level of experience. For it is still the level of goal-directedness that response-relations are dealt with, and these are not self-sustaining. Goal-directions have appealed either to the human orderer or to systems of totality for guidance and sustenance.

For that reason, McKeon's solution, just as Niebuhr's, misses the mark. McKeon writes:

If philosophers began with the fact of responsibility in its social context, they might explore and guide its extensions and applications without either deserting basic principles or negating the practical significance of principles by making the choice of principles the center of controversy.[8]

It misses the mark for the following reasons: (1) before the term can be applied either to human conduct or to social practice, responsibility must be sufficiently analyzed to yield the disclosure or the whereabouts of its source. Otherwise, the phrase, so fashionable among writers today, "on

---

[7] *Ibid.*, 8.
[8] *Ibid.*, 22.

being responsible," has no meaning either for conduct or for social practice. And (2) the contextual analysis that both Niebuhr and McKeon advocate cannot solve the problem beyond cultural relativism, which may well be sufficient on this level of analysis but not sufficient to get at the universal human meaning of responsibility. Such contextualism is a form of social holism in which responsibility has its source in cultural or regional totalities. Let me turn next to the relation of the human orderer to responsibility as I conceive or try to envision the "human" dimension of responsibility and of its source in man.

The Readiness for Responsibility

In the above section, the hidden reference in responsibility is the human orderer. Now it is the task to reveal his relationship to responsibility under the caption of "readiness for" responsibility. This phrase does not suggest that man is "ready for release" by some system of totality to be responsible to that totality. Unless man finds "releasement" for responsibility in himself as a human orderer, he can only practice responsibility to something or to some system of totality. At the moment I am not interested in showing how nature, being, life, or God, are responsible for man. I am interested specifically in the notion of "human responsibility" that derives from man's purposive being and accounts for these larger systems of totality. The phrase does not suggest generational responsibility, for nature is responsible for such stages of life. I am talking about its human development and its source in man, and this perspective has further consequences of vision toward order in nature, being, life, or God. The "readiness for" responsibility is precisely the human condition of ontological interaction that sustains the operation of choices, goals, ideals, and totalities. Unless it is assumed that man is authentically a human orderer capable of such creative participation in existence—capable of generating images of human nature and models of existence by its powers to immediatize and mediatize experience (and to be its gathering focus)—we cannot get beyond the notion of the responder, beyond responsive functions, or beyond the phrase "readiness for" shared responsibility. There is a prior sense of purposiveness that functions as this readiness for responsibility when man reflects on himself and describes human nature in terms of "human agency," "organism," or even as a "responsible person." It is within the thick of experience that man exhibits the capacity of model-making by participation and model-making by reflection. While it is not an omni-competent power, the human orderer is a significant factor to contend with in participation, especially in the production of images about human nature, symbolic forms, and systems of totality. It is precisely the fact of its modest power in existence that totalists have derived the belief that it is possible to get rid of the human orderer in some system of totality by going beyond the subject-object split. But as I mentioned earlier, this was a premature solution to the problem which leads to unnecessary compli-cations about man's relation to the world. The human orderer goes along to accompany all such ventures that would reconstruct life.

The more expansive notions of man-the-responder have a modest glimpse of what readiness for responsibility means. Because they invest the re-sponder with meaning-giving structures in his responses to stimuli, they soon lose sight of the fact. They allow for such "readiness for" meaning to man's mind but not to his purposive nature and for the fact that man gives such meaning-structures to experience by model-making participation in experience. The ontological perspective of man's purposive nature en-ables us to relate the human orderer to elemental modes of response to life, for which he is the gathering focus. This domain of man's creative par-ticipation has been totally neglected because immediate experience has been conceived, unjustly so, as the domain of lived experience where all mediations were left unjustified. The essence of living is participation in which the human orderer is himself involved on the primal level of en-counter. Immediate experience is only one kind of participation among others and as such cannot be severed from the human orderer to seek the instructions of totality on its own. Man's purposive being provides his readiness for responsibility. Once we sever participation from the human orderer (and even the notions of man-the-responder, or his response func-tions, do this), there is no way to recapture man's readiness for response-relations. Man is more than an interpreter of responses, more than a par-ticipant in situational directives because he makes all such things possible. A response is not responsible in itself, and neither is an autonomous action unless man is ontologically self-directing in such encounters. This is not to deny encounter experiences. It is to give them enrichment of meaning and empowerment by purposive being.

The history of thought has given rise to many models of responsibility even before the term came to be used as a noun in 1787. The moral dimen-sion of the term signified duty or obligation. When it was related to a religious system of totality, such responsibility was delegated "from above." In the empirical tradition, which was a reaction to religious unity, such terms implied delegated responsibility "from below." The model of responsibility that I am espousing is, in essence, self-delegated in the sense of ontological self-direction. Such self-delegated responsibilities come to light on the phenomenal level of goals, choices, and totalities. On the ontological level, goals have not yet been picked, choices have not yet been made, and totalities have not yet been formed. This neutral area of ontological self-direction, this groping for goals, choices, ideals, totalities, or for meaning in general, is what we mean by "readiness for responsibility." Purposive being mediates such response relations on a more specific, programmatic level on the phenomenal level of experience. This is the second stage of defined human purpose as self-direction. Human responses are thus prefigured or foreshadowed in purposive being as they express themselves in purposive participation. It is interesting that when such a notion is ignored and the human orderer is excised from primal participation in immediate experience, there is no way for theorists to get off the level of goal-directedness in defining response-relations. Yet this is not enough to account for the source of human responsibility. In the process of purposive participation, man evolves standards of responsibility, and criteria for standards of systems of responsibility, in the ongoing processes of life. Man's purposive nature cannot be extricated from primal experience. However, some of its plans can be canceled or thwarted. But then the human orderer reasserts itself in primal experience by reordering its plans, ideals, and so forth. This is enough to avoid the charge of relativism.

If one is to get at the source of responsibility, it is necessary to forego the easy option of dealing with response-relations on a purely external level. Such externality shows itself only after the human orderer has been severed from the notion of responsibility. For circumstantial or situational response-relations to be meaningfully operative in some recognizable human form, one must understand the nature of ontological readiness for such responsibility. If this is denied, there is no way one can go beyond the notion of responsibility to something or some system of totality. But the odd part is that human purpose is used in its holistic tendency to build up such systems of totality; only its forming and shaping capacity is denied once the totality assumes ontological priority to the human orderer. The readiness for responsibility, whether it is responsibility for a comprehensive view of man or a comprehensive view of life, is what gives man claims on responsibility.

Human models of participation determine our views of responsibility. If participation comes in models, theories of responsibility cannot be identified with universal responsibility *qua* responsibility. All we can do is make correlations with existence, to participate in existence, to have close-ups of existence in the experience of participation. The purposive model of participation offers such readiness for responsibility in the form of purposive being which some of the other models deny. Such "readiness for" is man's discovery of the human orderer in himself and in social existence. I believe we have to turn to ontological participation to overcome the credibility of responsibility on the action level. Goal directions in themselves or in the form of response-relations are not self-sustaining justifications. They point either to the human orderer or to totality for guidance. If participation is to make human sense, it must be anthropologized, as was indicated earlier. The same is true of responsibility. I turn next to the radicalization of responsibility involved in the ontological, participatory model of human responsibility.

6. Purpose and Responsibility

Purpose has been taken for granted in all past discussions of responsibility and in its earlier versions of accountability and imputability. The subjectivists have regarded it as a function of the subject self. The objectivists have thought of it as the function of the intellect. The term responsibility itself has both these dimensions when it functions as accountability and as imputability. Both versions of responsibility have assumed the traditional meaning of purpose (telos, goal, end, aim) as some form of goal direction for which intentionality has been the traditional synonym. The subjectivists delighted in the use of intentions or intentional actions; the objectivists, on the other hand, were drawn to the means/ends continuum to explain response-relations. Since I have defined purpose ontologically as man's capacity to be self-directing in existence, it is necessary to relate this dimension of purpose to the notion of responsibility. It is not necessary to deny purpose in terms of its traditional meanings. On the phenomenal, analytic, and artifactual levels, purpose is still regarded as some form of goal direction. It is only on the ontological level that purpose means a form of self-direction in terms of a functional ontology. My attempt to relate this theory to responsibility, in accounting for its source in the human orderer, I shall call the ontological model of responsibility.

I noted in earlier chapters that both freedom and determinism have no independent existence. They are, respectively, functions of the subjective and objective models of human participation. Hence, from my point of view, it is not necessary to relate freedom and responsibility, on the one hand, to the law of causality, which contemporary thinkers think is necessary to solve but so far have not been successful in finding a solution to the subject-object split, or the dichotomy of freedom and determinism.[1] Pur-

---

[1] R. B. Edwards, *Freedom, Responsibility and Obligation* (The Hague, Martinus Nijhoff, 1969), ix–xii.

pose is a mode of being in purposive being, and this is prior to such model-making. This means that the "purpose of action" is not self-sustaining. It also means that "responsive actions" are not autonomous and self-sufficing. They implicate either purposive being or some system of totality. By purposive being I do not, of course, mean a free-wheeling agent capable of acts of self-determination. Neither do I simply mean the self-action of self-government on the social scene. Such alleged self-performers are abstractions from man's capacity to be self-directing in existence. By analogy to the individual, society, too, is capable of social self-direction in terms of purpose-bearing groups and organizations. To account for individual and for social self-direction, we find the need to define the notion of ontological responsibility, to show the radicalization of responsibility. This is the opposite side of the coin, when earlier I talked about liberating the human orderer to give him claims over responsibility.

The first question we must answer is: Why have an ontological source for responsibility? Why have an ontologically functioning human orderer? The obvious answer is that this is the only way to explain the "hidden reference" in responsibility and man's "readiness for" responsibility. Man is not released into responsibility by some other power. If he is, then the topic of discussion is the responsibility of that other power. This is not "human" responsibility. But my point is that even when man has explained his "relation to" some such power in terms of "responsibility to" it, his purposive nature has had a hand in designing this other-than-human orderer.

The more important reason for such a model of the human orderer as the source of responsibility is that other notions of the human orderer have failed to give us the source of human responsibility. The most ambitious models were subjectivity and agency, or the reduced version of both, where subjectivity was defined specifically as agency or as self-agency. These models are inadequate because they sell man out to a system of totality or assume an unwarranted autonomy for such subjective functional acts. We have already indicated the inadequacy of placing the source of responsibility in systems of totality. Thus we have reached an impasse both in our images of man and in our images of totality to account for the source(s) of responsibility. The obvious need is to reconstruct a new model of man in terms of purposive being, to relate him to purposive participation and to responsibility. The model we proposed may be viewed in terms of the analogy of concentric circles. The first circle, beginning at an established point, represents man's purposive being as self-directing in existence. The second circle represents ontological participation, also running through the same point of reference noted in the first circle. The third circle would represent the experience of human responsibility as an outgrowth of the second circle. Each circle passes through the same spot in the first circle, representing the human orderer, and is meaningless without this directive passage. The first circle is one that symbolizes ontological experience as defining the possible conditions of human participation and responsibility.

The transition between the ontological and the phenomenal experience, from being to action, is really a transition from self-direction to choice-making, goal-seeking, responding (which are operational aspects of this potentiality in man for the readiness of responsibility). The distinction between being and action is not a separation. It remains a distinction. Ontological model-making is felt in human participation and responsibility when choices are made, goals and ideals are set and sustained, when responses are viewed in terms of meaningful situations. This purposive model of human participation and responsibility, which we have labeled an ontological model, is not free of model-making. But it is a model that allows for model-making on all stages of experience, whereas the other comparative models we mentioned identify their blueprint of existence with existence. By allowing for the process of model-making right from the beginning level of the ontological perspective of experience, we can account for the hidden reference in responsibility and view it positively as the readiness for responsibility. This means that man's capacity for self-direction is prior to man's drive for meaning which, incidentally, is not free of model-making either.

A Look at the Contextual Analysis of Responsibility

If choices, goals, and responses represent a human investment in experience, we cannot leave the problem on the phenomenal level unsolved. Otherwise, man has no real share in existence. Our claim is that man has a *being-share* in existence, and this prevents us from saying we understand existence *qua* existence. For we can understand existence *qua* the human orderer that is a participant in it. In short, we can have only close-ups, correlations, with existence. This is not as bad as it sounds because these are close-ups of existence from within a participatory situation and not outside its context. The greatest lived experience we can have in existence is participatory experience. To get a lived experience outside the context of human participation, apart from an ontological human orderer, is a sell-out of human life. There is much of this in current philosophy. The more we excise the human orderer from existence by the pretence of getting a greater story on human participation in existence, the more we tend to make life meaningless either for the human orderer in existence or for the naked Other as given in experience. Both terms of the participation are emasculated in such confluent views of human existence, as I noted in the last chapter.

Let me show the relevance of this model of responsibility to Professor McKeon's contextual theory of responsibility. McKeon states that the dimensions of responsibility are three:

It has an external dimension in legal and political analysis in which the state imposes penalties on individual actions and in which officials and governments are held accountable for policy and action. It has an internal dimension in moral and ethical analysis in which the individual takes into account the consequences of his actions and the criteria which bear on his choices. It has a comprehensive or reciprocal dimension in social and cultural analysis in which values are ordered in the autonomy of an individual character and the structure of a civilization.[2]

Though the individual and the community are partial sources of responsibility, the main source of responsibility appears to be the notion of a "reciprocal relation" between them. This is suggestive of the coresponsiveness mentioned in earlier chapters, where it was suggested that situationalism or contextualism is not its own but points to a system of totality beyond itself and, therefore, points to a principle of comprehension from beyond itself, as the source of real responsibility, that the individual and the community have a share in.

Responsibility is a slowly emerging process in history, and both evolution and history are the true sources of it. This is not "human" responsibility. The slowly emerging process of responsibility comes to have four basic elements in it: accountability, imputability, freedom, and rationality.[3] But the source of responsibility cannot be explained in terms of any of these four components. Thus McKeon pushes the source of responsibility beyond the subjective and objective dimensions of it to a sociohistoric to-

[2] McKeon, *op. cit.*, 5.
[3] *Ibid.*, 25.

tality. This yields him the principle of coresponsibility or that of reciprocal relatedness.

If one attempts to obtain the source of responsibility from phenomenal experience, the history of thought shows that this can be achieved in one of two ways: (1) place it in some system of totality, or (2) assume the autonomy of experience, of actions, of communal interaction on some functional level and to regard this autonomy as a form of self-sufficiency. My analysis indicates that the pluralism and relativism that results from this procedure is too high a price to pay for the sources of responsibility because it is self-defeating and ends up in claims to ultimacy rather than communication about shared responsibility and its possible source. The fact of the matter is that (1) self-government presupposes social self-direction, that (2) self-action presupposes self-direction, and (3) the principle of coresponsibility presupposes either a system of totality or a human orderer that builds such systems of totality. Thus all three dimensions of responsibilities require purposive being and the ontological model of responsibility to be operative. Contextualism as an approach to responsibility has no way of coping with the problem of sources.

It should be kept in mind that the *model* of purposive participation is the source of human responsibility. One may, if one wishes, call it a *metamodel*, to avoid the claim that the model of responsibility is identified with responsibility *qua* responsibility. This means that responsibility does not have its source in reality directly, but only indirectly, as it is filtered through the models of existence from within the matrix of participation. Of course, there is no necessity that this model of responsibility be the right one just because other models of the human orderer have failed in the history of thought. Its value is in its pragmatic worth. It enables us to solve certain problems, like the subject-object split, freedom and determinism, etc., in a better way than other models of existence do. In terms of its pragmatic value, it can be termed a metamodel. It accounts better for the human modeling power in the process of participation than do the others. It is better to assume this modeling and forming process in participation than to succumb to the tyranny of totalities. It has at least the merit of avoiding the charge of relativism, since the human orderer is prepared to order anew or reorder some of the goals, plans, aspirations. All I mean to assert at this time is that it is better to assume model-making on the level of being and action, not only in reflection and the meaning domain, than to assume uncritically the directives of totality in human responsibility.

The principle of reciprocal relations that McKeon is concerned with, as the basis of responsibility, is an attempt to substitute a dynamic historical process for stultifying choices in facing up to human responsibility. This speaks well for totality, but it misses the point for "human" responsibility. Perhaps Charles Horton Cooley was the first to provide a real base for such coresponsibility, at least for the American tradition. He said that the individual and society are merely two aspects of the real totality of the human condition. If this were not a totality that signified reality, I would agree with it. But as it stands, such a principle of reciprocal relations is a model both of the human condition (relating the individual to totality) and also a model of responsibility. Whether we entertain the goal of a responsible person, a responsible community (like a government), or a joint model of shared responsibility, purposive being is compresent with such models since it is a model setting forth the human modeling power in participation. Note such phrases as the following when we use responsibility in terms of our language: *belief in* responsibility, *acceptance of* responsibility, responsibility *as freedom*, the *confrontation of* responsibility, *on being* responsible, *education for* responsibility, *having* responsibility, the *weight of* responsibility, the *burden of* responsibility, *flight from* responsibility, *resistance to* responsibility, *deemed* responsible, *groping for* responsibility. These all presuppose a human orderer of responsibility, a readiness for responsibility on the part of purposive being participating in existence. We miss all this when we relate response to reaction and forget about the possibility of an ontological debate on the matter of relating response to self-direction. The language of self-reference is evident in such language usage. The posture we choose in relating ourselves to such language is the either/or disjunctive I mentioned earlier, of relating it to the human orderer or to a system of totality(s).

J. R. Pennock, in his introductory chapter to *Responsibility*, puts his finger on the pulse of the problem when he writes:

Responsibility, then, has various meanings in different contexts, some of them fairly precise; but if we are seeking a common core for these meanings, we must say that it means more than duty or dutifulness and more than accountability, although it includes these meanings. The "more than" points toward the exercise of discretion by deliberate and thoughtful decision in the light of a sound calculation of probable consequences and a fair evaluation of claims. . . . In fact, it is fair to say that "responsibility" has two primary meanings, or that what I have called the core of meaning has two facets, (a) accountability and (b) the rational and moral exercise of discretionary power (or the capacity or disposition for such exercise), and that each of these notions tends to flavor the other. In any particular application, either one may be dominant, but the other remains in the background. When we use the word "responsibility" to mean "accountability," it is usually when we have in mind accountability for some proper exercise of discretion. If I lend you a dollar, I speak of your "duty" to repay me; or I may say that I have a "right" that you should repay me. Put in accountability-responsibility terms, I would say that you are accountable for repaying me. But if you ask me how I can expect you to repay the dollar when you have lost it, I may reply, "that is *your* 'responsibility.' " On the other hand, when we use the word "responsibility" to refer to behavior of the "proper-exercise-of-discretion" type or to the disposition to exhibit such behavior, the notion of accountability for such behavior is generally in the background, even if only in the sense of accountability to conscience or high standards.[4]

We have already made our point about accountability as a *model* of responsibility. If Pennock means by the background of accountability in choice-making responses, as something suggesting more than a model of responsibility, then I would disagree. Before we relate choice-making and goal-making to such a background of accountability, implicating systems of totality, we must recognize the presence of the human orderer in his capacity of ontological self-direction in situations of choice-making responses. Neither theoretical nor practical reason is, in effect, really self-sufficient in its goal-making in response-relations. That is precisely the problem of the twentieth century, which has turned to the irrational in most aspects of life for some new sense of responsibility. The prevalence of the irrational, evidenced on a global scale in contemporary life, is enough to mar the image of a pure reason being the source and guide of human responsibility. Even the model of "practical reason" as the source of responsibility has been shipwrecked by the twentieth century. Responsibility is thus the demand of our purposive life, before it takes on the shades of meaning associated with accountability, deliberation, or choice-making responses. If we are to avoid schemes of totality which make authoritarian claims on life through idiosyncratic patterns of responsibility, we must regain some sense, if only a working sense, of a human orderer who is self-directing in existence although not self-sufficient in such participation. Thus if we have bungled some systems of responsibility, we stand a chance of coming up with others that will be more suitable for human living. The problem is not to have a mere responder, but how to make the responder responsible for the system of response-relations. When

[4] C. J. Friedrich (ed.), *Responsibility* (New York, Liberal Arts Press, 1960), 13–14.

the task is so envisioned, self-direction becomes a paramount trait of purposive being in the matrix of participation. We have to assume a human orderer even when man's search for responsibility is a groping or a developmental one. We have no other choice in the matter except the choice of losing ourselves in some system of totality. The burden of such a system, however, is more oppressive than the alternative we are advocating. If there is a common core of meaning in the notion of responsibility, according to the model of purposive responsibility, that phenomenon is ontological self-direction. This gives additional feasibility and justification to such notions as subjectivity, agency, and other models of the human orderer. It can function properly as a *metamodel*, without claims of ultimacy made on its behalf by pointing to reality. The purposive *model* of participatory responsibility remains a model that accounts for the human modeling power necessary for recognizing "human" participation. This is what I meant earlier by the fact that the human orderer anthropologizes the process of participation by models of experience.

The Radicalization of Responsibility

The radicalization of responsibility assumes that the category of the "responder" or his "response-functions" is a derivative notion. One must go beyond such a functional approach to a functional ontology in order to establish a case for the human orderer. This is not a humanism in the light of being, nature, life, or God. It is man in the light of the human orderer as he confronts himself (individually and socially) in the experience of responsibility. Such a human orderer is more than a responder to a system of totality. Thus the human orderer is more than simply an open awareness (defined subjectively or objectively as an open field or stream of experience); he is self-directing in his awareness and is present as such in choice-making and goal-making. This means that man has certain claims on responsibility. One need not deny the notion of the responder or his response-functions. These have a significance on the phenomenal, analytic, and the artifactual levels of response-relations. This also means that man is more than "purposive behavior." This model of man already presupposes the presence of purposive being which views itself in that image. On the phenomenal level, man retains his capacity to respond in experiences of responsibility both in acts of self-subjectification and self-objectification. But this is not enough to disclose the source of human responsibility.

My contention is that just the way we have separated purposes (goals) from man's purposive nature and come up with the external image of purposiveness defined as goal-directedness, so we have separated the human orderer both from the concept of the responder or from the notion of response-functions. Perhaps the separation of the human orderer from the phenomenon of responsibility has come about through inadequate or weakened notions of the human orderer. It is not that man hasn't tried in the course of history to make claims on responsibility; rather it is the fact that he has failed to establish those claims or to properly confront the human orderer in himself in responsibility experiences. When he has defined the human orderer as mastery of reason over the self, responsibility has been equated with reasonability. When the self was viewed in terms of the mastery of its emotional life, responsibility was identified with spontaneity. When the process of history was conceived as having a mastery over the self, then responsibility came to be equated with the dialectical processes of history and the dynamics of social forms. In conceiving of the human orderer in terms of the mastery of purposive being over the self, it is my intention to equate such mastery only with the notion of ontological self-direction in the matrix of participation without claiming omnipotentiality for it.

Obviously, man is not a sitting duck on the pond of existence. He is more than a catalyst in human participation; he anthropologizes participation. Even when he leads himself to believe, or is led by others to believe, that he is a creature of conditioning and self-conditioning, the human orderer has contributed to that image of man. The model of the conditioned man does not get rid of purposive being; it merely discards some of its plans by the consent of the human orderer who is present in such model-making ventures. Man is self-directing in such an awareness. This means that even when man substitutes the notion of "control" in the place of "responsibility" in such an image of man, ontological self-direction has had a shaping role to play in the construction of such an image of human nature. It is understandable why man "fights back" under such conditions or fights against the planned society. He is aware of being or of having been conditioned. This points to the human orderer even in the conditioned image of man. The conditioned man or the organization man is not the real man; he is a model of man. Now the totalists would have us believe differently, namely, that their model of the conditioned man is the real man or to be identified with the real man. We have disallowed this mistaken identification to every philosophy of man and to every comprehensive theory about totality, including our own view of man and totality. We are not gods. We have only man's work to do, even in our philosophizing.

What is the consequence of this for the organized view of man as the conditioned creature? The reply is that this is a temporary image of man, constructed by the experimentalists for the sake of objectivating knowledge, and the rest are claims to ultimacy for one's model of man. The average man knows this only too well. He ponders the philosophy of a planned life and wonders about his own idiosyncratic contributions in the midst of such rigid planning. He keeps resisting conditioning and the organization ideal of life, the ideal of this omnipotent variable in modern life. He wonders whether this is not the first reaction of man to establishing man's relations to nature and to society, that perhaps there are better relation patterns where his life would be lived out with more meaning attributed to individuality. If there is such a rigid continuity in life's experience, he wants to know why. Man is not passive to all this (or he shouldn't be). In the midst of it all he is dismayed and dreams about the radicalization of participation and responsibility. If he is not one, he wants to become a claimant of responsibility in the matrix of participation. He reorders that which fails to give him or his society a measure of satisfaction.

The mistake that experimenters and planners have made with respect to the conditioned image of man is to identify the model with man *qua* man. They have assumed, in their policies of control and conditioning, that by denying man certain goals and plans they have denied his purposive being as well. This is a great mistake and one which the experimenters hold with other totalists in the history of thought. To offset such confusion, and the possibility of the erosion of responsibility under mindless inquiry, it is necessary to concentrate on the possibility of reconstructing such an image of man that it will be more difficult to lose him in systems of totality. Man is not a virus in history that we should get rid of him in some system of totality. The real viruses are the systems of totality which make claims to ultimacy rather than offer evidence for their schemes.

Perhaps the notion of man-the-responder (or the reactor, or one who functions merely in terms of response-functions) is merely a hangover from totalistic schemes in the history of thought and from the part-to-whole logic that has dominated philosophy for centuries. But if these totalities are seen for what they are—models of existence rather than real and immediate cosmic reality—there is a chance we can postulate a human orderer beyond the receptive category of the responder both in terms of purposiveness and responsibility. I have already shown the relevance of purposive being to systems of totality; I have now to show its relevance to responsibility, which I will attempt to do in terms of the notion of the radicalization of responsibility.

One, the first thing that needs to be done is to break through the external image of purpose defined as goal-directedness and of responsibility defined as a response-relation. This is what they are on the phenomenal level of experience. But this level of action and counteraction does not yield the source for responsibility. When it is claimed that it does, it is some system of totality that governs man both in purpose and in responsibility. I know of only one way to avoid the externalization of both phenomena: by relating them to ontological self-direction. Man wants to be the center that radiates response-relations, even though he knows he does not control the universe. He wants to have claims on responsibility. He has the gnawing feeling that if he is not responsible *for* systems of responsibility he should not be responsible *to* them. He also knows that if he is not responsible for them, someone else is, and he is gripped by the prospect of totalitarian thought.

The first problem, then, is how to make man the gathering focus for response-relations rather than to place the source in some domain outside himself. We have seen that the case is otherwise with the other models of human participation. John Dewey will serve adequately in terms of the confluent model of participation on this topic. He writes:

The unification of the self throughout the ceaseless flux of what it does, and suffers, and achieves, cannot be attained in terms of itself. The self is always directed toward something beyond itself and so its own unification depends upon the idea of the integration of the shifting scenes of the world into that imaginative totality we call the Universe.[5]

Maurice Friedman, commenting on this passage, states:

The self is, indeed, always directed toward something beyond itself. Dewey sees this direction as toward the "Universe." It would, indeed, be unthinkable for man to live without some imaginative apperception of a "world"—a unified totality over against him of which he also sees himself as a part. But we may question whether this is enough, whether anyone ever attains unification of the self in reference to the universe. Does it not come into being rather in respond-

[5] Maurice Friedman, *To Deny Our Nothingness* (New York, Dell, 1967), 216.

ing again and again to one or another concrete image of man? "Mankind" and the "universe," "man" and "the world" are proper corollaries, but I, the self, need another I, other I's, even if at times in imaginative and fictitious form, if I am to become a real person and achieve personal unification.[6]

However, once the self is goal-directed to a totality, frozen in its track of meaning, he can only be a "functionary of" that system, a responder or a set of responsive functions in the stream and field of experience. It is the model of goal-directedness, defined in terms of ultimacy (totality) in each system of totality, which defines the image of each responder. There is no universal responder but only the responder defined by separate systems of totality. The "imaginative totality," however, is not so imaginative when it is construed as being real and immediate (even though incomplete). It is fed by the stream of concrete unitive experience. In this context, imagination is not the function of a human orderer (this is as true for Marcuse as for Dewey); it is the receptive servant of a real totality. It takes imagination to grasp the orderings of systems of totality.

Friedman shows some confusion on the matter when he questions the possibility that the self may not be unified by its goal-directedness toward totality, and then he loses the thread of meaning he has discovered in the questioning (in the very next sentence) and states that man can only be unified if he responds to ever-growing images of himself. What is this but goal-directedness toward oneself, imaged as a totality? One is unified, I would assume, by a plurality of temporary images of oneself. Friedman is too bound to Mead's perspective to be freed of Dewey's thought. Both need the responder as an assumption in a system of totality, whether that totalistic image be of the universe or of man. The fact that the self is "always directed toward something beyond itself" prevents both thinkers from arriving at a notion of the human orderer and at the source of human responsibility. The sell-out occurs in the receptive category of the imagination, which is impotent as a human orderer since it always mirrors the orderings of totality, whether through the past (Dewey) or in the present (Mead and Friedman). The fact is that once we go beyond the subject-object split, as the confluent model of participation does, the self can only be a set of responses in the stream or only a responder. It is the requirement of the prepurposive model of life (in contrast to ontological self-direction). Why must there always be a responder? The system of totality demands it, or the system of the total man imaged as totality. This is assumptive

[6] *Ibid.*

reasoning. We need a responder because there is no human orderer ontologically postulated. Once he is operative in participation, models of the whole man and the whole universe come to be seen for what they are: projected patterns of meaning in man's drive for understanding himself and the world around him. Whether such unification is external or internal, whether it deals with antecedents or consequences of acts (the usual conflict between subjectivists and objectivists), is a distinction that is posterior to a purposive being functioning ontologically as a human orderer in the matrix of participation. This requires the further radicalization of responsibility. The basis of such responsibility is thus man confronting the human orderer in himself. If the imagination is severed from the human orderer and allowed to operate as one elemental mode of response in the stream of experience, as a servant of totality, man has already lost the source of human responsibility. He can only be made to be responsible and can only show *responsibility to* something, either to totalistic images of himself or to totalistic images of the universe.

The fact is that the distinction between the isolated and integrated self is a posterior distinction to purposive being. That problem doesn't bother a lower creature like a cow. It bothers man as a purposive being. The integral self, a "relation to," requires a human orderer capable of ontological self-direction, as much as the isolated self, as subject of being. Both external and internal human directionality have been poorly defined because there was no adequate concept of the ontological human orderer. The problem of the source(s) of responsibility necessitates such a view. This problem can, of course, be ignored. It can be seen as a muddled question hung up on language problems that need further clarification. It is already taken care of by the system of totality, says the totalist. It needs only a typology to clarify such patterns of response-relations. Or all that has to be done is to trace its actual course of development in history to see its enlarging meanings in progress. But how can one be sure of the meaning of responsibility in individual and human conduct unless one first attends to its source(s)? The first requirement, then, is to analyze it as a "human" phenomenon rather than as a pie-slice of totality. Then one can proceed, as does J. R. Pennock, to worry its political uses, as in the following passage depicting the role of the social scientist as an adviser to governmental organizations:

They may be thought of as falling in one of two categories: the allocation of responsibility and the provision of conditions favorable for eliciting responsible behavior on the part of those to whom responsibility has been allocated. . . . Both tasks require knowledge of the prerequisites for the exercise and growth of effective responsibility. One consequence of the nature of responsibility is that it is something that can develop.[7]

My point, however, is that such growth can take place only if we assume individual or social self-direction. It is not simply a process of organic maturation, as in nature. When one identifies his model of development with evolutionary process itself, then it is totality, not individual or social self-direction, that guides responsibility in its growth patterns. That Dewey and Mead emphasized becoming one with the process of evolutionary striving rather than being passive to it is a way of saying that totality is responsible for human responsibility, which is rather far-fetched as a concept of "human" responsibility. No wonder Dewey refused to consider the antecedents of responsibility; he hated the prospect of being called another totalist, another Hegel, whom he allegedly outgrew. He would consider the theme of responsibility in the circumstances and consequences of actions performed on the immediate level of interaction and social encounter.

Two, it has been our discovery that deontologizing the human orderer in participation only leads to the ontologizing of the orderings of some system of totality. Maurice Friedman does not escape totalism when he postulates the fact that "concrete images" of man direct man in his responsibilities. His perspective does not lead to the radicalization of responsibility since it stays on the level of phenomenal interaction. The individual's response to the concrete images of man in history does not yield a human orderer in the matrix of participation. In terms of my view, man is self-directing in the search for models of human nature. Such concrete images are already products of man in the matrix of participation which is inclusive of the ontological human orderer. Such concrete images arise on the phenomenal level of goal-directedness and exhibit more totalistic goals. Friedman makes the same mistake as Mead and Dewey in severing the goals of life from man's purposive nature which postulates and orders such goals in the means/ends continuum. Thus placing the priority on goals, rather than on purposive being, is like placing the cart before the horse, or a set of response-relations or the responder before the human orderer. Concrete images of man, which perform such a guidance function for man, are merely external patterns of ontological self-direction in man's search for models of human nature in the wider search for meaning. In short,

[7] Friedrich, op. cit., 19–20.

self-direction is prior to the process of totalization or some of its set and cumulative concrete images.

It is important to come to grips with Friedman's perspective in his book, *To Deny Our Nothingness*, because it is a prevalent view of joint responsibility under the label of the confluent model of participation. Friedman states:

The image of man . . . is an integral part of man's search to understand himself in order to become himself, of his search for an image of authentic personal existence. . . . It implies a meaningful, personal direction, a response from within to what one meets in each situation, standing one's ground and meeting the world with the attitude that is rooted in this ground. Man cannot live without searching for authentic existence. . . . However . . . he must be concerned again and again with potentiality, choice, and decision . . . with discovering an authentic response to each situation he faces. . . . I must be concerned with what is authentic *human* existence and what is authentic existence for me in particular. These two can never be divided from each other, nor can they be identified.[8]

I am assuming that by "authentic" Friedman means "real," or what he calls "concrete image." The belief that man can be authenticated by goal-directed response-relationships, that such responses call man into being, is in essence an illusory belief because there are many models of goal-directedness and of response-relations, depending on which model of totality is discussed. There is no universal human responder on the phenomenal level. What it means, in terms of my thesis, is that on the phenomenal level of goal orientation, where systems of totality abound and where they originate, we cannot discover the source of human responsibility. If such a discovery is claimed, however, the source of responsibility is some system of totality.

To be directed by concrete images of man is a form of totalism built up externally by cumulative response-relations and external goal orientation. But we have seen that such goal-directedness demands either the ontological orderings of totality or that of the human orderer. The fact of the matter is that each such concrete image of man, posturing as the whole man, has its own model of the responder or of response-relations. Moreover, such smaller totalities implicate and reflect one's model of the whole universe. Thus even the concrete images of man are not their own; they are servants of totality. What this amounts to in terms of my thesis is that unless we

[8] Friedman, *op. cit.*, 17–18.

can get off the external track of meaning of goal-directedness and responses, we can neither liberate the human orderer nor radicalize human responsibility. The responder is like a broken bell unable to ring true because he is not a human orderer. The springs of action in experiences of responsibility are thus thwarted from the very beginning. The "image of man" is the work of the human orderer in the matrix of participation; it is not simply an embodiment of an attitude and of a response, as Friedman supposes. Man is not the product of either a personal or a social encounter, unless both presuppose a human orderer in the matrix of participation. When Friedman softens André Malraux's phrase, "we can fashion images of ourselves sufficiently powerful to deny our nothingness," by equating "fashioning" with "responding," he weakens an already weakened notion of the human orderer. Man's great virtue is to be ahead of such definition-making and model-making concerning human nature—and not only to be ahead of such a game, but a purposive being who directs man's search for models of human nature. We can more readily deny our nothingness if purposive being contributes to our becoming in the matrix of participation. Man is ontologically self-directing in personal and social encounters or he suffers the consequences, namely, those of totalitarian thought which would order dialectically, in terms of the unity of being and nothing, the meaning of human life. In the case of a totalistic view of life, such concrete images of man come about by "participation in the whole" (which a situationalism like Friedman's assumes). It is more advisable to insist that both models of the whole man and the whole of existence are designed by the modeling human power we have called the human orderer in the matrix of experience. Whether we respond to more particular concrete images of man (Friedman) or to more general totalities (Dewey and Mead) is really inconsequential. For one remains on the level of phenomenal experience where the source(s) of shared responsibility has an illusive character.

Three, another perspective which separates purpose from responsibility and prevents the radicalization of responsibility is the view that response-relations flow directly from the nature of human vitality, implicating such terms as growth, spontaneity, feeling, subjectivity, and power. All these concepts can perhaps be summarized by the phrase "human sensibilities," as elemental modes of response closer to the orderings of totality than to the human orderer. When power is added to spontaneity, as in Marcuse's writings, we strengthen human vitality, but the problem of the source(s) of responsibility is still very much in jeopardy. Human sensibility is revolutionized, but only to lead one into the omnipotential ten-tacles of another alleged real and immediate totality. This kind of vitalism, as was exemplified in chapter 1 by the young radicals and in a later chapter on totalistic participation by Marcuse, does not yield the radicalization of responsibility. Such a "practice of life" assumes, but does not demonstrate, the meaning of shared responsibility. Paul Tillich and Rollo May have shown some dissatisfaction with human vitality as an oversimplified guide to human life. Rollo May, facing the same problem in psychiatry, comments:

There have been a number of attempts to identify what we mean by vitality in the psychological sphere: such words as "aliveness" and so on are used, but without anyone's having much conviction that he has said anything. Does not intentionality give us a criterion for defining psychological vitality? The degree of intentionality can define the aliveness of the person, the potential degree of commitment and his capacity, if we are speaking of a patient, for remaining at the therapeutic task.[9]

May continues to quote Paul Tillich, his mentor on this topic: "Man's vitality is as great as his intentionality: they are interdependent. This makes man the most vital of all beings . . . to create beyond himself."[10]

Both thinkers, though they are correct in suggesting the alliance between vitality and directionality to get some sort of notion of shared responsi-bility, are mistaken, however, in reading off the human sense of directed-ness in terms of self-transcendence and goal-directed intentionality. This merely freezes, even paralyzes, some routes that human beings take in terms of ultimate commitment or concern. Neither Tillich nor May are appreciative of the fact that I have been espousing: that possibly such systems of totality are merely models of existence. Intentionality in both systems of thought is merely the servant of totality, which assigns both the "responsibility for" and the "responsibility to" in human participation. There will be a more extended treatment of this topic when we consider Rollo May in a later chapter. Meanwhile, the point I wish to make is that an "interdependent relation" may not be its own; it may also implicate totality, as it certainly does, in Tillich's and May's perspectives. It leads to a principle of coresponsiveness either between man and God or between man and nature. These may be solutions for totalists but not for one interested in reclaiming a notion of the human orderer in the matrix of

[9] Rollo May, *Love and Will* (New York, W. W. Norton, 1969), 245.
[10] *Ibid.*, 244.

participation. Neither is it a solution if the abstract directionality of self-transcendence is mistaken for a basic feature of the human orderer. Suffice to say that even while we experience a shared vitality on the human scene, this source of human empowerment may not be the source of shared human responsibility. Responsibility needs a directionality to be responsibility. The next question is: Which is the most fitting kind of directionality that yields the experience of human responsibility?

The radicalization of responsibility requires that the human orderer be the gathering focus of human vitality in terms of directionality. However, this is not a philosophy of will and self-determination, as a single isolated faculty. Will is one elemental mode of response in man's purposive being. It is not the human orderer in the matrix of participation. When the human orderer is functioning in purposive participation, will manifests itself in acts of self-subjectification. It is not the "moving mover in participation." It is but one aspect of the subject self in a triadic relationship. Its encounter experiences have meaning only because there is a human orderer that gives meaning to the acts of the will in participation. It is thus part of man's capacity for model-making in participation.

Four, what is the relation of responsibility to conscience when response-relations are radicalized? I have developed a theory of conscience elsewhere which, in summary, means the following. Conscience is an instrument of self-criticism. As such, while it may cancel some of the goals and plans of purposive being, it does not cancel the latter. Viewed in this light, conscience is a "functionary of" the human orderer. When the theory was developed I was unaware of the ontological possibilities of human self-direction. I tried deriving it from choice-making and goal-making on the phenomenal level of experience. Its guidance value was attributed to the "cumulative result of past self-directives." As such, it was a deposit, residue, storehouse not of past imperatives, but of past purposes. Man respects conscience for its deposit of past self-directives and for its ability to participate in the ongoing process of decision-making considerations.[11]

I can now add a new dimension to this theory of conscience as self-criticism. The radicalization of responsibility enables us now to regard self-criticism in terms of our understanding of our model of existence. Conscience is not only a storehouse of past purposive insights, it is also capable of anticipated insights in terms of the future because it functions as part

---

[11] William Horosz, *Escape From Destiny* (Charles C. Thomas, 1967), 159–68.

of our comprehensive outlook through models of existence. Once the human orderer is a vital part of primal experience, conscience, as a function of the human orderer in participation, has a new share in self-criticism. Even when the human orderer makes new alliances with being, nature, life, or God, it is self-directing in such "relations to." Conscience, as a function of purposive being in participation, has a share in this directedness and relatedness and functions as self-criticism.

Let us examine the resources available to us in mankind's conscience, an effective instrument of human self-criticism. As the storehouse of past purposes, it is of aid to us in current decision-making. In terms of the future, its prognosis value is related to our comprehensive models of existence. Since man has a share in existence and can come up with models of reality with claims on participation and responsibility, conscience has a new role to play in terms of self-criticism. Its function is that of self-criticism in purposive participation and responsibility. It attests to the resourcefulness of the human orderer in both kinds of experience.

Conscience is not its own. It belongs either to the human orderer or to some system of totality. Since we have rejected the primacy of totalities as guides to life, conscience can be viewed as an effective instrument of self-criticism as a function of purposive being in existence. Its denials and acceptances, or its beliefs and unbeliefs, have to do only with the choices, goals, plans, and totalities that purposive being comes up with in the matrix of participation. It is not a replacement for purposive being, as totalists would have us believe. Conscience thus keeps score of the human orderer's plans and goals in experience. Self-criticism has to do with its operations in participation, not with purposive being on the level of ontological self-direction. It is a phenomenal check and guide to man as he relates ontologically to patterns of participation. Conscience keeps purposive being informed of its actions and plans and runs a constant commentary on the operations of purposive being in the milieu of participation. Thus it helps to keep the human orderer in touch with his response-relations in experience.

The view of conscience as an instrument of self-criticism has always been disparaged by totalists, who would make it a servant of totality. When conscience is made the master of man in such a totalistic context, it assigns man his proper and fitting turning space in the system of totality. Now there is nothing to apologize for in viewing it as a function of self-criticism. Conscience is man's doing even when he uses it as a guide. It does not cancel the human orderer in experience; it merely monitors some of its plans. The alternative to this perspective is to make conscience the guardian-care of man's relation to nature, being, life, or God. In Heidegger it watches *Dasein's* prewired relationship to Being and functions as the "call of care." When conscience is related to the human orderer, its function of self-criticism is to help clarify the operational directives of purposive being in experience. This view makes of conscience a more participatory phenomenon in purposive participation. Since ontological self-direction is applicable to personal and social participation and to models of existence, the work of conscience is also extended as being the surveyor of the operations and activities of purposive being in existence. Thus it plays a part even in appraising our models of existence, especially in evaluating the concrete images of man and of society. The view that conscience is here to displace the human orderer in existence, or be its pedagogue from above or from below, is unnecessary, for it can never replace purposive being as a human orderer of its experiences. Thus man is the gathering focus even of the works of conscience. And its work of self-criticism is more responsible because it is more human in its activities.

Five, if man is responsible for systems of responsibility (like conscience), and not only responsible to them, and for the more totalistic systems of responsibility, then this is of the essence of the radicalization of responsibility. When man is self-directing in his response-relations, he has gone beyond the responder or beyond a set of responses in the stream of experience and become a human orderer in participation. Such a one can make claims on responsibility because he is self-directing in his response-relations. When responsibility is defined as "deputyship," as it is in the religious tradition of Dietrich Bonhoeffer, for example, what is emphasized as responsibility is the surrender of one's life to the other man in terms of self-giving.[12] From my point of view, whether the individual is a self-seeker or a self-giver is a distinction that is posterior to the human orderer as self-directing. The religious tradition of Bonhoeffer is more eager to relate the issue of self-seeking and self-giving to a system of religious totality than it is to see

[12] Dietrich Bonhoeffer, *Ethics*, ed. by E. Bethge (New York, Macmillan, 1965), 224–27. Bonhoeffer's concern was with the structure of a "responsible life," not with the sources of responsibility. It was already assumed that its source came from God. But in terms of my thesis, we cannot make such an assumption, and, consequently, we must regard it as one model of total accountability competing with other totalistic patterns of responsibility. In a sense, we are talking about a prior issue—human responsibility—before it becomes religious or moral responsibility.

it in relationship to man first. Once man is goal-directed toward God, his response-relations must always be outwardly directed. The primary meaning of such responsibility is that it is a unifying principle in that system of totality. However, other systems of totality may have other models of accountability other than that of "deputyship."

If we take another example, that of naturalism, man is first responsible to a system of natural totality even before he is responsible to himself. When a naturalist pronounces upon the responsibility or irresponsibility of consequential acts, he does so with this standard of totality in mind. On the issue of freedom, much depends on what the natural totality assigns man as turning space—for example, the contingency or chance-factor discoverable in nature. Man may exploit this contingency for his own ends and happiness, but the subject matter limits the alternatives for such choices. For man is answerable first to his relations to nature before he is answerable to himself. His positionality defines both man's dependence and possibility on nature's order and disorder. It is an odd requirement that man's freedom depends first on the accidental factors of nature and only secondarily on the human orderer. One's goal-directed commitment to nature makes of responsibility a unifying principle of that system of totality.[13]

The radicalization of responsibility assumes both the above systems of totality as models of existence for which man himself is responsible. Each model of totality has its own system of accountability which it claims to be universal (only because it has identified its model of existence with existence as existence). In Bonhoeffer's Lutheran perspective, it is assumed that man is both free and bound, therefore dialectically ordered by the Christian system of totality (or one model of this religious tradition). It is a sin to be self-directing in the system of totality with such an affirmation of faith. The same is the case with naturalism as a system of totality, but which is less dialectically ordered. Rather it is ordered by the objectivating methods of science which define man's turning space in nature. In both cases, man is not responsible for his responses to nature or to God because in a prior way he is committed in goal direction to one or the other by the system of totality, or by the alleged necessity of human nature, or the necessity of the spirit. In opposition to such systems of totality, I have maintained that the birthplace of responsibility is purposive being that assumes

[13] S. P. Lamprecht, *The Metaphysics of Naturalism* (New York, Appleton, Century, Crofts, 1967), 155.

146

the responsibility for such systems of responsibility as discussed above. The questions about man's origins in some system of totality cannot be properly raised unless purposive being entertains them in the matrix of participation.

Six, perhaps I can summarize the above points on the radicalization of responsibility by confronting once more my definition of responsibility: man confronting the human orderer in himself and in social existence. Considered negatively, the following things may be said about it. When the source of responsibility is placed in some system of totality (social, natural, religious, scientific), man does not experience such a confrontation of self-direction. What he does experience is an external meaning of responsibility in which he participates to varying degrees of obligation (without knowing why).

Because of past failures of defining the human orderer in the matrix of participation, modern man has tended to immerse himself in systems of totality. The alternative we have chosen is to reconstruct another model of the human orderer that would take responsibility for the systems of responsibility, such as totalities. It is what we do with our models of participation that decides the fate of human responsibility and its source(s). And the models of participation that I have reviewed in Part One of this volume have all chosen not to recover the human orderer in the matrix of participation. My contention here is that when we dispose of one model of the human orderer in the course of history, this does not of necessity mean that there is no human orderer in experience. It merely means the denial of some of the concrete images of man that we have constructed in the course of time. Man has the potential to come up with others. The metamodel that I have emphasized, in which purposive being is master of life in the matrix of participation, enables one to place the source of responsibility in man once more.

Considerations of the sources of responsibilities on the level of action and phenomenal experience have also failed us in constructing a model of the human orderer that was the source of responsibility. Such functional approaches have assumed too much autonomy, whereas, in fact, they have succumbed to some system of totality. The most recent failure has been the notion of "human agency" unsupported by purposive being.

Definitions of responsibility in terms of institutional role-playing have not gone beyond a relativistic typological study of responsibility; neither have they resolved the issue of personal morality with such role-playing morality. The point is that the role theory of responsibility is itself in need of a model of social self-direction.

The principle of "coresponsiveness" has also implicated systems of totality as the source of responsibility.

Put more positively, the human responder can be enriched in his response-relations within experience with the model of man as a purposive being in participation. However, in order to offer this enrichment, he must be liberated through purposive participation in experience and respected as such through the radicalization of responsibility. Such a metamodel is needed today to reaffirm man's confidence in human responsibility. Without it we face a crises in responsibility and perhaps of our humanity.

7. Interrogating Theories of Responsibility (I)

I have been utilizing a linguistic distinction between "responsibility for" and "responsibility to" in the previous chapters, which my point of view requires. The meaning of "responsibility for" has to do with the operational dimensions of purposive being in the matrix of participation. Should the distinction not hold up, and this is always a possibility, it does not mean the denial of purposive being; rather it means that I have to come up with another operational phrase that will designate the work of purposive being in experience. Thus far I have had no difficulties with the distinction and wish to maintain it in this chapter in criticizing five other models of responsibility. My concern here is to return to the five models of participation discussed in Part One to see what theories of responsibility they prescribe. The order of the material will follow a different pattern: youth and Marcuse on responsibility, Mead and Dewey on responsibility, and Polanyi on responsibility. This will give me additional opportunity to interrogate the theories of responsibility as I have interrogated their foundational models of participation.

Youth and Marcuse on Responsibility

They have much in common, only Marcuse has a power ethic to blend with the notion of social spontaneity. Since I have already given an extended treatment of the relation of responsibility to spontaneity in chapter 1, I have only a few more comments to add to this. My main concern in this section will be with Marcuse and this material will relate to chapter 3.

It has been my contention that the problem of youth and authority has been oversimplified. Many of the psychological or psychiatric discussions of youth never get beyond the problem of youth and authority. This is the way the problem looks in terms of a totalistic perspective. Let me discuss this matter in terms of Erik Erikson's resolution of the problem of youth and authority.

Erikson recognizes many abuses of responsibility in both stages of life, that of youth and adulthood. The adults are guilty in the way they have handled delegated power, both in terms of authority and permissiveness, because they have neglected an understanding of youth as a "stage of life" in the larger developmental context of history. They have misunderstood the meaning of "generational responsibility." According to Erikson, both kinds of adults, the authoritarian and the permissive, make decisions for the young which ignore "what reasonability and responsibility they may be ready for themselves."[1] The youth can respect only such authority that their course of development prepares them for or releases them for. Other kinds of responsibility are regarded by Erikson as rather artificial. Unless the responsibility that adults require of youth has its true source in history and evolution and is fostered by them, it is of the artificial variety.[2]

Obviously the author has identified his model of human development with the course of evolution and history. He has also identified culture and history with nature and evolution. With these two identifications he is more than willing to identify the "readiness for release" with "readiness for responsibility." He is thus willing to settle for the phrase "responsibility to" something as the deepest kind of responsibility that man can have. All that one need do is to be receptive to the source and directionality of responsibility dictated by one's stage of life, to be humanly responsible. When nature and history combine to produce the course of human development, as from a system of totality, they are jointly responsible for the course of human development. Man's true responsibility is to be responsible to one's stage of life and, through that stage, to be responsible to a biosocial system of totality. Erikson believes that such responsibility to a system of totality, which is not a model of existence but the real thing, is the height of human responsibility, and it leads to a global or universal response-relations among the generations in their quest for identity. He states:

What might, then, slowly emerge from delegated responsibility is a worldwide ethics superseding traditional moralities. I would call ethical such guidelines and interdicts as are based not on what is arbitrarily permitted or superstitiously

[1] *Newsweek* (December 21, 1970), 86.
[2] *Ibid.*

150

forbidden but on what liberated experience and informed intuition can agree on.[3]

In reading Erikson's book, *Insight and Responsibility*, one becomes so saturated with humanistic values that one tends to forget Erikson's commitment to Freud's system of naturalistic totality, in which responsibility plays a minimal role in human behavior. The "liberated experience . . . informed intuition" is the kind of experience that comes through psychoanalysis. It derives from a prepurposive model of totality, since the course of development takes place from below. If this is "reasonability," to be responsible to something but not for it, reasonability should be equated with the notion of "dependence" rather than with responsibility. It is also interesting to note that what is reasonability for Erikson is irrationality for the youth. Yet both tap the source of this responsibility by an appeal to a direct form of immediate experience. The Freudian belief "of underscoring the direction of what is given in development," which Erikson cosigns, is an untenable belief, unless one takes the liberty of identifying one's model of development with the course of development itself. But what guarantee do we have that the biosocial totality behaves as our theory says it does?

In the light of my theory, Erikson's attempt to read responsibility and its spontaneous development in terms of the youthful stage of life and its "readiness for release" is a way of blending human freedom and necessity that confounds the human intellect. It may be good Hegelian dialectic, but this is already a substitute directionality and source for human responsibility.

Such "spontaneous development" as the source of responsibility of youth at a particular stage of life that Erikson espouses is a way of placing the source of human responsibility in a system of totality. That it is more than a model of existence and its developmental course is merely a claim to ultimacy on the level of immediate experience where all mediations are left unjustified. There are many such models of human development. Erikson, however, overlooks this important fact. He believes that his model of totality is in tune with reality which through the life stages will make a proper distribution of shared human responsibility. This assumption is quite explicit in the passage below:

At any rate, the ethical questions of the future will be less determined by the influence of the older generation on the younger one than by the interplay of

---

[3] *Ibid.*

subdivisions in a life scheme in which the whole life span is extended; in which the life stages will be further subdivided; in which new roles for both sexes will emerge in all life stages; and in which a certain margin of free choice and individualized identity will come to be considered the reward for technical inventiveness.[4]

In this new and coming context of life, "the young adult specialist as the permanent and permanently changing authority" will take on increasing responsibility for the younger youth.[5] Erikson believes that the older youth will somehow reflect more faithfully the responsibility of youth as a stage of life. Whether such a situation would reflect a better partnership on each stage of life is really beside the point. If totality, through the developmental stages of life, is responsible for the system of responsibility at each stage of development, and for the shared responsibility among the generations of men, man may as well enjoy his leisure time, forget about responsibility, and submit to the directives of an effete Hegelian dialectics, where all comes out well at the end anyway, irrespective of human responsibility. Erikson has the optimism of Hegel's three-term dialectics even with respect to the breakdown of responsibility on all levels of life:

A new generation growing up with technological and scientific progress may well experience technology and its new modes of thought as the link between a new culture and new forms of society. . . . In this respect, assuming this hypothesis is true, the greatest strains will be on the youth. This particular generation, like its predecessors, may come back to some form of accommodation with the society as it grows older and accepts positions within the society. But the experiences also leave a "cultural deposit" which is cumulative consciousness and—to this extent I am a Hegelian—is irreversible, and the next generation therefore starts from a more advanced position of alienation and detachment.[6]

In Hegelian terms, there may be no predictable society "to come back to," according to Erikson, because in the triadic dialectics the third term, while it is inclusive of the old, is a stage of advancement beyond it. This means progress and the overcoming of alienation, if not for this generation then at least the next one.

If Erikson were in charge of the process of human development, rather than a theorist about it, his advice would be welcome. But the fact that he gives us a model about the course of human development for which he makes certain claims of ultimacy, such a directionality and such a source

[4] Erik Erikson, "Youth Today and the Year 2000," *Natural Enemies,* ed. by A. Klein (New York, J. B. Lippincott, 1969), 533.

[5] *Ibid.,* 532.

of human responsibility, is of dubious origin. First of all, the fact that he relates a pattern of dialectics to immediate experience is enough to show that he is dealing with "unjustified mediations" on the level of immediate or unmediated experience. In such a domain of immediacy there is no justification of right or wrong. The very standards that arise from immediate experience are thus assumptive. The point is, Erikson prefers a source for human responsibility that is outside the human orderer, and perhaps this is a way of searching for absolute participation through one's model of existence. Better yet, it is a model of existence searching for reality. The promise of liberation and insight is the promise of Erikson's model of existence and not the promise of life itself. Because it has placed human life under the directionality of a dialectical totality, supported by evolutionary and historical development, it means a new form of submission for man.

However, it must be said on Erikson's behalf that at least he does not label the New Left as a form of "new barbarism." Nonetheless, Erikson thinks in terms of the generations of men and of generational responsibility in his totality. The young radicals think in terms of their youth-specific culture requiring another spontaneous model of totality than what Erikson has in mind. Both totalities derive from an appeal to immediate experience. It is not the case, as Daniel J. Boorstin claims, that the youth serve the cause of "sensation" and reject the guidance of "experience," and that this is what makes them new barbarians. Boorstin comments:

The New Barbarism, in a word, is the social expression of a movement from Experience to Sensation. Experience, the dictionary tells us, means *actual observation of a practical acquaintance with facts or events; knowledge resulting from this*. A person's experience is what he has lived through. Generally speaking experience is (a) cumulative, and (b) communicable. People add up their experiences to become wiser and more knowledgeable. We can learn from our experience and, most important, we can learn from other people's experiences. Our publically shared experience is history. Experience is distinguished, then, by the fact that it can be shared. When we have an experience, we enter into the continuum of a society. But the dramatic shift now is away from Experience and toward Sensation. . . . Sensation is personal, private, confined, and incommunicable. . . . The sensation-oriented suffers an "identity-crisis": he is concerned mostly about the boundaries of that bundle of private messages which is himself. The experience-oriented seeks, and finds, continuity, and emphasizes what is shared and what is communicable.[7]

[6] *Ibid.*, 526.

[7] Daniel J. Boorstin, "The New Barbarians," *The Rhetoric of No*, ed. by R. Fabrizio, E. Karas, R. Menmuir (New York, Holt, Rinehart, Winston, 1970), 99. Cumulative

Though I sympathize with the broadened perspective of empirical philosophy in its definition of experience over the narrower limits of experience defined as "sensation," they are, nonetheless, both on the wavelength of immediate experience and profit from its unitive guidance. The difference is not all that great. Both views supplant the human orderer in directionality and responsibility by offering the directives and the response-relations of immediacy. Both views implicate a naturalistic totality as the guide of man. The very fact that we can point to the dimension of social spontaneity in the New Left disproves Boorstin's thesis that it is simply concerned with an "identity-crisis," concerned with "private messages." Let me put the matter as forcefully as I can. What is at stake is how both sensation and experience can be the source of human directionality without implicating some system of totality that rules human life. In terms of this question, I see little difference between the wisdom of experience and that discovered by sensation. They both share the wisdom of systems of totality, which in terms of my thesis derives from the wisdom and directives of the human orderer in existence. I anticipate similar problems of experience in Marcuse's view of responsibility which I shall discuss below.

In Marcuse's theory, sensation and experience are not antithetical terms. They are rather combined in the form of a "new sensibility" which Marcuse believes will usher in a new revolutionary era. The new blend of Eros and Reason, unified by the productive imagination, is to be understood not in terms of Kant's critique of judgment because it is meant as a revolutionary conception. If Marcuse were replying to Boorstin's article, he would probably attach the epithet of the New Barbarism to the advanced stage of capitalistic society rather than to the youth.

The "aesthetic universe" is the source of human responsibility backed by a biosocial system of totality. The centrality of this domain cannot be overemphasized in terms of Marcuse's perspective:

The aesthetic universe is the *Lebenswelt* on which the needs and faculties of freedom depend for their liberation. They cannot develop in an environment shaped by and for aggressive impulses, nor can they be envisaged as the mere effect of a new set of social institutions. They can emerge only in the collective practice of creating an environment: level by level, step by step—in the material

---

experience is as much in need of guidance as private sensations. The line between sensation and experience, defined between private and public, is a tenuous one. In either case, that line is defined by a system of totality and not by the human orderer in participation.

and intellectual production, an environment in which the nonaggressive, erotic receptive faculties of man, in harmony with the consciousness of freedom, strive for the pacification of man and nature. In the reconstruction of society for the attainment of this goal, reality altogether would assume a *Form* expressive of the new goal.[8]

Productive as the imagination may appear to be, the reader should note that the essence of the new life would consist in the pacification of man where his receptive categories would function at a maximum. The imagination, as an elemental mode of response, is solicited to do the work of reconstructing society on more erotic and adventuresome lines.

It is surprising that Marcuse prefers the artistic imagination to the religious expression of it. The religious imagination has been more effective than the artistic imagination in terms of its productivity in the world. But, I suppose, Marx's denial of the religious imagination as a revolutionary tool prevented Marcuse from utilizing it for the revolution. The point is, and this is a historical consideration, the religious imagination has a more impressive record than the artistic one, even though both are receptively conceived.

Is the demand for such receptivity the requirement of one's model of totality, or the demand of experience or history? Marcuse never faces this problem. It would appear to be a servant of totality in the reconstruction of the world. It certainly does not represent the human orderer in his participation in the world.

In his *An Essay on Liberation*, Marcuse deals with the issue of moral responsibility between two competing systems of totality. Obviously, each such system defines its own meaning of what is responsible or irresponsible. To avoid such a problem, Marcuse attempts to relate moral responsibility to the biology of the individual, which would give responsibility roots in man's instinctive life. The concrete goals of the revolution and the health of the new society both derive from this instinctive base that is, of course, free of ideology.

The rebellion would then have taken root in the very nature, the "biology" of the individual; and on these new grounds, the rebels would redefine the objectives and the strategy of the political struggle, in which alone the concrete goals of liberation can be determined.[9]

But there are many such models of biological responsibility (Hans Jonas

[8] Herbert Marcuse, *An Essay on Liberation* (Boston, Beacon Press, 1969), 31.
[9] *Ibid.*, 5.

and the biophenomenological perspective, and the theory of Edmund Sinnott), but none of them lead to the revolutionary consequences or to the species-being that Marcuse has in mind. What I am suggesting is that the placing of the source of responsibility in the metabolism or in some other biological function is already a sociophilosophical reading of man's biological life and of its alleged "needs." I think the appeal to biology as a support for the moral responsibility in a system of totality is merely another claim to ultimacy for one's model of existence and responsibility. There is nothing in human metabolism that it should be either evolutionary or revolutionary in its interests. Such impositions of meaning upon man's biological constitution are merely an attempt to find weighty evidence for one's misguided effort to make one's model of existence into something real. To label man's instinctual life as an "instinctual revolt" and turning this, by necessity, into a "political rebellion" is too much even for the imagination of man. It shows the magic talisman of the ideology critique doing its wondrous works in the midst of humanity. The very attempt to utilize the "infrastructure of man" (as part of the larger societal infrastructure) is an attempt to find new sanctions for what would be better left alone as a model of existence and responsibility. Marcuse's biological interests are thus to invest his model of human existence with some new sanctions and with claims to ultimacy.

It is part of Marcuse's optimism to believe that additional growth in capitalistic technology may modify historically those human needs that are beyond competition and aggressive performance, that it may even transform the assertive man with assertive freedom into a receptive man with receptive freedom (which knows its limitations in the necessities of social forms). The new sensibilities will reveal in practice "the potential of a nonaggressive, nonexploitative world." It is obvious that Marcuse is concerned with the exploitation of human responsibility in terms of global external institutions in capitalistic society. My concern has been to show another potential area of exploitation where human responsibility is related to a system of revolutionary totality. He has no fear about such exploitation because he has denied the model-making features of his system of totality marching through the institutions of the world. He states: ". . . the new sensibility has become a political force. It crosses the frontier between the capitalist and the communist orbit; it is contagious because the atmosphere, the climate of the established societies, carries the virus."[10]

10 *Ibid.*, 22.

If the human orderer in all its strength of mind and purpose cannot discover the proper harmony required for social living, how can Marcuse's "biological solidarity" find the way? The attempt to recapture the new sensibilities prior to the human orderer in the matrix of participation is doomed to defeat, for it immerses man in a system of totality from which he never recovers (unless man has a glimpse of it as a model of existence). Such biosocial solidarity Marcuse regards as elemental, instinctual, and creative. Yet he also has his reservations about the radical youth and the importance of spontaneity for the revolution. He comments:

> To be sure, within the repressive society, and against its ubiquitous apparatus, spontaneity by itself cannot possibly be a radical and revolutionary force. It can become such a force only as the result of enlightenment, education, political practice—in this sense indeed, as a result of organization.[11]

In short, it can work only in a perfect society, and until that stage of social life is reached, it needs the mediation of revolutionary organizations.

What we have here is responsibility to a vision of life but not responsibility for such a vision. The system of totality takes on the responsibility for that vision. It is little wonder that "a culture of receptivity" is required to put across the intentions of totality. The facts which lie before such a visionary system of responsibility are more than realistic. Such ideals are "impossible possibilities," with no God to help achieve such high aspirations. First of all, the miraculous change of man from an assertive and aggressive creature to one of sublime and meditative responsibility is a more than formidable task that an external revolution may not even touch, let alone solve. Secondly, the restructuring of society to allow for "the ascent of the Aesthetic Principle as Form of the Reality Principle" is similarly a formidable undertaking. Thirdly, the restructuring of the productive imagination from the ornamental role it has played in the history of thought, or from the role it played in relation to primitive life, is also a formidable task. In the light of my thesis, even if this were achieved, it would still not give us the human orderer we are seeking. In short, this is a task that only a system of totality could achieve. What this would necessitate is the work of "the totality" and not a model of existence. As far as the implementation of the erotic and aesthetic ideal of life is concerned, the task seems hopeless.

Moreover, the very ideal of the human orderer in terms of the imagina-

11 *Ibid.*, 89.

tion has been a successful one only in the field of art. Its receptive nature, its holistic tendencies, prevent it from functioning in the capacity of a human orderer in practice. We need more than imagination to construct a new model of man that will have ontological self-direction in personal and social encounters. Imagination has been a servant of totalities in the history of thought. Its essence of meaning is holistic or synoptic. But, then again, there is no point in talking about imagination as a universal abstraction. It is my imagination or yours, respectively. That is to say, man is self-directing in his imaginative quests even on the level of primal experience. The alternative is that imagination functions as a unifying principle in a system of totality that is both limited by it and orders the imagination. The human imagination is not its own. Either man or a system of totality claim ownership of it. Its productivity in practice depends on one or the other factor. Marcuse is only too eager to relate it to a system of totality because of its remarkable receptivity. The issue can be put in different words also, namely, that the "appreciative consciousness" means one thing when it is seen as a part of totality, and it means another when man takes responsibility for it in self-direction. Literally, then, the appreciative consciousness appreciates its master first of all.

What kind of responsibility can one expect from an "aesthetic universe" that has the foundational character of *Lebenswelt*? It is responsibility which is rooted in man's receptive freedom, as the artist's. The whole point of art, in terms of its historical perspective, is it never took responsibility for its creations but only for the climate of creativity. It first claimed to be inspired from above via the Great Analogy, in which the artist was a creator like God only in a creaturely manner. Later in history, art claimed to be inspired from below, as from the Freudian unconscious, etc. This was a way of showing responsibility to but not responsibility for one's creativity. How this would work out in society is a puzzle of the greatest magnitude. Who would take responsibility for such a society if all members of that society were capable only of responsibility to it but not for it? The obvious reply is: history as a totality. There is no social self-direction on the part of society. It is the tool of totality as the process of world history marches through the institutions of society. Thus the appeal to aesthetic directionality is an abortive appeal. It looks for directionality where there is a lack of it, in the aesthetic universe.

Moreover, such a *Lebenswelt* is only a model of existence, not existence qua existence, as Marcuse omnisciently claims it is. The term is borrowed from Edmund Husserl, as noted earlier, but there it represents the world of the *ratio* and not an aesthetic domain. Marcuse criticized Husserl for not being practically oriented, which is true, but he merely substituted another model of the "historical situation" which progressively revealed the truly universal beyond the domain of historical relativism. His critique of Husserl's concept of "essence" said, in effect, that Husserl neglected "the consciousness of specific groups and individuals" that generate consciousness historically and materialistically and with revolutionary fervor work for a more rational organization of society. Such essences cannot be left free-floating in a universal domain separated from the efforts of men to attain a rational society. Marcuse writes:

The dialectical concepts transcend the given social reality in the direction of another historical structure which is present as a tendency in the given reality. The positive concept of essence, culminating in the concept of the essence of man, which sustains all critical and polemical distinctions between essence and appearance as their guiding principle and model, is rooted in this potential structure.[12]

This would add a revolutionary dialectic, a form of methodological power structure, to the aesthetic domain, to share the responsibility for man.

However, when we add power to the aesthetic continuum, we do not derive responsibility of a human sort. The aesthetic comes to be dominated by a system of dialectics that owes its primary service to a system of historical totality that is not of man's making. Man is merely the servant of a dialectically ordered aesthetic universe. He is not responsible either for the dialectical march of history or for the aesthetic universe. The pacification of man is now accomplished. If we ask a pointed question, why is pacification such an important issue in a totalistic perspective, the reply is obvious. One cannot cross the boundaries of such a system of totality. Is this the equivalent of "humility" in the Christian scheme of life? Here, too, one cannot cross the boundaries of the religious totality, as "pride" often does. Such requirements on the part of totalistic schemes of life would have more legitimacy if it could be demonstrated how one's model of totality was the real and immediate *Lebenswelt*. To the extent that Marcuse's model of totality is still in search of its own reality, to that extent we must disregard his totalitarian claims on life. The fact is that he has given us a model of accountability which rests on the model of the aesthetic

---

[12] Herbert Marcuse, *Negations* (Boston, Beacon Press, 1968), 86.

Lebenswelt that is dialectically ordered. It is a goal-directed model of life demanding certain responsibilities of man to guarantee the goal direction. Such a goal-directed life can only be a model of life projected by purposive being on the plane of historical existence to help understand the meaning of the processes going on history. If this model fails in man's comprehension of history the human orderer can project other shapes and patterns to account for the processes of history and man's responsibility therein.

Let me underscore the point made above by a review of my thesis. In the light of my *metamodel*, every goal-directed pattern of life is a model of life and not life *qua* life. This holds true also for "the dialectics of liberation." The claim that it is otherwise is merely a claim to ultimacy for one's goal-directed model of existence. Unless there is a purposive being to originate and sustain such totalistic patterns of goal-directedness, in terms of a metamodel, we are left with the bedlam of relativism. The claim that dialectical concepts transcend the given conditions of history in the direction of another historical structure is thus a spurious claim. That man is advised to follow such a substitute directionality in life is man's own invention. The human orderer goes on all such trips beyond the subject-object split. It is in the sphere of man's capacity to be self-directing in experience that such goal directions arise, and the schemes of totality (with their special models of accountability) are nothing but ultimate goal directions. Such goals and totalities arise on the phenomenal level of experience. They are misappropriated by the totalist for purposes of his own convenience. A better term than responsibility for any system of totality is the concept of "control." This term conveys *responsibility to* but not *responsibility for* the meaning of one's life.

With this restatement of my position let me pursue the theme of rooting the source of responsibility in the aesthetic universe (Marcuse's *Lebenswelt*), "the Pure Land of Eros." Marcuse believes that the elimination of scarcity, of surplus repression, will give us a nonrepressive reality principle and society. Jack Jones, who pursues this theme in terms of the perspective of depth psychology, has a ready comment for Marcuse's perspective on this very issue:

Marcuse's third contention is easily refuted. The existence of art, play, and fantasy does not demonstrate that any "nonrepressive sublimation" is possible— only that *less* repressive sublimation is. This takes place within the context of and under the protection of the greater amount of repression required to establish and maintain whatever the cultural mode (artists, children, and fantasts do not create it). To say this, naturally, is not in the least to depreciate the value of art, play and fantasy.[13]

Marcuse's attempt to remove from society further repressive burdens (surplus repressions of the dominant form of society) may not give us a "non-repressive civilization." To be sure, it is a doctrine of hope, but for which world? Marcuse's reply is that it is for this world in terms of a restructured history dialectically wrought through the hands of labor.

George P. Grant, looking at Marcuse as an "orgastic gnostic," comments that in such a view of the liberated society there is no place for virtue and vice, just as there was no place for it in the Freudian image of man.

These gnostics have an answer to this criticism that is traditional among all gnostics. When people achieve genital primacy or orgastic potency, there will be no need for the idea of virtue, because the activities that the tradition called vicious will just disappear. Just as the Marxists, true to their dogma that the cause of evil lies in property relations, believe, therefore, that evil will largely disappear when that cause has been eliminated, so these gnostics unite as the cause of evil bad property relations and sexual repression and believe that the overcoming of both will lead to the good society. Here indeed we come close to the very center of modern man's image of himself. Evil is not in the free will, but arises from the realm of necessity. The most obvious implication of this is that it cannot be called sin.[14]

We could cite other criticisms of Marcuse that are just as potent as those of Jones and Grant. But it is not our intention to exhaust such a list of criticisms. There is a more basic problem in Marcuse that has not been reflected in such criticisms, namely, that the dialectics of liberation externally achieved in history is no guarantee that man will be internally liberated. We have worried this second problem, perhaps unduly, but the fact remains that a greater system of repression is imposed on man by a model of totality that poses as reality than any possible institutional oppression of man. If man is not his own, what good is circumstantial freedom? The real oppressor and aggressor are these models of existence and models of accountability when they function as real and immediate totalities. The real question is: How can man relieve himself of the burden of totalitarian thought, the illusion of absolute participation, and, above

[13] Jack Jones, "Herbert Marcuse and the Cunning of Revolution," *Michigan Quarterly Review* (April, 1970), 77.

[14] H. Schoeck and J. W. Wiggins (eds.), *Psychiatry and Responsibility* (Princeton, D. Van Nostrand, 1962), 131–32.

all (the greatest illusion), namely, that man reaches the dignity of his humanity by being responsible to such a system of totality but not responsible for it? Literally speaking, Marcuse jumps from the frying pan into the fire. If man is not his own, the aesthetic dimension and the union of Eros and Logos prepackaged by the human imagination will not help him much. Marcuse's blueprint of social health has the quality about it of a blueprint. It is a construct of human responsibility by man who has neglected the human orderer in himself. Perhaps he is too fearful or too apathetic to take the responsibility for his vision of communal health. If he is, he is a revolutionary only in externals. Inwardly he represents the pacification of man when he shows such receptivity to a system of totality that is not his own, or which has gone beyond his search for wholeness, to a totality that is external because it is beyond human participation (even though inwardly conceived).

DEWEY AND MEAD ON RESPONSIBILITY

Whatever else we may make of the confluent model of human participation, such as John Dewey's, it is a teleological model of man's relation to nature. With Dewey's strong emphasis on the experience of interaction that takes place between the organism and its environment, Dewey would like to claim more for it than as simply being a model of existence. We have called this attempt on the part of Dewey a mere claim to ultimacy for his chosen model of existence. It is, in fact, an implicit, unthematized, goal-directed model of man's relation to the world. Let me take the ideal of naturalistic "growth" as an example of implicit model-making. Growth is the ideal of human destiny in the matrix of interaction. This ideal of organic maturation, however, is as much a goal or ideal as any other, and as such it is the product of a purposive being participating in existence. Other things grow too, but they do not have growth as an ideal or an end. Things just happen to them; growth just happens to them. The need for such a distinction is imperative. When Dewey takes over the biological category of growth as an analogy to man, he wants to do more with it than that, namely, to make man goal-directed to nature and less passive toward the evolutionary process. He is trying his hand at a model of existence, like Hegel before him who postulated the relation of consciousness to the world in terms of experiential interpretations of that model. The phenomenon of "growth," as a goal, end, or ideal, does not grow out of life. It does not simply have a natural base. It is, in a real sense, the disclosure of purposive being in the matrix of participation that enables one to talk about a naturalistic totality unfolding in the world, as Dewey interactively interprets it. To say that the ideal of growth comes out of life itself is merely to identify one's naturalistic model with existence *qua* existence. It is a way of making "growth itself" a claim to ultimacy for one's model about growth.

Dewey's perspective on responsibility prevents man from being responsible for his growth, from being self-directing in his growth, or socially self-directing in such growth. Man can only be responsible to the phenomenon of growth itself. He carries the virus of growth, as Marcuse's man carries the virus of dialectical history on the move. The fact that there is prior purposiveness exhibited by man when he makes an alliance, either with nature or history, is totally ignored by both writers, because both of them claim that their view of reality is model-free, and they make this claim by an appeal to immediate experience where there is permission to practice unjustified mediations.

From growth, Dewey moves on to the notion of "continuity," which is a further abstraction from the model of growth ("it is through thought that continuities are experienced").[15] The next step is to utilize the realness of relations and the reality of continuities to make his claims of ultimacy for a system of naturalistic totality.

In terms of our perspective of the *metamodel* of purposive being, even a naturalistic form of goal-directedness is a model of human experience. The model of accountability which follows from such a system of totality thus bears the limitations and the possibilities of such a naturalistic scheme about life. Even when responsibility acts as a function in the stream of experience, it has this model-making quality about it, as I shall endeavor to show. The fact that it is a unifying principle in his system of naturalistic totality does not mean much because other totalists utilize responsibility as a principle of unification. As such, responsibility can only be true if man commits himself responsibly to the stream of experience for guidance and meaning. The real question is: Does the self contribute to its own unification in the field of immediate experience, or do the unitive experiences do this task for him? Ethical, aesthetic, and religious experiences help unify the self because man is no longer the human orderer

[15] Richard J. Bernstein (ed.), *On Experience, Nature, and Freedom (John Dewey)* (New York, Bobbs-Merrill, 1960), 208–209.

in such unitive experience. Such unitive experiences do for man what he cannot do for himself. They bear the instructions of totality in the context of situational immediacy.

Dewey's image of man, just as his model of total existence, has bearing on his theory of responsibility. When he reduces the self to its acts, or identifies selfhood with actions to pave the way for the importance of unitive experience, he has cleared the way for an external image of responsibility. It has something to do with the union of acts with their respective objects, and this provides the dominant direction of activity, not the human orderer.[16] Thus in one stroke Dewey disposes of the human orderer as a purposive being, ontologically self-directing in its actions, and of responsibility defined as man confronting the human orderer in himself. He also disposes of the inner dialogue in selfhood which European philosophies correct (Martin Buber, for example). This is not necessary, for the primal dialogue is between act and object in the stream of experience. This has similarities to what Sartre has done when he reduces being to action and then comes up with being as the result of choice-making and action. Sartre similarly loses the human orderer in the field of consciousness.

This prepurposive model of man, where the self has the *organism* as its *designatum* and where action has priority to the ontological human orderer of experience, yields external responsibility. A "response" is not the beginning of an activity; it is rather a "change, a shift, of activity in response to the change in conditions indicated by a stimulus."[17] Even the responder can be dispensed with quite readily. To say that this brings about the "whole self" integrated with unitive situations is rather misleading. The fact is, there is no human orderer either before the action, and there is no human orderer in the unitive situational experience. Unitive experiences instruct man even though he is part of the interactive situation. Dewey's definition of a motive makes this clear: "It is the movement of the self as a whole, a movement in which desire is integrated with an object so completely as to be chosen as a compelling end. . . . An object moves a person; for that object as a moving force *includes the self within it.*"[18]

This is the whole point, say, in *Art As Experience*, when the author weds the expressive act with the expressive object. This is primal unity

[16] John Dewey and J. H. Tufts, *Ethics* (New York, Henry Holt, 1932), 319, 321–22.
[17] *Ibid.*, 321.
[18] *Ibid.*, 322–23.

from below the self. Dewey's main target is the unity imposed on life "from above." But this very directionality of unitive experience and its processive formation, with growth as its paradigm case, shows it to be a model of existence. When Dewey disposes of rational unity from above in the interpretation of selfhood, as being abstractive in nature, he thinks he has reached the bedrock of selfhood, the real, immediate, integral, inter-active self as the live creature in an interacting environment. Whereas in my perspective, Dewey has come up with another model of unity for man and for nature, only this one is the abstract model, not so much of the ratio, as it is modeled by experience and participation. We do not escape model-making in participation. In fact, we need it to understand perspectival human participation. Dewey should have caught a glimpse of this truth from all his emphasis on the specificity of acts and from situations as all-inclusive unitive sections of the stream of experience. If this is not model-making by participation, I don't know what is. The need for ex-periential abstractions is rather obvious. The specificity and perspectival nature of human participation requires it for confronting and understand-ing the human condition. Dewey's model (which replaces the human orderer in participation) of actions, interacting with their objects—of "actions having guidance through their (own) intent:—their insight into their own consequences," utilizes intelligence, as a phase of unitive ex-perience itself, to give such insights to actions, as Dewey attributes to them.[19] This is tantamount to saying that there is a prior stage of inter-action between knowledge and action prior to the human orderer and his claim-making capacity. Such interaction is a method of totalizing experi-ence without the human consent of the human orderer and his directive powers. Such a requirement, that the human orderer first be absorbed in processive actions in processive situations and second that he give up his directives for those of unitive experience, is the demand of a model of existence and not the requirement of life itself. The human orderer as a purposive being projected such a plan to deny its directives in the field of experience, which does not necessarily deny purposive being, as Dewey claims it does.

There is another reference where Dewey holds to the principle that "any-thing that is has something unique in itself, and this unique something

<hr/>

[19] Paul Schilpp (ed.), *The Philosophy of John Dewey* (New York, Tudor, 1951), 521.

enters into what it does."[20] How can this be, if in the present doing of something, it is determined from below? Suppose a man is a human orderer or a purposive being that is somewhat "unique in itself." How does he enter uniquely into what he does in terms of Dewey's perspective? He is neither antecedently recognized nor consequentially important as a director of unitive experience. Why does Dewey refuse to apply this principle to man as a human orderer in participation? Moreover, if functionalism is all that Dewey respects, how does he know that something which is unique in itself? If his method does not provide for knowing that which is "unique in itself," how does he know that it enters fully into what it does when he reduces the self to an identity with its actions? Let me be more specific now on the issue of responsibility in Dewey.

First of all, Dewey discusses the topic of responsibility in relation to freedom and determinism. Freedom is functional and circumstantial. It has to do with those choices and actions which promote real growth. It is thus a servant of naturalistic totality. The term responsibility is also functional in terms of a prospective bearing. This would mean that Dewey regards responsibility as a function of actions with regard to their inner actions with things, objects, and persons. He does not consider the source of responsibility in terms of its antecedents in the human orderer. His external view of freedom obviates such a necessity. Dewey writes:

The possibility of a desirable *modification* of character and the selection of the course of action which will make that possibility a reality is the central fact in responsibility. . . . A human being is held accountable in order that he may learn; . . . in such a way as to modify and—to some extent—remake his prior self . . . the question is whether he is capable of acting differently *next* time; the practical importance of effecting changes in human character is what makes responsibility important.[21]

Obviously, this is not an explanation of human responsibility as a generic human trait, though it may be a way of talking about responsibility in relationship to education. We noted earlier the religious model of accountability which tied responsibility to the notion of beliefs in creation, etc. Dewey simply refuses to deal with the sources of human responsibility. It is a meaningless search for him, it appears, because it may lead beyond his basic postulate of interaction between the organism and its environment. His system of totality prevents such a search. The fact is that the question

[20] Bernstein, *op. cit.*, 283.
[21] Dewey and Tufts, *op. cit.*, 337.

of antecedents and consequences in the considerations of responsibility are secondary to purposive being, for the distinction presupposes such a self-directing human orderer individually and in social existence. So does the topic of learning. Dewey contends that with man's increase in the capacity to learn there develops a larger capacity for choice-making, deliberation, and, therefore, an enlargement of the meaning of responsibility as accountability. Is this an identification of reasonability with responsibility? The issue bears close scrutiny. Dewey offers the following formula for relating freedom to responsibility:

There is an intrinsic connection between choice as freedom and power of action as freedom. A choice which intelligently manifests individuality enlarges the range of action, and this enlargement in turn confers upon our desires greater insight and foresight, and makes choice more intelligent. There is a circle, but an enlarging circle, or, if you please, a widening spiral. . . . Freedom consists in a trend of conduct that causes choices to be more diversified and flexible, more plastic and more cognizant of their own meaning, while it enlarges their range of unimpeded operation. . . . Our idea compels us . . . to seek for freedom in something which comes to be, in a certain kind of growth; in consequences, rather than in antecedents.[22]

Apparently, the concepts of freedom and responsibility are functions in situations of immediate interactions implicating a system of naturalistic totality. Dewey must define these two functionaries of a naturalistic world-view in terms of the limits and possibilities of his model of existence. We have already shown that purposive being is required, however, to state the human ideal of growth, that man is self-directing in his growth. The human orderer is also significantly present to the distinction "between choice as freedom and power of action as freedom." However, since I have not yet developed the relation of purpose to reason in terms of my theory, I do not want to push this point too much at this time, except perhaps to say that the goals of the mind in such intelligent choice-making cannot be separated from the human orderer. What the goals of the mind mean for naturalism is hard to assess. There is much that is written about the point that teleology is always manifest in a medium (mechanism). This would imply that purposes are empirically grounded. There is a prior concern, however, the problem of antecedents, which naturalism neglects: namely, what is the relation of the mind as a function to its goals as functions of a function?

22 Bernstein, op. cit., 276, 280.

And, what is the relation of these goals to purposive being, defined as a human orderer, as being ontologically self-directing in existence?

Dewey states that "what men actually cherish under the name of freedom is that power of varied and flexible growth, of change of disposition and character, that springs from intelligent choice. . . ."[23] In terms of my theory of the functional use of freedom, it means the way we use our purposive nature to contribute to our becoming. The former freedom is the servant of situations implicating totality. In the latter case, freedom is the servant of the human orderer in the matrix of participation. Thus the ontological capacity for self-direction is present in the principle of selection and choice-making considerations. Dewey's position leads him to a consideration of the harmony between freedom and determinism in the experience of inter-action. My theory achieves the harmony of the two in relation to purposive being. Because Dewey solves the problem of freedom and determinism outside the human orderer, his theory of responsibility can only be an external image.

That is the reason why social and empirical conditions are so important as contributors to the meaning of responsibility. In the place of the human orderer, Dewey requires the interaction of past experience with present situations in the anticipation of the future. Dewey remarks, "There is no source save past experience out of which the concrete stuff of new aspirations can be formed."[24] He believes that such socionatural conditions "enter integrally and intrinsically into the formation of character, that is, the make-up of desires, purposes, judgement of approvals and disapprovals."[25] This, however, is an odd requirement for one who neglects the antecedents of human actions in the consideration of human responsibility. What is the funded experience of the past but a reliance on antecedents to responsibility? The point is that man is already ontologically self-directing when he solves his present problems and defines the meaning of responsibility in the now by an appeal to past experience and in the light of future experimentation. Such a selective use of both time dimensionalities cannot be stated adequately apart from purposive being operating in experience. Moreover, blind habits, or intelligent habits, developed in the present, also fall short of the self-direction required to guide man in his growth process if we define man as being self-directive in his growth. Responsi-

---

[23] *Ibid.*, 284.
[24] Dewey and Tufts, *op. cit.*, 380.
[25] *Ibid.*

bility, before it can be a process of growth and development, is first the experience of man in confronting the human orderer in himself and in social existence. The ideal of being a completely responsive person in one's actions is a secondary consideration to such a primal encounter as self-directing. The fact that man is held accountable in the improvement of his future conduct presupposes the purposive being that Dewey's theory denies. The notion of man as a self-performer of his acts is merely an abstract source of such concrete acts and, therefore, cannot function as the source of responsibility. Moreover, Dewey is rather unclear on the notion of human agency which appears to be lost in the interaction between the organism and its environment. The organism may well be the *designatum* of the self, but purposive being is already assumed in imaging man in terms of the analogy of the organism rather than in terms of another model, say, that of a machine.

From the above considerations, Dewey's prime concern is with the process of acquiring responsibility in terms of a prospective outlook through a philosophy of action. The self in such a context is only a "factor within experience" and the environment, as a factor in that confrontation or interaction, is a "direct constituent of direct experience." Such empirical considerations of responsibility have a tremendous role to play on the phenomenal level of experience. But even on this level, Dewey's perspective, empirical as it is, is only one model of accountability competing with other models of responsibility interpreted experientially. Dewey has no right, short of omniscience, to insist on the identity of his model of existence with existence as existence. His identification of selfhood with action is one of the claims to ultimacy in this direction, of claiming more for his comprehensive view of existence than his model would allow as a model of human participation and responsibility. Moreover, the very attempt to relate freedom and responsibility "with the possibility of growth" is a second claim to ultimacy in Dewey's model of existence that is in search of reality.

Freedom is not the capacity for growth unless man is viewed as a human orderer who is the directing force of that freedom, either within or without experience. The potentiality of freedom needs to be directed in its possibilities. It is not its own. The same is true with responsibility. Response-relations are directed either by the human orderer or by a system of totality, or it is an empty claim or some form of control of human life. There is a strong possibility that Dewey's processive interpretation of the self, and of freedom and responsibility, is itself a model of process and a model of man, requiring an identity to link them. Man is more than a creature of organic maturation. If it is the case that he is self-directing in his growth, then "the quality of becoming" is not the domain of such virtues or of selfhood, unless man contributes creatively to that process of becoming by model-making through his purposive being. Dewey's statement about growth, which follows, is just another claim to ultimacy for his image of man and model of totality: "We set up this and that end to be reached, but *the* end is growth itself."[26] Dewey contradicts himself, after he has assigned man his positionality in nature by making him goal-directed to nature and to the process of evolution, when he says: "To make an end a final goal is but to arrest growth."[27] In a system of naturalism, while the totality is not complete, man is irrevocably goal-directed to nature, which is equated with his destiny. What is this but a form of "ultimate" goal-directedness, an ultimate end? Dewey works himself into these confusions because he confounds his model of becoming with the process itself and identifies his comprehension of nature with nature itself. In all these moves, Dewey plays the part of a human orderer which he denies in his theory of human responsibility. He plays the game of antecedents but denies the same privilege to others.

Dewey's muddle can be pinpointed further, namely, his belief that once he has rejected some form of external or transcendental unity (as an intruder into experience) which he regarded as an abstraction and model, that he was safe inside experience and free of such abstractions and model-making. But every totalist suffers from this illusion, namely, that he can only defeat a model of existence by real existence itself, until another totalist comes along and plays the same trick on his predecessor. Dewey writes: "If such a person would set his thought and desire upon the *process* of evolution instead of upon some ulterior goal, he would find a new freedom and happiness. It is the next step which lies within our power."[28]

Thus Dewey fails to distinguish between his model of process and "the process of evolution." Yet there is a certain real sense in which a purposive being has preferred the ultimate goal of process and the ultimate goal of evolution as a final interpretation of life and its destiny to that of a substantive explanation of life. This would indicate that the "first step" also lies within man's power, that man's purposive nature is a part of such

[26] *Ibid.*, 340.
[27] *Ibid.*
[28] *Ibid.*, 340–41.

primal experience and its model-making is evident in the matrix of such participation. Process as an ideal cannot be separated from process itself. Put differently, process itself cannot be discovered apart from a model of existence and thus requires the mediative notion of a purposive being in the very matrix of participation. Otherwise we merely compound the difficulties with awkward language about the directionality and responsibility in human life. In terms of my theory, direction of movement is not yet human directionality and neither is it human responsibility. Movement may be its own organization, but this is not yet responsible organization. Unless man is self-directing in his organizing and growth, even growth itself and process itself can't do much for him, for he is not in a position to know what to do with them. The further identifications of the self with situations of new growth can have meaning only if a person is ontologically self-directing in such growth. If this is the case, purposive being must be a prior postulate to a goal-directed life, whether it be that of naturalism or existentialism or some other school of thought.

I noted above that Dewey is not against all antecedents of action but only against the immediate subjective antecedents. He admits the funded experience of the past as a form of antecedent directionality that is of constructive benefit in illuminating the present for us. I also noted that the unity from below is also a model of existence when the claims of ultimacy are removed from one's model of existence. But the most damaging belief to a perspective of responsibility is the belief that subjectivity is only a parenthesis in the life of objectivity. This reduces the human orderer to a set of functions in the stream of experience never to be recovered by Dewey's theory. Dewey must do things in spite of his theory about life. The solution I have suggested is that the subjectivist's criticism of the objective model of life be taken seriously, namely, that it remains an abstract model of existence. Similarly, the objectivist's critique of subjectivism must be taken in all earnestness as being an abstract model of life. They are, in fact, both models of human life. The appeals of the objectivist convince only the objectivists. The appeals of the subjectivists convince only the subjectivists. They don't convince each other. Why should we be convinced by either side? Why don't we take the word of each "by the other"? In terms of my theory, both the subjectivist and objectivist perspectives are simply models of man, concrete images, parading one at a time, as the real man. Neither makes claims on reality. What each does is, that in the midst of reality, they come up with concrete images of man and of totality.

What is more important to do is to relate the concept of naturalistic continuity first to the human orderer before it is related to nature. Before it is a paradigm of nature, continuity is a horizontal human directionality that relates to the ontological capacity for self-direction. It is true that emergent things grow out of nature, but that they are not identical with that from which they emerge cannot be stated as a belief about evolution without some notion of a purposive being. Such growth and development, when identified with the concept of continuity, is the work of a purposive being. Continuity does not grow on trees. It is the way we size up nature and its meaning of growth by participating in existence as purposive beings. If nature is responsible for man in terms of his total potentialities, our purposive being has had a hand in fashioning this kind of model of existence. Purposive participation is prior to such participatory schemes in totality. The confluent model of responsibility remains a model because the naturalistic perspective of life is a model. It derives its image and has an awareness of its function from externals or from the sphere of betweenness, the field of interaction. Like the life of purpose in the school of naturalism, responsibility takes on the image of externality.

I turn next to George H. Mead's objective model of participation and responsibility to size up the full implications of this external image of man. He outdoes even Dewey in his attempts to derive responsibility from externals.

If "response" is the central meaning of responsibility, what is to prevent us from completely externalizing the meaning of this concept? That is precisely what happens in Dewey's and in Mead's perspectives. The objective model of participation gives us another external image of responsibility. Even a most generous interpretation of Mead, who regards the "me" and the "I" as two responding sides of the self, is just another way of supporting the external image of responsibility. The same thing happens, of course, with the notion of purpose defined as some form of goal-direction; it, too, becomes externalized in its meaning. At best, Mead gives subjectivity a parenthetical turning space in the domain of objectivity, relegating it to the area of indeterminate experience. We have the same emphasis upon the limitations of intentional experience as in Dewey. Even the internalized self is the product of such externalization. But the point is that even objective and externalized experiences do not stand on their own; they implicate the orderings of totality. Mead exploits the external meaning of responsibility in terms of communal solidarity more than any other naturalist. In the final accounting, man is responding to responses of responses until he has lost his capacity completely in the matrix of communal solidarity of the human orderer and even of the social orderer of experience. The end result is that the experiences of internalization and reflexivity are merely instrumental conceptualizations of putting across the external meaning of life. They are the reactive experiences of the person to totally externalized response-relationships. Thus even the inward man becomes a symbol of the outward social man completely naturalized by the relations evolved in emergent situations.

Perhaps the best way to label Mead's account of responsibility is to call it a liturgical dramatization of social responsibility. In such a situation, the Oxford English Dictionary informs us that the response follows a read lesson, which adds nothing to the meaning of the lesson itself, but merely gives it a certain embellishment in musical overtones. This may well be the case with Mead's view of responsibility, in which nature is responsible for the social act and the latter is responsible for the social gesture, language, and symbolization. These, in turn, are responsible for the self in response-situations. Social behaviorism is the source of responsibility, although society itself is not socially self-directing but implicates a naturalistic totality. That such a social behaviorism may itself be a model of lived experience, depending on another naturalistic model of totality, is a possibility that does not occur to Mead.

The philosophy of the act is in control of the human orderer and his response-relations to life. For the human act is the dramatic event that is model-free. Although these actions are instrumental as the bearers of responsibility, they are at the same time socially conditioned acts. In this instrumentalist context, the human act has a dynamic life of its own as it moves from stage to stage carrying man's responsibilities on its shoulders. These action–response-relations are mediated by the significant symbol and the vocal act, which is to say that individual acts are regulated by the social acts. The chain of command in response-relationships is from Nature to Society to Society's Media to Man. If we add to this directionality the framework of functional holism that sees the individual as an insignificant part in the whole, then responsibility is seen as being discharged from the whole to the part. Man is manipulated by totality. This is nothing new in the history of thought; it is merely a new arrangement of external responsibility by another scheme of coherence. That such systems of totality may be projects of human self-direction first does not appear to trouble Mead. But holism in itself does not solve the problem of pluralism in its surroundings.

This processive view of responsibility, through the symbolic conversation of gestures in a context of social objectivism, enables man to be goal-directed in a twofold manner. On the one hand, he is goal-directed to himself, and on the other, he is goal-directed to others. Responsibility is built up the way meaning in general is built up. Anselm Strauss points out the central issue in the process:

The important point is that typically human meaning arises during co-operative group action. In simpler terms, we may say that every group developes its own system of significant symbols which are held in common by its members and around which group activities are organized. In so far as the members act toward and with reference to each other, they take each others' perspectives toward their own actions and thus interpret and assess that activity in communal terms. Group membership is thus a symbolic, not a physical, matter, and the symbols which arise during the life of the group are, in turn, internalized by the members and affect their individual acts. . . . That the organization of responses requires an actor who also acts toward himself: one must be simultaneously his own subject and object.[29]

The phenomenon of responsibility, as a processive experience, similarly derives from the communicative process, as does the process of meaning in general. What is of interest here is that man need not be ontologically self-directing in such symbolic interactionism. One needs only to define the self as an object to itself in the act of self-objectification. This gives us the object self. There is no need for acts of self-subjectification because such experiences can be derived from acts of self-objectification. Neither is man's purposive nature needed to mediate the acts of self-objectification in learning to take others' roles toward self. This perspective of man introduces the external meaning of responsibility in Mead's writings. Man is not his own, either as subject or object self. These facets of selfhood are molded by symbolic interactionism in the milieu of communal solidarity that is supported by nature in various forms of emergence. Thus the social acts are the carriers of responsibility, or rather responsibility is a function of social behaviorism.

Richard Niebuhr gives an excellent account of such "social solidarity" as being the source of responsibility. He is a faithful disciple of Mead, who comments:

[29] Anselm Strauss, *The Social Psychology of George Herbert Mead* (Chicago, Chicago University Press, 1956), xiii.

Our action, is responsible, it appears, when it is response to action upon us in a continuing society. A series of responses to disconnected actions guided by disconnected interpretations would scarcely be the action of a self but only of a series of states of mind somehow connected with the same body—though the sameness of the body would be apparent only to an external point of view. Personal responsibility implies the continuity of a self with a relatively consistent scheme of interpretations of what it is reacting to. By the same token it implies continuity in the community of agents to which response is being made. There could be no responsible self in an interaction in which the reaction to one's response comes from a source wholly different from that whence the original action issued.[30]

Once the commitment is made to the central meaning of responsibility as being response-relationships, the path to externalization is set. The logic of the situation leads us forthwith to social solidarity, where the individual agent socializes in the continuing community of agents. But the question persists, nonetheless, who is responsible for such systems of responsibility? Both Niebuhr and Mead reply that it is the system of total responsibility that is responsible for the individual's responses. This is where we part company with the external image of response-relations. Unless man is responsible in such relational activities as a self-directing participant, why should he be responsible to the system which he is not responsible in shaping? Because Niebuhr has no alternative to goal direction and response-relations, he disengages purposiveness from *fitting* responses. Having discarded man's directive agency to make room for external responsibility, he moves, with Mead, to social responsibility as being the common source of individual responsibilities. All individual action originates in the social act. But it should be kept in mind that even the social orderer of individual responses is really a responder to other directives, namely, nature's emergence pushing its claims of directionality in the human collectivity. Thus natural solidarity backs social solidarity, which, in turn, backs individual responsiveness to this entire system of responsibility. The concept of emergence is a central feature of social behaviorism and represents Mead's basic belief that "reality exists in a present."[31]

Maurice Natanson, in his fine exposition of the "metaphysic of time," states that Mead's approach to the structured act "from the standpoint of

---

[30] J. M. Gustafson and J. T. Laney (eds.), *On Being Responsible* (New York, Harper, 1968), 35.
[31] Maurice Natanson, "G. H. Mead's Metaphysic of Time," *Journal of Philosophy* Vol. L (1953), 776.

the actor" takes him beyond strict behaviorism and beyond the stimulus-response mechanism it espoused. This is certainly true, and I regard it as an improvement over behaviorism. But there is another issue that must be considered, namely, how does the concept of the "actor" fare as a human orderer in the matrix of participation. Mead gives us only the interplay of responses between the "I" and the "me," as two aspects or foci of the self. To the extent there is dialogue between the self as subject (I) and object (me) it is an external dialogue internally displayed and one that would not please Martin Buber, for example, who is interested in a more subjective evaluation of such a dialogue.

Natanson is quick to perceive some of the difficulties of Mead's position, although he is sympathetic to Mead's point of view:

Earlier we said that for Mead every "I," i.e., every original and individualistic act of the self, is unpredictable and can be grasped only in the completed deed: the "I" is always seen and grasped from the standpoint of a "me." In other words, the "I" comprehended is always an "I" which has been incorporated in a present "me." This concept has important implications for the theory of the self, implications which Mead himself does not develop. If the individual can understand his "I" only as it exists in a "me," he can never see himself in his actual acts as they occur in a present, but only in reflection can he comprehend or grasp the "I" aspect of himself. It is only the *other* who can see us as we are in our acts, in our performances, in our unique "I" aspect. That the act of self-reflection is one in which a past content is considered in a present. The basic point of criticism here is that Mead's consideration of the "I" and "me" aspects of the self implicitly involves a temporal analysis apart from which the philosophical problem of the nature of the self cannot be handled.[32]

It is Natanson's contention that the early position of Mead in *Mind, Self, and Society* was still in the tradition of behaviorism in defining the subject-object dialogue in terms of the communicative process. With Natanson's interests in the phenomenology of Alfred Schuetz, he now feels that this dialogue should be reconsidered in terms of Mead's philosophy of the present which Mead did not develop fully.

Let me state the contrast as sharply as I can between Mead and my theory on the issue of the subject-object dichotomy. Mead resolves the subject-object problem by going beyond a theory of man to nature. Next, since society is an emergent from nature, Mead hastens to make the communicative process, the field of symbolic interactionism in a community of agents, the actual solution of the subject-object split. My resolution of the

[32] *Ibid.*, 777.

split is that the dialogue between subject and object is mediated by purposive being, that it is first a problem of a theory of man before it becomes a problem of man's relation with nature. Solving the subject-object dichotomy by social behaviorism is precisely what gives us an external view of human responsibility which, in turn, implicates a socionaturalistic totality.

This is not to say that mine is an internal solution and that Mead's is an external one. The problem is more complex. By making subjectivism and objectivism into models of man which are mediated by purposive being on the plane of ontological interaction, I have undercut the primacy of the distinction between the internal and the external. The distinction is, after all, posterior to purposive being. When Mead considers social behaviorism, he considers such objective behavior as being real and immediate on the level of action-encounter. For Mead, objectivism is not a model of man. But we have the same phenomenon in subjective participation which regards this kind of experience as being real and immediate. This position also disregards the model character of the subject self. Thus for the objectivist, the external is the real, and for the subjectivist, the internal is the real. Each claim to participation is alleged to be free of model-making and projection. The subjective view considers the internal as ontologically prior. The objective view considers the external as the more primitive experience. In terms of my theory, the distinction of internal and external is a function of each model respectively. From my point of view, purpose is not the function of the subject or the object self. They are functions of man's purposive being participating in existence. Subjectivity and objectivity are ways in which the human orderer conceives himself in experience. Thus while the subjectivists may push the reality claims of the internal against the objectivist's view of the external, and vice versa, it is not necessary for my theory to enter this conflict. Purposive being is required to mediate internal as well as external experience.

Let me take Mead's notion of the "I" as a case in point. The "I" is an I-process of responsiveness. It is a part-function of the whole self implicating a system of social behaviorism. In this context, the "I" is reduced to a position of near impotence. The self as "I" is advised to be goal-directed to itself by the generalized Other or by society, a community of responding agents. The self as "I" is goal-directed to itself in society by the "Other." The "I" does not even have the capacity to be goal-directed of its own power. This is true both of the individual and of society. Both can only respond to messages of goal-directedness coming from without. The self responds to society and society responds to nature. What I am suggesting is that the I-response or the I-process is not its own even in the experience of intentionality. This is true both in the case of the objective and the confluent models of participation. Man is responsible to another's goal-direction even when he is goal-directed toward himself.

This is the end result of social behaviorism with respect to the self, and it has an ominous ring for responsibility. Why should man be *responsible to* such goal-direction if he is not *responsible for* such goal-directedness himself as a human orderer? To say that Mead is not concerned with the source of human responsibility, that he is not concerned with *what* the self, the I, the we, and the group, are, but that he is merely concerned with their functional relationships, is, I think, an easy way out of the problem. Such a functionalism assumes an autonomy that makes ontological commitments to the self and society, yet, as a form of derivativism, it cannot sustain such a position of autonomy. At any rate, the consequences are disastrous for human responsibility. Man is advised to follow another to become what he is. Why should man be responsible if he is given no claims on responsibility, if he is not even responsible for his own goal directions but can only respond to them externally? If there is no human orderer as a self-directing being, why should he be either responsible to or responsible for responding to the goal-direction of the Other or of responding to himself in goal direction? This consequential theory of responsibility, of responding to one's own acts or to those of another, makes sense only in terms of an antecedent and present human orderer in such choice-making responses.

The fact is that when the I-process is considered as a part-function response in the context of social behaviorism, man is not even a true responder in such response-situations. He is, in fact, an actor who is capable of role-playing but whose roles are defined by social behavior, and those in turn are designed by nature. If responsibility is pushed back (beyond the subject-object problem beyond a theory of man) from the individual to society and from society to nature, what meaning can there be to Mead's belief "that reality exists in the present"? If it comes "from below," how present is the present? Man may be the receptor of such real intentions in the present, but those directives are not the creations of the present. What this implies is that a system of socionatural totality directs the process of symbolic interactionism in and through the communicative process. The present is only the place where the past directs when reality emerges in the social present.

In terms of my theory, it is not only the concept of the "I" that is troubled (which for us means that man is self-directing in existence), but also the notion of sociality. The social structure is also goal-directed to nature, but this goal-directedness is not of its own choosing. It is the work of nature in social interactionism. When social forms are deprived of social self-direction, and also deprived of giving birth to goal directions, society, too, can only respond to the directives of nature in the present milieu of interactions. Thus sociality is as much a problem as the I-process concerning the issue of responsibility. There is no human social orderer prior to social roles, rules, and relations. There are only the workings of nature in the processes of social interaction. However, what is needed is some measure of human responsibility, besides the notion of social solidarity, to account for human interaction. Mead tries to overcome this deficiency by postulating a theory of mutual determination that leads to the principle of co-responsiveness. However, I noted earlier that such coresponsibility implicates a system of totality which is insufficient for human directionality. Let me examine more carefully the relations of role-playing in society to the issue of social self-direction, which Mead neglects, as a prior consideration to a rule-directed society. Let me approach the issue through the writings of Dorothy Emmet, who is sympathetic to Mead's perspective and respects the social sciences.

Emmet's solution to the subject-object dichotomy, between personal and impersonal role-morality, is to link both of them in terms of the notion of the "role." This, too, is external mediation of the problem imitative of Mead's perspective as defined by the social sciences. Such a role stands for "a part sustained by an individual or succession of individuals, but a part which has been to some extent formalized by custom and prescription."[33] The author believes that the notion of role links the functional, purposive, and creative aspects in a philosophy of human action. In a book written eight years later, she pursues the same theme in more detail by insisting that role-making goes below the level of roles, rules, and relations and is actually found to be relationships between people.

Emmet's solution—"to see how each survives in the other"—with respect

[33] Dorothy Emmet, *Function, Purpose, and Powers* (New York, Macmillan, 1958), 275–76.

to persons and roles, even if it were successfully resolved, would only give us a new version of the principle of coresponsiveness and would implicate a system of totality. At any rate, Emmet's solution is that it is possible to combine individualism with role-playing without absorbing the "person in the persona."[34] This sounds more like a programmatic solution than a theoretical resolution of the problem.

If one justifies the relationship of subject to object by role-playing or the communicative process backed by the social community, there is still the problem of social self-direction to account for, which is a prior process to the existence of roles, rules, and relations. Unless this is accounted for, role-playing implicates the orderings of a system of totality. In such a framework, there is no point in liberating the individual because his "turning space" is defined by the system of totality. Of course such role-making in a rule-directed society is a more hospitable subject matter for science than the creative aspects of society which bring about such roles and rules. Emmet allows an account of "previously structured commitments and expectations within a network of relationships," but this is not social self-direction.[35] If there is no such social self-direction in a culture, what credence is there to the goal directions which it initiates in public if it is capable of such original goal direction on its own? How can society responsibly direct the individual if its sense of responsibility is derivative? A rule-given society is not yet a socially self-directing society. Neither Emmet nor Mead show a concern for personal and social self-direction. They merely take this for granted in some sense and proceed with the functional analysis of the importance of impersonal relationships in human life and how they sustain the individual.

The "persona," like Mead's "actor," leaves the individual with an external sense of responsibility in the matrix of interaction. The task is still before us: that of liberating the human orderer from "the supreme art of gesturing and responding" which is the hallmark of man in Emmet's and Mead's perspectives. The use of "significant symbols" must still be related to a purposive being or to society's purpose-bearing institutions in order to recapture the significance of human responsibility. If man is not his own in the act of responding either to himself or to the "generalized Other," then the principle of coresponsibility becomes a rather meaningless phrase. Both authors are caught in the functionalism in the debate between freedom and

[34] Dorothy Emmet, *Rules, Roles and Relations* (New York, Macmillan, 1966), 154.
[35] *Ibid.*, 201.

determinism, and they are unable to reconstruct the human orderer and his sense or claims on responsibility in the objectivist framework. Man is absorbed by a system of totality from which he never recovers but in which he is given a "turning space" which conditions him to accept what the totality has to offer. If man's self-steering depends on the expectations of others, and if his self-expectations depend on the "generalized Other," then one has properly acquiesced to his positionality in nature and to a consequential theory of responsibility. In such a context, it is no longer possible to have meaningful discussions of the human orderer. One can only respond either to his own acts or to the actions of others because selfhood has been reduced to a philosophy of action. Such a control of human life by symbolic interactionism can give us only a mass of human responsibility.

Let me conclude this section on Mead by saying that my critique of Dewey's position is applicable to Mead. The latter has, in fact, given us a more positive reading of external responsibility in terms of role-playing. The attempt to harmonize individualism with the impersonal domain of roles in a rule-directed society may only be the requirement of the objectivist model of participation and not the demand of life itself. Even if this move were successful, which it is not, it would merely yield the principle of coresponsiveness in the communicative process, which would be a way of admitting the orderings of totality in social behaviorism. Behavior is not its own. It belongs either to a human orderer or to a system of totality. Not to consider the antecedents of the problem, or to consider the presence of the human orderer in consequential acts, is a way of dismissing the problem. Objectivism and the confluent model of participation have not elevated the notion of human responsibility; neither have they shown a preferential status to human values in general. Pragmatism has leveled down values to the level of facts instead of lifting the facts to the level of values. The human orderer has been lost to a system of totality by a discipline claiming an autonomous philosophy of functionalism. Functions have more in common with systems of totality than they do with purposive being. Thus a functionalism such as Mead's has a way of delivering man to a system of totality where man's experiences of responsibility are in jeopardy. At best, man can only show *responsibility to* such a system of socionatural totality, and even then the goal directions which it entertains may not be its own.

In terms of my perspective, I find difficulties even with a goal-directed life if it is devoid of ontological self-direction. But even this kind of goal-directedness is undermined by Mead's perspective. Responsibility can have human meaning only in terms of man's purposive life. Unless man confronts the human orderer in himself and in social existence, what we have is control of life (by a system of totality) rather than human responsibility.

POLANYI'S VIEW ON RESPONSIBILITY

There is a phrase which Polanyi uses—"self-set standards" or "self-set ideals"—which describes the responsible subject self as agent in his perspective. This is to be seen in the context of a philosophy of commitment in which the subject declares its own goals and sustains them with a tenacity and a passion that we have come to call "commitment." Responsibility has its source in the goal-directed subject self in the framework of an anthology of commitment to those goals. More specifically, it is man's understanding (in terms of *Verstehen*) that is the source of human responsibility. But this merely sets up the problem of responsibility because neither the subject self nor its understanding nor the goals of the mind are really their own. They are functions of a larger totality which determines and guides them. In this section I shall examine Polanyi's concept of responsibility by centering attention on such terms as subjectivity, freedom, calling, and commitment.

It is the subjective understanding, not merely the calculating reason of the positivists, that is the source of responsibility in the matrix of intentional experience. While I sympathize with Polanyi on the issue of antipositivism, his view of subjective participation between the knower and the known is not adequate to describe the human orderer in existence. The subject self is tied to a system of totality which imposes certain patterns of meaning upon the intellect and man. The entire perspective is dominated by the part-to-whole logic. It is Polanyi's contention that the participation of the knower in the known is a way of shaping and forming knowledge, that it does not invalidate objective knowledge, although it may impair its objectivity somewhat. The real problem in such a system is whether the subjective understanding can give us an adequate knowledge of the human orderer that is not absorbed by a system of socionaturalistic totality. Understanding and goal-seeking are both functions of subjectivity, but the latter is not its own. It is the top level of emergent evolutionism following directives from below. This immediately sets up certain insurmountable problems for the notion of responsibility. Let me begin the analysis with the concept of commitment.

The notion of "selfless subjectivity" is the basis of the "ontology of commitment." This gives rise to the lower self (the self of private convictions). It also gives rise to the higher self (to personhood with its cargo of beliefs, self-compulsions, and commitments). As Polanyi views it, "Since the two poles of commitment, the personal and the universal, are correlative, we may expect them to arise simultaneously from an antecedent state of selfless subjectivity."[36] The freedom of this selfless or intelligent subjectivity is the freedom to relate to a system of totality. Man's responsibility to such selfless objectivity is essentially a response "to things that are purely of the mind." Both subjectivity and responsibility are thus related to the lower levels of reality. In such a context there is no need for self-direction because the process of thinking takes place in the conflict with bodily desires. As Polanyi states:

Mental passions are a desire for truth, or more generally, for things of intrinsic excellence. Desire for these things of the mind, pursued for their own sake, will conflict in general with desires of the body, so that the pursuit of truth will become an act of self-compulsion. And this holds also in a more essential context, namely in respect of choices taken in the exercise of personal judgment. . . . The theory of personal knowledge says that, even so, a valid choice can be made by submitting to one's own sense of responsibility. Herein lies the self-compulsion by which, in the ideal case of a purely mental achievement, the utmost straining of every clue pointing toward the true solution finally imposes a particular choice upon the chooser.[37]

Thus the essence of personhood appears to reside in the self-seeking understanding that is prior to ontological self-direction as I have used the term. The drive to understand is a subjective drive, a universal urge, self-transcending, that doesn't stop until it reaches a system of totality. The ontology of commitment is designed to guard the relationship of subjective goal direction to totality.

The whole point of commitment is that the subject self bends toward the system of totality which would give it wholeness and universal knowledge. Man acts as he believes he must. Freedom as a "relation to" is a way of talking about necessity. In this ontology of commitment, the person moves from passion to confident utterance to accredited facts to total commitment

[36] Polanyi, *Personal Knowledge*, 313.
[37] Polanyi, *Study of Man*, 62.

in a system of totality. If I were to simplify this, I could say that personal responsibility to universal knowledge and to the larger sphere of experience, interspersed by varying degrees of commitment, is the essence of human participation and also a way of gaining explicit, objective knowledge through personal commitment and personal knowledge (tacit, unformulated knowledge).

Commitment is a term that defines the subjective reference of goal-directed activity on the part of the subject self, along with such terms as intentionality and self-transcendence. The means/ends continuum would be the objective reference in such goal-directedness. But Polanyi has no interest in this. More specifically, commitment concerns the "universal intent" of the person's understanding. The language of commitment is used to talk about intentional experiences of the mind, as in the following passage:

Here the personal comes into existence by asserting a universal intent, and the universal is constituted by being accepted as the impersonal term of this personal commitment. . . . The freedom of the subjective person to do as he pleases is overruled by the freedom of the responsible person to act as he must.[38]

Is this a way of talking about the responsibility of goal-directedness in a system of totality, where neither the subject self nor its personal understanding is its own? What point is there in speaking of "self-set ideals" in a framework of "self-compulsion" and "commitment"? Commitment is a way of sustaining and carrying on with the goals with the ultimate intention of guaranteeing the goals of the mind. Is such responsibility to the belief in pure mental achievements, and to the goals of the mind in the framework of commitment, the essence of human responsibility? Responsibility to the drive to understand (with its drive for universality a built-in feature of it) does not yield responsibility for human knowledge because personal knowledge is not its own. To be caught up in a world of one's own self-seeking and self-compulsion does not give us a human orderer even when it is viewed as a responsible self or in terms of responsible choices on the top level of the evolutionary scheme of reality.

Although Polanyi avoids the determinist fallacy to a certain extent—"by committing himself to a personal knowledge of the human mind as a seat of responsible choices"—he does not avoid placing the source of human responsibility in a system of totality more subjectively oriented.[39] This

[38] Polanyi, *Personal Knowledge*, 308–309.
[39] Polanyi, *Study of Man*, 89.

brings up a certain problem that needs to be pointed out because Polanyi vacillates between the "responsible agent" and "responsible choices" in the framework of totality. If subjective human agency is not its own, how can its choices be responsible and its goal directions trustworthy? The main thrust of the meaning of responsibility appears to be in choices and rational acts in the context of commitment. The way Polanyi views it, "the study of man must start with an appreciation of man in the act of making responsible decisions," and it must end with the belief "that a passionate comprehension necessarily appreciates the perfection of that which it comprehends."[40] The philosophy of commitment is a way of bridging the two beliefs. Let me offer several criticisms of the ontology of commitment.

One, it is surprising that one who is so interested in a theory of personhood and holds that personal knowledge is at the base of more objective knowledge should ignore the human orderer by placing the ontology of commitment ahead of man's capacity to be self-directing in existence. Apparently, the drive or craving to understand and the totalization that evolves through the universal intentions of the mind are prior to human self-direction. The ultimate commitment of man to this drive to understand is apparently a prior responsibility. However, if we place a philosophy of commitment to guarantee ultimacy of goal direction, the way is open for obscurantism and dogmatism in philosophy.

Two, the commitment is not only to the subject self, but a commitment of subjectivity to a scheme of totality which places the human orderer on a secondary status. Thus man is not self-directing in his understanding. The universal nature of the mind follows a "calling" and is ruled by its "positionality" in the system of totality. The self-seeking subject, through its understanding, is obligated by its compulsive nature to have commerce with totality, to appreciate its comprehensive directions, to grasp with passion or feelingful awareness "the intimations of order in reality." The responsible choices, which it allegedly has, are imposed on the chooser by the system of totality. Particular experiences point beyond themselves to a system of comprehensive totality, which the mind follows through with passionate concern and commitment. The essence of responsibility, or of "submitting to one's own sense of responsibility," is a way of submitting to this drive for understanding, of showing commitment to the goals of the mind. Responsibility is thus a unifying principle in Polanyi's system

[40] *Ibid.*, 36, 71.

of totality, and the concept of commitment is merely a way of guaranteeing that it remains so.

Three, the fact that man "can sustain purely mental purposes" by a philosophy of commitment proves nothing if the drive to understand implicates a system of totality and if the understanding is separated from the human orderer who is self-directing in such participation. Is this really an opportunity for the exercise of pure thought and its universal intentions as the author thinks?

What then is our answer to those who would doubt that man made of matter, man driven by appetites and subject to social commands, can sustain purely mental purposes? The answer is that he can. He can do this under his own responsibility, precisely by submitting to restrictive and stultifying circumstances which lie beyond his responsibility. These circumstances offer us opportunities for pure thought—limited opportunities and full of pitfalls—but all the same, they *are* opportunities, and they are ours; *we* are responsible for using or neglecting them.[41]

This is the upshot of Polanyi's prepurposive model of responsibility (prepurposive in that such goal-directed responses are prior to self-direction). Responsibility, as a higher level of personal operation, is seen in terms of its embodiment in lower levels of its being and is, therefore, liable to failure.

Human responsibility too is subject to a similar intrinsic limitation; it can operate only if embodied in human beings who are liable to failure. For no responsibility is taken where no hazard is to be met, and a hazard is a liability to failure. Moreover, while men are by nature subject to lust, pain and pride, which makes them liable to dereliction of duty, these self-centered drives are indispensable elements of a responsible commitment. For only by staking our lower interests can we bear witness effectively to our higher purposes.[42]

Is this view the demand of life, or is it the requirement of a prepurposive model of human knowledge and experience? The position is paradoxical, to say the least. Polanyi deludes objective knowledge in terms of personal knowledge in a framework of commitment and then loses the subject self and its sense of responsibility in an objectivating world-view in which it is given a minimum of turning space for choices and response-relations. The paradox can be put in other terms also, namely, that it is necessary to sacrifice *responsibility for* in order to achieve *responsibility to* in the participation of the knower in the known. If this is the universal firmament

41 *Ibid.*, 68–69.
42 *Ibid.*, 67.

of universal obligation in a system of totality supported by passionate commitment, responsibility comes off rather weak. The point is that the subject self loses its essence as a human orderer and is incapable of truly responsible relations because the universal intent of the mind is separated from the human orderer and from man's search for wholeness. The subject self comes not only to appreciate the system of totality, but it actually follows out the directives of totality.

The issue of "self-centered" or "outward centered" drives of the spontaneous self-seeker and the seeker of universal truth is posterior to purposive being and his self-direction. These are already models of goal direction and response-relations. Lust, pain, pride, etc., are secondary moralistic considerations of responsibility. Such issues do not touch the source of human responsibility. Whether the self is self-giving, selfless, selfish, or self-seeking, these are abstractive expressions of the capacity of purposive being to self-directing in participation. Such terms are given content by each system of totality. What is pride for the Christian totality is a sign of creativity and health in Aristotelian or social-science perspective. Such moralistic views of responsibility are by-products of systems of totality which assume prior purposiveness to be operative on the human plane of interaction. The levels theory of reality that Polanyi shows concern for is similarly guided by prior purposiveness which his theory of responsibility does not account for. The fact is that the "ideal of a responsible choice" can operate only if one assumes the presence of self-direction in such human selection. Either that, or it is the "calling of man" in a system of totality which is Polanyi's choice.

The "unique responsibility" on the plane of human interaction which Polanyi espouses is not so new or incomparable. Every totalist plays the same game in defining responsibility by man's positionality in a system of totality. This is another arrangement of the same theme. Polanyi merely accepts societal patterns of responsibility as defining man's positionality in responsibility. Or he compares such "acts of choice" to "acts of discovery," where both are regarded as acts of submission to given goal-directedness, to self-set ideals. Man is fixed by commitment to given goal directions. Such patterns of purposiveness are always models of participation. They do not have the primacy, immediacy, or reality that Polanyi attributes to them. The fact is that if man as a human orderer is not responsible for such goal-directed responses, then totality is. The second alternative, in terms of what I have said about it, is even less free of model-making than goals because they are more assumptive, ultimate goals. The human orderer is the source of such goals, totalities, and response-relations. No philosophy of commitment will obviate this fact because commitment itself depends on this purposive movement in the human context.

Let me summarize this section on Polanyi's theory of responsibility to point up its inadequacies: (1) Polanyi freezes human goals and responses by a philosophy of commitment; (2) human responsibility is put at the service of the quest for universal knowledge (knowledge for its own sake); (3) Polanyi's "sense of calling" determines both the limits and possibilities of human responsibility; (4) reason, which is not its own, is the source of such responsibility; (5) the commitment of such responses is blind self-seeking enlightened by derivative goals; (6) submission to a scheme of totality is identified with man's primal responsibility; (7) no amount of "indwelling" can rescue the human orderer in the quest for responsible relations and choices in such a system of totality; (8) the mind, which is at the source of such responsibility although not its own, is yet postulated as a "comprehensive feature of man," symbolizing the whole man on the top rung of the evolutionary ladder; (9) such an indwelling understanding is closer to the directives of totality than it is to the directives of the human orderer; and (10) the "process of mutual reliance," which Polanyi regards as social responsibility, is nothing but the principle of coresponsiveness which implicates a system of totality as the source of human responsibility.

The tragedy of this perspective is that man is called upon to be responsible to something that is beyond human participation and beyond his responsibility, namely, the system of totality: "While it then lies beyond our responsibility, it is yet transformed by our sense of responsibility into part of our calling."[43]

[43] Polanyi, *Personal Knowledge*, 324.

8. Interrogating Theories of Responsibility (II)

This chapter is a continuation of the critique of systems of totality as the source of human responsibility. I have hopes of extending the critique to three other theorists of responsibility—Richard L. Rubenstein, George A. Schrader, and Martin Buber—and conclude the chapter with an overall critique of totalistic schemes of responsibility exhibited in the last two chapters. It is my firm belief that any explanation of responsibility in terms of one of its components, like accountability, answerability, liability, or imputability, is inadequate to define its source. When such themes are expounded by systems of totality they turn out to be goal-directed models and response-relations of this experience. There is no way to avoid the issue of pluralism and relativism once this path is taken. The only communication left to man is, "*My* totality is real and *yours* is artificial," or, in terms of the second person, "No, *mine* is real and *yours* is artificial."

The most likely objection to my theory is: If you postulate the whole of existence as an ontological model, what else is there that is real? One cannot reduce living and real wholes, living traditions and communities, to abstract categories and ideologies because they symbolize human "solidarity," and such holistic solidarity is always to be preferred to an ideology or a model. In short, the objection is likely to be that I am having commerce with "mosaics" rather than with real life. Such is not the case, however, for in the midst of reality we come up with close-ups of reality or with models of existence in which the human orderer has had a forming and shaping hand in the matrix of participation. I am not denying reality but only asserting the relevance of purposive being to it and accepting the fact of purposive participation as a mediative factor of such models of existence. In fact, a prior question is called for: How were such schemes of totality hypostatized by immediate experience to begin with? Let me proceed further with the analysis of totalistic schemes of responsibility, interrogating the source of responsibility in each scheme.

RUBENSTEIN ON RESPONSIBILITY

Richard Rubenstein's *Morality and Eros* presents a theory of responsibility in the context of naturalistic totality with religious overtones. The author wishes to preserve a balance between the pagan gods of Dionysos and Apollo in order to free man for a naturalistic responsibility. The tense equilibrium takes the following form:

Freedom must be wild and ecstatic. It must also be ordered and disciplined. Only in the fulfillment of adult sexual mutuality can order and discipline be successfully integrated with passion and release. . . . The household gods of a consuming fulfilling marriage are both Dionysos and Apollo.[1]

What is odd about this combination is that the family, which is fast deteriorating in our culture, has become the exemplar of human responsibility. It is difficult to pin down why marriage is the norm for the authentic life, whether this is the traditional Jewish emphasis on the subject or whether it is the demand of Rubenstein's philosophy of the body. Perhaps it is trying to make the best out of a bad sociological institution.

Rubenstein is known as a radical Jewish theologian who has rejected the Old Testament God as Lord of History. This involved a transcendent system of totality, a God who ruled the earth from above, which I call the postpurposive model of existence. In reaction to this model, Rubenstein now prefers a naturalistic unity of life, a prepurposive totality, coming from below. The rejected system of totality is now regarded as artificial or abstract, and the naturalistic one is seen as something real and immediate. In terms of the second alternative (the naturalistic one), both the pagan gods seem to be operating in the natural universe, but the dominant god is Dionysos:

Dionysos and Apollo are in reality masks of the God who abides after the death of God. That God is not the perfect, unchanging Creator and Lawgiver who stands in isolated splendor outside his creation. He manifests himself (so to speak) in the dynamic, ever-changing structure of reality itself. After all, God manifests himself in and through Mother Earth and the material cosmos.[2]

---

[1] R. L. Rubenstein, *Morality and Eros* (New York, McGraw-Hill, 1970), 39.
[2] *Ibid.*, 40.

Dionysos, in particular, symbolizes "art, life, creative passion, or . . . body."

Why has Rubenstein substituted the prepurposive view of total unity for the postpurposive model of totality? Rubenstein holds that God as Lord of History has failed the Jewish people in the death camps of Europe. As a consequence, the new Jewish theology must begin after Auschwitz. Such a theology must explore the possibility of reality in the present. Rubenstein holds with Mead that reality exists in the present, not in the Jewish past. Perhaps he has been influenced by the dominance of the prepurposive model of life so omnipresent in our culture that the reasons he gives may simply be rationalizations or justifications of this influence. At any rate, nature is to be utilized in terms of Eros-derived impulses symbolized by Dionysos, driving man, by nature's possibilities in him, to new heights of adventures of the body for the enrichment of life itself. I mention this theological structure of responsibility to show how Rubenstein became disenchanted with one real and immediate system of totality and then accepted another, more fashionable today, as the new source of human responsibility. In his *The Religious Imagination* there is the same interaction between the psychoanalytic view of life (the prepurposive model) and the more traditional Jewish faith with its postpurposive version of responsibility. He justifies the mingling of the two models by saying that paganism is an "honorable and a responsible religious path." But the question lingers on: Is it a responsible religious path for the traditional Jew who is bound to the postpurposive model of existence?

The essence of man, in terms of the new-found system of totality, is that he is a self-seeker. What is most important to the natural man is the fulfillment of his bodily needs as Eros manifests them. The body makes judgments, seeks solutions in various situations, and experiments with life. Thus, in terms of this religious naturalism, *homo religiosus* must first meet the demands of the body, of Eros and Dionysos. In short he must pay new homage to the new system of totality in which responsibility is once more, as in every totality, a unifying principle in the system. The unconscious has much to say in directing man's sense of responsibility; so does spontaneity and other terms implicating love and ecstacy. Order, however, there must be. And this is provided by a system of totality which harnesses the power of the passions of Eros. Man can only be responsible to such derivative impulses and spontaneous outpourings of love. The system of naturalistic totality is responsible for Eros.

What is of interest in this new system of responsibility is that the old patterns of responsibility are rejected by the new standard. There is an attempt to read off past Jewish life and its religious meaning in terms of the prepurposive model of existence, as in the following passages:

Just as irrationalities of the personal life such as dreams, slips of the tongue, cleansing rituals, jokes, eating and evacuatory anxieties had proved to be keys to the unconscious strivings of the individual, the irrationalities and superstitions of religion were understood to play an analogous role in the life of the group.[3]

David Bakan has commented that both psychoanalysis and religion have a common concern. He tells us that both agree "that the manifest is but the barest hint of reality, that beyond the manifest there exist the major positions of reality. . . ." From earliest times far too much has happened to the Jewish people that defies simplistic explanation for anyone to rest content with a vision of Judaism which takes its practitioners at the manifest meaning of their words. I have attempted to penetrate beneath the surface in a few crucial areas of concern to Jew and Christian alike. Without the aid of psychoanalysis, this project would have been impossible.[4]

Rubenstein continues to say that the Jewish fear of idolatry, of ascribing the reality of the whole to the part, was a perennial preoccupation in history. He himself has the fear that applying psychoanalysis to the Jewish tradition may involve him in idolatrous actions. But the point is that every system of totality defines the content and significance of idolatry for itself. One in a naturalistic tradition need not have any such fears because idolatry is a foreign term in the prepurposive model of totality. Is this a hangover from the postpurposive model of totality in Rubenstein's perspective? What is of greater interest, however, is how the model of existence controls the meaning of a system of totality of which the author is not even aware.

I mentioned there were religious overtones to his naturalism in which Rubenstein moves from the concept of the death of God to the death of man. The name for this new religious Ground of Being (the naturalistic totality) is Holy Nothingness. As a product of negative mysticism, it is a system of totality placed at the beginning of life, to which man returns after an adventurous bodily existence in a world that remains silent to his queries. The final system of totality which dictates human participation, directionality, and responsibility is thus a naturalistic system of totality with mystic overtones. What is man's responsibility in this system of totality?

[3] R. L. Rubenstein, *The Religious Imagination* (New York, Bobbs-Merrill, 1968), 1.
[4] *Ibid.*, xix–xx.

The source of human responsibility is in necessity, in human facticity, in the universal urges that drive his bodily life, be they Dionysian or Apollonian. Man is a self-seeker because he must be a self-seeker. The universal urges in this define the search. Man not only takes "head trips"; he also takes "body trips." The trips define his responsibility. The Eros in man is this source of human directionality and responsibility. The irresponsible pagan god, Dionysos, is the source of human responsibility. Apollo, in a somewhat weakened state, is to check its wild and ecstatic escapades through the body in existence. It is a universal drive in all human morality and existence. Mysticism, nature, and the body are thus responsible for man's sensitivity to response-relations in life. Man learns the rest pragmatically, experimentally, as to what goes and what does not. Self-seeking, not self-giving or God-seeking, is the source of human responsibility. It is learned from Eros, from within, and from circumstances, from without. In practice, man learns quickly that in looking out for himself he must simultaneously look out for others. We already know this doctrine as "enlightened self-interest," with all the liabilities it carries.

This perspective affords an interesting contrast to other models of spontaneity I discussed among the youth, where spontaneous self-seeking or social self-seeking was shaped by the revolution of totality rather than by enlightened self-interest. Both views presuppose either the orderings of totality or the human orderer that is self-directing prior to such self-seeking. Both views presuppose a pattern of spontaneous responsibility, moving in two different directions, and implicating the orderings of totality rather than the directive of man. Rubenstein merely gives pragmatic and religious orientation to such vitality. Let us take a closer look at man in his relation to totality in Rubenstein's perspective.

There are certain primary responsibilities that man is required to perform in this system, as in other totalities. As a bona fide self-seeker, man should first take care of the body and fulfill its universal cravings, for he is simply an "exemplification" of embracing totalities in which God is the ultimate totality. Apparently, each man is merely a wave in the ocean of God, disappearing in due time to make room for others. "Have fun as a *wave!*" is Rubenstein's advice. Thus man is a part of the "self-unfolding of God's life." To this Rubenstein adds a touch of "negative mysticism," where things have their beginning and Nothingness and to which they return. Meanwhile, Rubenstein prescribes for the adventures of the body, for "the body and its timetable" is the only hope man has. The upshot of this view is that "Death is the price we pay for life, love, joy; so too is our unredeemed resistance. . . . All we have is this world. Let us endure its wounds and celebrate its joys in undeceived lucidity."[5]

Is there any point in talking about responsibility concerning the self-seeker in such a nihilistic context? Man is not responsible for himself. He is only responsible to the universal needs of the body. It is simply a matter of coordinating such universal urges and to see that each need gets a share of fulfillment. But this the body knows even without the concept of responsibility. It does what it must. This is its freedom. Pragmatic enlightenment in such a context is a superfluous theory. It is merely a way of guaranteeing that the self-seeker is successful in its self-seeking. But what is the point of it all if Nothingness shadows every fulfillment of the body? The body must contend with the "irrepressible aspects of earthly existence." It is interesting that such Eros-derived impulses for one writer lead to a spontaneous anarchic society and for another to Holy Nothingness.

Unless there is a radicalization of responsibility, there is no way in which man is to account for such totalistic schemes of responsibility. There is no way to legislate the claims of spontaneously derived systems of responsibility by an appeal to immediate experience, for immediate experience is itself in need of a standard of directionality and responsibility. Before man's destiny is fixed by final ends, we must assume that man is self-directing in such faith-seeking. Before he commits himself either to self-seeking, or to self-giving, or to Holy Nothingness, we must presuppose a questing purposive being. What is more, even when such systems of totality are successful, they give us only models of responsibility and goal-directedness. They are just as perspectival as the systems which produce them. When the self-seeker is guided by blind Eros and wild Dionysos, and by the pragmatic policy of enlightened expediency, the human orderer has already been subsumed by a system of totality. Why "accept life" with its "limitations and ironies"? If the cosmos is meaningless and the seeker is not in charge of human directionality, why should the self-seeker accept any responsibility for any kind of a good life, even that of the body? Because it is man's one and only life? This is no justification for the choice of being responsible. How can we be responsible if neither man nor the cosmos is responsible for human directionality?

In attempting to solve the problem of the self-seeker in existence in the

[5] Rubenstein, *Morality and Eros*, 196.

framework of determinism and freedom (learning in the direction of determinism), Rubenstein makes some analogies which break down precisely at the point where the self-seeker is defined.

The waves are caught in contradictory tendencies. They are the resultants of forces which allow them their moment of somewhat discrete existence. At the same time, they are wholly within the grasp of greater tendencies which ultimately collapse them into the oceanic ground out of which they have come and from which they have never really separated themselves. So it is with all life.[6]

The greatest example of this is human love, an expression of intimacy which is yet borne by the grip of universal forces. Although the given originating Ground is meaningless, it produces some bit of meaning through the body and Eros which makes life bearable. Rubenstein says we cannot press the metaphor too far. The self-seeker in responsibility is not like the wave that has neither identity nor is self-seeking. It does not apply at all. This is merely the demand of the prepurposive model of the Ground of Being, one variation among many, depending on the system of totality being claimed on the grounds of ultimacy. Rubenstein forgets who projects such systems of totality and such symbols of totality as the Ground of Being (Nothingness). Nay, he has no way of accounting for the human orderer in response-relations in existence. All he can do is follow the needs of the body; they have their own strivings in the long haul of Eros through existence.

In concluding this section it is important to state that the basic problem the self-seeker faces in "the grip of universal forces" which drive it is its ownership of individuality, how it can conceive of itself as a human orderer in this fate-ladened context. In terms of my theory, unless man is ontologically self-directing, the self-seeker is immersed in a system of totality for which he is not responsible but to which he is called to be responsible. This is the demand of every totality upon man. That is the reason why we reject it as the source of human responsibility, namely, that it leaves him with a schizoid attitude as a "responder."

SCHRADER'S VIEW ON RESPONSIBILITY

A more philosophical perspective of responsibility, also in the existential tradition, is provided by George A. Schrader in his chapter on "Responsibility and Existence." Responsibility is read off in terms of the concept of "liability." Can liability function as the source of responsibility? Schrader

[6] *Ibid.*, 186.

believes that it can if liability is thought of in terms of a system of Being which adopts Heidegger's perspective. I have already stated that any such attempt to define responsibility in a system of totality by one of its component terms, like accountability, liability, or imputability, comes out as a model of responsibility supported by a model of ultimate goal-directedness (the system of totality). For Schrader, however, liability as the essence of responsibility is model-free and represents "responsibility itself."

In fact, Schrader holds that "to exist is to be liable." One's existence requires responsibility for oneself. Moral views of responsibility are derived theories from this ontological perspective of responsibility. It is the way one faces his destiny in the system of Being, or faces up to facticity or the necessity of being. Schrader states:

Man's original liability is not simply that he exists, but that he "has to be." He confronts his existence from the first moment of his awareness as a problem and an object of concern. Man does not exist in the way that a stick or a stone exists but, as Heidegger expresses it, he "ex-sists," that is, he transcends himself in a reflexive relationship.[7]

Professor Schrader gives Heidegger's ontological perspective a valuational reading. He also ignores certain qualities of Otherness in Heidegger's system of being. He does not realize that concepts like "care" and "conscious as the call of care" are not humanistic or attitudinal notions. They are rather technical terms defining *Dasein's* goal-directed relationships to the system of being. Man, as an instance of *Dasein*, is similarly goal-directed to "the Being of beings." Man, therefore, is not his own, and his first responsibility is to the system of being. The primary meaning of responsibility in Heidegger's ontology is that of a unifying principle safeguarding the system of totality and man's relation to it.

The source of responsibility is not in the subject of being because the subject of being belongs to the system of being. Schrader believes otherwise when he states:

If to be a man is to be a subject and to be a subject is to be reflexively related to oneself, we have found an ultimate ontological basis for human responsibility. Man is responsible, in the first instance, because he is burdened with the ontological necessity of responding to himself in the sense of having to answer to himself for what he is and does. . . . To be is not simply to be liable; it is the original human liability.[8]

[7] C. J. Frederick (ed.), *Responsibility* (New York, Liberal Arts Press, 1960), 43–70, 45–46.
[8] *Ibid.,* 48.

My disagreement with this passage is that the subject self is not a human orderer but belongs to a system of totality which orders its being. In its given possibilities, it is prewired to return to the house of Being. The essence of the subject self is to return to the totality which is at the beginning of its destiny and the fulfillment of its destiny. This is authentic being. If the subject is thus outwardly (through inwardness) goal-directed to Being, man cannot be responsible "in the first instance." He cannot be *responsible for* the necessity of his being in the system of Being, into which he has been thrown (*Geworffenheit*); he can only be *responsible to* the intentions and directives of Being. In short, this is a model of liability in terms of man's experience of goal direction to the system of Being. Even if Schrader were correct, the notion of "original human liability" could not be sustained because the primary meaning of such responsibility is still the model of a goal-directed life. Being goal-directed to oneself, whether in Mead's social objectivism or in Heidegger's subjectivism and intersubjectivism, still leaves us with a model of experience and responsibility. Goal-directedness, in terms of my theory, presupposes ontological self-direction as the precondition of goal direction.

The anthropological perspective is of secondary importance to Heidegger. Whatever humanism there is in Heidegger is defined in terms of man's relation to being. In such a system, man is not responsible for a system of responsibility like that of Being. It is a prepurposive model of responsibility because man's ontological self-direction is secondary to intentionality or to man's goal-directed responsiveness to being.

However, there is merit in Schrader's perspective in that he places original human liability prior to moral views of responsibility: "Responsibility is the necessity of caring for oneself, of answering to oneself."[9] Where Schrader goes wrong is placing the source of responsibility in a system of general ontology rather than conceiving the human orderer in terms of an ontological capacity for self-direction, which makes such a system of general ontology a possibility. This miscalculation on Schrader's part roots the source of responsibility in a freedom that is equated with destiny and fate. Responsibility has its source in the system of Being, and the subject of being must abide by its intentions if it is to achieve authenticity. The fact that man identifies himself with the directives of being is evidence of the fact that there is prior purposiveness exhibited which is more primal than the goal-directed experience itself. The fact is that the potentialities are not

[9] *Ibid.*, 48.

his own. They are prewired by Being and ordered by its directives, advised to return home to its Source of Being.

How is moral obligation subsumed under ontological responsibility? Schrader states: "Ought statements do not in themselves *found* a concern but only *determine* it."[10] My concern over the subject self as a possible human orderer is the same as Schrader's concern over moral responsibility, namely, that both views of responsibility merely actualize prewired possibilities, that man is not self-directing in one's potentialities in either case. Just as one is obligated in moral responsibility to ontological requirements, so the subject self is obligated to a system of general ontology. It has been my experience, showing concern for totalistic ventures in philosophy, that every totalist redefines the notion of possibility or potentiality to suit his totalistic perspective. Another good example of this is John Dewey's perspective of potentiality.

But it also means that these powers are not unfolded from within, but are called out through interaction with other things. While it is necessary to revive the category of potentiality as a characteristic of individuality, it has to be revived in a different form from that of its classic Aristotelian formulation. According to that view, potentialities are connected with a *fixed* end which the individual endeavors by its own nature or essence to actualize, although its success in actualization depended upon the co-operation of external things and hence might be thwarted by the "accidents" of its surroundings—as not every acorn becomes a tree and few if any acorns become the typical oak. . . . When the idea that development is due to some indwelling end which tends to control the series of changes passed through is abandoned, potentialities must be thought of in terms of consequences of interactions with other things. Hence potentialities cannot be *known* till *after* the interactions have occurred.[11]

In terms of my theory of the human orderer, unless man is first self-directing in his potentialities, whether it be Aristotle's, Heidegger's, Schrader's, or Dewey's, to account for the prior moves of a purposive being in establishing systems of responsibility, there is no way out of the problem of relativism that the totalists create in redefining potentialities to suit each respective system of totality. Unless man has the possibility to be self-directing in his potentialities, even when these are related to systems of totality, there is no way to reclaim the human orderer as a significant contributor to human participation.

[10] *Ibid.*, 49, 52, 55, 70.
[11] R. J. Bernstein (ed.), *On Experience, Nature and Freedom (John Dewey)* (New York, Bobbs-Merrill, 1960), 237–38.

While I sympathize with Schrader's effort to place ontological human responsibility as something prior to moral responsibility, I am not too happy with his solution, namely, that ". . . the normative ought only expresses the necessity of responding to one's facticity. . . . The ultimate responsibility is existence itself."[12] The reasons for my dissatisfaction are: (1) that "existence itself" is a model of existence; (2) that "responsibility itself" is also a model of liability; and (3) that "the necessity of responding to one's facticity" is similarly a model of the factualness that obtains in existence, for one's "positionality" in Being is a changing one, as it is in nature. The point is that man's purposive being mediates all such claims, including the goal-directed responses of responsibility. General ontologies are a dime a dozen. The human orderer invents them to suit his fancy or, in more serious moments, to seek a better understanding of life through models of existence and more generalized patterns of meaning.

If man's ultimate responsibility is existence itself, this already presupposes an identification of one's model of totality with existence. It is a way of disconnecting man's search for wholeness of responsibility from the human orderer and a way of binding man to a system of totality. The fact is that within existence we are responsible for models of participation and responsibility. The claims to reality which are model-free are beyond man's grasp, both in participation and in imagination and thought. Man is not omniscient when he thus goes beyond the subject-object split; he is all too human in such ventures. The human orderer goes on all such trips beyond the alleged dichotomy. Responsibility is first man's business before it becomes the task of existence or being, or of man's relation to Being, Nature, Life, or to God. If the second alternative is given primacy, man can only be a "responder," if that, in such a system of totality. In return, he obtains a pie-slice share of its intentions. The interdependence of fate and freedom in the ground of being is a dialectical ordering of life for which man ought to be held responsible and not only held responsible to it. Such a dialectical ordering of life is a secondary, substitute form of directionality, as I noted earlier. Schrader's appreciation of the Heideggerian perspective fails to account for the Otherness in Being that holds man in its grips. The essence of man is not in the reflexiveness of consciousness, as Schrader holds, but in that to which consciousness points, to the system of Being that holds man bound to its directives. A dialectical ordering of life is not the original hu-

---

[12] Friedrick, *op. cit.*, 70.

man condition of responsibility unless the model of totality is given primacy to the human orderer. In that case, a dialectical form of directionality is the servant of such a totality. In terms of my theory, both are posterior to purposive being and both exhibit goal-directed patterns or models of life. They are not phenomenological descriptions either of existence or its inner workings and dynamics. In Schrader's case it is otherwise, as the following passage indicates:

In the case of self-responsibility I have maintained that the ultimate condition is the reflexivity of self-existence. I have interpreted responsibility in this context as itself a mode of relatedness of the self to itself. If we enlarge the context to include other beings, we might expect the same fundamental conditions to obtain. . . . To have a world at all is, like existing, a liability.[13]

However, reflexivity is merely a dialectical way of speaking about the unity of consciousness. This presupposes that the unity of consciousness is the source of its outward-going goals and ends. My position maintains that self-direction is prior to such unity, reflexivity, and intentionality and understood as a form of goal-directedness. For self-consciousness may be only the use we make of consciousness in our purposive being. But the main point is that if such unity is presupposed as the primal condition of goals and response-relations, then it is still a derivative form because it implicates a system of totality. Unless man is self-directing both in reflexivity and in intentional experience, consciousness is the servant of totality, as it turns out to be the case with Heidegger's and Schrader's perspective. Every mode of relatedness, unless man is self-directing in and through them, borrows its directionality from a system of totality and requires that man be guided by such real, immediate, given relationships. The fact that Schrader binds responsibility to the ground of being indicates that he would prefer to relate self-existence to a system of totality.

Responsibility does have ontological roots, but this is not to a system of being, defined by a general ontology. In this perspective, man is merely a "destiny that destines." If it is the case that "to exist is to be liable," then we must find satisfactory answers to these questions: To whom or to what? To man or to a system of totality? Unless there is a transworld system of totality writ large in the sky to legislate among such totalitarian schemes of thought, there is no point in making such claims to ultimacy, reality-claims, for every totalist has the privilege of playing the same game.

[13] *Ibid.*, 43–70.

The traditional meaning of purpose as *telos* or goal has influenced our concept of responsibility as having the basic meaning of a response-relationship. So long as this attitude prevails, we can neither construct a theory of the human orderer nor radicalize responsibility. We cannot escape immersing man in such systems of totality, for totalities are nothing more than ultimate goal directions. If purpose has an ontological relevance, it is possible to undercut the external meaning of purposiveness, responsibility, and the currently popular image of man.

Buber's Theory of Responsibility

Buber's attempt to go beyond the subject-object split (which belongs to the I-It world) to the sphere of *the between,* or to the community of the I-Thou relationship, is in effect another system of totality subjectively and intersubjectively conceived. Buber has made a valiant attempt to construct a theory of man, of personhood beyond the level of thinghood, on the level of immediate experience. The emphasis is on person-to-person confrontation and of personal confrontation with the Eternal Thou. The very contrast between a "free man" and the "self-willed man" is a good case in point and exemplifies the theory of personhood rather well. The free man has an encounter-stability that the self-determined man does not possess. Buber states:

But he knows that he must go out with his whole being. The matter will not turn out according to his decision; but what is to come will come only when he decides on what he is able to will. He must sacrifice his puny, unfree will, that is controlled by things and instincts, to his grand will, which quits defined foredestined being. Then he intervenes no more, but at the same time he does not let things merely happen. He listens to what is emerging from himself to the course of being in the world; not in order to be supported by it, but in order to bring it to reality as it desires, in its need of him, to be brought—with human spirit and deed, human life and death. I said he believes, but that really means he meets. . . . The self-willed man does not believe and does not meet. He does not know solidarity of connexion, but only the feverish world outside and his feverish desire to use it. . . . The unbelieving core in the self-willed man can perceive unbelief and self-will, establishing of a purpose and devising of a means. Without sacrifice and without grace, without meeting and without presentness, he has as his world a mediated world cluttered with purposes. His world cannot be anything else, and its name is fate.[14]

[14] Martin Buber, *I and Thou* (New York, Charles Scribner's Sons, 1958), 59–60.

Where does the free man turn to find the source of responsibility? He turns to "the act of relation" and finally to "the supreme relation," the subject of being before the infinite. He turns to the sphere of "the between."

Manfred Vogel, characterizing Buber's ethics as the "middle way" between the ideal requirements of the ethical and ethics guided and determined by the authentic capacity of the human being, gives a fine description of the significance of the sphere of "the between" that is the source of human responsibility.

For Buber's thought is by its very essence the overcoming of the ontological cleavage between the objective and the subjective. Ultimately, being is neither in the object nor in the subject. It is in the relation, in "the between." Object and subject are secondary, immerging from and held in the relation. Here is the one chord (the relation) of the two notes (the object and subject). Thus, being in "the between," opting for the objective as against the subjective or conversely for the subjective as against the objective is not feasible for Buber. Rather than polarization (either objective or subjective) Buber's stance must be mediating (between the object and the subject).[15]

Vogel, however, does not realize the fact that such a sphere of betweenness implicates a system of totality and cuts down on the participatory role of the human orderer in existence, which is a deliberate calculation on the part of the mystically inclined Martin Buber. Man does not rest until he has an encounter experience with the Eternal Thou. Thus "the authentic capacity of the human" depends not on the human orderer himself but upon a system of totality, a world-order, not the ordered world. Buber himself states that the more man is mastered by "individuality," the more the self sinks into unreality. Man's essence is to be discovered in communing with the community and finally in communing with an Eternal Thou. The whole point of Buber's philosophy is that man is not self-directing in such encounter experiences. His nose is made out of wax and he is led by the qualities of life disclosed by the sphere of betweenness. Even his definition of man as spirit reflects this when he conceives it as "a response of man to his Thou." Like the pride of man, when the spirit "adjudges to itself mastery over its work" it annihilates the "absoluteness of the absolute."

Buber moves beyond the subject-object split by an appeal to a direct form of immediate experience, only he does this in the personal and intersubjective sphere, whereas the pragmatists made similar appeals to immediate

[15] Manfred Vogel, "Buber's Ethics of Contemporary Ethical Options," *Philosophy Today* (Spring, 1969), 3–18.

experience on more objectivating grounds. These are obviously two different models of direct experience, yet each school believes it has a philosophy of pure encounter experiences when it makes such an appeal to direct experience. Man's purposive being is secondary to both schools of thought, which prefer the directives of immediate experience. Yet the pragmatists deny an encounter experience with God or the "way of God" that is so important in Buber's perspective. Obviously, Buber is giving a more mystical reading to direct experience than the pragmatists do.

What happens to the notion of responsibility when it is placed in the sphere of betweenness, in the personal, dialogical sphere of the I and Thou that has claims on reality through encounters? Buber's reply is that this approach gives man a "reality of responsibility" and not a model of accountability.

> Responsibility presupposes one who addresses me primarily, that is, from a realm independent of myself, and to whom I am answerable. He addresses me about something that he has entrusted to me and that I am bound to take care of loyally. . . . To be so answerable to a trusting person about an entrusted matter that loyalty and disloyalty step into the light of day . . . this is the reality of responsibility.[16]

Such a reality of responsibility involves both nearness and distance, as in the passage below:

> The spirit's service of life can be truly carried out only in the system of a reliable counterpoint—regulated by the laws of the different forms of relation—of giving and withholding oneself, intimacy and distance, which of course must not be controlled by reflection but must arise from the living fact of the natural and spiritual man. Every form of relation in which the spirit's service of life is realized has its special objectivity, its structure of proportions and limits which in no way resists the fervour of personal comprehension and penetration, though it does resist any confusion with the person's own spheres. If this structure and its resistance are not respected then a dilettantism will prevail which claims to be aristocratic, though in reality it is unsteady and feverish: to provide it with the most sacred names and attitudes will not help it past its inevitable consequence of disintegration.[17]

The "form of relation" really means "the form-criterion of response," in which one responds to a Thou and where the Thou requires such responses. The essence of responsibility appears to be in this mutual, though not

[16] Martin Buber, *Between Man and Man* (Boston, Beacon Press, 1957), 45.
[17] *Ibid.*, 95.

equipollent, response-relationship. The human orderer is reduced to the capacity of responding to the Thou of community and to the External Thou. Man thus becomes a responder to the quality of life depicted in the sphere of betweenness. Apparently, this is real responsibility for Buber. Man is thus bound to the world of community that is "turned to God." As Buber views it: "That is man's true autonomy which no longer betrays, but responds. ... Man, the creature, who forms and transforms the creation, cannot create."[18] With this comment Buber makes reference to the Creator/creature distinction which symbolizes the religious totality to which man responds. The system of total participation is equated with lived life and *real responding*.

What is most interesting about Buber's theory of responsibility is that man finds fulfillment in the life of dialogue even when he is not ontologically self-directing in such encounter experiences. This represents a theory of responsibility in which man is "permitted to lean his responsibility on something"—in this case, on a system of totality.[19] This lean-to theory of responsibility shows man how to be *responsible to* a system of totality, or to a world-order, without making him *responsible for* it. It "points him to" a Thou relation in community and with an Eternal Thou, with fixed goal-directedness that is severed from the human orderer and his capacity to contribute to his becoming, individually and socially. Buber is apparently reacting to Nietzsche's extreme individualism and his doctrine of the "will to power." Instead of formulating a better concept of the human orderer, Buber chooses to go beyond the subject-object split to the sphere of betweenness in order to resolve it and to immerse him in a system of totality. Responsibility would dictate that if one construct of the human orderer has failed us historically, it is time to have another rather than to despair over the possibility of such reconstruction.

Man is a problem of the *dialogue*, when viewed in terms of a concept of the human orderer. What I mean by this is that if the individual is not self-directing in such a dialogue, why should he be responsible to it? The same is applicable to the community. Buber wishes to evoke the power of the community, as well as the forces of spirit and nature, to explain man. But if the community is not socially self-directing first and is a pawn in a system of totality, driven by its dialectical intentions, how can community remain a human dimension of existence? The social self-direction of the

18 *Ibid.*, 103.
19 *Ibid.*, 92.

community is prior to the possible reading of the community as a form of communion with totality. If man is not the gathering focus of dialogue, totalitarian thought results from the advocacy of a life of dialogue "between man and man," and between "man and God." Unless we accept this as a postulate, we are stuck with a lean-to theory of responsibility. At best this is just another totalistic model of human accountability protected by the canopy of mysticism. It is an existential exploitation of immediate experience to gain favorable access to one's God and to one's community. That this should be a necessity of life rather than the work of purposive being is merely to identify one's model of existence *qua* existence and then label it a real and immediate system of totality. Buber has the same problem as other totalists, namely, how to move from his model of the world (the ordered world) to a world-order or to cosmic reality with religious overtones. Just to pronounce upon their separateness is not enough, as in the distinction between the free man and the self-willed man. Whatever there is of an alleged world-order that is not an ordered world can only be seen through comprehensive models of existence, and these are just as perspectival as other totalistic schemes. Even the world-order per se is a model of existence mediated by purposive being. The alternative plan is to identify our model of existence with existence as existence and then to disclaim the identification by claiming its reality.

Buber has thus failed to sustain subjectivity as a human orderer by immersing it in a system of totality, first in community and the life of dialogue, and then in the dialogue with the Eternal. All the claims about the reality of the person, the subject self, thus come to naught, just as the claims about the reality of the object self in the philosophy of transactionalism come to naught.

The fact is that both subjecthood and objecthood, as definitions of man, are models of individuality and particularity. Each implicates a system of totality mediated by the human orderer as purposive being. As "human orderer," man must be there as a presupposition and also enter into the structure of both kinds of activities. The inquiry as to which self is more real and which is a construct is a mistaken methodology and a misguided ideal. Such distinctions already presuppose a human orderer in the matrix of participation. To call one or the other "real" is a claim of ultimacy for one's model of selfhood. At most, it can be only a reality-claim, and such claims cannot be made without the human claimant as "human orderer." Getting rid of the human claimant by placing him in the sphere of betweenness, in the life of dialogue, merely postpones the solution of this vital issue. Unless man as human orderer takes responsibility for such model-making and reality–claim-making about himself, there is no way we can make man the source of human responsibility. The fact of the matter is that Buber assigns totality as the source of human responsibility, but this totality is in competition with other totalitarian claims. Such totalistic reality-claims are in competition with the human claimant and his reality-claims.

In Buber's case, man's being-in-community is a model of man as "responder." Totality defines the rules for such response-relations, and these are in competition with other models of the "responder" similarly dictated by other systems of totality. In short, man as human orderer cannot even claim control of responsibility for the dialogue in which he finds himself. The sphere of betweenness, as the life of concrete dialogue (where man is addressed and he answers), is thus the bearer of "responsibility for." Man can only respond in and to such dialogue. He is not responsible for it. Unless man confronts another claimant, there is no responsibility in Buber's sense because there is no primary address or claim to which man can answer. One is responsible to everything one "meets," but one is not "responsible for" what one meets. Buber gives a religious reading to immediate experience. But existence does not call man to responsibility unless purposive being mediates such claims about existence and immediacy. This is quite evident in the contrast between Buber and Kierkegaard. Kierkegaard's encounter philosophy requires no such dialogue and no such community to empower the individual, as Buber's encounter philosophy requires. The supreme dialogue with God suffices for the individual without the mediation of community. They are essentially two models of the "responsible person." The "I of Relation" has a different significance for Buber than for Kierkegaard. Thus the concept of responsibility in the concrete means whatever demands the system of totality puts upon it, for the directives of immediacy have their gathering focus either in a system of totality or in the human orderer as participant in existence. There is no neutral ground of immediacy that is the source of human directionality which is not itself in need of some mediation. The responsibility of the concrete can be a responsibility to the concrete only if someone or something takes *responsibility for* it. Human vitality in itself yields no responsibility, neither does the vitality of immediate experience.

That Buber uses immediate experience to authenticate man in a system of totality is obvious enough. Why should man be more authentic when he gives his life to a system of totality—"where the whole claims you, and you must answer Him"—and more than a mere man, if every such system of totality is only a model of existence? Whether responsibility, concrete or abstract, depends really on the totality in question. This is a secondary issue. If man is not responsible for such systems of total responsibility, it does not matter whether the content of responsibility is concrete or abstract, monological or dialogical, because responsibility is itself in some measure of jeopardy as a human experience. If man can only be responsible to but not responsible for it, why should the matter fall on his shoulders at all? "Living in responsibility" is not one kind of experience, for such an experience is mediated either by a system of totality or by a purposive being. Thus even "responsibility itself" or "real responsibility" is not really its own. It needs a sense of directionality before it can be a proper or fitting response. In Buber's case, the authenticated man and authentic responsibility both require a system of totality to be genuine. But such a system of totality is already a model of existence which requires of man to be responsible "for that in which before God he participates. . . ."

Dialogue with community or with God is a necessity of life only if that necessity has been mediated by purposive being in participation in existence. He does not believe in community first, or in God first, and then participate in existence next. These are products of purposive participation in existence, and there is no responsibility to either community or to God unless man first confronts the human orderer in himself and in social existence. To be authentic, the life of dialogue thus needs the participation of a purposive being or it becomes a servant of some system of totality. If purpose has an ontological relevance to existence, it cannot be cut out of the life of dialogue or community. It must share the primal responsibility for such dialogue, for the system of responsibility postulated as the "sphere of the between." The trip beyond the subject-object split is man's invention, and he must take responsibility for it, as for the absolute distinction between immediate and mediate experience. Such a "commitment to relationship" is posterior to purposive participation and responsibility. If it is prior to purposive being, the "commitment to relationship" is a hidden "commitment to a system of totality." The current definitions of immediate experience support such exploitation because direct forms of immediacy are themselves products of totalistic thinking. What needs to be explored in such cases is the "unjustified mediations" which justify all our knowledge.

An Overview of Systems of Responsibility

Saul Pett of the Associated Press made the following comment in his evaluation of our times:

Where we are, most thinkers agree, is an untended garden, overgrown and wildly seeded, in which human purpose has been obscured. We have much of what we don't want and have almost forgotten what we do want. "It is not so much that the pace is fast but that it is somebody else's pace or schedule," says Paul Goodman, social philosopher. The poets and the philosophers and the psychiatrists agree: men must somehow regain control of their lives.[20]

The above passage is relevant to what we have said about systems of totality and responsibility in several respects. First, totalities are in a very real sense "untended gardens" in that the human orderer has not fashioned or formed them and has no control over them, from the totalistic point of view. Man is only responsible to them and not for them. Second, the only way to establish control over them and over human life is to liberate the human orderer to be self-directing in human participation and in the invention of such systems of total responsibility. Third, the most troublesome aspect with regard to total systems of responsibility is, in terms of my theory, that man is advised to live his life in fitting responses to such totalities, that it is, in fact, "somebody else's pace or schedule."

Let me state some of the "signs" by which we can pinpoint or notice systems of responsibility over which man has lost a good deal of control. (1) When the experience of responsibility requires a dialectical ordering, it is a sure sign that both man and his experience of responsibility is guided by a system of totality. (2) When responsibility is defined as a "unifying principle," this is a sign that a form of totality orders its response-relations. (3) When responsibility is defined as a form of "acceptance" or "commitment," these are sure signs of totality at work in human responsibility. In addition to these signs, there are others, namely: encounter experiences (individual and social), concepts like "reaction" and "response." The surest way to spot signs of totalistic responsibility is by noting the patterns of goal-directedness which underlie the patterns of response-relations. These I have called intentional models of experience, accepted by the totalists as something primitive or primal in experience.

There have been two varieties of such goal-directed patterns of responsibility, namely, pre- and postpurposive. Response-relations were explained

[20] *Norman Transcript* (February 15, 1970), 4.

either from below or from above, and some, like Martin Buber, have used both models, the community and the Eternal Thou, to explain the life of dialogue which is the source of subjectivity and objectivity. When either of these two designs for living is used to construct responsibility (whether abstract or real), there is no way to appreciate responsibility coming from the human orderer, from the ontological capacity to be self-directing in existence. All that one can do is to follow the inspiration of Rainer Maria Rilke, who remarked: "A play of pure forces/ That no one touches unless he kneels and admires" (*Sonnets to Orpheus,* II.10). When such patterns of goal-directedness are pushed to the point of ultimacy, that is to say, beyond human participation, and acknowledged as reality-claims, this is nothing but totalitarian thought on its knees admiring systems of totality.

Another sure sign of totalistic schemes of responsibility is man's attempt to go beyond the subject-object split in such a way that the human orderer is excluded from such primal participation. In this sense, such a trip is beyond human participation. Unless man is a subject-object dialogue mediated by his purposive nature, the life of dialogue or the life of totality is devoid of meaning.

My critique of systems of totality and their models of accountability is not derived from any existential motif. Kierkegaard, for example, inveighed against system-building on the grounds of real existence. He titled some of his books *Fragments* and *Postscripts* in order to avoid system-building and practice direct discourse. This is not my motivation, for "existence itself" is as much an *"existential* construct" as any other conceived in the matrix of participation. The same may be said of the naturalistic view about existence or natural complexes. Whether such competitors of system-building (of a rational variety) are subjectively encountered or objectively encountered schemes of life, they, too, involve model-making by participation and invoke the human orderer's capacity for self-direction in the very matrix of participation. Having commerce with encounter experiences, whether subjective or objective in character, is a way of trusting the directives of immediacy to those of human purpose. This is already a sign of invitation for totality to step in, whether as a structure or as a process, to order human life and its meaning.

My criticism has concentrated on the following problem: when man has lost his claims on responsibility, there is no way provided by systems of totality for him to function beyond the role of a "responder" and "responsibility to." There is no justification to limit the phenomenon of responsibility to such a schizoid belief, for systems of totality result in the problems of pluralism and relativism. Their ultimate form of communication is through various forms of reality-claims or by claims to ultimacy. I have refused to play this game of whether a system of total responsibility is real or unreal, for any decision reached on such an issue can only be in terms of a claim to ultimacy for one's existence. Such claims are made only by denying the purposive formation of them. The problem of totality may be viewed as an instance of failure on man's part to shoulder his responsibility for systems of responsibility.

When systems of totality are given prior status to the human orderer, who is excluded from such primal experience, they require goal-directed living from man. Of man they require that he "confirm himself" or "conform to" such systems of totality. The radicalization of responsibility that I have insisted on views responsibility from a deeper standpoint. It already recognizes prior purposiveness at work in and through such acts of confirmation, conformity, and identification. This view sharpens man's sense of responsibility, makes him responsible for goal-directed patterns of living, whether these are conceived from above or from below, subjectively, objectively, or totalistically. Such goal-directed models of living prevent man from recognizing the human orderer in himself and in social existence in experiences of responsibility.

Systems of totality have their origin on the phenomenal level of goal-experience. They have no ontological status unless these phenomenal goals are transformed and fixed by some system of totality, as when they are theologized, naturalized, ontologized, essentialized, etc. The attempt to make goals and responses into fixed patterns of totality, whether highly structured or processive and thus to make them function as the domain(s) of such goals, is to cut the lifeline between human goals and man's purposive being. In terms of my theory, goals and responses have only one ultimate source, namely, in man's purposive nature, in the metamodel which places ontological self-direction prior to goal direction. Men have placed the source of responsibility in systems of totality only because they were unable to locate its ontological source in man or to have a model that would give it such location.

Perhaps the best way to summarize this section and the last two chapters would be to say that notions of the "responsible person," "responsible community," "responsible government," and "responsible decision-making considerations" come alive when responsibility is defined as man confronting the human orderer in himself, in social existence, in systems of totality, and in systems of general ontology. This is the missing link in all these notions. The effort at totalization, identity, or unity and destiny must be viewed as projects of purposive being in the matrix of participation. When purposive being is the foundation of response-relations, responsibility wears a human face and no longer hides its face in systems of totality.

Are Systems of Totality Homologous?

To raise the question is to get at the crux of the matter between my theory and the totalistic perspectives discussed in this volume. Some thinkers believe, and Paul Ricoeur is among them, that it is possible to have a "common structure" of meaning among such schemes of totality. Ricoeur states that "between one totality and another there can only be relations of homology."[21] The task, then, is to discover such "homologous relations," to note the progress in philosophy. Ricoeur attempts to legislate between the prepurposive totality of Freud and the postpurposive version of Hegel. What is of interest to note, however, is that Ricoeur, who finds a common structure between the two totalists, does so only in terms another system of totality which offers a new blend, also dialectically ordered, between the dialectic of archaeology (Freud) and teleology (Hegel), which finds the interplay of that theme in each writer. That is to say, Ricoeur does find a common structure among these two totalists, but it comes out as the third totality, mediating the other two. Perhaps this is the clue to the homologous relations among systems of totality.

The common structure can never be stated universally. It can only be stated by another system of totality making reality-claims or claims to finality. Ricoeur's alternative, a third totality to resolve the other two totalities, is a linguistic totality that relies on a hermeneutic reading of symbolism. The search for a comprehensive language to account for all of man's activities and symbolic forms in culture is a much-needed undertaking, Ricoeur believes, because the "unity of human language" is the big problem of the day. How do we combine Freud and Hegel, psychoanalysis and philosophy, the prepurposive model of existence with the postpurposive version of totality? But what this analysis amounts to is another system of totality and not the common structure of all systems of totality. That precisely is the problem.

[21] Paul Ricoeur, *Freud and Philosophy* (New Haven, Yale University Press, 1970), 461.

It is not necessary to get into Ricoeur's system to feel the insurmountable nature of his task. The latest totality, making claims of ultimacy and reality-claims, wins the day. It becomes thus another goal-directed pattern for living, similarly dialectically oriented. The relations of homology do not help us to understand the game of totalities and their oppressiveness with respect to human living. The "common structure" in all such totalities is always stated by the last totality, which finds the others partially deficient and artificial and assumes that the latest one is the real and immediate totality. Each such conciliation between schemes of totality ends up on the rocks of pluralism and relativism.

Let me state the case negatively. If systems of totality have anything in common, it is something negative, not positive. Each totality is a model of existence in search of its own reality. Each one plays the game of reality-claims and makes pretenses to claims of ultimacy even when it absorbs previous patterns of totality or when it combines several of them into one new totality. This is not a substantive "common structure" indicating homologous relations among them. It is really a failure to understand the game of totalities in philosophy as a species of totalitarian thought. That this is so in Ricoeur's philosophy is only too obvious.

Each totality can solve the problem of a common structure among totalities only for its own system of totality but not for the others. The others require similar action in terms of their form and content. Thus there is no homologous relationship among totalities, only more totalities. Perhaps I can raise a more serious topic for consideration. If there is a common structure among systems of totality, one would hope that they would give man some measure of security in terms of the theme of universal, original, human responsibility. A review of the literature has shown bankruptcy at this point. All we have come up with is competing systems of responsibility adhering to each respective system of totality. This is more of a test case of a common structure among totalities than coming up with another system of totality, as Ricoeur had done.

Responsibility is not a bridge built between man and man, between man and the world, that is built by systems of totality. There is nothing common to either systems of totality or to systems of total responsibility except claims to ultimacy or the reality-claims of a model of totality and a model of responsibility. Responsibility is man confronting the human orderer in himself, in social existence, in systems of totality and systems of total responsibility. It is the purposive being building bridges between himself and his communities or the world. If responsibility is a bridge between man and his communities, it has been engineered by the human orderer in the matrix of participation. Totalists are only too eager to cut the link between man's purposive nature and his goals and responses, but this is nothing but man's yearning for absolute participation in the midst of perspectival human behavior. When totalists do succeed in stating their respective cases in history, their career is short-lived, for the reality-claims are soon discovered by other totalists. History is itself a proof of the fact that systems of totality are perspectival schemes of holism furthering or hindering man's search for further meaning in the matrix of participation. Even through such systems of totality and responsibility, when man reaches beyond himself to his communities, he does so as a purposive being, as a human orderer, whose model-making is felt even in experience and participation. In responsibility, man reclaims his creations and thus contributes to his becoming and to his communities.

9. Theories of Psychological Integration and Man's Drive for Totality

Schizoid behavior is no stranger to humanistic psychology, but it seems strange to hear it espoused as a theory of human responsibility. Carl Rogers, in a rather personal remark, characterizes the whole pattern of responsibility in current ego psychology when he states: "I certainly feel responsible *to* the participants, but not *for* them."[1] This is Rogers' way of relating, as a participant and facilitator, to encounter groups. The main trust is placed not in the human orderer, but in the "group process" which has its own ineffable manner of changing and directing human behavior. But how can man be whole again if he is incapable of manifesting "responsibility for" the meaning of his life? How can he be authentic if his search for wholeness is divorced from the whole that would heal him?

Such reflections as the above will characterize this last part of the book as I attempt to point out the possibilities of responsibility in the contemporary theories of psychological integration. The intent of the chapter is to point up the model-making quality of such concepts as unitive experience, encounter experience, and participation in the whole which humanistic psychology takes for real. This is not an easy task, for humanistic psychology takes its commitment of man to a system of totality(s) rather seriously. But it is important to examine some of these reality-identifications to see what claims of ultimacy are made for the process of totality and what is left over for the human orderer to do in terms of responsibility. The fact that there is no common structure of meaning to these various systems of totality in humanistic psychology, but only models of totality, makes necessary such an analysis as I offer below.

In order to give some system to the analysis of this chapter, I shall deal with William James on unitive experience, Carl Rogers on encounter experience, and Erik Erikson's theory of man in totality. The remaining

[1] Carl Rogers, *Encounter Groups* (New York, Harper and Row, 1970), 46.

chapters will concentrate on James Bugental, Erich Fromm, and Rollo May on how they relate man to their respective systems of totality and what this does to the notion of human responsibility. In short, my concern will be with the philosophical implications of scientific humanism and how it pertains to the human orderer in the matrix of human participation. The guiding thread through this literature is the competition between man and systems of totality for the source of human responsibility. This thread may be difficult to see at times because there is much syncretism, eclecticism, and transitional thinking in current theories of psychological integration. Some of these ambiguities in ego psychology have been alluded to by the psychological theorists themselves. George Klein, for example, has pointed to the persistent problem of alternating between explanation in terms of *process* and explanation in terms of *motivation* in the study of the ego in psychoanalytic theory.[2] But these problems go deeper than methodological considerations. They go to the heart of human responsibility. Can the new philosophy of science advocated by humanistic psychology get at the source of human responsibility, or must it content itself with more phenomenal perspectives of the matter? Will the drive for totality in theories of psychological integration give us anything more than a schizoid theory of human responsibility? If it cannot go beyond this predicament, can this somewhat new discipline in psychology speak meaningfully about the "whole man"? Perhaps the analysis below will enable us to formulate some answers for such questions.

JAMES ON UNITIVE EXPERIENCE

The interpretation of reality as process gives a dynamism and a unity to James's functional thought that is still quite relevant to humanistic psychology today. My concern in this section is to lift out for emphasis James's thinking on consciousness as a *field* or *stream*. When James relates these two notions to existence as process, he does so on the level of immediate experience and participation. This means that consciousness is a given structure as field or stream, that is to say, it is not a descriptive model of experience. It is actually the way experience is in its flowing nature. Thus it is model-free. Such unitive experience is prior to the human orderer and actually guides human life in the fulfillment of meaning. The stream of

[2] G. S. Klein, "The Emergence of Ego Psychology," *The Psychoanalytic Review,* Vol. 56, No. 4 (1969–70), 521–22.

consciousness authenticates man. Man does not authenticate unitive experience. Bruce Wilshire considers this a "phenomenological breakthrough" in James's thought.[3]

Phenomenologically oriented humanistic psychologists choose this non-pragmatic side of Jamesian thought, centering on the notion of "the stream of thought, of consciousness, or of subjective life" from chapter nine in volume one of the *Principles of Psychology*. There is a flowing character to experience, to human encounters, and in our experiences of totality. Carl Rogers, for example, states: "The individual risks being himself in process in the relationship to others. He takes the risk of being the flow that is himself and trusting another person to accept him as he is in this flow."[4] Both James and Rogers regard the self as a process, as a more complicated flow of things than when it is simply regarded as an object. The "object" is already an abstraction from the larger fringe or marginal dimension of experience.

What is most noticeable in this line of thinking is that processive human experience is basically unitive in nature and has the function of a pedagogue in human experience. It teaches the human being how to live and how to be authenticated in the stream of lived experience. Perhaps the image of a swimmer in water, even while coming up for a breath of air is nonetheless sustained by the stream in which he swims, is the most apt description we can give of processive living. For James, such feelingful awareness of living experience itself that is model-free is of the essence of life. The basic question which keeps coming up for me is whether human participation in existence is prior to such an identification of process with existence, or whether the processive nature of life is first and human participation something dependent upon it. In terms of my thesis, a processive view of life which supports unity as being built from below involves as much model-making in participation and experience as some other encounter philosophy. In process philosophy, it is most difficult to reconcile the perspectival nature of human actions (their specificity) with the continuity of becoming. A philosophy of relations does not want to face up to this problem. It hides the problem within immediate experience.

A model-free unitive experience has been a basic problem from my perspective throughout this entire volume. It is no different in the case of

[3] Bruce Wilshire, *William James and Phenomenology* (Bloomington, Indiana University Press, 1968), 119-23.
[4] Rogers, *Encounter Groups*, 125.

James. The problem is that James identifies his model of the human consciousness with consciousness itself. The model of consciousness as field or stream is literally consciousness itself as consciousness. Thus it needs no mediation either by reason or by purpose. This point of view requires omniscience, which James does not have. It involves a theory of purposive mediation or a holistic use of human purpose, to state the unitive case for consciousness, as coming from below, as process. After all, the whole point in calling consciousness a stream or field is to get at the unity or totality of conscious human experience. Whatever else such a search may involve, it involves the mediation of consciousness by purposive being. James denies the forming capacity of human purpose of such unitive experiences. Unitive experience is borne from below, it is part of the cargo of meaning that processes themselves bear, and such processes are not models of experience. This presupposes a continuity of experience with nature, its connections in nature, and this is free of abstraction and model-making. Underlying this perspective is a belief in the reality of the part-to-whole logic and a shift from parts to wholes which both psychology and philosophy have come to emphasize. James discovered the shift in the study of British empiricism when he broadened the notion of experience to go beyond mere sensation, the narrow meaning of experience. James felt that in this shift the "part" was an abstraction but that the "whole" of experience was not. This was real and immediate; this was existence as process. The assumption of both philosophy and psychology has been the same ever since, namely, that wholes, unities, totalities, and experience as field or stream are model-free and thus free of abstraction and human projection. Thus unitive experience is more accessible immediately than is the "part" and sensational experience. This broader version of experience gave it the quality of cumulativeness, continuity, and relatedness and made it more amenable for learning and meaning-giving functions in life.

My objections to model-free unitive experience are the following: One, the postulate of conscious experience as field or stream is already a model of conscious experience and not consciousness *qua* consciousness, just as the postulate of experience *in* nature is a model of experience. This involves the mediation of consciousness by man's purposive nature in terms of its holistic tendencies. In our levels approach to purpose, the unity of conscious experience arises on the second level of purposiveness, the phenomenal level of goal-directedness. Thus both the empirical notions of continuity and wholeness, both of which symbolize unitive experience, derive from the second level of purpose, and this depends on ontological self-direction as the primary meaning of purposive participation in existence. In terms of my theory, it is not possible to state the case for the unity of experience, either from above or from below, without the mediation of purposive being. Unitive experience is as much an ideal or a goal, even when postulated developmentally and naturalistically, as any other end or aim. Such unities don't grow on trees. When naturalism rejected postpurposive unity, the unity which came from above and which it regarded as artificial (an intruder into experience), it assumed that the unity which came from below via process was model-free and, therefore, not fashioned by human purpose. This is the case once more of a claim to ultimacy, a reality-claim or reality-identification (of identifying one's model of process, development, and growth) with the course of nature itself. Is this the requirement of one's model of experience in nature or the demand of life itself? The postulate of continuity of experience with nature to which both James and Dewey adhere may simply be the demand of our purposive being in the matrix of our participation and not the nature of things themselves.

From my perspective, naturalistic goals, like the ideal of unitive experience, cannot be stated apart from man's purposive nature, which is its source of mediation in terms of its holistic use. To deny purposive being a forming quality to such schemes of unity is to play god by assuming an identity of one's model of existence with existence itself and then to claim that it came from below, from a system of totality also not of our own shaping and making. This is a reality-identification that totalists make to immerse the human orderer in a system of totality(s). From my viewpoint, such goals and projects are operational aspects of man's purposive nature ontologically conceived; they are the results of purposive participation in existence and not the work of existence as process from below. Moreover, the holistic use of purpose, as that used in postulating unitive experience, is a secondary use of purpose and a product of ontological self-direction, as are all goals whether immediate or ultimate. I believe that James takes holism from the phenomenal level of experience and gives it naturalistic fixation on the plane of immediate experience. Thus holism becomes a form of structure in immediate experience. Put differently, such unitive immediacy is used to give the character of permanence to flux and change in experience. It is a "ladder of ascent" in human participation without having recourse to the human orderer. Unitive traits, events, qualities, relations, values, ends, and events thus become a substitute for purposive participation in existence. In the light of my thesis, James gives a holistic, purposive mediation to the unmediated sphere of consciousness by calling it a field or stream. The stream of consciousness is thus a realm of unjustified mediations, which is a way of seeking permanence in the midst of change. Since James has identified his model of conscious experience with consciousness itself, he is unaware of this prior purposive mediation. Consequently, he does not think of himself as a model-maker on the level of lived experience when he equates consciousness as field or stream with consciousness *qua* consciousness. The fact is that the confluent model of human participation is the deciding factor in calling consciousness a field or stream.

Two, when James asks the question, "Does consciousness exist?," his reply is that it does not exist as a substance or as some entity, but that it exists as a process or function. The processive consciousness is thus free of model-making. What does it mean for consciousness to exist as process or as function? That it exists as self-consciousness? Why did James not take the second step implicated in his answer? That consciousness exists only as man is self-directing in his self-consciousness, that it is a model of consciousness and not the processive consciousness *qua* consciousness. Self-consciousness is the use we make of consciousness in our purposive nature. What is in question is the autonomy of self-consciousness as a function. The alternative we face in this regard is that it is not its own, that it belongs to man as a human orderer or to a system of totality. The distinction between consciousness and self-consciousness is thus posterior to purposive being as a primitive.

I am not saying that the human consciousness is only a model of consciousness. It is more, of course, but we experience it through the mediation of our purposive being, through models of participation and models of existence. The "stream of consciousness" is already mediated by purposive being when it is postulated as unitive experience, as being a unity, field, or stream. It already presupposes that mediation, only this is denied by processive thought which wants to get at the real and immediate in experience. Unless man is ontologically self-directing in self-consciousness, there is no point in calling it self-consciousness. Its goal-consciousness is an operational aspect of this phenomenon we have been calling the human orderer.

Three, James's attempt to go beyond the subject-object split to state the case for unitive experience, to the notions of "pure consciousness" or "pure experience," is thus an abortive effort. It is neutral only with respect to the human orderer since he has to follow its tendential leads but not with respect to a system of naturalistic totality. Even as a system of "neutral monism," "radical empiricism" has certain commitments which are ominous for the human orderer in spite of all the praise that James heaps upon the concept of the individual. Pure experience, it is claimed, is unmediated experience, unmediated and prior to the subject-object distinction, according to James. But the human orderer goes along, we have seen, on all such trips beyond the subject-object split. Though man's purposive nature forms such totalistic unities, its shaping capacity is denied by empiricism. Purpose is made a reactive phenomenon to the unity that comes from below and imparts its meaning-giving structures to life. One may even call it purposive alienation. What is of interest to note is that purposive being asserts itself even in the denial of some of its participatory goals and plans, just as the will asserts itself in will-less thought. The postulate of "pure experience" as a neutral kind of immediate unity is, from my perspective, a fictitious entity if it is conceived as something ontologically prior to purposive being. Even the decision to stay neutral is in fact a decision. It is a decision to seek unity in a system of totality by an appeal to immediate experience. It is a decision to deprive the human orderer of his ordering capacity in the stream of unitive experience. The choice that we confront is not so much a distinction between mediate and immediate experience (the line has been drawn to indicate an absolute distinction) as it is posterior to purposive being. But who or what is the gathering focus for both kinds of experience? It is not enough to make claims of ineffability about immediate experience. We must understand its relationship to the human orderer and its relations to systems of totality. For the notion of direct participation cannot be adequately understood apart from the concept of directionality.

Four, there is a tendency in James, in spite of his pluralism, to emphasize a functional holism. Although it is an incompleted world-view, such terms as pure experience, marginal (fringe) experience, real relations in experience, structures in experience, the distinction between knowledge by acquaintance and knowledge about, and even the way he relates the unconscious to conscious experience would suggest the bent of his thinking to account for the meaning of life in terms of some processive view of totality. Once James has established the unitive foundation of experience in his radical empiricism, which has phenomenological overtones, James is not worried about his pluralistic universe running askew. For the dynamic multiplicity evidenced in the world has a processive totality as its gathering focus. Those who view James phenomenologically are correct, of course, to conceive his radical empiricism as a system of totality, as coming prior to his pragmatic pluralism. I question such a system of totality if it is conceived as something prior to man's purposive being. This can only be a preconceived notion of the world with ominous implications for man. Let me call this point of view of consciousness as field or stream and his theory of processive totality a prepurposive comprehension of the world in its entirety.

James as a physiologist can never be discounted even in his most mature thought. It is an important element in the prepurposive model of totality in which the organism is goal-directed to nature and interacting with the total environment in terms of an evolutionary perspective. Unitive experience is also preconceived in this matter, as growing from below and which is prior to human purpose and intervention. That James views man as being goal-directed to nature is a central preoccupation with him. This is understood by him to mean a real organic connection and directly experienceable as such. Part of this world-view is his conception of immediate experience as being relationally structured, also goal-directed or intentional, and as holistic. In this context, the object of thought, in the context of marginal experience or in its horizon-structure, is "the ultimate totality of the thought's total object" (Bruce Wilshire). His functional world-view is thus built up by unitive experiences and horizon-structures, applicable to both things and objects and man, and such encounter experiences flowing in the stream of life provide meaning for lived experience. This is to suggest that if consciousness exists as a function and is real as a field or stream, then the choice we face is whether such a consciousness implicates a human orderer that conceives his life in participation as a stream or field, or whether this implicates the intentions of totality at work through the totalistic tendencies (like feeling-tendencies) in experience.

James chooses the second alternative, which denies the role of man's purposive nature on the ontological level in primal experience. Pure experience is the domain of human goals and the resolution of the subject-object split since it is prior unmediated experience to such a distinction. Thus James alienates man from his purposive nature to bring him close to a processive system of totality by an appeal to immediate experience. In identifying consciousness with stream or field, James deprives man's purposive nature from a shaping or forming role of unity in experience. Such unity is the work of model-free processes and not that of the human orderer. Yet it is only man that thinks of the world in terms of totalities and unities. This appears to be the prerogative of a purposive being who chooses to see his life in terms of the patterns having a developmental course. James alienates man's purposive nature from primal experience and seeks to establish a relational notion of permanence by an appeal to direct experience. Thus the directives of immediacy, the servants of totality, are preferred to secure the meaning of life for man to those of the human orderer in purposive participation in life.

Five, perhaps I can state my main objection to the view of unitive experience more forthrightly in this last section. The question is not, as James supposed, whether purpose does or does not relate to primal encounter experiences of this unitive variety. Such a question is really academic. The real question is whether we use the forming and modeling power of human purpose holistically or self-directively. Which has prior status, ontologically speaking? Since, to me, schemes of totality originate as fixed patterns of goal-directedness, the holistic use of human purpose is secondary to man's ontological capacity for self-direction. This is a prior problem to the issue, whether processive reality is real or unreal or whether such totalities have a common structure to them, even within the empirical school of thought itself. Thus the question is whether we play the old traditional game of final purpose as the ultimate meaning of purposiveness and of life, or we think of it first ontologically and then proceed to show its relevance to unitive experience and to systems of totality, whatever their brand or school of thought. The very fact that James struggled with the problem of the "One" and the "Many" indicates that he tried to solve this problem, unsuccessfully, because he had no way of relating it meaningfully to an existent human orderer. The Jamesian point of view betrays his bent toward Bergson and the Romantic movement, which had a fondness for the "immediate wholeness of the whole." Man is more than an injection into the whole by immediate experience, reposing there on the ground of totality. He is purposive in such ventures of thought and experience.

If this is the case, the reality-identification between wholeness and existence is just another claim of ultimacy, only this time for the processive model of totality. But even this model of existence or "participation in the whole" has traces of human participation in it. No case for holism can be stated without a certain use of human purpose. The question is, which is the more authentic interpretation of man's purposive life in the domain of lived experience. The process thinkers have made a holistic use of human purpose in the form of positive alienation. In denying the modeling power of man's purposive nature, they have implicated man in a system of processive totality with ominous consequences for the human orderer. They deny purposive participation and responsibility for man on the level of primal experience. If this charge is correct, then we must face the issue of whether schemes of totality are built up primarily by a system of goal direction or by ontological self-direction that is prior to such ultimate goals.

Six, there has been a prevalent tendency among the naturalists to relate purpose to the works of the mind and not to lived, immediate experience. I suggest that this is a way of seeking permanence in the midst of change. One may question the assumptions of change but not those of permanence. This narrow view of purpose (and even here the primary concern was to relate teleology to mechanism or to a medium as the bearer of the intentions of totality) enabled the empiricists to establish the claim that immediacy belongs to the pre-reflective stage of experience (with which I agree). But purpose is more than a function of the human mind, and the goals of the mind cannot be separated from the human orderer. If this is the case, then such prereflective unitive experience is not necessarily prepurposive in character. Just because it is prereflective, it need not be prepurposive. The human orderer is there appraising the relation of reason to experience before both themes are related to a scheme of processive totality. Though consciousness as stream or field is prereflective, it is not prepurposive. The notion requires a holistic use of human purpose in James's view, but this is unaccounted for in his theory. Another way to say it is to insist that even "knowledge by acquaintance" requires purposive mediation (of a more participatory kind) as does knowledge about experience. One is just as bound to abstractions by participation as the latter is bound to the abstractions of the mind. Both exhibit the model-making power of man's purposive nature. To say that knowledge by acquaintance is free of such modeling power is to separate man's affective life from the human orderer and to relate him in this condition of helplessness to unitive experience implicating a naturalistic system of totality. The problem we face is whether we make unitive experience the directive force of human life or acknowledge the human orderer's capacity to shape and form unitive experience as part of his search for meaning in the larger quest for wholeness. These reflections on unitive experience should help us to confront the patterns of model-making in the psychologies of encounter which follow.

ROGERS ON ENCOUNTER EXPERIENCE

The conflict between encounter philosophies is very much in evidence in the writings of Carl Rogers. I shall touch on the matter only in terms of his latest book, *On Encounter Groups*. That is to say, he runs together the subjective and the objective principles, existential and naturalistic encounters, and the ambiguity of explanation in terms of process and in terms of motivation is really an inheritance from this conflict. Rogers is plagued with this problem even in his later works. George Klein views the problematic relation of these two different theoretical enterprises in humanistic psychology with grave concern:

Two different theoretical enterprises are implied in these two models of explanation. Current ego psychology tries to straddle them, with no gain to either. The confusion in its explanatory focus is evident in the way in which ego "functions" are conceived. In *process* explanations, talk about ego functions focuses on perception, memory, learning, in their *formal*, operational aspects, but *not* on the aims, purposes, and intentions to which these functions are put and the settings in which they are involved. Proceeding in this direction, ego psychology becomes almost indistinguishable from traditional academic psychology in its concern with intelligence and cognitive processes; it is certainly not distinctively psychoanalytic.[5]

On the one hand, there is process explanation with ultimate reliance and trust placed upon the "group process" and the change and directives it affords the individual. On the other, there is the motovational explanation, the reliance on the individual's contribution and directionality to the group process. I believe that in the final analysis the problem is weighted in the direction of process itself as the bearer of human meaning and the subjective experiences are merely instrumental, parenthetical, to a better science of man and, therefore, to more objective appraisal of the whole man.

Naturalistic encounters are still preferred and given primacy over subjective and intersubjective phenomenological data, for this is reachable only indirectly from the scientific point of view. Self-oriented experiences are thus utilized for more objective goals. Man as object is replaced by man as process, both individually and collectively. Part of the phenomenological task, then, is to get at "more process quality," since the variables of inner experience cannot be measured directly. But the goal, Rogers contended as early as 1963, is to achieve more operational meanings of this inner world

[5] Klein, *op. cit.*, 522.

of personhood. Thus Roger's attempt to bring more closely together the subjective and objective aspects of life suffers still from a precarious imbalance because the subjective component of experience plays only a parenthetical role in this solution. By the fact that it is accessible only to indirect procedures, whereas processive explanations are more amenable to more direct procedure, would make existential encounters that much less significant.

Rogers believes the best way to harmonize them is through functional procedures: "We will be attempting to discover the functional process relationships which hold for the inner world of personal meanings, and to formulate these with sufficient precision that they may be put to empirical test."[6] But the whole point of existential philosophy is that man is more than the sum total of his functions, which is to say that a functional approach cannot get at the irreducible subject-self. This does not disturb Rogers' phenomenological approach. Even though his method does not reach this self beyond its functions, he still claims "a view of man as subjectively free, choosing, responsible architect of the self."[7] Man is thus a person who in the midst of process creates himself. But Rogers' methodology can only get at the functions and not at the real process of creativity itself in such personhood formation. Rogers is to be admired, however, for attempting to expand the categories of science to deal with experiences in addition to behavior. Great as this effort is, it is dogged by the possibility of failure if the goal is to achieve genuinely heuristic theories "leading to the discovery of significant functional relationships having to do with human life."[8] Part of the anticipated failure of such an approach is, even postulating its success, that the irreducible subject self is not even touched by such a method.

What I am suggesting is that it is precarious to blend the processive thought of William James and the intersubjective personalized world of Martin Buber. They offer us two models of encounter, naturalistic and existential, which are not so readily harmonizable. Such immediate experience comes to us in terms of models of existence which relate to the human orderer. It is not a solution to say that a person must risk himself to the ongoing process because such unitive experience is a model of human

---

[6] Carl Rogers, "Toward a Science of the Person," *Humanistic Psychology* (Fall, 1963), 90.
[7] *Ibid.*
[8] *Ibid.*, 92.

participation and not real participation *qua* participation. The fact that man "risks being himself in process" involves more than a functional point of view. There are philosophical problems that are unresolved in this psychology of integration which suggest a synchretistic approach where all the food is not digested properly. Let us take a closer look at this problem.

Rogers is very much troubled by the psychological fact that modern man is alienated from his feelingful life. He would remedy this through group therapy, sensitivity sessions, where the group process would release its healing balm. There are many stages of growth and change involved in going through such an experience in encounter groups. The last stage, in particular, is worth noting in such a processive experience. Rogers comments:

Feelings previously denied are now experienced with both immediacy and *acceptance*. Such feelings are not something to be denied, feared, or struggled against. This experiencing is often vivid, dramatic, and releasing for the individual. There is full acceptance now of experience as providing a clear and usable referent for getting at the latent meanings of the individual's encounter with himself and with life. There is also the recognition that the self is now becoming this process of experiencing. There is no longer much awareness of the self as an object. The individual often feels somewhat "shaky" as his solid constructs are recognized as construings that take place within him. The individual risks being himself in process in the relationship to others. He takes the risk of being the flow that is himself and trusting another person to accept him as he is in this flow.[9]

In this context, "acceptance" can only mean being *responsible to* the promptings and directives of immediacy or spontaneity. Such self-acceptance, both individually and socially conceived, is prior to ontological self-direction as defined in this volume. Acceptance is a feelingful response to the directives of spontaneity. Risk-taking is also a form of action-immediacy. The entire meaning of such "self-responsibility" (which is discussed in stages four and five of group growth via encounter experiences) is in the context of *responsibility to* but not *responsibility for* the growth process.

While this process explanation is not reductive—not as impersonal as tension reduction, equilibria, discharge, and object, and is suggestive of motivation, self-direction, and goals—the language is deceptive and ambiguous. Personal terms are used to describe an impersonal process of functional relationships (acceptance, risk, recognition, trust, etc.), but there is

---

[9] Rogers, *Encounter Groups*, 125.

no "human orderer" in the matrix of purposive participation. What counts is the confluent model of participation where the unitive experience guides both the individual and the group. This implicates a system of totality rather than the human orderer. What else can be made of the statement, "He takes the risk of being the flow that is himself. . ."? If man is "the flow" in the larger impersonal process of the flow or stream of experience rather than a human orderer in participation, why the personal language to describe the impersonal growth?

The subject self is not his own. It is a derived inner process from the larger impersonal stream of experience. It implicates a system of totality as its gathering focus. Is this final purpose explained from below, *via* process, rather than from above? Is this processive interaction, the interplay of processive forces, the laced part of the football conceived as a whole? The fact is that processive explanations do not escape the traditional meaning of purpose defined as some form of goal-directedness. It accepts commerce with totalities, which is a natural outgrowth from viewing purpose externally. Is such a totality not an intruder from the outside if it is conceived as being beyond human participation, as every totality must be by definition? If this is the case, what possible meaning can be given to such feelingful or spontaneous relationships which derive from encounter groups? Rogers, accepting the research of Betty Meador, comments:

They became closer to their feelings, were beginning to express feelings as they occurred, were more willing to risk relationships on a feeling basis, whereas these qualities had not been characteristic of the group initially.[10]

What is one closer to, in such self-related feelings, in such a context? Is it to processive totality or to the human orderer? If one is closer to totality, why the language of self-reference and the I-Thou relationship? There is nothing about the *flow* of experience that it should be either personal or impersonal, of itself. This is already a purposive reading of human experience, shaped and formed by purposive participation in existence. It

---

[10] *Ibid.*, 125. In short, processive growth is already on its way, and it is attributed to the encounter experiences. Growth motivation, in this case, is an ambiguous situation, for it represents the character of the process and not motivation. This is no longer striving after goals in the ordinary sense of human striving; it is processive striving, which is a "continuing process of becoming" in which the specificity of acts is run together with the process of becoming itself. Such an attempt to fuse growth and motivation on the level of immediacy, prior to purposive participation, is the weakness of syncretism in humanistic psychology.

is a processive model of existence, not processive existence *qua* existence. That Rogers takes process as something real and not as a model of existence is evidenced by the fact that he is willing to measure it and quantify it by offering a Scale of Process. Human responses need not even be identified in the stream of experience because what counts is the unitive experience that comes out of such encounter. It is this that has the capacity for self-direction, not the human orderer. But I insist that this kind of self-direction implicates a system of totality which orders and directs so that human directionality is already a derived, reactive phenomenon. The subject self and the feelingful group are both lost in a system of totality. Situational immediacy in that case is the servant of processive totality. Self-responsibility can only be self-expression. Spontaneity is the servant of totality. One can be responsible to it, but not for it. To plead for the ownership of selfhood in terms of feelingful acceptance is thus a misguided effort. Human responsibility does not "bubble through into awareness," though human vitality may. That is precisely the problem of relating human responsibility to spontaneity, as I noted at the beginning of this book. The flow, changingness, and spontaneity of the stream or field of experience do not necessarily yield responsibility, unless it be the model of responsibility evoked by some designed system of totality.

If human participation does not define and design the goal directions of life, a system of totality(s) does it for us. This is what happens when we place our "trust" in "group process." The price may be too high for such growth, for becoming "more fully functioning persons." The process of organic maturation does not define human responsibility. Only man's purposive participation in existence gives us that. The "process of change" or "feeling responsible" may not be the proper sources of responsibility. Unless the human orderer is the gathering focus of such changes and feelings, there is control of man by some system of totality and not human responsibility. There is as much totalitarian thinking in psychology as in philosophy.

Rogers places his trust in the confluent model of participation and responsibility. The most this model can yield is the principle of coresponsibility. This does not give us the human orderer and purposive participation in terms of the thesis of this book. The subject self fails to be a human orderer in existence, just as the encounter group fails to be a socially self-directing group. It implicates a system of total directionality of the group. The "whole man" theme is a popular topic of humanistic psychology. That whole man implicates a system of totality. Man is completed by a processive totality to which he is goal-directed by the part-to-whole logic I discussed earlier. Thus the "acceptance of his total being" can only mean the acceptance of a model of totality as the real and immediate totality. This rests on reality-identifications I have rejected. Such a processive totality may yield "real feelings" where "real persons emerge," but this is not the human orderer. It is a model of man in a model of totality for which claims of ultimacy are made. The free-flowing qualities which characterize such a life are derived from the directives of totality. If one encourages mindless and purposeless encounters as the essence of human responsibility, which trust in a processive totality apparently requires, there is no way of reclaiming either the human orderer or purposive participation and responsibility in existence. Such "change-producing" insights may be liberating for a scheme of totality but not for man. The path to obscurantism and dogmatism is strewn with the litter of such commitment relationships. Unless the human orderer has ontological status in participation, such "commitment to relationship" is a hazard. We have recognized this in religion and politics, but not yet in psychology and philosophy. If man is not self-directing in such relational experiences, on the primal level, why should he be so trustful of them or committed to these relations? Trust "in some sort of process movement" already presupposes ontological self-direction in the commitment to a processive totality which that implies. It is a commitment to the ultimate ideal of "growth." It says, in effect, give yourself over to process and it will transform your life into growth; it will do for you what you cannot do for yourself. Thus the trust in human sensibilities, when divorced from the human orderer as its gathering focus, can be disastrous. Unless man is the gathering focus for such elemental sensibilities, totalities usurp this power and man surrenders the contributions of himself to the processes of becoming.

Growth, I noted earlier, is as much an ideal of life as any. Only in this manner can there be meaningful talk about "responsible growth." Growth is neither the father of human responsibility nor its child. To relate responsibility to growth spontaneously is to confuse it with human vitality or with simplistic change or flux. Responsibility is not a career or a temporal span. The notion of a "responsible career" in a span of time is itself in need of explanation. The real problem is not that of relating growth to pain and suffering, as Rogers does, but to ontological self-direction, purposive participation and responsibility. Growth as a preset ideal is preconceived by purposive being in relating himself to a scheme of purposive totality. Human growth does not grow on trees or in encounter groups, unless purposive beings participate in such encounter experiences. As a form of goal-directedness, the ideal of growth is a quest in self-direction. We cannot conceive of growth or the process of organic maturation on the human level without purposive being. The philosophy of naturalistic encounters, like existential encounters, is a posture of relationships by participation. Unless man takes responsibility for such encounters, there is no point in talking about responsible growth.

The purpose of this chapter is not to deny the significance of unitive, encounter, and totalistic experience, but to show the ontological relevance of purposiveness to such experiences. I am as concerned about the "feeling of unreality, of impersonality, and of distance and separation that exists" among people as is Carl Rogers. But we do not overcome such alienation, loneliness, and isolation by relating ourselves to a system of totality that is somehow prior to purposive being. This is courting a greater sense of alienation. Neither do we solve the problem by postulating the role of the human orderer in the subject self and its existential encounters. This courts another system of totality. If what is needed is a vigorous philosophy of human participation in existence, man's purposive nature must play a vital role on the level of primal experience. Otherwise we keep playing the game of totalitarian thought, and there is no profit in this, for each alleged system of totality makes man obedient to its own claims of responsibility. To identify with such totalities on the level of immediacy is to confront such schemes of totality in total human weakness. To deny the role of purpose in shaping such totalities is a manifestation of such weakness, for we refuse to take *responsibility for* our comprehensive designs on life.

Rogers is caught in the middle of the subject-object split. His view of social spontaneity leads to growth, Rogers claims. Among the radicals, I noted earlier, social spontaneity leads to the revolution of totality. That spontaneity comes in brands or models of existence is only too evident. The appeal to immediate experience to make these models of existence real simply manifests the ubiquitous nature of man's purposive nature in participation. Processive explanations are just as much caught up in abstractions as are motivational explanations of the ego and its functions. They are different participatory models. To solve the subject-object split by a processive totality is to solve the problem outside a theory of man, and the human orderer goes on all such trips beyond the subject-object split. After all, an encounter group is a planned encounter experience. Its participants are purposive beings. They give themselves to the situation and risk their lives in the flow of experience. Already they are more than "responders" in the flow of processive totality. To deny this is to court the dehumanizing factor of totalitarian thought.

In the final run, this may be more alienating than those at the focal point of attention. What good is it to save man in process if the latter implicates a system of totality which makes a sport out of man's search for wholeness? This may be more damaging in the long run than the "institutional rigidities" an encounter group is designed to escape. Unless man is self-directing in his encounters, with all the ontological status and weight we have given it, man will continue to capitulate to models of totality whose reality he will have to assume because he has divested himself, to begin with, from purposive participation in existence. The point is that whether we choose processive or motivational patterns of explaining the ego and its functions, such explanations are posterior to purposive being if man is regarded as a subject-object dialogue mediated by his purposive nature. Any other meaning of self-direction and self-responsibility plays the role of a servant of some totality. More is needed to liberate the human orderer than the notion of freedom in process, for man is not the gathering focus of such freedom defined as a "relation to." That Rogers is caught in a problem between man's humanity and his science is only too obvious. Giving the subjective self and its experiences a parenthetical role in the system of processive totality is an ambiguous answer for one interested in the "person." If he is looking for a homologous relationship between the subjective and objective models of totality in order to bring the subjective and objective principles together, it is my considered opinion there is no such common structure. There are only models of totality with their reality-claims. Feelings of commitment to relationships, to totalities, while they may be heartwarming and intense, simply give us a schizoid pattern of human responsibility. They immerse life in totality, but they do not guide us. These problems will come to light more as we consider some of the systems of totality in the psychological theories of integration. We turn now to Erik Erikson's view of man in totality.

ERIKSON ON TOTALITY

The above analysis of unitive and encounter experiences has undermined our confidence with respect to man's claims on responsibility. Thus a closer look is called for to see how man is immersed in systems of totality in theories of psychological integration. Erikson's work in ego psychology is as good a place to start as any. He himself has witnessed the "humanistic crisis" in psychology, and he attempts to give certain solutions in terms of a Freudian interpretation to some aspects of this crisis. He speaks out on behalf of the totalistic view in many respects: (1) by making the central problem of modern man focus on the quest for identity or unity; (2) by showing a concern for a world-wide ethics in some universal sense; (3) by absorbing the human orderer in a socionaturalistic totality that includes several orders of existence, such as the somatic, the social, and the personal (in terms of the configurations of mode-zone relationships); (4) by making development and "generative responsibility" the real guides of man; (5) by placing the source of human responsibility in an evolutionary perspective that is inclusive of historical assignments for man; and (6) by making man's purposive nature a secondary and reactive phenomenon to this processive understanding of the ego and its functions.

Perhaps the best place to start is with the role of human purpose in this entire configurational approach to man. Purpose is something acquired in infancy to manage the world of play. Thus it contributes to the "ego strength" of the child in its efforts to handle the beginning world of the imagination. Purpose gives the child mastery over the world of play. More specifically, it derives from "fantasy and play," and this is carried over into the adult world in the form of "play-acting" and "role-playing." Though Erikson takes the world of childhood play seriously (it is as important to the child as thinking is to the adult), purpose is something that is posited at the beginning stage of the life cycle and continues to play this less serious role in adult life. It provides seriousness for the child and lightheartedness for the adult if confusion is not to be confounded by this utterance. Its role in adulthood is to confront the irreversible purposes of reality in the developmental process in each stage of life, and thus comes upon harsher times than it did during the period of infancy. But it originates as an ego function in early childhood to help govern that nebulous world of play and imagination.[11]

Erikson accepts the traditional meaning of purpose as some form of goal-directedness and gives its unifying function a psychoanalytic reading. Thus the seeds of identity are sown at the beginning of the life cycle. The ego's

[11] Erik Erikson, *Childhood And Society* (New York, W. W. Norton, 1950), 185.

function is thus related to its drive for unity, wholeness, integrity, mastery, strength, and synthesis. This drive for unity takes place in a context of the confluent model of participation and responsibility in which man is inter-actionally already goal-directed toward a socionaturalistic totality. To find authenticity, the ego must find its fulfillment in a real and immediate totality. Erikson works out the course of this development in eight stages of life, wherein each stage has the burden of relating man to the larger system of totality that is immanent in the world. The meaning of purpose in this context, as Erikson conceives it, is:

Purpose, then, is the courage to envisage and pursue valued goals uninhibited by the defeat of infantile fantasies, by guilt and by the foiling fear of punish-ment. It invests ideals of action and is derived from the example of the basic family. It is the strength of aim-direction fed by fantasy yet not fantastic, limited by guilt yet not inhibited, morally restrained yet ethically active. That man began as a playing child, however, leaves a residue of play-acting and role-playing even in what he considers his highest purposes.[12]

But what is good pablum for the children at play hardly suffices as the serious source of human goal-directedness and response-relations. People do not live and die for goals playfully. The fact of the matter is that Erik-son cannot give us any serious consideration of human purpose because man is tied to the apron strings of totality, as in the passage below:

One can only conclude that the functioning ego, while guarding individuality, is far from isolated, for a kind of community links the egos in a mutual activa-tion. Something in the ego process, then, and something in the social process is—well, identical.[13]

In fact, Erikson holds that "this mutual activation" or "communality of egos" is itself actuality, reality, and not merely a "recognition of the factual."[14]

Since the pattern is now set for a system of totality, to which man is integrally related and configurationally goal-directed, there is really no longer any room for a human orderer but only the need for an actor and play-acting. Is this a purely "methodogenic" problem? Is this the demand of his model of existence, or the requirement of reality itself? The fact is that once Erikson postulates a system of totality and lines up the ego func-tions in the direction of identity-seeking in the framework of ultimate goal-

[12] Erik Erikson, *Insight And Responsibility* (New York, W. W. Norton, 1964), 122.
[13] Erik Erikson, *Identity, Youth And Crisis* (New York, W. W. Norton, 1968), 224.
[14] *Ibid.*, 328.

direction, there is no need for a serious consideration of purpose or for purposive participation in existence.

Moreover, the inhibitions of purpose by such phenomena as fantasy, guilt, punishment, and other possible flaws of its operation in experience are problems which arise only at the phenomenal level of experience. They do not arise on the ontological level of self-direction, which is the prior meaning of purposiveness. Even if purposiveness is blocked in some of its goals and plans, as is quite likely on this level, this need not obliterate the need for a human orderer. In fact, it calls for a model of purposive being to counteract such phenomenal problems and reorder some of the goals and plans that have been blocked.

Erikson gives us a goal-directed model of the ego in its many functions. Sartre gives us another goal-directed model of selfhood, etc. The point is that there are many models in which the self is goal-directed to itself in larger systems of totality. Why should one prefer Erikson's model over Sartre's, who has less respect for the unconscious strivings of man than Erikson? Erikson views totality as having an "adjustment and survival value." I am certain that Sartre has worked out similar justifications for regarding his model of totality as the real and the immediate one. The point is that such "wholeness synthesis" between man and the world is the design of purposive being in its search for wholeness. Erikson writes: "When the human being, because of accidental or developmental shifts, loses an essential wholeness, he restructures himself and the world by taking recourse to what we may call *totalisms*."[15] The ego achieves this restructuring by relating itself to a system of totality in its more primitive functions, not as a human orderer. Totality, in this case, is a *gestalt* with a sense for an absolute boundary. The ego's search for wholeness or identity is fulfilled only when it makes fitting responses to a real and immediate totality. It does this in the community of egos through mutual activation, in terms of Erikson's theory of psychosexual development. George Klein, who thinks a great deal of this approach, remarks:

Erikson's is a configurational, rather than an energic, conception of psychosexuality; qualitative aspects of mode (apparatus) and zone are fundamental. If one were to look at these in the conventional psychoanalytic framework, one would have to say that such mode-zone applications are simultaneously ego-drive structures. But, obviously, the latter terminology and the tripartite model of ego, superego, and id, whose sense rests on the assumption of distinguishable

[15] Erikson, *Insight And Responsibility*, 93.

energic forces, simply do not suit such a schema as Erikson's, in which the configurations of mode-zone relationships *are* the "drive structure."[16]

What this amounts to is that the ego achieves restructured patterns of totality through more processive rather than reductive drive structures. Man can only be responsible to such drives, whether they are reductively or more processively conceived, and not responsible for them. Erikson's solution to the two kinds of explanations in ego psychology, the processive and the motivational, is to make the drive structure in the ego's strivings and functionings more complex socially and more holistic. But it does not add anything to the schizoid attitude of human responsibility that such a totalistic view has. This is most noticeable in Erikson's discussion of "ego strength" or "ego integrity." For the ego is supposed to be doing what we generally conceive the human orderer as doing, but it is not such a human orderer. It is rather an actor playing roles assigned to it by a system of totality. Note how Erikson sweats the problem of ego integrity:

Lacking a clear definition, I shall point to a few constituents of this state of mind. It is the ego's accrued assurance of its proclivity for order and meaning. It is a post-narcissistic love of the human ego—not of the self—as an experience which conveys some world order and spiritual sense, no matter how dearly paid for. It is the acceptance of one's one and only life cycle as something that had to be and that, by necessity, permitted of no substitutions: It thus means a new, a different love of one's parents. It is a comradeship with the ordering ways of distant times and different pursuits, as expressed in the simple products and sayings of such times and pursuits.[17]

The question is not how one defends his life-style or life cycle, which has come about by an accidental coincidence by fortuitous forces, but how such a life-style has come to be and how it maintains itself with some sense of the human orderer about it. The unity of selfhood, which is a problem for philosophy and psychology alike, has persisted for some time. Humanistic psychology is content to construe the problem in terms of ego involvements or ego functions. Erikson's favorite term for it is ego identity or ego integrity. Let me put the problem another way. We do not help matters too much by answering the first question (Who am I?) by seeking first an answer to the second question (Where do I belong?), for there is prior purposiveness involved in such a quest for identity, namely, man's ontological capacity to be self-directing in his quest for identity, whether this be in himself or beyond himself in some system of totality. There is no

[16] Klein, *op. cit.*, 523–24.
[17] Erikson, *Childhood And Society*, 232.

common structure or a homologous relationship between the ego process and the social process unless one has first identified his model of existence with the reality of processive totality. Erikson needs a theory of human purpose to establish the quest for identity and a relationship between the two questions raised above, which his theory of psychosexual development does not account for. There is no common quest for identity undifferentiated by purposive being. Human identity comes in all brands and models, just as do all goal-directed designs for living. The appeal to immediate experience does not absolve man from having responsibility for such designs in living. If there is need for totalisms, it is postulated by purposive being, even the alleged model-free configurational approach of Erikson.

Ego psychology lacks a concept of the human orderer. Man's drive for unity in himself and beyond in systems of totality assumes a drive structure but not a capacity for purposive participation. My complaint has been that unless man confronts the human orderer in himself and in the social milieu, ego strength can only be postulated in some system of totality which deprives man of his claims on responsibility. The "humanistic crisis" in psychology has centered on the need for such totalisms on the part of man and their possible survival value. Yet we have discovered that such models of totality are a dime a dozen, that they deprive man of his rightful claims on responsibility if they are taken as real and immediate. Humanistic psychology never gives an adequate description of how such totalisms "humanize" or authenticate man beyond his own search for wholeness.

Erikson's failure to define ego integrity in the matrix of totality is understandable. Once man is immersed in a system of totality, his primary responsibility is to the system of development. If ego strength comes from the outside and identity is viewed as the problem of one's belongingness to totality, the source of responsibility, too, must come from the outside. Man is not the gathering focus of the principle of unification, of the drive structure. They reflect the directives of totality. Man can only be *responsible to* such a drive, but not for it. Even when Erikson moves to the larger sphere of "generational responsibility," to the responsibility of the human race universally conceived, the same schizoid attitude toward responsibility prevails. But the questions persist: Why should one be committed to the unification of personality, of the human race, and to the unification of the world? Why should one give his life over to some system of totality when such schemes are of our own making? Unless man is a human orderer, capable of exhibiting in himself the source of human responsibility, why should he be *responsible to* anything? Man "at his most balanced" best is an ideal of ours, like the well-rounded personality; it is not something that a psychosexual development teaches us, or the historical course of evolution. This is the meaning we impose upon the course of events and the shape we try to give our lives. Ontological self-direction is thus prior to such a drive structure that has a built-in unifying principle that is goal-directed to nature. Such a commitment already presupposes our desire to relate to nature on the primal level of experience. It is the product of purposive participation in existence. Erikson's postulate—"the readiness for release"— already manifests this prior purposiveness which his theory does not account for. Unless we take this much for granted about man, responsibility can only mean that man confronts the orderings of totality within himself through his drive structure. But this is not "human responsibility," but nature's. This is what happens to totalistic schemes of responsibility: he must give up the best that is in him, to fit into the orderings of a system of totality. Yet such systems can only be models of existence and existence *qua* existence. If Erikson could show us how his model of the course of development is the developmental course itself, as existence *qua* existence, we may turn a listening ear. But such omniscience is beyond man. He can only come up with models of reality by purposive participation in existence. To speak with assurance about things that are beyond human participation, as totalisms do, is the height of irresponsibility. Such tactics prevent man from ever establishing his claims on responsibility. This means that when we underscore "the direction of what is given in development," we cannot hold this belief in isolation from man's search for wholeness via nature. There is prior purposiveness exhibited in such a belief that Erikson's theory of positionality (man's place in . . .) does not account for. If purpose has an ontological bearing on life and is not mere child's play (as Erikson holds), then such commitment to nature's developmental course must be seen through our models of existence.

If human strength depends on a "total process" that directs both the generations of men and the structure of society, then the self can never surmount its role as being the "regulator" of this process. Since the strength of the ego comes from the total process in its developmental course through history, responsibility can only be a unifying principle of the processive totality. But this already presupposes an identification of Erikson's model of existence with existence *qua* existence. But this is a model of totality competing with others in psychology.

10. Responsibility and the Authentic Life

In James Bugental's humanistic psychology we have another model of totality in search of reality. The totalism advocated by the author is "existential unity" rather than processive unity, or the two modes of encounter are run together as in Rogers. The appeal to immediate experience is essential for this new model of totality as it was for the others. S. S. Bindman thinks that such an appeal to immediacy is an essential trait in humanistic psychology: "Humanistic psychology represents, in part, a return to the dictum of Ernst Mach: physics is the science of mediated experience, and psychology is the science of immediate experience."[1] That such a science rests on indirect procedures does not appear to be a problem to this school of thought. Along with an emphasis on immediacy is a strong commitment to more holistic points of view than in traditional psychology. Bindman does not know what to make of this, what this really means in practice. I have attempted to show that for human responsibility it has ominous consequences in practice in that it commits man to a system of totality based upon unjustified immediate experience.

The existential unity which Bugental espouses has an ontological base: "Being is ultimately a unity, but I can only experience that unity wordlessly."[2] Thus it is free of abstractions and model-making. It is encountered by feelingful or basic awareness. To the extent we talk about it, we invent and construct our approaches and perspectives of this existential unity. To the extent we discover it, we remain mystically silent before it. The task for communication and for living is "to restore the ontologic unity" that is already there in its wordless state. For us, coming in contact with the unity

---

[1] S. S. Bindman, "Subject and Nonstatistical," *Contemporary Psychology*, Vol. 16, No. 3 (1971), 158. This is a review of *Challenges of Humanistic Psychology*.

[2] J. F. T. Bugental, "Values and Existential Unity," in *The Course of Human Life*, ed. by C. Buhler and T. Massarik (New York, Springer Publishers, 1968), 383.

of being means reachieving that unity which is already there beyond a multiplicity of perspectives and beyond the experience diversity. But any commerce with the unity of existence, with the indivisible, is a way of shadowing the unity, and thus we can only experience it in its fragmentive forms. I suppose this is really strong language to put across the *immediate* nature of existential unity.

Subjectivity and the Authentic Life

In order to achieve the science of immediacy, humanistic psychology has emphasized the importance of subject matter over methodological procedures as having prime importance. Lived experience is not a subject matter of the science of humanistic psychology. The subject is more processive, more immediate, and more aware than the object self, the part-man, the nonparticipant, the one who is not feelingfully aware of his life. This is the real self, while the object self is a construct. In Bugental's perspective, the subject is given ontological priority over the object self. It is thus responsible for its actions in situations. The term "I-process" refers to the person as pure subject. It has a double meaning: as being-aware-and-choosing and that of agency. The subject self is equated with the whole man when it is tuned into the system of Being that is this wordless unity of existence.

Subjectivity, however, is not the human orderer that I have postulated, for it implicates a system of totality. Bugental's vision of the authentic life is well expressed in the passage below:

A person is authentic in that degree to which his being in the world is unqualifiedly in accord with the givenness of his own nature and of the world. . . . Authenticity is a term used to characterize a way of being in the world in which one's being is in harmony with the being of the world itself. To say it differently, we are authentic to that degree to which we are at one with the whole being (world); we are inauthentic to the extent that we are in conflict with the givenness of being. . . . By authenticity, I mean a central genuineness and awareness of being. Authenticity is that presence of an individual in his living in which he is fully aware in the present moment, in the present situation. Authenticity is difficult to convey in words, but experientially it is readily perceived in ourselves or in others.[3]

Authentic responsibility would, then, mean relating one's search for whole-

[3] J. F. T. Bugental, *The Search For Authenticity* (New York, Holt, Rinehart, Winston, 1965), 31–32, 33, 102.

ness to the system of being. Responsibility is really a commitment to a system of totality wherein it functions as a unifying principle.

There are elements both from Husserl and Heidegger in Bugental's perspective, whether he gets it directly from there or from the European existential psychologists. The Husserlian element is that one does not question the *Lebenswelt* but only this and that aspect of this world-reality. One merely tunes in on it by commitment. Such questionings merely fragment the existing unity. This is obviously a claim to ultimacy for one's model of existence. But it also has mystic connotations, to the effect that the *All* transcends even the "totality of existence." The Heideggerian element is the emphasis on the system of Being wherein *Dasein* (of which man is an instance) returns to being to achieve an authentic life.

The harmony that Bugental postulates between man and the world is derived from immediate awareness of self and world. Here Bugental sides with phenomenology over science in order to hold the belief that the world is a "construction" of basic human awareness and transcendence. The subjective and intersubjective world is real and immediate; the objective world is "inferred." Thus he does not find the convenient "identity" between the ego process and social process that Erikson thinks is important to his configurational approach to ego psychology. There is no "common structure" between man and the world even when my world and yours overlap. However, communication between my world and yours is possible, and this is what the therapeutic relation depends on. Thus the harmony between one's being and the being of the world is postulated on an individual basis, not on the basis of communality of shared activations, as in Erikson. It is a harmony based on the distinction between values and beliefs.

Values are the basic conditions of being, and beliefs are the individual's responses to such values. The realm of values so defined functions as a unifying agent in life. And the conditions of being-values mediate man's harmony with Being. One confronts such conditions of life by immediate form of experience, Bugental holds:

Our values are expressed in the manner in which we confront the existential givens of being. The point of confrontation is the point at which value is created, is actualized. All authentic values can, ultimately, be traced back to these givens, I believe. Thus all values deal, ultimately, with courage and dread, with being and nonbeing, with life and death.[4]

[4] Bugental, "Values and Existential Unity," 385.

What, then, is man's relation to the world? The authentic relation of man to the world is the response of courage to a system of Being. The authentic life "reachieves" the unity of existence through values, the given conditions of being, even though his views of those conditions and of the unity of existence is perspectival and fragmented. However, Bugental is certain there is that unity of existence in the system of being that the unitive experience of encounters can capture or actualize. When this takes place, and there is some harmony between the givens of being and our beliefs, life is authenticated on the level of primal immediacy. The "wordless unity of the fact of existence" is available to man for possible authentication, for harmonious relation, for identification between one's being and the being of the world. The authentic life, then, consists of linking man's fragmented life with existential totality and the mystic All through feelingful awareness. Basic awareness is thus a reality-feeling and awareness of totality and the conditions of being. Man is not ontologically self-directing in such awareness, as I shall point out later.

The distinction between values and beliefs is a way of relating values to totality rather than to the human orderer. The path to such a totality is humanistic psychology as the science of immediacy which invites all the problems of phenomenology and its *constituted* world-totality, which is a constructed world-view and yet not a construct, etc. The conditions of immediacy thus lead to the conditions of the given in the system of Being. There is an identification here between one's model of existence and existence *qua* existence, where values are hypostatized into the conditions of the given. The notion of ontological subjectivity is regarded as being real and has priority over the object self. Yet subjectivity ignores the demands of the human orderer in participation and sides in with a system of totality. If subjectivity fails to convey the notion of the human orderer in existence, why should the notion of "unique immediacy" be more than a model of subjectivity? If its task is to blend in with the conditions of existence, how, then, is it unique? The notion of ontological freedom, the self's capacity to practice "ontological options" in existence (that is, in lived experience) fares no better. Freedom, like subjectivity, is the servant of totality. The science of immediacy, from the standpoint of my theory, depends on the subjective model of human participation, and this we have discovered is as much a model of participation as some others.

Bugental's distinction between *values* and *beliefs* has many undesirable consequences. There is no conflict possible on the level of values because these are the bedrock conditions that totality imposes upon us through the system of Being. Conflict can arise only on the inferred level of beliefs. While values arise at the point of subjective interaction with existence, these "value-actualizing decisions" and the conditions of existence themselves are the work of Being. Neither the subject self nor his ontological freedom with its flare for "ontological options" are decisive as concepts of the human orderer. Man can only *respond* in the matrix of immediate experience, either in courage or in dread, to these existential *givens* in life. His list of existential values support totality rather than the human orderer. They are: wholeness, rootedness, identity, meaningfulness, and relatedness.[5] It appears in this context that responsibility has its source in existential values enumerated above, not in the human orderer. This means that existential confrontation is not purposive or self-directive confrontation. It suggests a being-confrontation in which purpose defined as self-direction has no ontological status. If this is the case, responsibility can only be a unifying principle in the system of totality. Man is capable of *responsibility to* but not *for* the realm of values and the system of responsibility which they guard. Responsibility is thus tied to the notion of self-transcendence, in which subjectivity transcends itself to implicate totality, which is a subtle form of goal-direction and, therefore, a model of directionality and an abstraction from man's capacity for ontological self-direction. Man is not a human orderer in this science of immediacy, even though on occasion he acts like one in personal encounter.

I mentioned some of the difficulties with Bugental's model of subjective participation and with the notion of ontological subjectivity in order to point up the fact that subjectivity may itself be a model of existence rather than a bastion of immediacy and real participation. To the extent that Bugental reads subjectivity phenomenologically, it is a prepurposive model of personhood manifesting itself through the immediacy of phenomena. To the extent where Bugental's mysticism dominates, there is a postpurposive reading of subjectivity as spirit. Bugental is not aware of the fact that these are already two models of subjectivity, both of which are goal-directed to different schemes of "world-loyalty."

Participation Through Ontological Options

In the above section it was suggested that Bugental identified his model

[5] *Ibid.,* 388.

of authentic being with the process of authentication itself, that he made no effort to distinguish processive from phenomenological encounter. Thus it is necessary to pursue the theme of "ontological options," where real values arise and for which totality is responsibility. Phrases like "the choice of oneself," "total choice," "choice confronting contingency," "responsibility of choice," "respond to our being," and "the response of courage" would all seem to suggest that the personal self of encounter is a real human orderer. But this is not the case at all. The ontological self is merely responding to the call of Being in terms of "active passivity." Unless man as a human orderer is the gathering focus for the responses of dread and courage, he cannot be the source of human responsibility. Nor is he supposed to be. What is it, for example, that gives rise to choice-making and goal-seeking? Bugental replies: "From contingency arises anxiety, but equally it is integral to the possibility of choice."[6] Thus only the "whole person," not one who is self-fragmented and divorced from his own feelings of immediacy, can confront the world of finitude and contingency threatened by the possibility of nonbeing. Choice-making thus has its source in a general ontology and not in the human orderer. This is the first point at which the source of responsibility is spelled out.

What happens to the subject-object split in terms of this theory of choice-making? Unitive experience is its source of inspiration and not the human orderer. Bugental is clear on this matter: "Except for its immense importance, this overcoming of the subject-object split might be subsumed under the recognition of the wholeness of experience. It is certainly a part of that recognition."[7] Only lived and immediate experience can satisfy the conditions of such wholeness. The feeling of rootedness in all mankind, in the system of being, is thus the overcoming of the subject-object split. Bugental continues:

World no longer seems out there and in opposition; rather the boundary between I and world is experienced as fluid and changing with one's awareness and experience. Similarly, one no longer feels the split within himself. The *Me* or *Self* is recognized for what it is, a scrapbook of the past, interesting, personal, but static and not binding upon the liberated I that lives in this minute.[8]

What happens when one lays claim to one's being in a system of totality? To be sure, one does go beyond the subject-object split to a system of to-

[6] Bugental, *Search For Authenticity*, 196.
[7] *Ibid.*, 275.
[8] *Ibid.*

246

tality, but this is only a solution for that particular model of totality. There is no common structure or homologous relationship among systems of totality. Thus each totalism solves the subject-object split in its own peculiar way with no hope of a universal solution to the bifurcation. This would indicate that the respect which Bugental shows for the wholeness of experience as a tool of humanization and actualization is unsupported by the evidence. If "a way of being in one's life" means reifying a model of existence that is identified with cosmic reality, then the promise of authenticity is an illusion. What is of interest in humanistic psychology at this point is that there is a stronger commitment to more holistic points of view, yet no homologous relationship among these different systems of totality has come up. Each writer appears to be operating in his own *Umwelt* with no cognizance of other totalisms existing in the field.

Bugental owes his holistic point of view both to Heidegger and to mysticism. I noted before that the former is a prepurposive model of totality and the latter a postpurposive version of it. This would imply that there would be a competing source of human responsibility, were Bugental aware of the significance of model-making with respect to systems of totality. In Heidegger, "the Being of being" is at the beginning of the life process and prewires man's potentialities for a return to Being, from whence it came. To which model of totality should man conform? To Being or to the All? When we consider all these ramifications of how subjectivity and choice-making implicates systems of totality, we are at a loss to discover the source of human responsibility.

Next let me examine some further consequences of man's "ontological options" to see what subjectivity participation in the realm of immediacy implicating a system of totality really means for Bugental. He calls it "complete awareness and full feelingful assent." The basic meaning of awareness is the universal urge for self-transcendence. I have criticized this notion in *The Promise and Peril of Human Purpose*, where it was concluded that self-transcendence is only a form of goal direction as an elemental model of response and an abstraction from man's capacity to be ontologically self-directing in existence. In Bugental, self-transcendence is goal-directed to the All and provides the path for ontological freedom, emancipation, and self-actualization.[9] Bugental continues: "Awareness is the medium through which we invent-discover our being. Awareness is our

---

[9] *Ibid.*, 277.

being, in the process of be-ing."[10] Subjective participation in being is thus self-transcending participation. Self-transcendence is thus a basic feature of subjectivity and its capacity for "ontological options."

Spontaneity is another trait. This means that on the level of personal encounter there is no model-making and no abstractions. Feeling knows best what life is all about, not the human orderer. Both these notions, self-transcendence and spontaneity, which define the core of selfhood, implicate man in a system of totality. Man is advised to be responsible to that system and to identify with its directives and values as the given conditions of reality. Human participation is the "consequence of a genuine committedness is living rather than a cause or evidence of it."[11] I shall spell out the relation of responsibility to commitment in a later section. Meanwhile, suffice it to say that human participation in existence is secondary to "participation in the whole," in this case to two models of it: the Heideggerian and the mystical. Both responsibility and commitment are prior to ontological self-direction. As Bugental views it:

Commitment is not a subscription to something external to the person's own life. . . . [It] is an awareness, an attitude, a clear and feelingful recognition of being fully present in the moment, making the choices of the moment, and standing by the consequences of those choices whether anticipated or not.[12]

Not much is accomplished in humanistic psychology by rejecting the reality of the object self and the naturalistic totality which that implies, for this school of thought merely comes up with the reality of the subject self which implicates a phenomenological system of totality. For the subject self to be real, it is felt that it must touch a real totality. Bugental is unaware of the fact that commitment to the immediacy of selfhood can be just as external as commitment to a real object self if and when subjectivity implicates a system of totality that is beyond human participation. The wholeness of experience is that elusive externality to which one commits himself in choice-making in the realm of direct experience. The appeal to direct experience or to momentariness is really the gateway to totality. The "now" or "today" is used as an "integrating factor" of life. The present is thus the "operational unit" of goal-setting. But all these phrases and experiences require a theory of purposive being to be operative in the present.

Unless man is self-directing in his awareness, unless he is self-directing

[10] Ibid., 283.
[11] Ibid., 338.
[12] Ibid.

in his time dimensionalities, unless he is self-directing in making the distinction between the fragmentive and a whole life, these terms and phrases come off rather superficially. The danger which exists in such theorizing is that if man is not present in self-direction in and through such choice-making, his subject of being will not save these experiences from superficiality. The point is that they become tools of totality if we discount the integrating factor of man's purposive nature through the capacity of self-direction. Such choice-making is an external affair unless man is present to himself in self-direction. That life is a whole or fragmentive is an issue that a purposive being must decide on. This third-force psychology has no theory to account for the source behind the unifying powers of selfhood. It simply assumes a wordless unity and the identity of selfhood without accounting for the principle that actually unifies selfhood in its quest for wholeness. The fact is that a system of totality, as a model of existence that is mistaken for a real and immediate totality, can be just as oppressive and external as the institutional fragmentation of life that we are experiencing in modern society.

Bugental is more eager to relate choice-making considerations to a system of totality than he is in seeing them as expressions and operations of the human orderer in the matrix of participation. Hence his appeal to unitive experience in the field of immediacy, which is a servant of the directives of totality. When such choices reflect the underlying unity or identity of the I-process, they implicate a system of totality. Life becomes a matter of the "reactualization" of existential unity that reflects a system of totality. Such "existential oneness" displaces the human orderer in the matrix of participation. Man's being has priority to his purposive nature. In the light of my theory, when unitive experience is bifurcated from the human orderer, however intense or dynamic it may be, is more a totalistic than a human virtue.

What kind of commitment does man's drive for unity and totality require of him? Why is commitment to immediate experience so vital to humanistic psychology? Is it because man wants to feel his way into totality through his model of existence? I believe that this is merely a reality-claim for one's model of existence in the absence of a theoretical accounting for a human orderer. The main reason for such commitment on the primal level of experience, prior to ontological self-direction, appears to be that immediacy is the gateway to totality. It is real totality that invests life with wholeness. Thus man is given a chance to "re-experience his wholeness"

249

and his "responsibility in and for his own actions." In his actions and choices he can reenact the wordless unity of existence that would make him whole once more. Subjective participation thus means being conscious of a real totality and of submerging oneself with immediate totality. There is no wholeness in the subject self itself. Thus its search for wholeness must terminate in some real system of totality.

Thus subjectivity does not escape externalization in spite of its depths of inwardness. Such participation refers "to the freely chosen expression of one's being in action" or to the "authentic person's commitment to his own being in the world," which is really an expression of the "authentic person's identity."[13] So long as one is goal-directed to a system of totality, unitive experience, of being goal-directed to oneself, is essential to such an approach. But this may simply be a solution by one system of totality. Since there is no common structure among systems of totality, this may be a stopgap, a temporary solution to the whole issue. When the subject self is advised to confront the wholeness of experience and a real totality, it is a myth to talk about self-actualization. It is a myth because the self is not its own, and it does not confront either the underlying unity of its own I-process or the underlying unity of a real system of totality as a strong human orderer. It confronts them in rudderless striving, mindless inquiry, and primal encounter that is void of purposeful being. Self-actualization is merely awkward language about an emasculated human orderer that must inevitably capitulate to a system of totality in order to experience wholeness. Although this total program is conceived in immediacy, it has an external and programmatic aspect to it. Commitment is to something external, even though inwardly conceived, because it sets its sights on the wholeness that is beyond human participation. When man is advised to conform to the ontological given conditions of Being in order to be authentic, his purposive nature has no ontological status, for he is not a human orderer. When man is advised to be "unqualifiedly in accord with" such a system of totality, when it is only a model of existence invented by a groping science of behavior, the path is open to obscurantism and dogmatism.

That one should desire to be "at one with the whole of being" through feelingful awareness is as much an act of purposeful being as any other. This is another model of man's "participation in the whole." In all such

[13] *Ibid.*, 343.

RESPONSIBILITY AND THE AUTHENTIC LIFE

totalisms, the notion of Otherness seems rather central. It is so also in Heidegger's "ground of being." When Bugental translates Heidegger into humanistic psychology, he conveniently ignores the centrality of Otherness in his system of Being. Thus when man is advised to conform to being, this involves more than self-actualization; it involves conformity to the Other that is always beyond the scope of human participation. The same is true of Bugental's search for the All in mysticism. The directives of the Other take over where subjectivity shows its impotence or its lack of human ordering capacity. This third-force psychology has substituted an intersubjective totality for an objective one in which it can submerge man anew. The humanism is thus deficient because it emphasizes values that are beyond human participation. Such conditions of the *given* as wholeness always elude man's search for wholeness.

The Idea of Authentic Responsibility

The central meaning of responsibility is the "affirmation of one's being as the 'doer'" which is equated with the subject self as agent to the exclusion of the object self to which things are done.[14] Behind the responsible doer is the system of totality as the source of subjective responsibility. It is a form of confrontation with totality in the midst of unitive experience. As a form of "existential confrontation," responsibility is a way of facing up to the system of Being, to face up to anxiety with courage, to give meaning to being-in-the-world in the larger system of Being. Thus it is a form of unifying principle serving the cause of totality. It obliges man to experience the "givens" of being in a system of totality.

Among the *givens* of basic human awareness, however, there is a conspicuous absence of self-direction. What dominates is a form of goal direction underlying human finitude, potential to act, choice, and separateness. Many of these traits of awareness derive from Paul Tillich's theology. The givens of awareness thus relate primarily to a system of totality rather than to the human orderer. Thus responsibility can only be a function of man's relatedness to totality, as in the passage below:

The actions we take are not random, however. We discover that we experience concern about the actions we take as they affect the awareness we have. Thus we discover that we have *responsibility*. Responsibility expresses our involvement in the world and heals the breach that contingency creates, restoring us

[14] *Ibid.,* 23.

to relatedness to the world of which we are aware. . . . There are important psychological consequences of this experience of responsibility and its basis, our potential for taking action. These are the two forms of existential anxiety: guilt and condemnation.[15]

Thus the "potential to take actions" is the source of human responsibility. It is one of the givens of awareness (which is not self-directing). The second aspect of responsibility concerns the consequences of those acts, abounding in guilt and condemnation, the effects of our action-relations to totality. If the self is not its own but implicates a system of totality, then its actions also are derived from immediacy and are not their own. The human agent, as the source of responsible actions, thus breaks down. It is part of the stream of unitive experience and is, in fact, dismissed as a human orderer in that stream or field. Subjectivity is itself guided by unitive experience or the wholeness of experience. The implications of this for responsibility are ominous. It is an existential confrontation with totality, with unitive experience, with encounter experiences as man tries desperately to fit into the system of totality and be submerged by its stream.

The correlate of the "potential for action" is an "ontological given." "Responsibility" is the "subjective experience" in this context and derives from the human potentiality for action. When man contributes to the stream of unitive experience, he is responsible. But his actions do not reflect a human orderer in the stream. They reflect a subject doer only. And he is not his own. Man is a responder in the stream of experience. His actions and choices are correlated with totality and unitive experience, not with the human orderer. What this amounts to is that totality is the source of responsibility. But if totality is only a model of existence, not cosmic reality itself, responsibility has been misplaced at its very source. Thus the definition of responsibility as an "existential confrontation" is a way of dissipating its source in universal immediacy. The science of immediacy, psychology as a third force, fails to recover man's claims on responsibility. It merely substitutes another model of existence for an objective totality. But it has been my discovery that subjective totality can be as external in its meaning as the objective model of existence. Thus even an existential perspective of totality is a model whose abstract nature is hidden by the unjustified mediations in the realm of immediacy. The abstract nature of subjective totality must be fed constantly by the stream of unitive experience to be credible, yet such unitive experience already presupposes the immanence of such

[15] *Ibid.*, 37.

a totality at work in existence. In this context, the concept of responsibility can only mean some form of encounter therapy, where feelings of responsibility are separated from the human orderer and his purposive participation in existence. If there is an existential unity below the level of communication, totality as the mystical and the unspeakable, it has been designed by man's purposive nature and must be vitalized and revitalized as an abstraction by unitive experience.

Concern for actions need not reflect human attitudes or self-direction. This Heideggerian term, which Bugental uses uncritically, is the guardian of *Dasein's* relation to Being. It is not an anthropological term and does not suggest human responsibility for one's actions. Care merely carries out the intentions of the system of Being. It is the servant of the Other in the system of Being. The commitment to totality is prior to the commitment to man in both writers. Responsibility is the servant of authentic man, and man is authenticated only if he is goal-directed to the system of Being. Otherwise he is inauthentic. In this context, responsibility does not bear the stamp of man's directionality. It is a sentinel function in the system of Being. It carries out the directives of totality. If responsibility is only the "subjective correlate of the existential given of the ability to take action," man has not yet confronted the "human orderer" in primal experience; he has just resigned himself to the fate of responsibility in the system of totality. But the alternative of whether man confronts the wholeness of his being in the system of Being or adjusts to the rules of society, as purported goals of therapy, presupposes a prior purposiveness that Bugental's theory does not account for.

CRITIQUE OF ONTOLOGICAL FREEDOM

The ontologically free subject of being is a post-Freudian view of man and suggests a new potential of man who is more than an object. But this freedom may be just another empty word suggesting a general ontology which has man in its grip; it is not suggestive of the self-directing human orderer with a stake in such a general ontology. The general ontology assigns man the proper positionality in terms of ontological options. In my perspective, it is a prepurposive model of freedom, since purpose as self-direction is excluded from primal encounter experience as is man's intellect. The model of human accountability is also one of commitment to totality prior to self-direction. One is advised to fully confront the existential anxieties of being in the system of Being, not to play the role of purposive participation in existence. Responsibility is this responsiveness on the part of existential man, the authentic one, to such encounter experiences. When one conforms to Being through one's being and its feelingful awareness, one is most responsible because one is, then, most authentic. Responsibility is the posture of the authentic man committed to a system of Being. While man is not responsible for Being he is advised to be responsible to it. This schizoid attitude of responsibility derives, in part, from the notion of ontological freedom, which I shall criticize below.

One, ontological freedom implicates a system of totality. The requirement that such a totality be real and immediate is the price the psychologist pays in having to relate ontological freedom to a system of being that is prior to the human orderer.

Two, human potentialities are prewired, as Heidegger's *Dasein* is (for a return to Being), so that human fulfillment requires a real and immediate totality for authentication. Yet it is a model of existence only parading as a real and immediate totality. I have found no common structure among such systems of totality to speak of. One can claim formal homologous relationships among them, but this amounts to a discussion of geometric patterns only. The fact is that the purported universal thread that is supposed to be common to them often turns out to be another scheme of totality with new reality-claims of its own, as I noted earlier about Paul Ricoeur's perspective. Thus man is not self-directing in his potentialities that would bring about his self-actualization. Such self-realization is dependent on the possibilities of the given totality operating in unitive experience and in encounter situations or upon the interaction of man with the given conditions of his being. But such values that arise from this fear of intersubjectivity are really the manifestations of Being's intentions. Unless man is self-directing in his potentialities and in his basic awareness of life, self-actualization can only be a derivative process which ontological freedom cannot restore into a human orderer. The fact is that the task of life, according to Bugental, is to reachieve that unity of existence which is there in its mystic slumber, wordless in its indivisibility, but omnipotent in its claims upon life.

Three, choice-making confronts all the major themes of a system of totality, but it never experiences the presence of a human orderer in ontological self-direction. He is replaced by the unitive experience that serves the intentions of totality. From my point of view, such choice-making on the phenomenal level of experience is an operational aspect of ontological

254

self-direction, just as goal-seeking is. The attempt to view freedom in terms of one's being is an attempt to make it a primitive term. This enterprise is a failure because the subject of being implicates a system of totality that controls the possibilities in such being. For choice-making takes place in the stream of experience where it is not in command of its situations or encounters. In fact, it is rather led by them. Purpose and reason are both excluded from primal experience in choice-making. Feelingful awareness, which best describes the stream of experience, is the matrix in which choice-making operates. Thus a being-encounter is not a purposive encounter in terms of self-direction; it is not encounter as self-directing.

Perhaps the implications of Bugental's perspective will become clearer if we state some of the significant experiences of the authenticated man. Such experiences are prior to ontological self-direction. They are: fantasy and imagination, the experience of suchness, the freedom of awareness (of self-transcendence, not of ontological self-direction), and creative emptiness. Let me take them in the order listed. Fantasy and imagination play a significant role in the emergent authentic man, the man who knows his goal-directed relations to a system of Being. This aesthetic dimension of man, suggesting a certain artistry of living, is a "way of stretching and celebrating the freedom of awareness" and thus relates to ontological freedom and its options that I discussed above.[16] The aesthetic dimension here does not lead to revolution, as in Marcuse. The aesthetic dimension, in fact, refers to the wholeness of experience. It may even be the appeal of immediate experience as a field or stream. It has qualities of self-transcendence where the I-process communes with the All in mystic splendor. In this religious context, it is a lure from beyond, from the future, from the Eschaton. It relates to a postpurposive model of totality and not to the Heideggerian emphasis on the system of Being which is at the beginning of the life cycle. In short, fantasy and the imagination, to the extent they celebrate ontological freedom and its options, to that extent it is imagination serving a system of totality of which man's being is a functionary.

The experience of suchness is another feature of the authentic man, and this involves a kind of mystic rapport with life, a kind of "silent communion of the viewer and the view," as in the following passage:

Suchness is the aware opening of one's being to the givenness of all being in which the gap between one's own being and all being is transcended. . . . In

[16] *Ibid.*, 399.

suchness we transcend apartness and know oneness without straining, without thought, without self-consciousness.[17]

Apparently Bugental thinks that the height of living is to be discovered by crawling into life rather than participating in it. Is this a way of seeking the permanence of immediacy to stave off the flux of experience? Is this a form of transcendent escape to a system of totality?

The mystic notion of suchness is a good example of submerging the human orderer in a system of totality that is regarded as real and immediate. It is a way of being a creative coworker with the process of creativity itself, and this flows in from below and from above man. It involves the total self-giving of the subject self in open and free awareness, in ontological freedom; it involves "total awareness, with all one's awareness being devoted to the intercourse with the panorama." Is this the experience of instant being in the system of Being?

The language of closure and openness concerning freedom and awareness is in essence a prepurposive discourse about a prepurposive model of man. It means closure with respect to the human orderer and an openness to totality. It has nothing to do with the human potential. It is rather a new form of determinism about human potentialities. Man is free only to actualize that which a system of totality or a system of Being intends for him. He thus has the ontological option to feel his way gropingly into the system of responsibility that is assigned to him through the potentialities of being.

The third feature of authenticity is the freedom of awareness or the ontological freedom I criticized above. Such "full awareness is a kind of interpenetration with that to which we attend: This is the element of suchness that is evidenced when we overcome the separation between observer and observed. Full awareness transcends the subject-object dichotomy."[18] This is a good example of how ontological freedom serves the intentions of totality rather than the human orderer. This is what happens when subjectivity, unitive and encounter experiences, are deprived of the mediation of purposive being in the construction of such systems of totality. The whole mistake rests on one simple misidentification, of identifying one's model of existence with existence as existence.

Before there can be such a thing as ontological freedom, defined as open,

[17] *Ibid.*, 400.
[18] *Ibid.*, 401.

direct, and free awareness, there must be "directed awareness." The question now is, Who does the directing of human awareness: man as a human orderer or a system of totality that orders man? Bugental considers the notion of self-transcendence as a basic feature of man. I do not view this term as a primitive because it is an abstraction of ontological self-direction, a form of goal direction, and a servant of totality. It leads to all sorts of ultimate goals. Totalists have been fond of this term throughout history. When ontological freedom is given its foundation in the universal urge for self-transcendence, its freedom of awareness can only be expressed in terms of a goal-directed awareness. There are many such models of goal-directed awareness in the use of self-transcendence as a basic feature in a theory of man.

The fourth feature of the authentically emergent man is the concept of creative emptiness. This is the ebb and flow of immediacy in us, and of listening to it, which liberates us from the bondage to the Self. It is the opposite of role-playing attitudes. "To know my being in pure I-process terms, freed of the substantive qualities of the Self, still eludes me. Yet there is the potential for ultimate creativity in the very emptiness of the fact of being, in its openness to whatever we will write."[19] Creative emptiness is the experience of "the pure subject of being." It is really the essence of pure irreducible subjectivity as over against the object self.

What is most evident in the above characterization of authenticity is the absence of the human orderer in the notion of subjectivity and ontological freedom. In fact, the only way the subject of being can be regarded as real and immediate is by relating the subject self to a system of real and immediate totality. Thus ontological freedom or open awareness is essentially a freedom within the system of Being, with which we identify our human freedom. Thus the whole matter hinges on the fact of whether a system of totality is real and immediate or whether it is a model of existence, as I claim it is. If it is only a model of totality, then ontological freedom is not a victory for the human orderer. It is rather a functionary of a system of totality.

Four, in further criticizing the notion of ontological freedom as a field of openness between beings and Being, it should be noted that such fields of unitive experience come in many brands or models, depending upon the dialectical patterns that have been used to design the unity in such en-

[19] *Ibid.*

counter experience. Since such unitive experience assumes the underlying unity of totality within immediacy, ontological freedom has its source outside of man. The only way man can claim it for himself is to claim immediate rapport with such a system of totality, which is what the theory of self-actualization presupposes. It is interesting to note that in discussing the many characteristics of the process of actualization, there is no mention of self-direction or of the human orderer or the relation of man's purposive nature to primal, encounter experience. What this amounts to is that Bugental is more preoccupied with Being's potentialities in man than with man's relation to these potentialities.

What happens to the concept of responsibility in the context of ontological freedom? If such freedom is itself derivative, the system of totality becomes the source of human responsibility. The primal meaning of responsibility is commitment to a system of totality with which one has identified the subject of being. This is essentially a therapist's view of responsibility, to give the patient an increased sense of wholeness with himself and the cosmos. It means having the ability to stand behind one's words and deeds and thoughts. Thus being responsible for the patient is tantamount to curing him, as Hellmuth Kaiser remarks: "Anything that increases the patient's feeling of responsibility for his own words must tend to cure him."[20] This view of responsibility is essential to good therapy. It is also a sign of health for the patient wins through to identity and self-transcendence. Bugental himself advises such authentic commitment where a person genuinely accepts responsibility for his feelingful life or for his total being. Such a reachievement of a responsible identity is accomplished by authentically relating to the existential unity discoverable in a system of being. Such an identity is a growth-motivation experience and not the goal of a human orderer in existence. The commitment Bugental has in mind is not external to a person's life. From my perspective, it is a goal-directed external model of responsibility because it is prior to ontological self-direction and prior to the interests of the human orderer. The very fact that a person accepts responsibility in courage or rejects it by fleeing from it in dread or anxiety shows the operational aspects of an ontological human orderer which Bugental's theory excludes. An awareness of the givens of being is not enough to account for human responsibility in the sense that I am using it, where man confronts the human orderer in himself and

[20] H. Kaiser, "The Problem of Responsibility in Psychiatry," in *Advances in Psychiatry*, ed. by M. B. Cohen (New York, W. W. Norton, 1959), 237–38.

society, because man himself has fashioned the systems of totality in which such given conditions of existence are given meaning and definition.

Six, our last critique of ontological freedom and the responsibility it evokes is concerned with the status of the ontological givens of existence. The basic "given," I have noted, was existential unity, which I have denied and claimed that such givens cannot be stated apart from human motivation and apart from purposive being and its mediative functions. Bugental has great respect for the given conditions of being as he has defined their meaning in the system of totality. It is his model of existence which defines the nature and the status of the givens. The upshot is that man should show respect for the givens of existence by being *responsible to* them. Such given conditions are the counterparts of purposive participation in existence. They provide the unitive structure that underlies the stream of experience. What is to be said of this view which holds that these given conditions are the bearers of the intentions of totality? Are these givens merely the demand of Bugental's totalistic perspective of existence, or is it the requirement of life itself?

I think it is the requirement of the subjective model of participation, which defines the givens differently than the objective model of participation, which Bugental now prefers to the scientific world-view. This perspective derives from the identification of his model of existence with existence *qua* existence. It is a claim to ultimacy by an appeal to immediacy and the identification of reality with immediacy. The "givens" as "unifying agents of Being" provide for the unification of selfhood and the existential oneness with all being. The very fact that the givens play this existential role of unification is indicative of the fact that subjective participation in existence lacks a human orderer, that it must be unified from below or from above itself, that is to, from beyond itself. The function of unification, however, can only be maintained if it can be shown how the model of totality is more than a model and an abstraction from human participation in existence. To leave the issue of the given in the hands of feelingful awareness for the guidance of life is a risk I am unwilling to take if these untutored elemental responses to life, like courage and anxiety, are not themselves meaningfully related to the human orderer. Unless man is self-directing in such elemental modes of response, the responding agent cannot be a responsible person in participation.

The upshot of Bugental's theory of responsibility, which rests on ontological freedom, is that responsibility itself is just as *angst ridden* as the subject of being which is insecure unless it works out a feelingful intimacy with a system of totality. To make *anxious responsibility* the *standard* of human potentiality in the healing arts is to emphasize the risk-taking side of life. But such courage in the face of being may be called something else when the lid is taken off the risk-taking, as in the identification of one's model of existence with existence *qua* existence. There are risks enough in the precarious conditions of life without making out a case for surplus risks that come from mistaken identifications about what is real and what is not. Feeling one's way into a standard of responsibility is the greatest risk of all because spontaneous feelings, while they give us vitality, do not give us the human sense of responsibility. Such feelings are already committed to a hidden standard of responsibility which the system of totality intends to order.

When responsibility is made the subjective correlate of the given conditions of being, its encounters are goal-directed experiences that no longer have the benefit of the human orderer. These are untutored responses and are themselves in need of a pedagogue. Bugental's perspective demonstrates that when responsibility is made a function of subjectivity, it, too, must fall prey to the system of totality, along with the subject of being. In contrast, when it is made the function of an ontological human orderer, which mediates the principle of subjectivity in its theory of man, then man becomes the source of such systems of responsibility as Bugental has in mind. Commitment to any system of totality that requires ontological priority to the human orderer is a species of totalitarian thought, whether it is practiced in psychology or philosophy. Unless man is the gathering focus for response-relations, there is no way to escape this tendency toward totalitarian thinking.

Unless man can show *responsibility for* becoming the subject in his world of experience and account for being the experiencer of experiences, he serves a system of totality, one of his own making but one which is attributed to the Other. This leads to a schizoid theory of responsibility that is ridden with anxiety and risk-taking. It is not enough to create meaningfulness in life if that creativity comes from below or from above man, for man is not responsible for such creativity. He can only follow its directives when it manifests itself to him in the matrix of participation. Acceptance of responsibility means acceptance of creativity also. When man contributes to his becoming as a human orderer, in the capacity of ontological self-direction, he manifests responsibility for the creation of meaningfulness. He not only understands what he creates but stands behind such acts of creativity in the role of a purposive being. Re-experiencing the wholeness that is the wordless unity of existence lacks the quality of being *responsible for* one's creations. The wholeness of unitive experience merely leads man into the trap of totality and claims of ultimacy for which there is little justification.

II. Responsibility in Fromm's Constellation of Totality

The charm of Erich Fromm lies in the fact that he is a complex dialectical thinker but a simple and clear writer. I hope to unravel in this chapter some of the turning points in his thinking on the issue of human participation, directionality, and responsibility. These three terms are essential to his constellation of totality. Fromm himself has faced the dilemma of whether to root responsibility in a human orderer or in a system of totality, and he chose the latter alternative. He derives subjectivity from objectivity and defines participation and directionality in terms of man's dialectical positionality in nature. These decisions involve him in certain philosophical perspectives of man which he himself has labeled humanism. I am concerned in appraising the philosophical implications for the human orderer and his responsibility in Fromm's humanistic system of totality.

There are several ideas that commit Fromm to a system of totality which he believes is model-free. One is the notion that each person carries within himself "all of humanity," that he is the bearer of the universal. Mankind, as a smaller totality, implicates the larger totality of nature which Fromm conceives dialectically. Hence responsibility, which symbolizes freedom rather than unfreedom, also bears the stamp of the universal. According to Fromm, "The humanistic conscience is its readiness to listen to the voice of one's own humanity and is independent of the orders given by anyone else."[1]

Fromm has been a popular spokesman for the antiauthoritarian humanistic conscience which implicates mankind and the larger totality of nature. He himself has encouraged those elemental modes of response in man which support unitive experience and totalistic participation in life. But he has bound man to a system of dialectics which submerges man in a system of totality from which it is difficult to extricate the humanity of

[1] Erich Fromm, *The Revolution of Hope* (New York, Harper and Row, 1968), 82.

262

man. This dialectical view of man is another feature which commits man to a system of totality rather than to the human orderer. Man is involved in nature but rises above it in reason, imagination, awareness, and transcendence. As a "freak of nature," man reflects that stage of evolution where life is aware of itself. This self-awareness need not imply a human orderer in existence. In fact, life's awareness of itself in its totality implicates a system of real and immediate totality. Man's amphibious nature is what gives him feelings of loneliness and separateness which he would overcome by committing himself to a system of totality that is more than a model of existence. This very precarious condition of man drives man for wholeness, to come up with a new sense of transcendent unity which is different from that original unity of existence that man had as a piece of nature. To seek that oneness with nature which primitive life experienced is a form of retrogressing. Fromm is interested in a new dimension of unity based on basic human awareness of totality in himself and beyond. This progressive search for wholeness in a real and immediate system of totality goes beyond mere animal survival. As Fromm views it: "The wish to be alive 'beyond survival' is the creation of man in history, his alternative to despair and failure."[2] Man's search for wholeness is not yet self-realization. Without a real and immediate system of totality which would crown this quest, man remains a bundle of contradictions with the ensuing feelings of separateness and loneliness. Man must be more than an animal to reach such integral unity with totality, yet he is not a human orderer that is self-directing in human participation. While he practices love and reason to search for this new equilibrium, he can reach authenticity only by being implicated in a system of totality. For it is the "whole man" that utilizes love and reason in its drive for unitive experience, and this implicates a human striving that has intimate ties with totality.

To be sure, man has a more dynamic role to play in such a system of totality, but he is not self-directing in his awareness, for such self-transcendence implicates man as being goal-directed to a system of totality. On his own, man is never free of the basic rift in his nature, between nature and his awareness of it, but in a system of totality it is possible for him to achieve a new sense of unity. That such a system of totality is real and immediate, not a model of existence, Fromm makes clear by emphasizing the significance of birth and of the continuous nature of the birth process in

---

[2] *Ibid.*, 86.

life as the individual and mankind together strive to achieve a new sense of their wholeness.

The problem, then, which the human race as well as each individual has to solve is that of being born. Physical birth, if we think of the individual, is by no means as decisive and singular an act as it appears to be. . . . Actually, the process of birth continues. . . . Birth, then, in the conventional meaning of the word, is only the beginning of birth in the broader sense. The whole life of the individual is nothing but the process of giving birth to himself; indeed, we should be fully born, when we die—although it is the tragic fate of most individuals to die before they are born. . . . The birth of man began with the first members of the species *homo sapiens*, and human history is nothing but the whole process of this birth.[3]

This, then, is a third aspect in Fromm's effort to relate man to a system of totality that is more than model-free. Man is part of the creative process in relating his search for wholeness with a real and immediate system of totality. Fromm believes that no man escapes this alternative of regression and progression in his drive for wholeness, that "all essential human cravings are determined by this polarity."[4] He concludes his book, *Man For Himself*, with the same message: "Man's main task in life is to give birth to himself, to become what he potentially is. The most important product of his effort in his own personality."[5]

As a neo-Freudian, Fromm emphasizes culture and history as significant parts of the new and real totality. Being a piece of nature is no longer a workable totality for man. The real totality has now the Marxian image stamped upon it. In order to claim immediacy and reality for this new sociohistoric totality, Fromm is eager to transfer the meaning of biological birth to sociohistoric continuity to give credibility to the process of creation that is model-free. The real nature of man is now newly and dialectically ordered. Man is goal-directed toward a sociohistoric totality. Since this goal-directedness is real and not a model of human participation of history, it determines all human purposes and achievements. Consequently, man's search for himself can only be accomplished by immersing himself in the creativity that is totality. This is what Fromm means by "life aware of itself" and by the injunction to "practice life." When man rejects Fromm's model of existence, he falls into the category of "alienation."

[3] Erich Fromm and R. Xirau, *The Nature of Man* (New York, Macmillan, 1968), 309–10.

[4] *Ibid.*, 311.

[5] Erich Fromm, *Man For Himself* (New York, Rinehart, 1947), 237.

Fromm has identified his model of existence with existence as existence. To arrive at the experience of oneness with all that exists (what I have called "participation in the whole") thus comes at a great cost. Fromm believes that it is still possible to have a notion of individuality as a separate entity in such a holistic context. Perhaps, but this is not the "human orderer" we have been seeking. Within the system of totality, man has the freedom of *alternativism*, which is a freedom determined by man's biosocial nature and life's awareness of the contradiction that man himself is in nature. This means that man has freedom within the structures of his existence. He has the freedom to respond to the system of totality (dialectically ordered) by affirming its directionality and responsibility as his own. The self achieves its real nature by making the system of totality its main responsibility. Here, freedom is nearly synonymous with destiny. This is brought out by the dialectical relation which holds that man is a "constellation of forces structured in a certain and ascertainable way" and "life aware of itself."

It is freedom rooted in transcendence, which is that universal urge in us that finds its total fulfillment in the system of totality. The primary directionality is this capacity for self-transcendence, which Fromm has taken from its theological and philosophical orbits of meaning and placed in the individual organism. This universal urge is similarly goal-directed toward totality. Since it provides the primary guidance for man's freedom, it can be said that freedom, too, is goal-directed toward the hoped for unity in the system of totality. Fromm remarks:

The basis for love, tenderness, compassion, interest, responsibility, and identity is precisely that of being versus having, *and that means transcending the ego.* It means letting go of one's ego, letting go of one's greed, making oneself empty in order to fill oneself, making oneself poor in order to be rich.[6]

THE PATH TO SELF-REALIZATION

Fromm's perspective requires that man give up his capacity for ontological self-direction to find realization in a system of totality. Man must empty himself of being a human orderer and make himself poor in this ability in order to find fulfillment in totality. Direct experience in the form of spontaneity is the bearer of the directives of totality and is the means to self-realization. Spontaneity can overcome the externality in alienating experiences. Such immediacy of self-expression enables one to confirm

[6] Fromm, *Revolution of Hope*, 85–86.

himself in the system of totality by affirming its intentions and structures and making them one's own.

The path to self-realization is discovered also by self-transcendence, in which human freedom is rooted. This universal urge is dialectically controlled and goal-directed to the sociohistoric totality. Self-transcendence is a primitive feature of man's essential nature, for it is that basic awareness of life that enables man to progress toward his destiny. It is a quality of organismic life, a finite and temporal notion, deepened by psychoanalytic meaning. In Fromm's perspective, it is the equivalent to "self-transformation," the vehicle by which one achieves the new unity. Might it not be an insecure wish, however, if man is a basic contradiction, with no deity to help him extricate himself from the contradiction that he is?

The search for wholeness by the act of love is central to Fromm's plan for self-realization. It is an elemental mode of response on the part of man, an "act of penetration," which grasps the meaning of union better than any other mode of response. Fromm claims that

In the act of fusion I know you, I know myself, I know everybody—and I "know" nothing. I know in the only way in which knowledge of that which is alive is possible for man—by the experience of union, not by any knowledge our *thought* can give. The only way of full knowledge lies in the act of love; this act transcends thought, it transcends words. It is the daring plunge into the essence of another person, or into my own.[7]

Speaking of the "limitations and dangers" of psychology, Fromm continues: "Psychology becomes a substitute for love, for intimacy, for union with others and oneself; it becomes the refuge for the lonely, alienated man, instead of being a step toward the act of union."[8]

Love, along with other spiritual qualities, is the "leap" to unitive experience, to encounter experience, to realization in a system of totality. It is thus a greater asset than knowledge in reuniting man with totality. If man is to continue the process of birth in self-realization, he should "take the leap into the act of commitment, concern, and love." Central to man's integrating experiences are the act, the commitment, the leap, the act of love, and, Fromm adds, "the responsible act of commitment."[9] All these terms and phrases suggest an appeal to immediacy as the path to totality.

[7] Erich Fromm, "The Limitations and Dangers of Psychology," in *Religion and Culture*, ed. by Walter Leibrecht (London, SCM Press, 1959), 33–34.

[8] *Ibid.*, 35.

[9] *Ibid.*, 36.

Man's search for wholeness of experience is an immediate yearning. The cry of loneliness and separation is the basic motivation for unitive experience and totality.

The unconscious also has a great role to play in the path to self-realization. As Friedman suggests:

> One source of such transcending . . . is his unconscious, which to Fromm is neither good nor evil, rational nor irrational, but both—all that is human. The unconscious is the whole man, the universal man, minus the social part. . . . "To become aware of one's unconscious," therefore, "means to get in touch with one's full humanity and to do away with barriers which society erects within each man and, consequently, between each man and his fellowman."[10]

When the concept of the unconscious is related to spontaneity, self-expression means a prepurposive search for wholeness and relatedness. It is prior to ontological self-direction, for man's elemental modes of response are separated from the human orderer. In fact, they implicate a system of totality which operates its intentions from below. The admonition to "practice life" can only mean a commitment to a system of totality prior to man's capacity for self-direction. The prepurposive model of totality is thus the lure for both the individual and mankind. The goal which Fromm envisions for humanity is to transform the unconscious to consciousness, to have rapport with the wholeness of existence. Spontaneity and productive work are essential to the realization of such union.

Spontaneity plays such a significant part in self-realization that it is essential to examine it more critically to see its implications for human responsibility. As a form of subjectivity, it relates to the concepts of the "whole man" and the system of totality. As a form of derived experience, it needs a system of totality to make it real, and, in turn, spontaneity is needed to breathe life into the abstraction of totality. As a form of subjectivity, it is itself in need of directionality and responsibility. Fromm's appeal for relatedness and union depends on these basic human sensibilities, on man's elemental modes of response. Unitive experience thus needs spontaneity to give it processive permanence in the midst of change and flux. In Fromm's system, however, a dialectical totality is in control of human sensibilities and not the human orderer. The latter is alienated from such elemental acts because the primary drive for the lonely and separate man is the need for wholeness. Because the human possibilities are prewired by the system

---

[10] Friedman, *To Deny Our Nothingness*, 235.

of totality, the self-expressions of spontaneity are proper responses for their realization.

The human orderer is thus dissipated in life's awareness of itself. The goals man makes are not his own. They reflect the basic schism of his nature. The choices he makes are similarly dominated by the alternatives that life sets up for him. His entire life, in fact, is controlled by the system of totality which has invested him with its sociohistoric possibilities. The primary task, then, is to reunite with the system of totality, to open the path to spontaneous experiences, the source of unitive experience in its myriad forms and the path to human responsibility. Spontaneity means that man is created from below and he must first be responsible to its directives *via* self-expression. However, one is not responsible for this creativity and self-expression. The act of continuous birth and the creation of ourselves is not our own. We can only be responsible to its directives. Thus Fromm's belief in the importance of spontaneity as a guide to life becomes the basis for the schizoid theory of responsibility I noted in other humanistic psychologists. Yet Fromm calls this form of immediacy "positive freedom" or "the process of growing freedom." It is thus a freedom of relating to a system of totality. Both the immediacy of self-realization and the immediacy of totality are thus free of model-making and abstractionism on the level of lived experience.

Perhaps the best way to focus on the problem of spontaneity is to see it as the central motivating factor of man in his relationship to life and joy. Fromm viewed this effort as "strengthening the life-loving side in oneself," as he characterized the biophilous conscience. Friedman's criticism of Fromm's perspective is very much to the point on this issue when he writes:

Fromm cannot capture *man* in the sheer love of life since man's relation to life is different from that of the rest of life. Life is not worth loving and enjoying unless implicit in the concept of life is living well. Growth is not necessarily a good unless implicit in the concept of growth is growth in a direction that realizes positive values. Fromm's syndrome of growth does indeed imply such values—love, independence, openness—but for that very reason his scheme is circular. His ethics of growth rests on another set of ethics which in turn he seeks to ground in the ethics of growth.[11]

Fromm's image of man as a "completely human being" suffers from the same fate as the notion of growth. Neither can be stated in terms that are model-free or free of human valuation. There is an ideology critique in

11 *Ibid.*, 238.

Fromm, as I noted earlier in Herbert Marcuse. They have in common the Marxian image of man as a social being. I am in agreement with Friedman's criticism of Fromm's position, but I would carry it a step further. One cannot identify his model of existence with existence as existence, as Fromm has done in relating man to the totality of life. This is the basic confusion. The further ethical conclusions follow this mistaken identification. It is necessary now to be more specific in criticizing Fromm's notion of spontaneity.

One, spontaneity is the servant of totality and does not liberate the human orderer, as Fromm supposes it does. He is correct in speaking of "our fear of spontaneity" as a modern problem of alienation. He deals with alienation largely in terms of external and cultural conditions. He offers a simplistic solution to it by turning inward, to existential subjectivity, to achieve the "act of oneness" with life or to have "a total intuitive grasp" of life in its lived presence. Fromm believes that subjectivity in the form of spontaneity is the bridge by which man transcends the ego and unites with a system of totality and has the benefit of the guidance of unitive experience. It is interesting, however, to note that spontaneity is characterized as being real only if it implicates a larger system of totality that is similarly regarded as being real.

Two, spontaneity is a prepurposive model of subjectivity. Subjectivity can also be viewed postpurposively. Fromm confuses these two models of spontaneity, just as he runs together existential and naturalistic modes of encounter, assuming they are one thing. Why it should be called a form of positive freedom and growing freedom is difficult to see because it is freedom within the structures of existence, freedom depending on the total person in a system of totality. It is goal-directed freedom, and spontaneity itself is goal-directed self-expression. Both come under the orbit of meaning that I would term "active passivity." In this context, spontaneity means receiving the directives from totality, to which one has committed himself, to which he is responsible. Man does not have the freedom for purposive participation in existence, that is to say, he is not self-directing in the structures of existence. The positive freedom that Fromm's productively oriented person has is free in relation to totality but not in relation to his purposive nature. Man's goal-direction to totality is prior to self-direction, as I have used the term.

Three, Fromm mentions the child and the artist as the great exemplars of spontaneity. The whole point about both is they bear no burdens of responsibility. The child is exempt from it and is not accountable till a certain age. When the artist endorses the pre- and postpurposive model of immediacy and creativity, he is not responsible in and for his creativity either. If he looks at creativity *from below*, then nature or the unconscious is responsible for the creative life. When he looks at it *from above* (in terms of the great analogy to God), then God or some Other is responsible for his creativity. Spontaneity means to practice something, to give self-expression, but not to be responsible for it, or for its participation, or for its directionality. Has Fromm given a premature discussion and solution of the relation of spontaneity to freedom? Or is this a calculated game for the system of totality as against man, the human orderer? In either case, self-realization through the system of totality is a precarious gain. If it is a gain at all, it is on the side of totality, as I noted. In terms with its linkage with responsibility, it can only mean "responsibility to."

Four, spontaneity is not its own; it belongs either to the human orderer or to a system of totality. In fact, it is a way of breathing new life into an abstraction called totality. Thus to have a science of immediacy is somewhat premature because there is a prior problem that must be faced: how such a form of immediacy is related or identified with reality, and also whether spontaneity, as a direct form of experience, is controlled by our models of existence. Unless such freedom is first related to a human orderer and self-direction, its capacity for self-expression can only mean adherence to the directives of totality.

Five, the self-expression of our potentialities presupposes the self-directing character of purposive being. Otherwise there is no self to express itself. Since man's given potentialities are not his (but those of a given totality), he has some freedom only of actualizing what is there as given by totality. Potentialities, too, must then be related to directionality. Since Fromm does not relate them to man, he relates them to totality. He justifies all this by an uncritical belief in the immediate wholeness of experience, a romantic version of life. Unless we assume that in some real sense man is self-directing in human participation, the concept of self-realization is a myth. Unless man is self-directing in his potentialities, there is no way to firm up notions like the "acceptance" or the "spontaneous affirmation" of our powers. Human vitality in the form of creativity and dynamism is insufficient to account for human responsibility either for one's own life or for a system of totality. Perhaps Fromm's drive for perfectionism is so strong that the drive for wholeness must terminate in a real and immediate totality instead of a model of existence. Besides being a philosophic problem, it may also be a psychoanalytic one.

Six, if spontaneity is real only because subjectivity is real, and the latter is real as a completely human being only if a real system of totality is assumed, the model of creativity which follows this order of things must be prepurposive. This model requires that one be responsible to creativity or to spontaneous activity but not responsible for them. One can only be "genuinely related" to them but not a human orderer in such activities. This is the confluent, pragmatic model of participation where life cooperates with Life to sustain itself in meaning. That this leads to a schizoid theory of responsibility does not trouble Fromm in the least, as the following remarks make clear:

Ours is only that to which we are genuinely related by our creative activity, be it a person or an inanimate object. Only those qualities that result from our spontaneous activity give strength to the self and thereby form the basis of its integrity. The inability to act spontaneously, to express what one genuinely feels and thinks, and the resulting necessity to present a pseudo self to others and oneself, are the root of the feeling of inferiority and weakness. Whether or not we are aware of it, there is nothing of which we are more ashamed than of not being ourselves, and there is nothing that gives us greater pride or happiness than to think, to feel, and to say what is ours.[12]

But unless man is ontologically self-directing in integrating feeling with reason and the creative existence with his own notions of creativity, there is no point in talking about self-development. Thus in going beyond the subject-object split through spontaneity, Fromm, like Erikson, postulates an identity between the I-process and the social process and settles for man's relationship to the world in terms of "one structural whole." But if this is a model of existence in competition with other totalisms which postulate other patterns of the part-to-whole logic, then the sacrifice of the human ordering capacity is in vain.

Seven, perhaps the most central meaning of spontaneity for Fromm is its commitment to relatedness, in which man "confirms himself" or identifies himself with totality. In his book, *The Revolution of Hope*, Fromm makes this rather explicit: that man has the "need to be related to man and nature and to confirm himself in this relatedness."[13] Prior to this remark, Fromm is impressed with Marx's position on the passions, which he defined

[12] Fromm, *Revolution of Hope*, 69.
[13] *Ibid.*

as "man's faculties striving to obtain their object." Fromm quotes Marx approvingly in the following manner:

In this statement, passion is considered as a concept of relation or relatedness. The dynamism of human nature inasmuch as it is human is primarily rooted in this need of man *to express his faculties* in relation to the world rather than in his need to use the world as a means for the satisfaction of his physiological necessities.[14]

This is a way of endorsing one's model of goal-directedness with a claim to ultimacy by saying that such goal direction is the very necessity of human nature. But the Christian makes a similar claim about his God that a Marxian makes about the totality of history, that it is a real, immediate, and an ultimate totality. Every totalist who identifies his model with existence *qua* existence makes this claim of "necessity of human nature" at one time or another. It is a way of competing with other systems of totality. Spontaneity is merely an unjustified mediative device to help man "confirm himself" in this relational totality. This is what I have called a mistaken identification of one's model of existence with existence itself. But this may be the requirement only of the pre- and postpurposive models of existence and not the demand of life itself. The fact is that "life aware of itself," understood in terms of spontaneous awareness, may not be the most responsible life. Is this a form of masochism, to use one of Fromm's favorite terms, to give away the directives of our purposive nature to a system of totality and then to plead for it in spontaneous receptivity?

Eight, the relationship of spontaneity to responsibility breaks down in Fromm's perspective, just as it did in the first chapter on the radical youth, primarily for the reason that some sense of directionality is needed to relate to spontaneity for it to be the positive value that Fromm thinks it is. Friedman senses the problem in Fromm's writings, but he comes up with a rather similar alternative himself. Friedman writes:

Insofar as the image of man is concerned—the direction to authentic personal existence—he has left us with an affirmation of man and of "self-realization" without the direction that would make these terms meaningful. . . . Growth is not necessarily a good unless implicit in the concept of growth is growth in a direction that realizes positive values. . . . We cannot define ourselves or our potentialities apart from the direction we give them, apart from what we become in relation to others. This direction, this becoming, implies a movement toward the authentic, toward values, toward the image of man.[15]

---

[14] *Ibid.*

[15] Friedman, *To Deny Our Nothingness*, 237–38, 240.

Friedman's perspective is both a criticism of Fromm's view, to the effect that he absorbs the image of man in a system of totality and thereby does not allow the "image of man" sufficient directive agency in human life, and an alternative to Fromm's perspective in which the "image of man" is a vital directive force or power which functions "as a direction of movement which shapes the raw material of the given into authentic personal and human existence."[16]

It is necessary to move beyond the perspectives of both authors in order to liberate the human orderer from systems of ultimate goal-directedness. The conflict between particular goal direction (Friedman) and more totalistic goal direction (Fromm) is not the central issue in this case. The problem is how to go beyond the "image of man" (the total man) and the "image of the universe" that has been identified with existence itself. Unless goal direction is related to ontological self-direction, we have no other alternative but to submerge man into a system of totality or to follow the various myths of the "whole man" in the history of thought. Both authors exemplify the confluent model of participation to varying degrees. Fromm commits the total man to a system of totality through spontaneity which invests man with wholeness. Friedman attributes directive power to images of man. The fact is that the human orderer is self-directing in both forms of totalism. Both relate significantly to man's search for wholeness as a self-directive effort on the part of man's being in the matrix of participation. The above views cannot integrate *responsibility for* with *responsibility to*, to human choices and goals. Fromm's insistence that "there is only one meaning of life: the act of living itself" can only relate "life's awareness of itself" to a form of "responsibility to." This is insufficient for a "human" concept of responsibility. Such spontaneous activity is better than compulsive or automatic behavior. But unless man is self-directing in his activities (and the notion of "human agency" fails to qualify here), there is no way in which the self can make claims on responsibility and exhibit responsibility for his choices and goals for images of himself and systems of totality.

Nine, John Schaar's critique of spontaneity in Fromm's writings is primarily concerned with its shortcomings in terms of goal-directedness. It provides "no guides for the end of actions," in fact, "it draws away from the aims of action." Schaar comments: "The ethic of spontaneity, then,

---

[16] *Ibid.*, 17.

emphasizes the form of life and neglects its substance and aim."[17] That this concept provides an antidote to "conformity" is somewhat misleading, Schaar thinks, because spontaneity is still left with a lack of a positive vision of a good life. Thus he recommends a civilization that has a serious concern for goals and vision, that is capable of placing restraints and rules on spontaneous living. "Truly productive men do not live for living. They live for ends, for purposes and ends outside themselves."[18]

The basic difference between Fromm and Schaar appears to be that Fromm recommends the ends and goals discovered in the stream of unitive experience and Schaar views them in a nonprocessive manner. Thus they adhere to two different models of goal-directed designs for living. Consequently, it is not enough to challenge spontaneity, to insist on the fact that it lacks the traditional meaning of purpose defined in terms of ends, aims, or goals. Schaar simply gives us another dimension of goal-directedness, or rather another arrangement of it. Both views fail to liberate the human orderer in the matrix of participation. They stop short of ontological self-direction that gives meaning to each model of goal-directedness, whether it is within the stream of experience or beyond it.

The positive freedom disclosed by spontaneity in Fromm's writings, which is beyond the coercive character of instinctive mechanisms (the addition of Marx to Freud), is insufficient to state the case for the human orderer in the matrix of participation because it implicates a system of totality rather than man's contribution to his becoming. Spontaneity thus lacks the notion of directionality in its self-expressive movements and a consideration of ontological purposiveness. The goals and choices this allows man are those provided by the structures of given existence. It is the freedom of self-expression in the structures of existence in terms of prewired possibilities. The determinism of possibilities or of human potentialities is more difficult to observe than a determinism that is fixed into patterns of actualities because one has to wait for the actualization of such potentialities to take notice of the determinism. If freedom of self-expression can only win its freedom by being bound to a real and immediate system of totality instead of a human orderer, it is a freedom that is inherent in the chromosomes and in the total process of history, in short, in the evolutionary process itself. Man can only be *responsible to* such a process but not *responsible for* it. It is not the freedom of man's purposive nature to contribute to human be-

[17] John Schaar, *Escape From Authority* (New York, Basic Books, 1961), 306.
[18] *Ibid.*, 110.

coming, which shapes and forms the very character of unitive experience and schemes of totality.

The definition of spontaneity "as the total affirmation of the self" indicates the failure of Fromm to liberate the human orderer in the process of participation. The confirmation of such participation in the whole of existence is the work of an alleged real and immediate system of totality. It is not the human orderer that "confirms himself" in such relatedness but an individuality that lacks precisely this quality and ability to confirm itself. If it has this capacity to confirm itself in a system of totality, this is denied to it in theory. Thus the unity that spontaneity is said to introduce into human life, though warm and feelingful, is ignorant of the positive values which direct and give design to such unity. The postulate of a unitive spontaneity already assumes a human orderer in practice which is denied in theory. Fromm already makes a holistic use of purpose to introduce spontaneity as a unifying principle of selfhood. Such unity presupposes ontological self-direction and purposive participation in existence. Unless spontaneity belongs to a purposive being, and he is its gathering focus, it is incapable of manifesting either purpose or responsibility. It can warm the heart of man with unconscious designs for living. It does not, however, liberate the human orderer to be humanly aware of life as he participates in it. The limitations and dangers of this perspective will show themselves as we consider Fromm's view of the relation of responsibility to the humanistic conscience in the pages which follow.

Responsibility and the Humanistic Conscience

Responsibility is a slippery term in Fromm's constellation of totality. The author is so preoccupied with the relation of man to society and to totality, and of the relation of values to man's inherent nature and to facts, that he neglects to relate these topics to the human orderer. If we raise the question, why should man be responsible "for himself," we are at a loss to find a reply. When it is Fromm as pragmatist who is speaking, the answer appears to be that man is a problem-solver, that if he has the problem of loneliness and separateness he will go about solving it and look out for himself in the process. But aside from the fact that man is problem-oriented, there is no account given of why he should be so predisposed. There is one passage which anticipates Fromm's reply, and it reads as follows:

It is one of the properties of the human mind that it cannot remain passive in the face of contradictions, puzzles, anomalies, and incompatibilities. Inevitably

275

it wishes to resolve them. . . . Since the existence of such dichotomies generates such complex needs as the need to restore the sense of equilibrium between himself and nature and the need to understand the why and wherefore of the universe, an orientation or frame of reference becomes necessary. . . . [In order to be a problem-solver man must] acknowledge his fundamental aloneness and solitude in a universe indifferent to his fate, to recognize that there is no power transcending him which can solve his problem for him. Man must accept the responsibility for himself and the fact that only by using his own powers can he give meaning to his life. . . .[19]

If man is not a human orderer in the matrix of participation, however, how can he use "his own powers" for self-realization? Fromm's obvious reply is that man makes an alliance with the system of totality that helps him utilize his own powers for his own good. But this already presupposes an identification of one's model of existence with existence itself and an identification of one's interests with the directives of totality. In short, as Friedman reminds us, "one must *already* have meaning in life, meaning that can be actualized through man's meeting with life,"[20] in order to seek such a meaningful relatedness to a system of totality and identify with its intentions. There is prior purposive participation that is required to account for such identification. In short, man must be a human orderer before he can be a responder to the world or to a system of totality.

Another problem concerns what Abraham Kaplan states is the central problem in Fromm, namely, the tendency to deduce values from facts, from man's assumed inherent qualities.[21] When Fromm appeals to man's "own powers," he has in mind these inherent qualities, like in the passage above where he refers to the inherent disposition of the mind to be a problem-solver. It is, however, difficult to separate the goals of the mind from the human orderer. Consequently, I look at this as an awkward pragmatic terminology to account for self-direction in the practice of human participation where there is no such self-direction in theory. The mind is an adaptive function of life and not a self-directing agency. We have run into similar problems with John Dewey's perspective. The fact is that man is more indeterminate in his basic nature than what Fromm is willing to account for in terms of his theory of positive freedom. Man is also more self-directing and purposive in participation than Fromm gives him credit

---

[19] J. A. C. Brown, *Freud and the Post-Freudians* (London, Cassell, 1961), 153–54.

[20] Friedman, *To Deny Our Nothingness*, 233.

[21] Abraham Kaplan, "The Heart of Erich Fromm," *The New York Review of Books* (April 8, 1965), 33–35.

for. Thus a theory of organic maturation cannot account for the liberation of the human orderer, who would, then, be in a position to help himself through his own powers. Fromm's productive man is not a human orderer; he is part of a system of totality whose burden of responsibility he bears and carries out.

This is further documented by Fromm's theory of freedom defined as alternativism. Of this, Kaplan says that it is "in striking accord with the conception of John Dewey. . . . The character-structure of the free man . . . is under constant pressure from social forces as well as from inner compulsions."[22] The theory of responsibility which results from such alleged positive freedom is the study of response-relations in terms of their consequences. Thus it suffers the fate of the confluent model of participation and of the pragmatic theory of responsibility noted earlier. If man is a part of a larger interactive network of things and receives primary guidance from unitive and totalistic experience, it is difficult to see how man can be responsible for himself. Thus the admonition that "man must accept the responsibility for himself" is a form of simplistic moralism. If he is not his own, how can he be responsible for himself? He can only be responsible to one of several alternatives that sociohistory provides for him. He can make his way in this structuralist context in terms of feelingful responsibility, but this is not the human orderer that I have described in previous chapters.

Moreover, becoming aware of what we truly are, in terms of our inherent qualities, has about it a certain quality of impotence when compared with the purposive model of participation. First of all, we do not know what we truly are in terms of our possibilities; we know these potentialities only after they have been actualized, when it is too late to do anything about them. Secondly, to become what we are may simply mean to conform to a model of existence rather than to actual laws of human nature. Thirdly, if the human orderer has no ontological status in such participation, how do we know what we are doing when we go through these procedures? There is another sense of impotence which Kaplan notes: "With Freud and Marx he shares the postulate that to understand is to transcend; consciousness of who and what we are reveals our true interests and directs us to their fulfillment."[23] From my perspective, self-transcendence, as a form of goal-directedness, is more the servant of totality than man's effort

[22] *Ibid.*, 34.
[23] *Ibid.*, 33–34.

to order his life or to integrate his experiences into meaning. In all these respects, then, the appeal to the facts of human nature or to its inherent laws for directionality is a way of obeying the dictates of totality, of being responsible first to the system of totality and of not being responsible for man's choices, goals, and designs for living.

The truth of the matter is that Fromm is more eager to exhibit the risks of the live creature in its confrontations with life than he is to show how he is responsible in those confrontations. Thus he is much closer to Freudian permissiveness than he would declare. The individual is basically a self-seeker in a larger structure of totality. This is an abstraction from the human orderer's capacity for self-direction. Since man is only a self-seeker, he cannot truly be *responsible for* himself. Whether man is a self-seeker or a self-giver in situations of relatedness, we must attribute the directionality of some such movement to the human orderer if the concept of individuality is to have any meaning at all. The issue of whether man should be for himself or for the other is posterior to the purposive being and his purposive participation in existence.

Fromm's positive image of man is in terms of productivity, which is giving birth to the potentialities inherent in human nature. A person that is productive is capable of exhibiting love relations and other spiritual qualities. In short, he is capable of showing care, responsibility, respect, and knowledge. He shuns all authoritarian paths. Responsibility in this humanistic context of productivity is defined as "my response to a request which I feel to be my concern." It is thus a *feeling* of responsibility. In terms of this humanistic conscience, man is a responder and an answerer. To be responsible is equated with "to be ready to respond." Responsibility is an aspect of the act of love. Both are conceived as elemental modes of response for which man is not the gathering focus as a constituent element of love. Responsibility can only be stated negatively, as a responsibility to one's feelings. Both love and responsibility are unifying principles in man's quest for wholeness. The ultimate lure for both is a system of totality that is regarded as real and immediate.

Perhaps we can get at the matter more quickly by Fromm's concept of "well-being" as it is perceived by the humanistic point of view. The most forthright comments on this theme are to be found in *Zen Buddhism and Psychoanalysis*. His concept of well-being is reminiscent of Paul Tillich's method of corollation, where man asks the questions and religion gives the answers. In the case of Fromm, it is life that gives the answers. It is also reminiscent of James Bugental's position when Fromm defines well-being as being "in accord with the nature of man." This is well-being in terms of direct and immediate experience prior to ontological self-direction. It is reminiscent of Heidegger's system of Being minus its value connotations. In terms of Fromm's own words:

Well-being is the state of having arrived at the full development of reason: reason not in the sense of merely intellectual judgment, but in that of grasping truth by "letting things be" (to use Heidegger's term) as they are. Well-being is possible only to the degree to which one has overcome one's narcissism; to the degree to which one is open, responsive, sensitive, awake, empty (in the Zen sense). Well-being means to be fully related to man and nature effectively, to overcome separateness and alienation, to arrive at the experience of oneness with all that exists—and yet to experience myself at the same time as the separate entity I am. . . . If it is all that, it means also to be creative; that is, to react and to respond to myself, to others, and to everything that exists—to react and to respond as the real, total man I am to the reality, to everybody and everything as he or it is.[24]

Relating oneself productively to world-totality means living according to that reality and its laws and acting within the structures of world-totality. In terms of the goals of psychoanalysis, such well-being is reached by the attempt "to make the unconscious conscious—or, to put it in Freud's words, to transform the Id into Ego."[25] Fromm continues:

If one pursues the aim of the full recovery of the unconscious, then this task is not restricted to the instincts, nor to other limited sectors of experience, but to the total experience of the total man; then the aim becomes that of overcoming alienation, and of the subject-object split in perceiving the world; then the uncovering of the unconscious means the overcoming of affective contamination and cerebration; it means the de-repression, the abolition of the split within myself between the universal man and the social man; it means the disappearance of the polarity of conscious vs. unconscious; it means arriving at the state of the immediate grasp of reality, without distortion and without interference by intellectual reflection; it means overcoming of the craving to hold on to the ego, to worship it; it means giving up the illusion of an indestructible separate ego, which is to be enlarged, preserved as the Egyptian pharohs hoped to preserve themselves as mummies for eternity. To be conscious of the unconscious means to be open, responding, to *have* nothing and to *be*.[26]

[24] Fromm, D. T. Suzuki, and R. De Martino, *Zen Buddhism and Psychoanalysis* (New York, Harper & Brothers, 1960), 91–92.
[25] *Ibid.*, 95.
[26] *Ibid.*, 135.

Such "full union, the immediate and uncontaminated grasp of the world," is Fromm's biggest illusion, for it identifies the model of existence with existence as existence, and this presupposes omniscience on the part of the psychoanalyst; it puts him in a class even beyond that of the "high priest." It is quite obvious that the effort to deliver the unconscious into consciousness is an effort of a purposive being, a human orderer, which Fromm's theory does not account for. It is an act of self-direction to relate oneself to the world that is model-free. Fromm, too, is obliged to view the wholeness of the universe through human participation, just like the rest of us. That is to say, he, too, must see the entirety of existence through a model of existence. To identify his model with existence itself is a claim of ultimacy for the model. One does not proceed from model-making to lived experience that is free of participatory abstractions, as Fromm supposes.

Fromm wants a humanism without a human orderer. This request itself is a request to be liberated by immersing oneself in a system of totality. It is a path that a purposive being takes on the level of primal encounter. The very effort to go beyond the subject-object split is doomed to failure because such a design is the work of a human orderer. His preference for meditative thinking that is imitative of Heidegger's *Gelassenheit* is a way of courting negative mysticism that is similarly immersed in immediacy. Whether man is a self-seeker "for himself" or an other-seeker or the seeker of totalisms, such movement presupposes not only directionality but, on the human level specifically, self-directionality in the matrix of participation. Thus Fromm wants human emancipation without a human emancipator. His concept of individuality lacks that which it needs most to operate as an individual, namely, self-direction.

Making the unconscious conscious does not get rid of the human orderer; it presupposes him as a purposive being. In transforming the id into the ego, the ego is not lost but finds itself in the process of self-direction. Fromm's theory ignores this important fact. He prefers the prepurposive model of human directionality. This means giving ultimacy to the unconscious as a prepurposive source of directionality. Since it is the custodian of total man and total humanity, it appears to be the ultimate in directing man to a life of meaning. The cost of discipleship to the total man, the universal man, the world citizen, and to totality, is the negation of the human orderer as a contributor to his becoming in the matrix of participation. This is idiocy: to exchange the human orderer for the whole man. It is, in fact, a form of masochism, in which man gives up his powers to totality and then begs for them in return in order to transform himself through his own powers.

The presence of the human orderer is seen also in man's search for unity by relating feeling and reason to obtain the image of the total man and of relating this partial totality to the real system of totality. Yet Fromm's theory does not account for the human orderer in these moves of purposiveness. How does one love a whole? He loves it by loving his idea of it. Fromm loves his model of existence so much that he makes claims of ultimacy for it. The fact is that he cannot make the transition from his model of existence to existence itself by unitive experience, like the concept of the total man, because such unity is itself the product of purposive being. We participate in existence first before we come up with designs about the total man or the total universe. Because both of them are products of purposive participation and model-making by experience, we cannot claim a reality-status for them apart from man's search for wholeness. It is because man is a purposive being that he goes on the quest for wholeness. This is not the request of a scheme of totality. The contrast between my view and Fromm's is that Fromm prefers the directives of immediacy and the intentions of totality to those of man's purposive nature in achieving the good life. I believe that what Fromm wants is impossible to design without a consideration of a purposive being.

Fromm's dependence upon Heidegger and Zen Buddhism shows his preference for the directives of immediacy. But how can he judge the point that immediacy is of one color in both schools of thought? I think that immediacy comes out in two different models of direct experience, and these are controlled by two respective models of existence. They are two different kinds of encounter. Just because both deny the role of the human orderer in the sphere of immediacy does not necessarily make immediacy a unified sphere of being. To postulate such unity for immediacy is already a holistic use of purposive being in participation. Such unity does not follow from the "very nature of man." It is this very nature of man that is itself the problem of this discussion. The "power to act creates a need to use this power" is true only for a purposive being. The use or misuse of power we cannot leave for immediacy to decide for us. Fromm's pragmatic solution to this dictum—"the power to act creates a need to use this power"—is a meaningless gesture unless we can point to a human orderer who gives meaning to such acts. Otherwise we are merely a witness to simple physiological motions.

Fromm's attempt to escape the omnipotentiality and narcissism of the ego leads him to a greater form of narcissism, to the omnipotentiality of a system of totality. It is not so much the love of life that drives him, but the love of a model of existence which he equates with existence as existence. This needs psychoanalytic treatment as much as the wayward characteristics of the ego. Fromm mistakes the model of existence with "ways of being." Thus when one *participates in the whole*, or when one experiences the "total experience of the total man" (and shows an appreciation of the unconscious as the voice of total humanity), this is already an abstraction from man's purposive participation in existence; it involves all sorts of mistaken identifications, hypostatizations, and reifications. Every totalist loves his model of totality so much that he wishes it to be cosmic reality itself. But such a model of existence, which allegedly solves the subject-object split, is only a reality-claim, a claim of ultimacy for one's model, a feeling of reality (or reality-feeling). It is the spurious claim of "an uncontaminated grasp of the world," when all along it is fashioned and formed by purposive being in the process of participation. Like Bugental, Fromm discounts the Otherness of "the Being of beings" in Heidegger's thought, which oppresses the individual in being's goal direction to Being.

Such concepts as love, care, responsibility, respect, and knowledge that make up the characteristics of the productive man and productive thinking, as in *Man For Himself*, are in essence the guardians of man's goal-directedness to the system of totality. Man can only be "for himself" through a given totality. In this context, responsibility is a unifying principle in the system of totality. It has a guide other than man the human orderer. In such responsibility, man does not confront the human orderer either in himself, in society, or in the schemes of totality that have dominated the history of thought. Its basic meaning is that of "response," which is a hangover from totalistic thinking about man.

The upshot of this digression on the "well-being" of man is that the "humanistic conscience" implicates a system of totality more valuational than Heidegger's ontological approach to totality and more existential than Dewey's naturalistic approach to the problem. Fromm does not even trouble himself to differentiate between such divergent models of encounter as we find between Heidegger and Dewey. He lumps them together indiscriminately to arrive at a constellation of totality which is still another attempt to state the case for a third system of totality. Neither is Fromm concerned with a discussion of a common structure among such systems of totality which his position obligates him to clarify. These are some of the basic assumptions underlying the notion of the humanistic conscience, which is "our own voice," the "voice of the human race," the voice of "unitive experience," and the voice of a "real and immediate totality." It functions as a magic talisman to overcome human alienation in a fragmented world. But Fromm is unaware of the new "repressedness" and "alienation" created by his narcissism for a real and immediate totality, which the humanistic conscience is responsible to but not responsible for.

Fromm's frame of orientation, frame of devotion, frame of commitment, is not fashioned and formed by purposive being. Is it a new form of authoritarianism that has escaped the author's attention in his concern for humanism? I would call it ideological authoritarianism. Fromm has struggled so long with the problem of authoritarianism that this form of it may be a residue of his thought, scars of the battle. He has fought it so long he can no longer recognize its subtler versions. Unless man as a human orderer is the source and origin (the *fons et origo*) of such totalistic models of existence or systems of responsibility, we have to face the prospect of ideological authoritarianism. Once we disconnect man's search for wholeness (via self-direction) from totalisms, we are on the way to being submerged in systems of totality.

Fromm's "constellation of totality" is a syncretistic product of many schools of thought. We noted its pragmatic and existential sides. There is also the modern vitalist or romanticist view of wholeness to which Fromm subscribes. Of this, Bruce Wilshire writes:

Not just the concept of the whole, but the whole in its concrete immediacy of nature, not just accurate knowledge about nature, but sensuous intuition of it and active involvement within it as process—that is the earmark of the romantic.[27]

Is this man's claim of closeness to experience or the demand of totality upon man's search for closeness and wholeness? Fromm and the romanticists take the latter. The humanistic conscience, which is the source of responsibility, implicates this immediate system of totality, where immediacy that is model-free is equated with totality. In Fromm's view, this leads to an uncontaminated version of the image of man and of the entire universe.

[27] Bruce Wilshire, *Romanticism and Evolution* (New York, G. P. Putnam's Sons, 1968), 15.

But can the mind and imagination of man come up with more than a model of existence in its entirety? Fromm subsumes the reason under the whole man theme. The whole man is master of its reason, then. Does this come any closer to equating the immediacy and wholeness with cosmic reality? The reply is obviously negative in the light of my theory. There are many reasons for its rejection. Even if the mind is a "slave to the idea of unity" in its "insatiable search" for "all possible experience," this is no guarantee of the existence of totality and does not warrant the identification of immediacy with absolute being. Konstantin Kolenda remarks that this goal of the mind, to embrace "all there is," is frought with difficulties in the Christian scheme of religious totality.[28] I would say, in addition, that this peril exists for every totalist, not only the religious totalist. The "gap between conception and existence" cannot be bridged by the mind, even when, as in Fromm's case, the whole man is in charge of the mind. Fromm's *psychological misuse* of reason's striving for wholeness of knowledge is that he identifies this model of reason about the wholeness of life with life itself. I have suggested, on the other hand, that the mediating link between thought and existence is the "model of existence," which never identifies model with existence itself but only provides correlations with it in participation. "Participation in the whole" is thus an abstraction of purposive participation in existence. The gap between concept and existence is not closed by a "mistaken identification," but there is correlation and commerce between the two by the mediating link of "model of existence." This is the product of purposive participation in existence, in which purpose has an equal share in primal experience. Such model-making by participation is as close as we can get to life, in our love of life and in our strivings for systems of totality. Purposive participation is thus the deepest kind of lived experience we can have. Philosophies of encounter which advocate more intimacy with existence, than such models of existence, are caught up in the narcissism and omnipotentiality I noted above in Fromm's totalism. Fromm is correct to relate the mind's search for universality with man's entire search for wholeness, but he is wrong in going from that

[28] Konstantin Kolenda, "Thinking the Unthinkable," *Journal For The Scientific Study of Religion* (Spring, 1969), 72–78. The author concludes that religion need not "postulate an entity which purports to answer to the highest demands of reason." Perhaps this is also the reply to Fromm: that humanistic psychology need not postulate a Whole, Totality, or Unity (which are logical notions), to answer to the highest demands of reason. When this is practiced by psychology, the "whole man" becomes the servant of totality.

resultant model of existence to existence itself. The "whole in its concrete immediacy of nature" is already a model of existence. One can go beyond it only at his own peril, by claims of ultimacy for his model. Fromm shares this illusion with romanticism and vitalism.

Can the mind come up with more than a model of existence? Can the perspectival participator in existence come up with more than a model about the whole of existence? My reply to both questions is in the negative. What each kind of experience gives us is a model of ultimate goal-directedness which requires the metamodel of purposive being in participation even to operate. Thus man is responsible for systems of ultimate responsibility. The "humanistic conscience," as Fromm defines the notion, does not make man human; it makes him "whole." Wholeness in itself is neither human nor inhuman. It is what we do with it in our purposive being that makes it human or inhuman. If man is somehow made responsible for such total systems of responsibility, wholeness can have a wholesome effect upon human life. However, if man is submerged in systems of totality (which define his individuality and humanity prior to his purposive nature), there is no way to claim that wholeness is a "humanizing" factor in life.

The conclusion I reach is that Fromm's constellation of totality cannot be the source of human responsibility because it is itself only a model of existence and not a real and immediate wholeness equated with the entirety of the universe. Thus the replacement of the id by the ego in a system of totality does not make man any more *responsible for* systems of responsibility than the id did before it. Turning the unconscious into conscious considerations, if the consciousness is dominated by the structures and processes of totality, is an academic solution.

12. Responsibility and the Daimonic

Rollo May makes an earnest effort to construct a notion of the human orderer in terms of wish, will, and intentionality only to lose him again in a system of totality. His differences from Freud, in this post-Freudian image of man, are rather pronounced and take the form of "psycho-synthesis" rather than "psycho-analysis." It is man as unitary being which impresses him. But for sake of contrast it is necessary to point to the defensive nature of the Freudian image of man. Freud rejected two views of the human orderer: (1) as the isolated subject self with will as its master; and (2) as the rational self where reason was the master of life. Such constructs of selfhood are no longer acceptable to Freud or to modern man. In their place, Freud postulated man in a system of naturalistic totality with a world-view of its own. The father of psychoanalysis claims, however, that this is not a new *Weltanschauung* because it is part and parcel of the scientific view of life. It can thus adhere to the scientific world-view, which is an incomplete model of existence and makes no claims to being self-contained.[1]

This new perspective placed the source of human responsibility, if any was left, in a system of totality whose laws defined the nature and status of man's affective and mental life. The will of man was replaced by the unconscious as the guide to life, and the latter was the servant of the system of totality with which Freud identified the value of man. Even the construct of man as "self-seeker" finds an uncertain place in Freud's system. The human orderer is thus lost in a system of determinism, an object among others, determined by the laws of nature and the directives of totality. Central to this preoccupation was that man suffered a great deal from "narcissistic illusions" in conceiving of himself as the human orderer.

[1] S. Freud, *The Complete Introductory Lectures on Psychoanalysis*, ed. by J. Strachey (New York, W. W. Norton, 1966), 645–46.

"Narcissism" is, for Freud, "the libidinal complement to egoism." Since the will and reason have failed as constructs to define the human orderer, the ego must be properly fitted anew into a system of totality—"the ego is not the master of its own house."[2] It is overruled by both the sexual instinct and by the unconscious drives of man. Man is incapable of proper decision-making because the conscious mind is given meager impressions, incomplete information and perceptions in order to make solid judgments. This rules out the mind as being the master of the self and the will as well. Since man is not in control either of his sex life or his other drives, neither of his will to power nor of his mind, he fails to measure up to the standards of a human orderer. In these circumstances, to postulate a human orderer is merely a case of a "narcissistic investment" in our own capacities. There is no call for such psychological extravaganza in the midst of the world's realities.

The neo-Freudians have been concerned in their ego psychology to correct some of these Freudian inadequacies about the ego as a part-function. Their current concern is "psychosynthesis" or the definition of man in terms of relatedness and productive love, in short, a more holistic model of man. Some among them, like Rollo May, have followed Adler's concern for the individual in the midst of totality. Their concern is more with the problems of integration and synthesis, of relating man's affective life to the meaning of life.

May believes that Freud's view of the will has undermined man's sense of personal responsibility, which he notes in the following passage:

In describing how "wish" and "drive" move us rather than "will," Freud formulated a new image of man that shook to the very foundations Western man's emotional, moral, and intellectual self-image. . . . Man's image of himself will never be the same again; our only choice is to retreat before this destruction of our vaunted "will power" or to push on to the integration of consciousness on new levels. I do not wish or "choose" to do the former; but we have not yet achieved the latter; and our crisis of will is that we are now paralyzed between the two.[3]

It is precisely this new level of integration of the human orderer that I shall examine in this chapter, to see whether it is a new form of submergence of the individual to a system of totality or whether it is actually

[2] J. Rivere (ed.), *Collected Papers of Freud* (New York, Basic Books, 1959), 347–56, 355.
[3] Rollo May, *Love And Will* (New York, W. W. Norton, 1969), 182–83.

the liberation of the human orderer. I noted earlier that ego psychology can be as involved in systems of totality as much as the id. Perhaps this is at the heart of the psychosynthesis in the current movement of humanistic psychology.

Part of May's central vision of man is the mythological world-view, if not a moral one, is the notion of the "daimonic in man." The daimonic is a servant of a system of totality, but it also has other meanings in May's writings. May states, for example: "The daimonic arises from the ground of being rather than the self as such. It is shown particularly in creativity."[4] But May fails to tell us that it is a prepurposive model of creativity, as something coming from below man and welling up within him (to which man is responsible but for whose creativity he is not responsible). It is both a positive and a negative power, both divine and diabolical. It is a "generative process" in either case. Since it is an aspect of the ground of being, it functions as the source of human vitality.

More conservative Freudians find the notion of the daimonic rather troublesome. Michael Beldoch, for example, thinks it is next to useless as a concept of psychological analysis:

It would seem that the daimonic is a term for all psychic seasons, of all psychic functions. Sometimes it is ego, sometimes id, sometimes conscious, sometimes unconscious; sometimes it is evil, sometimes it is beyond good and evil. Close reading finally leaves one with the feeling that what May mostly means is what Freud meant by the Id, but without the obligation felt by Freud to be as parsimonious and as internally consistent as possible in his definition.[5]

Beldoch selects five conflicting views of the daimonic to illustrate his dissatisfaction with this mythological phenomenon. But he misses the most important aspect about this drive for human vitality, namely, that it is the servant of totality. Man has responsibility to it, but he is not responsible for its creativity and directives. In short, man's responsibility to it is that of being a proper responder to its directives or intentions.

All that is required of man is to direct, redirect, or channel this creative natural force of the daimonic in order to live a vital, feelingful life and be attuned to the system of totality. Whatever else is done to it by man, it should not be repressed, for this vital power, then, takes its revenge upon man. May advises man to accept the daimonic, to channel its energies and

---

[4] *Ibid.*, 124.

[5] Michael Beldoch, "Love And Will: A Placebo for Despair," *Psychiatry and Social Science Review*, Vol. 4, No. 4 (1970), 3.

directives without letting it possess him completely. This is precisely the point that is crucial in May's system: If the daimonic is the servant of totality, why should man balk at the fact when it possesses him wholly? May continues that "the destructive side can be met only by transforming that very power into constructive activities."[6] However, if it is prior to good and evil as well as the servant of totality, whence the origin of this destructive side? In fact, its very task is to mold man to fit responsibly into the system of totality. May is not concerned with this issue; he is unaware of the contradiction. His primary concern is man's *responsibility to* the daimonic power that is available to him in the ground of being. This mythological power May regards as an "existential reality" which guides man in specific situations and enables man to assert himself with vigor and vitality. Without it, man remains apathetic. If this natural power is regarded as the source of human vitality and reverenced as such, what does responsibility to it actually mean? Does integrating it with his consciousness mean identifying with its directives? If May is calling for a reconstruction of its directives through will and intentionality, this activity can only be understood in some receptive sense. Man is not a human orderer in the psychosynthetic perspective of his relatedness to the world. Expressing the daimonic power in the act of love may not be sufficient to reconstruct the intentions of the daimonic. The problem appears to be that the human orderer can do very little in facing up to the wayward aspects, the destructive side, of this creativity in life. Let us then take a closer look at the human orderer in terms of May's intentions.

May's rejection of the deterministic model of man, as being only a model of man, enables him to side in with existential thinking on the subject self and the whole attempt to recover the human orderer in terms of some form of the dynamics of subjectivity. Man's quest for identity is very important for him. He also notes the fact that it is notably lacking in modern life, which suggests "this inner experience of impotence" on a mass scale. His solution to such impotence and apathy is to integrate will with a more integral view of personality to offset its impotence. As early as 1953, May was searching for a more holistic perspective of human directionality, as in the following passage: "The self is the organizing function within the individual and the function by means of which one human being can relate to another."[7] The will as an isolated faculty is thus rejected and made

[6] May, *Love And Will*, 130.
[7] Rollo May, *Man's Search For Himself* (New York, W. W. Norton, 1953), 91.

a "conjunctive process," along with the act of love, wish, and intentionality, as in his latest book, *Love And Will*. In all these terms, May is appealing to man's elemental modes of response to the ground of being and to the daimonic force operative in life. These terms have more in common with a system of totality than they do with a human orderer; hence the phrase "conjunctive processes." May continues:

The interrelation of love and will inheres in the fact that both terms describe a person in the process of reaching out, moving toward the world, seeking to affect others or the inanimate world, and opening himself to be affected; molding, forming, relating to the world or requiring that it relate to him. This is why love and will are so difficult in an age of transition, when all the familiar mooring places are gone. The blocking of the ways in which we affect others and are affected by them is the essential disorder of both love and will. Apathy, or a-pathos, is a withdrawal of feeling; it may begin as playing it cool, a studied practice of being unconcerned and unaffected. . . . Apathy . . . is a gradual letting go of involvement until one finds that life itself has gone by.[8]

May thus defines the human orderer as a responsible person in terms of moving out or "in the process of reaching out." Reaching out toward what? Obviously, toward a dialogue with the daimonic in oneself and in others and eventually toward the system of totality which directs our human possibilities. It is this "reaching out"—the responder—that May mistakes for the "independent person in his own right" or "an identity in one's own right." The problem is that man's uniqueness is defined by his wholeness, and this, in turn, is defined by a system of totality rather than by man's capacity to be self-directing in existence. May favors ontological freedom, as Bugental does, only to lose it in a system of totality, along with subjectivity. Thus responsibility for one's unity is in essence a responsibility to the system of totality with which one has already identified his concern, but this prior purposiveness is not accounted for in May's theory about man. It is necessary to pursue this theme of "unitive being" in May's psychosynthesis because it is at the heart of the issue of human responsibility. To measure human responsibility, the ultimate criteria, for May, is unitive being and experience, among them being "honesty, integrity, courage and love of a given moment of relatedness." Responsibility, as one of the psychological goals, is such a unifying principle of life and gives significance to the movement toward integration.[9]

[8] May, *Love And Will*, 29.
[9] May, *Man's Search For Himself*, 276.

The Contributions of Wish, Will, and Intentionality
to Unitive Being

The relation of wish to will can perhaps be put in Kantian terms: wish without will is blind and will without wish is empty. According to May, wish gives the will a sense of empowerment and the playful vision of imagination. "Will is the capacity to organize one's self," May contends, "so that movement in a certain direction or toward a certain goal may take place. Wish is the imaginative playing with the possibility of some act or state of occurring."[10] It is a dialectical relationship. Wish, as one term in the polarity, is the contribution of the Freudian unconscious or the contribution of the daimonic in man. Will involves self-consciousness and choice-making considerations. Although will is basically goal-directed in its movement, May sometimes uses the term "self-direction" to speak of its "mature" behavior. Whatever else this relation may involve, the central meaning of the relation of this polarity is that it is a dialectical ordering of life. It is a way of salvaging the Freudian image of man in a new blend of unitive being. As I noted earlier, dialectics is a servant of totality. Whether will is the capacity to organize one's self or the self is conceived of as the organizing function in the individual, is not the crucial issue (though problematic); what is crucial is how both are dialectically ordered. Both will and the self are organized and organizing, but they do not have the capacity of a human orderer that is ontologically self-directing in participation. May senses this need to go with the construction of unitive being, and he suggests the integration of wish and will in the concept of intentionality "which cuts across and includes both conscious and unconscious, and both cognition and conation."[11]

In relating wish to will, May is concerned to relate vitality to directionality. The question is, does this directionality, which is combined with human vitality, sufficiently describe the liberated human orderer that we have been seeking in participation? Does the concept of intentionality sufficiently define the liberated human orderer? May's first concern, however, is to discuss the issue of how both wish and will point beyond themselves to the notion of intentionality. This term, too, takes on holistic implications, as in this passage: "By intentionality, I mean the structure which gives meaning to experience. It is not to be identified with intentions, but

[10] May, *Love And Will*, 218.
[11] *Ibid*.

is the dimension which underlies them; it is man's capacity to have intentions. . . . Intentionality is at the heart of consciousness."[12] I shall later challenge this assumption of "structure" and "capacity" in man for intentionality, to the effect that this is only a model of goal-directedness falling short of the liberated human orderer, that May has missed the human orderer in his construction of unitive being. For the moment, let me first pursue the theme of integration between wish and will and intentionality.

As a phenomenologically oriented psychologist, May takes the intentionality and its goal-directed patterns of experience as reality; it is the carrier of the meaning of reality. Thus it is not a goal-directed model of experience, not a form of projectionism, abstractionism, or subjectivism. Freud, imitative of Brentano (whose classes he attended), attributes intentionality to the wish-world, to free associations, dreams, and fantasies. May, along with modern interpretations of intentionality, would also attribute it to man's conscious life and to objects, both of which are operative in the larger field or stream of horizontal experience. Thus intentionality is suggestive of two things: goal-directedness in experience and unitive experience, or the structure of meaning in both. It is the outward-directed meaning from subject to object or the outward-directed meaning from object to subject. It is that "structure" which gives meaning to experience. Thus for Husserl, to intend meant the meaning, the act, and the movement toward something. This is what he meant by the "consciousness of" as a primitive form of experience. This perspective already presupposes experience as a unity, field, or stream, and also as immediacy. The intentional man or experience are in the category of the "responder." It is an outward movement from a unitive center of action. In Husserl, it implicates a transcendental totality and the totality of the *Lebenswelt*. In May, it is suggestive of a socionaturalistic totality. In either case, intentionality is the servant of totality(s), fed by the stream of unitive experiences and their meaning structures.

The crux of the matter between May's perspective and mine may be put simply: May believes that a unity of experience, or a unity of man-in-the-world, stands behind all such intentional experiences; my view, on the other hand, holds that such unity is already a result of purposive self-direction, that it is a model of unity as stream or field, that as such it cannot

[12] *Ibid.*, 223–24.

be the source of intentional experiences. Ontological self-direction is thus prior to intentional experience, however understood, as the bearer of the meaning of reality. May oversimplifies matters at this critical juncture of his discussion of intentionality by giving us a dictionary solution of the problem, following Webster's authority:

Now a fact which may be surprising to many readers, as it was to me, is that the first meaning given for "intend" in Webster's does not have to do with "purpose" or "design," as when we say, "I intend to do something," but is rather, "to mean, signify." Only secondly does Webster give the definition "to have in mind a purpose or a design." Most people in our voluntaristic Victorian tradition have tended to skip over the primary and central meaning and to use the concept only in its derivative meaning of conscious design and purpose. . . . The more significant aspect of intention is its relation to meaning.[13]

What comes as a greater surprise to May, along with the phenomenologists in many quarters, is the rather assumptive nature of such unity that is presupposed by the basic meaning of intentionality. Unity, rather than being the directive agency of man, is itself in need of directionality, of purposive being as ontologically self-directing to be operative. It already makes a holistic use of purpose to function in a unitary way. Unless man is self-directing in such meaning, the structure of meaning implicates a system of totality, the unity of which is similarly fashioned or formed by purposive being. That May is quite serious in recommending such unitive being as the guide of man is evidenced in the following passage: "It is in intentionality and will that the human being experiences his identity."[14] And this presupposes the unity of consciousness which can function as "consciousness of." Moreover, this view of consciousness implicates a system of totality. Such subjectivity is made real by being completed by a real and immediate system of totality. I denied this belief because it is simply a model of existence. The *I-can*, which is presupposed in such an I-process, already presupposes a human orderer that is self-directing in designing unitive experience on many levels. The conflict is not with rationalism, as May supposes, but between some version of totalistic unity and the human orderer.

Intentionality thus presupposes a commitment to unitive experience prior to self-direction. Its goal directions are primary. Design and purpose come out of such primary goal-directedness in primal experience. This does not

[13] *Ibid.*, 228–29.
[14] *Ibid.*, 243.

mean, however, that intentionality is not designed or formed, as May pre-supposes. It is designed by the system of totality rather than by the human orderer. It may not be a voluntarism, understood in terms of an isolated will, but it is a form of totalism, calling for a commitment of man prior to his purposive being.

Any theory of meaning which denies man's capacity to be self-directing in the quest for meaning, even of a highly structured kind, implicates a system of totality, even when such intentional acts and experiences are assumed to be neutral. For the unity of consciousness (as stream or field) implicates a larger transcendental unity or a system of totality. This commitment to preformed unity is a claim to ultimacy; it is a power-claim, or agency-claim, for a system of totality. Purposive being is prior to the issue of whether life is fragmented or unified. It is an issue that only a purposive being that is self-directing can actually raise. His participation in unitive experience is thus the result of his participation in existence. Such "partici-pation in the whole" is the result of purposive participation. The unitive nature of intentional experience, its many patterns of goal-directedness, are also such results of purposive participation in existence. Intentionality is, in fact, a model of experience and not the uncontaminated immediacy and reality which May thinks it is. May's additional appeal to Heidegger's concept of care, understood as "to take care of," merely confirms my critique. Care is not man's attitude toward life, in Heidegger's perspective; it is rather the guardian of *Dasein's* relation to the system of Being. Care and conscience are both servants of total relatedness. They already pre-suppose the primal unity in the system of Being. Unitive experience, in the form of intentional experiences, is merely a way of breathing life into this abstraction of totality. Yet human identity and intentionality both pre-suppose the reality and immediacy of such a system of totality, which I think is only a model of existence.

This perspective of intentionality has ominous implications for a system of responsibility which I shall unravel later in the chapter. Meanwhile, it is necessary to point out the psychoanalytic dimension of intentionality. May believes this deepens the notion of intentional experience. But such a move comes at a great cost, namely, the severance of intentionality from human purpose and the relating of it to the unconscious and to a system of totality and the equating of freedom with necessity. We have already seen how the distinction between the intention and intentionality has pre-pared the way for this. On this new level of consciousness, wish and will, which represent unconscious and conscious intentions, have intentionality as their structure of meaning, and the latter refers to a "state of being" and involves the "totality of the person's orientation to the world at the time."[15] The basic meaning of intentionality is thus removed from the human orderer and related to a system of totality. It thus makes way for the pre-purposive model of life and creativity, for it pushes intention from the domain of conscious purpose to a more totalistic framework, "to the deeper, wider, organic plane of intentionality."[16] This move enables man to give himself over to another ordering power, other than the human orderer, whose ordering is more total, feelingful, and organic. Man is guided by the realm of intentionality, by a meaning-giving structure that is not his own because it comes from beyond the subject-object split. May continues: "Not solipsistic, intentionality is an assertive response of the person to the structure of his world. Intentionality gives the basis which makes purpose and voluntarism possible."[17]

Emotional unity is thus prior to purposive and rational unity. There is a unity of existence which transcends man's search for wholeness and dictates the terms of man's integration. The psychoanalytic interpretation of intentionality endorses this resurgence of the primacy of feeling and its unitary experience as a guide to life. The strategy is to go beyond the subject-object split to endorse a meaning-giving structure that is prior to the human orderer and his purposive participation in existence. Unitive experience is given the privilege of guiding human life, and this implicates a system of totality. Like the daimonic in man, intentionality, too, is the servant of totality. These two will be reinforced by another servant of totality, Eros, which will complete the three guides of man in the system of totality.

MAN'S RESPONSIBILITY TO IRRATIONAL DRIVES

Eros is the third mythological directionality of man. It is man's urge for relationship and procreation. As a form of love, it lures man from ahead and beckons him to respond to patterns of goal-directedness. This form of love is basically an "urge for union." Man is *responsible to* Eros, just as he is responsible to the daimonic in life and to the structure of intention-

15 *Ibid.*, 234.
16 *Ibid.*, 234–35.
17 *Ibid.*, 233–34.

ality. These three elemental modes of human response have their gathering focus not in the human orderer, but in a system of totality. Eros is the openness of man (imaginative, emotional, spiritual) to world-reality beyond and around him. This form of love, May states:

Eros is the binding element par excellence. It is the bridge between being and becoming, and it binds fact and value together. [Both Eros and intentionality] presuppose that man pushes toward uniting himself with the object not only of his love but his knowledge. And this very process implies that a man already participates to some extent in the knowledge he seeks and the person he loves.[18]

What is the relation of Eros to purpose? Purpose is a function of Eros and of man's total feelingful life, since feelings are intentional. This means that the human orderer is a *functionary of* the irrational drive of Eros, the daimonic, and of intentionality. Purpose is correlated with freedom, with open possibilities and the future. For example, May makes the distinction between the "reason why" and "purpose for." The former is connected with determinism and the latter with freedom. As May views it, "We participate in the forming of the future by virtue of our capacity to conceive of and respond to new possibilities, and to bring them out of imagination and try them in actuality."[19] May views this as the process of active loving. It is the source of active responsibility. The author continues:

I am proposing a description of human beings as given motivation by the new possibilities, the goals and ideals, which attract and pull them toward the future. This does not omit the fact that we are all partially pushed from behind and determined by the past, but it unites this force with its other half. Eros gives us a causality in which "reason why" and the "purpose" are united. The former is part of all human experience since we all participate in the finite, natural world; in this respect, each of us, in making any important decision, needs to find out as much as he can about the objective facts of the situation. This realm is particularly relevant in problems of neurosis in which past events do exercise a compulsive, repetitive, chainlike, predictable effect upon the person's actions. Freud was right in the respect that rigid, deterministic causality does work in neurosis and sickness.[20]

But Freud was wrong in applying this to all human experience, even to that area of life which shows purposive behavior. A person that is conscious of his actions views possibilities differently and sees them in the context of responsibility and freedom.

[18] *Ibid.*, 79.
[19] *Ibid.*, 91–92.
[20] *Ibid.*, 93.

But the work of purpose is restricted to being a reactive phenomenon to man's irrational drives, like Eros, the daimonic, and the structure of intentionality. If man is goal-directed to a system of totality, and these guides serve the totality, the turning space for purpose is rather limited and responsibility is viewed in a truncated form. If these actually guide human life, push man from behind, lure him from beyond, or silently make claims upon him from below, responsibility can only be a reactive phenomenon to these irrational drives and not a dominant contribution to one's becoming. Responsibility is not the product of self-direction. As a unifying principle in the system of totality, it can only function as a self-regulating principle or show only a *responsibility to* these drives. To emphasize the total response of man in encounter situations is not liberating the human orderer to be self-directing in participation. The total response in that case means following the intentions of totality.

These irrational drives are goal-directed patterns of living. They are the bearers of the directives of totality. Man's purposive nature is barred from their primal encounter with life. What counts is the totalism which they symbolize, as in the following passage: "We love and will the world as an immediate, spontaneous totality."[21] But the question is, does one ever go beyond the model of existence by such acts to actual and real participation in cosmic reality? Such "willing by participation" is still model-making. May is fond of this triumverate of irrational drives, since each drive puts man in touch with totality and has an out-going quality in its striving. While each of these emphases points to a deeper dimension in man, this deeper dimension is achieved by implicating a system of totality that is regarded as real and immediate. As May views it, "Each requires a participation from us, an openness, a capacity to give of ourselves and to receive into ourselves."[22]

What can responsibility mean in the context of this totalism? Of the three forms of drives, May chooses intentionality and develops its relationship to responsibility. But it should be kept in mind that the structure of intentionality is prior to the human orderer and his capacity for ontological self-direction. The domain of actions seems to be the center of responsibility, as in the following passage:

By my act I reveal myself, rather than by looking at myself. The imputation

21 *Ibid.*, 324.
22 *Ibid.*, 308.

that is correlated with intentionality is not a speculative matter, but an act which, because it always involves responding, is responsible.[23]

This passage shows *responsibility to* these allegedly autonomous actions, but it does not show *responsibility for* these acts. When pressed for the source of such actions, May admits a human agent as the self-performer of his act, exhibiting qualities of striving characterized by self-transcendence, as in the following passage:

> It is significant at this point to note the great number of terms used in describing human actions which contain the prefix "re"—re-sponsible, re-collect, relate, and so on. In the last analysis, all imply and rest upon this capacity to "come back" to one's self as the one performing the act. This is illustrated with special clarity in the peculiarly human capacity to be responsible (a word combining re and spondere, "promise"), designating the one who can be depended upon, who can promise to give back, to answer.[24]

The responsible person, for May, is, then, the self-transcending responder as the source of his response-relations. It is this transcending agent that "puts himself on the line" and participates in encounter experiences. There is a problem, however, with this perspective. Human agency is a model of men acting. It is not a specific act; it is rather the source of such actions and responses. As a "source," human agency is a concept, a universal, a model, and not the real man, unless one identifies the notion of human agency with a particular individual. How do we go from concept to existence in this particular case? Notions of human agency, like May's, are rather troublesome on this account, unless they presuppose purposive being that is ontologically self-directing in existence. Without the human orderer, the notion of human agency dissipates itself in a system of totality. What good is it to make man the source of his acts if he does not confront himself as a human orderer in his actions? If he is not his own, and is himself a derived product and guided by the irrational drives of Eros, the daimonic, and the structure of intentionality, of what good is the self-transcending human agent as the source of human responsibility? The fact is, May can only show human responsibility as a responsibility to, but not as a responsibility for.

May often uses response and responsibility together as a redundant phrase. Response is the central meaning of responsibility; it is not another

[23] *Ibid.*, 238.
[24] Rollo May, E. Angel, H. F. Ellenberger (eds.), *Existence* (New York, Basic Books, 1958), 73–74.

experience to be coupled with responsibility. The attempt to derive responsibility from the concept of response with the belief that somehow the responding acts themselves manifest the meaning of responsibility is thus an irresponsible procedure. Moreover, such spontaneity, I noted as early as the first chapter, does not yield responsibility. It is itself in need of it. The problem is with what is revealed when "by my act I reveal myself." In May's perspective, man does not reveal himself as a human orderer; he reveals himself as a functionary of totality and of unitive experience under the guidance of three irrational drives (mythologically conceived, at least Eros and the daimonic). Man is a dialectically oriented creature whose purposes are secondary to this dialectical design for living. The total man is a model of man, dialectically conceived. In order to safeguard the totality of human existence, May sacrifices the human orderer as a contributor to his becoming. The total man is not a real man; he is a goal-directed model of existence. His capacity for self-transcendence and agency are goal-directed universal urges. Whether man is whole or fragmented is a decision that purposive being must make about life. This is not the work of dialectics.

May's speculative view of the structure of intentionality, which is a departure from the descriptive view of it in phenomenology proper, leads him to further speculations about the relations of this term to human vitality, as in the passage below:

Intentionality and vitality are correlated by the fact that man's vitality shows itself not simply as a biological force, but as a reaching out, a forming and re-forming of the world in various creative activities. The degree of one's intentionality can thus be seen as the degree of one's courage.[25]

Through this correlation, May hopes to give us built-in goal direction to assure man of his destiny in a system of totality. Before we relate intentionality to courage we should be clear of its relation to the human orderer and self-direction. For there are many models of goal-directedness, each claiming inclusion in a real and immediate system of totality. May's model is one such competing design for living and not the whole of existence or the whole of man. He has a narcissistic investment in both these models (of man and of totality) and would make them real and immediate for the reader's consumption and therapy.

His view of responsibility reflects this confusion:

[25] May, *Love And Will*, 245.

Responsibility involves being responsible to, *responding*. Just as consciousness is the distinctively human form of awareness, so decision and responsibility are the distinctive forms of consciousness in the human being who is moving toward self-realization, integration, maturity.[26]

Thus responsibility is a reactive phenomenon to the primary movement of Eros, the daimonic, and the structure of intentionality in man. Responsibility is a functionary of another more basic directionality in which man is mythologically oriented to cosmic reality. When May speaks of responsibility personally or socially (as coresponsiveness), it already presupposes a commitment on the part of man to these irrational drives. Such commitment is prior to ontological self-direction and is a form of obscurantism. It is a secondary unifying principle in man, along with responsibility. The primary unifying agents are Eros, the daimonic, and the structure of intentionality.

The ascriptive view of responsibility which May holds hinges on the notion of "imputation." This is the narrower meaning which ascribes an act to an agent. My point above was that such a theory presupposes a self-directing human orderer which May's theory does not account for. To be goal-directed to one's self, to fully confront one's existence with all its irrational drives and spontaneity, does not make one responsible for one's existence unless one simultaneously confronts the human orderer in himself. The mere responder is not the source of human responsibility. He is the servant of a system of totality which assigns him the system of responsibility. The human agent is himself in need of responsibility in such a system of totality. When one turns to one's existence in goal-directedness and conceives of one's self as a human agent, one is, then, reacting to a model of one's self which is controlled by the larger model of existence which one mistakes as being real and immediate.

The Unity Beyond Purpose and Will

May's narcissistic investment in the image of man and the model of totality has led him to hypostatize both forms of unity, a trait which he shares with humanistic psychology in general. Total participation in the whole of existence is the driving force of this narcissism. However, being in love with one's image of man and model of totality does not make these totalistic schemes real and immediate. They remain on the model-making

[26] *Ibid.*, 267.

level. Thus every effort on the part of man to go beyond the subject-object split involves the efforts of the human orderer. Even when man denies actual and possible goals and plans, he does so with his purposive being which remains intact to come up with other goals and plans. The unity beyond purpose and will is thus a unity postulated by purposive being, whether it be the contribution of the mind or of human participation. Every such totality of the person's orientation to the world is a self-directive move on the part of purposive being to reach out for community. To postulate man's drive for wholeness in primal experience, prior to purposive being, gives us encounter experiences that are unaccounted for (in terms of justification) in immediate experience. May has reasons for going beyond will as an isolated human faculty, for it has failed as a human orderer, but he is unjustified in going beyond human purpose to the structure of intentionality that is prior to human purpose. For the very unity that is the basis of such intentionality of experience betrays the work of purposive being. This, at any rate, is what I wish to show in this section.

May's attempt to bypass voluntarism, to submerge man in a system of totality, is an ambiguous and defeatist program. Will has functioned as a human orderer against deterministic models of man and against mind-oriented rationalistic philosophies. Self-determination was its alleged strength as a human orderer. This is a form of human agency where man is viewed as a self-performer of his acts. As an isolated faculty, it had a tendency to be solipsistic and impotent. In the course of history, a will-oriented philosophy has failed to liberate the human orderer. May is thus correct in wanting to bypass voluntarism to account for a new image of man. But he is wrong in his strategy to submerge man in a system of totality through the irrational drives of Eros, the daimonic, and the structure of intentionality. The anticipation of community, love, and closeness comes at too great a sacrifice, the sacrifice of the human orderer. His humanism turns out to be another form of totalism. Thus his attempts to reconstruct a human orderer out of the debris of voluntarism must be judged a failure. Part of this failure is due to the fact that he holds unity to be the driving force of man's destiny. In terms of my theory, it is a form of ultimate goal direction, a model of experience designed by purposive being in its efforts to be self-directing in experience. Thus ontological self-direction is required as the *precondition* of such unity and as the *condition* to sustain man in his quest for wholeness. Without this requirement, there is no way to avoid the hypostatization of our images of man and models of totality. That May has succumbed to such reification is only too evident in his writings. It has led him to a philosophy of commitment prior to self-direction.

In the light of my theory, will is an elemental mode of response in man's purposive nature, which is the gathering focus for all such elemental modes of response, including the act of love. The alternative to this position is that such responses serve a system of totality(s). We have denied the third possibility, namely, the autonomous subsistence of such acts, choices, and responses, since they implicate a system of totality(s). Will as a function of the subject self has failed as a model of the human orderer because subjectivity, to be real, had to be incorporated in a system of totality, as I noted in the subjective model of participation. Man's purposive nature is mediated both of will and subjectivity. The failure to relate both to an adequate notion of purposiveness has undermined man's claims to responsibility. Thus I sympathize with May's attempts to go beyond voluntarism as a model of the human orderer. The only objection I have is that the total man is taken to mean the real man, and the only way the total man is real is by being regarded as part of a larger real and immediate totality. To be sure, there is a "crisis of will," but the resolution of the crisis in the direction of a system of totality, in my view, simply perpetuates the crisis. The faculty of an isolated will should instead be reconciled to a new model of the human orderer instead of submerging man in a system of totality. The impotence of will, which is its inner crisis, can be resolved, and the will can be given empowerment in the concept of a purposive being. Will is an aspect, and one aspect only, of man's ontological capacity to be self-directing in existence. For man's purposive being mediates the subject, of which will is a function, in various forms of self-determination. The latter is an abstraction from ontological self-direction. Whether man is driving in his experiences or the driven (the issue of free will and determinism) is an issue that is posterior to purposive being. Both are models of man, as subjectivity and objectivity also are.

The crisis of will, as May postulates it, is a crisis of the "presence or absence of power." This may be true of the will on the phenomenal level of experience where one runs into the problem of cross-purposes, of the implementation of purposes. We are considering a prior problem: how will relates to ontological self-direction and how it is an important component of the human orderer and in purposive participation in existence. The presence or absence of power, important as it is on the phenomenal level where human directionality takes on specificity in terms of goals, choices, ideals, plans. Even the view of Freud, that man is "lived by the unconscious," somehow presupposes a certain way of looking at ourselves in terms of purposiveness on the part of the human orderer. Let me list below some of my objections to the alleged theory of unity toward which man is goal-directed in love and will.

One, May states that the "microcosm of our consciousness is where the microcosm of the universe is known."[27] Such conscious knowledge of the world presupposes the unity and self-transcendence of consciousness prior to intentionality. It also involves consciousness in a larger system of totality. I believe that even this perspective of the world requires the mediation of purposive being. For self-consciousness presupposes the use of consciousness in our purposive nature. To have the world at our doorstep, in spontaneous immediacy, and to regard such an immediate, spontaneous totality as something more than a model of existence, is an oversimplification of the problem and involves the "narcissistic investment" I mentioned earlier. To love one's model of existence in love and will, noble as these virtues may be, does not give man the prerogative to identify his model of man with man per se or his model of existence with existence as existence. May utilizes three irrational drives (Eros, the daimonic, and the structure of intentionality) to breathe life into the abstraction of totality. This abstract unity derives from below, as all three irrational drives (inside and outside of man) make clear. Unity from below is as much a model of totality as unity from above. The only way to escape the problem is to postulate a human orderer (in terms of a metamodel) that goes beyond such images of man and models of totality, functioning as their source. I shall comment on this point in the conclusion.

Two, any effort to go beyond the subject-object split to postulate such a field of unity, whether of man or of existence as existence, presupposes a human orderer that is self-directing in his search for wholeness.

Three, when purpose functions to create such patterns of ultimate goal direction and attributes a dialectical unity and directionality to such totalisms, this is apparently an example of positive or purposeful alienation. Man's purposive nature, while it denies its directives and intentions by making them secondary to such goal-directed designs for living, does not deny itself as a purposive being. When such totalistic patterns fail man's

[27] *Ibid.*, 324.

search for meaning and understanding, the human orderer comes up with other schemes of totality in his search for wholeness, meaning, and understanding. If this is the case, May's distinction between purposiveness and intentionality is unwarranted.

As a form of responding, the total person responding to the total world, as the structure of intentionality is intended to convey, is ultimately still a form of goal-directedness. It is a goal-directedness that is ultimate and postulated as something prior to man's purposive nature. In short, the forming and shaping capacity of such unitive experience is denied to purposive being. This is purposive alienation. Commitment to this prepurposive structure of goal-directedness, prior to ontological self-direction, is an attempt to give man a substitute form of directionality in the place of purposive being. May's attempt to combine willing and knowing in acts of commitment to such a totality is a move in the direction of obscurantism. Unless the human orderer is the gathering focus for the goal-seeking of the will and the choice-making of the mind, it is rather easy to lose both to a substitute form of dialectical design of human life. Commitment is a form of goal direction with fixation on its mind. Perhaps this is the ultimate if man's ultimate meaning in life is to be achieved through an image of himself as a responder. Such commitment does seem to express the heights to which a responder can aspire. My attempt to liberate the human orderer, to go beyond the category of the responder, is simply to make purposive being the mediator of response-relationships, to establish man's claims on responsibility. While the psychoanalyst may have vocational biases in disconnecting purpose from the structure of intentionality in order to relate the structure to the unconscious and to the interaction between organism and its environment, this should be recognized for what it is, a bias, and not the course of human life itself. The fact is that the category of the responder is a hangover from the schemes of totality that have tyrannized man when he was submerged in such systems of responsibility. The responder gives us neither the liberated human orderer nor the source of human responsibility. It is May's preconception of unity, applied to his image of man and to his model of existence, which requires of man to be a functionary of both models—in short, to be a responder.

Four, the responder is a sufficient category to account for man's choices, goals, ideals, and schemes of totality in terms of goal direction. Whenever such goal-directedness is practiced, the responder implements such patterns. Its movement is external, the process of reaching out, like the meaning of purpose as goal direction is external. Intentionality is a synonym for goal-directedness as we have understood the meaning of purpose traditionally. It has a legitimate place on the phenomenal level of existence; it provides subjective unity to goal-seeking as the outward direction of meaning from subject to object, just as the means/ends continuum provides the objective reference to such goal-directedness. Intentionality may well be the deepest meaning of purpose defined as goal direction. To make it into a speculative structure of intentionality which is prior to purposive being and ontological self-direction is to miss the point. Intentionality, even when it goes beyond the subject-object split as a structure of being and as an epistomology, is still a form of goal direction and as such presupposes ontological self-direction. Such an intentional structure is a way of submerging man in a system of totality because the dominant image of man is still that of a responder in commitment to a system of totality. What I am suggesting is that such a transcendent unity, which comes from below man, is itself in need of human directionality and presupposes a human orderer that is responsible for totalisms and for systems of total responsibility. Intentionality is itself in need of ontological self-direction. The alternative to this thesis is rather dismal. It means that intentionality plays the role of a servant to the directives of totality. It binds man to a system of totality and does not liberate the human orderer for purposive participation.

Five, there are many models of the responder, depending on the numerous systems of totality. Such totalisms dictate the content and meaning and scope of the category of the responder. In terms of May's perspective, it means that "the process of reaching out" (some form of self-transcendence) also comes in many brands. For Tillich and Niebuhr, "reaching out" is a quality of the spirit. For Heidegger, "reaching out" is the quality of *Dasein* defined as existence. For May, the structure of intentionality "as a reaching out" is the capacity of the organism in its total environment. Each system of transcendent unity dictates the terms of the responder in his response-relationships. Obviously, what is needed is to account for this model-making power in terms of a theory of man to make sense out of these various models of man imaging himself as a responder in response-relations. It also means that we cannot identify our model of the responder with the very process of reaching out. Such a transcendent unitive experience is a model of experience and cannot be equated with lived experience itself.

May is rather touchy on this issue, especially when one of his constructs is in danger of being demolished. He actually believes that if his definition of man should fail us, man will never recover from the damage to his image. Take for example his comment about the daimonic in man:

Not to recognize the daimonic itself turns out to be daimonic; it makes us accomplices on the side of the destructive possession. . . . The denial of the daimonic is, in effect, a self-castration in love and a self-nullification in will. And the denial leads to the perverted forms of aggression we have seen in our day in which the repressed comes back to haunt us.[28]

Why should this be the case? The obvious reply is that May has identified his construct of the daimonic with the nature of man. He has identified, moreover, his image of man with man per se, the narcissistic investment I mentioned earlier. Is this a claim of ultimacy for one's model of man? That man is daimonic-ridden is a mythological construct of man which cannot be identified with the real nature of man. May thinks that man's life is guided by such stories or myths. He denies the fact that man is self-directing in such myths and in myth-making, in their creation and use as designs for living. His is a myth-ridden psychology. In such a world-view, the rejection of a mythical construct is tantamount to the rejection of man himself. But this is an obvious mistake. What is in jeopardy is one's construct of man and not human nature itself. To argue as May does is to assume an identity between an image of man and the real man himself. Unless one makes a distinction between such a dialectical construct and man himself, this confusion will not be avoided. Claims for "living" dialectics are really claims of ultimacy for one's model of human directionality; they are power-claims invented by purposive being to cope with the problem of meaning in life. Any dialectic which denies the role of the human orderer in framing such a substitute directionality for life is viewed, in the light of my theory, as such a claim to ultimacy. These are speculations of the mind prompted by human purpose and not descriptions to be identified with the human condition itself or the real man.

Six, the concept of unity that is beyond the subject-object split, beyond purpose and will, comes in many models and brands. Thus it cannot be the source of human responsibility. Such a perspective fails to liberate the human orderer. In fact, it prevents man from confronting himself as a human orderer in experiences of responsibility. Such unity plays down man's claims on responsibility and creates the schizoid condition of sep-

[28] *Ibid.*, 131.

arating *responsibility for* from *responsibility to* in a theory of "human" responsibility. What is needed is not a preconceived notion of unity beyond images of man and models of existence, but a reference to the human orderer that makes such totalistic schemes of man and existence a possibility. Unity is man's contribution to a theory of man and the universe. It derives from his modeling power in participation. Loving and willing "by participation" is a form of model-making, not an identification with lived experience or with the whole of experience. The unity of existence or the unity of emotions cannot be stated apart from the holistic use of purpose. As a form of goal direction, it presupposes ontological self-direction.

Seven, in fact the concept of self-transcendence, involved in such a transcendent unity, is a sure sign, just like a dialectics, of a preference for totalism in understanding man. Self-transcendence is used by totalists as a basic feature of man to submerge man in a system of totality. In the light of my theory, this is a substitute form of human directionality when it is severed from man's purposive being and given an ontological priority to man's purposive nature.

Eight, May's attempt to disconnect purposiveness from the structure of intentionality, to make room for a transcendent unity that comes from below, is perhaps the best way to submerge man in a system of totality. His philosophy of encounter, of the "total man" as a unitive being "participating in the whole," comes at the expense of the human orderer. But if man is to confront himself as a total human being with full human potential, this confrontation must be mediated by purposive being. Otherwise man has no obligation and responsibility to confront himself in existence. Before man is goal-directed to himself, to his existence, he must be self-directing in the matrix of participation. The overall speculative structure of intentionality in May's writings fails to liberate the human orderer and his claims on responsibility. Unless one's courage in facing up to existence has the support of a human orderer, it is a mindless and purposeless encounter needing further justification beyond the assumptions of immediacy. Feeling one's way into the standards of life is a dangerous precedent to set, especially if there is no way to connect spontaneity with responsibility. If our desires are to be based on needs and necessities, as May believes with the anarchists, these needs and necessities can take on human form if they are mediated by purposive being. Otherwise there is no connection between these supposed needs and necessities and one's desire for life. Because purpose is a secondary construct in May's writings, he has failed to give us an adequate theory of responsibility. Man is pushed from behind, lured from above, pulled from the front, moved from below; but in all these instances, he is not his own in his purposive life. He depends on substitute forms of directionality. This is hardly the standard for a "responsible person."

Many of May's creative insights suffer shipwreck by his drive for totalism. This is, in fact, the fate of responsibility in the field of humanistic psychology. It cannot go beyond a *responsibility to* irrational drives, to unitive experience, to systems of totality. The desire for a science of immediacy has substituted the directives of immediacy for man's purposive nature and its possible contributions to man's becoming. The drive for identity has supplanted the human orderer. Such unity, however, is not self-sustaining. It invites the prospect of totalistic claims on human life. The humanism in humanistic psychology is a form of totalism(s). It fails to liberate the human orderer and his claims on responsibility.

If such totalisms are merely models of existence, there is an insurmountable difficulty that humanistic psychology must face up to. It may be good psychology, but it is certainly muddled philosophy. The "process of reaching out" or the "push toward a direction of action" may be sufficient to discover the human "responder" in a system of totality. But it is not sufficient to grasp the human orderer or his claims on responsibility. While this may satisfy the human imagination, it is not a sufficient condition for participation in existence. If human life is to be redeemed from the tyranny of such totalisms, "commitment" must follow ontological self-direction. May's advice that man should choose his relationship to what determines him, in elemental modes of response (defined as conjunctive processes), is one of those free ontological options (discussed earlier concerning James Bugental's perspective), which is tantamount to "loving fate." This dialectics of freedom and necessity and the principle of coresponsibility which it yields (to the effect that we are cocreators of our fate), is a way of serving a system of totality. There are many models and brands of coresponsiveness. Each system of totality determines the content and relationship of such mutual determination. The confluent model of human participation thus loses the human orderer in the matrix of participation. To the extent humanistic psychology follows the confluent model of participation, it shares its liabilities with respect to the human orderer and responsibility.

The emancipation of man from one scheme of totality to another is as much a misguided effort in humanistic psychology as it has been in philosophy through the ages. *What man needs is emancipation from the very schemes of such totalities. Such totalities are but the human productions of man's search for wholeness.* They are not something to be found out there, in alliance with reality. They lead to dictatorial and authoritarian claims upon human life. The "whole man" of humanistic psychology, which is allegedly beyond the mere human search for wholeness of meaning and experience, is a prey to such dictatorial claims. The only emancipation worth having is one that recognizes authoritarian claims in the appeal to totalities beyond man's search for wholeness—even in psychology.

13. Conclusion: Some Reflections on the Crisis

What this volume has attempted to convey is a sense of the widening crisis which pervades our views of human responsibility. At the starting point I said that when man "lost his hold on life" there ensued a breakdown in human responsibility. If life is not worth living, what is the point of responsibility? But as the volume progressed, a greater crisis in responsibility began to manifest itself: even when man "had a hold on life" and felt rapport with it, it was possible for him to experience a breakdown in responsibility, to experience impotence in overcoming the gap between *responsibility for* and *responsibility to* some of the issues of life. Thus even in the midst of feeling exuberant about life's vitality, man may feel a loss in having lost his claims on responsibility. This alienation from responsibility has encouraged some to hide out in some local enclaves in systems of totality. It does not follow, then, that the more vitality and intensity of experience that one possesses, the more responsibility he will show toward life. Responsibility has its source in purposiveness, not in human vitality. Responsibility comes from purposive being on the level of primal experience. It is precisely this source of response-relations that our highly technological society has denied. If a man can lose his sense of responsibility at the height of his human vitality, the crisis of responsibility is real indeed.

There are two basic factors that have contributed to the breakdown of responsibility: (1) the separation of choices, goals, ideals, images of man, and schemes of totality, from man's purposive being; and (2) the separation of the human orderer from his acts of responsibility, or the separation of the responder and the answerer from its source in purposive being. Having been neglectful of the source, we have botched responsibility on the phenomenal level of response-relations. Even the warmth of being wrapped in the bosom of some system of totality and having psychic rapport with it does not get rid of the nagging problem that manifests itself in the popular belief: the more life, the more responsibility. The two clauses seem to be at variance with each other. The more the gap between *responsibility for* and *responsibility to* widens, the more man is at a loss to deal meaningfully with human aspirations and with acts of choice-making in response-relationships.

My attempt in this volume was to hold together the two basic themes of responsibility as two facets of one experience, to avoid a schizoid theory of responsibility, and to prevent the submergence of man in some system of totality where he is incapable of holding together these two dimensions. Some may view this attempt as a matter of epistomological confusion between the genesis of desire and the subsistence of acts of choice, between responsibility for and responsibility to, between the source of responsibility and the actual response-relations we experience on the phenomenal level of experience. The choice we face here is between epistomological niceties and the possible erosion of human responsibility. To regard questions of genesis, questions of sources of responsibility, is not a muddled question, something to be passed up for an ascriptive view of responsibility.

Many of the Anglo-American analysts are advocating an ascriptive theory of responsibility. Their attempt is to understand responsibility in terms of the philosophy of action. Responsible acts are to be explained not by causal descriptions, but by ascriptive responsibility. Such responding acts are intentional, involve societal rule-following, and require fitting responses to appropriate rules in a given society. Myles Brand, in his fine introduction to *The Nature of Human Action*, comments that human action is behavior "to which responsibility can be ascribed," that the focus of attention is on "performing an action" and not on its causal origins in terms of some individual agent. Ascriptive responsibility shifts the focus of attention to moral and social rules of behavior. It is thus a form of holism which views society as a rule-following culture to which man is answerable and accountable. The real question in ascriptive responsibility is whether one is psychologically and socially fit to be guided by rule-directed culture. When responsibility is construed in terms of "performing an act" in the context of ascriptive behavior, the issue of the source of responsibility is totally ignored and the sense of "crisis" is dismissed.[1]

In practice, the distinction between the genesis of acts and the performance of acts amounts to a separation in current theorizing about responsi-

[1] Myles Brand, *The Nature of Human Action* (Glenview, Ill., Scott Foresman, 1970), 18–21.

bility. The choice between antecedents and the consequences of acts, as a prior choice and purpose, is not accounted for by this distinction. Human choices and goals, as well as response-relations, cannot be accounted for by the autonomy of actions. Such acts implicate either a human orderer or a system of totality which orders such acts. Such functions do not exist on their own. Logical analysis of them does not invest these functions with existence. Thus the effort to get at the source of human responsibility on the level of action, whether actions are viewed causally or ascriptively, is an ill-fated enterprise. It creates a cleavage between responsibility for and responsibility to.

Whether one postulates an individual agent or social agency to account for human responsibility, the problem is the same. The human agent is a model of man in relation to his actions. This model is identified either with an individual person or with an actual social group in order to relate agency to actual behavior. In ascriptive responsibility, the agent is rule-directed society. Because the model-making quality of agency is not recognized as such (it is regarded as real and immediate), the problems of responsibility are misconstrued. The fact of the matter is that the human orderer as a purposive being is prior to descriptive and ascriptive explanations of human responsibility, and he is not accounted for in this kind of theorizing. The fact that man is present as a human orderer in acts of responsibility, and the source of such distinctions as the one between genesis and the subsistence of choices, is not a matter that can be brushed aside so lightly. There is no awareness of the crisis of responsibility among these thinkers because they are content to deal with responsibility only on the phenomenal level of experience and choose to ignore the problems concerning its source. Such action philosophies assume the immediacy of acts, which implicates a system of totality, and think of responsibility in terms of some system of totality. While I have not made a special study of the analytical view of responsibility, there seems to be a predilection for a holistic point of view toward responsibility.

In the light of my theory of responsibility, it is essential to keep the sources (problems of genesis) together with the performance of response-relationships. This integrative perspective is lacking in ascriptive views of responsibility. What does it mean to ascribe responsibility to a person for his thoughts and acts, for his performance-functions? It means that man confronts himself, affirms himself, as a human orderer in such response-relations. He faces up to himself, his thoughts and actions. The self-performer of acts is a by-product of the human orderer, an abstraction from ontological self-direction. Man does not take directives from his acts and their performances. These already presuppose a purposive being capable of exhibiting the human orderer in the matrix of participation. Even the recognition of impotence or lack of performance ability in situations testifies indirectly to the human orderer in the matrix of participation; man feels guilt, despair, impotence, lack of will, etc., in these frustrating situations. The goals and plans of the purposive being are being thwarted, denied, frustrated. Purposive being feels the sting of the situation. This does not mean, however, that purposive being is denied. Otherwise the problematic situation would not be viewed by man as a "crisis." He suffers with the situation as a problematic situation only because he is a purposive being, a human orderer, and views the problem as a "crisis."

One need not make claims of omnicompetence for the human orderer, as older forms of humanism did. What needs to be done is to make claims for the human orderer "in the matrix of participation." Wherever there are goals, choices, ideals, aspirations, selections, images of man, images of totality, the unitive experiences of situations, or encounter experiences, the human orderer is in the midst of them in participation. These experiences presuppose ontological self-direction. He has already mediated such phenomena, and the imprint of his model-making powers are present in participation. This affirmation of the human orderer in the matrix of participation is not Nietzsche's will to power and self-determination. Such self-determination is an abstraction from purposive participation in existence. It is a form of self-performance that assumes ontological self-direction. Man is a model-maker in participation. This metamodel of man does not claim omnipotentiality for the human orderer. It merely insists on an adequate theory of purposive participation that can lay claims to human responsibility.

The very term "crisis" attests to the continuous relevance of the human orderer to such problematic situations. That man experiences the contradictions and problems of a transitional era as a "crisis" already points to the human orderer in a problematic setting. It is there that man experiences (on the phenomenal level of goals, choices and response-relations) impotence in goal-seeking, choice-making, vision-making, or his helplessness in model-making; it is his "crisis," as problems read off in terms of a crisis situation. It is the presence of the human orderer in self-direction that turns the problematic situation into a "crisis." He is waiting to perform, showing concern, attempting to resolve. He does not want impotence to reign. A crisis is a groping for goals, a search for a specific directionality, a time of stock-taking. Far from being a denial of a purposive being, the term "crisis" attests to the human orderer in the matrix of participation. It is purposive being ready for participation, ready for responsibility through ontological self-direction. A crisis is not a "lack of will" or a "lack of purpose," it is rather the search for goals and choices; it is looking for a way out of a problematic situation. A problematic situation can appear as such only to a purposive being for whom problems become situations of crisis. These are prompted neither by subjective or objective conditions; they are generated by purposive being in the matrix of participation. The modeling power of the human orderer is already present in relating problem with crisis. The problem is an opportunity for a crisis situation only because man confronts the human orderer in himself. That such situations arise is no surprise to man, for man is incomplete and finite. His goals and plans are not all-encompassing, not all-embracing, not totally integrative. He must order experiences anew and reorder, as well as revise, his goals and plans as he relates directionality to human vitality. Once we separate *responsibility for* from *responsibility to*, there is no way to distinguish between problems and problems that become crisis situations. My attempt to go beyond the responder, beyond actions and their performances, is to liberate the human orderer as the source of response-relations. Without him there is no crisis situation, only a problem (if even that).

What is needed, then, is not the postulation of unity beyond purpose and will, but an adequate view of the human orderer that is responsible for response-relations in a self-directing manner. What is needed is a meta-model that will account for this modeling power in the midst of participation. Such a human orderer is already present in self-direction when distinctions arise between responsibility for and responsibility to, between descriptive and ascriptive acts, between causal and teleological explanations. They are concerns of purposive being who has a sensitivity and a readiness for responding only because he is a human orderer and can confront himself as such in the matrix of participation.

The metamodel of the human orderer recognizes man as a model-maker in experience, in fashioning images of himself and of existence in the very matrix of participation. We have recognized this power of man in thought, but not in experience and participation. The concept of purpose as ontological self-direction enables us to introduce model-making as an ontological concern of man. As an ontological concern, it lays claims on responsibility. This volume has emphasized the continuous relevance of the human orderer to images of man, images of totality, and images of human responsibility. Just because human self-direction is not omnipotential, it does not mean that man's life is inconsequential in participation and in response-relations. Those who refuse to take responsibility for their responses in participation are the same ones who refuse to confront the human orderer either in the individual or in society. Yet they insist on showing "responsibility to" when the springs of action and the sources of responsibility have already dried up in them. This would indicate they prefer the orderings of totality in which the human orderer is submerged and no longer capable of showing "responsibility for."

This metamodel is more than simply an "embodiment of an attitude and response." It envisions a human orderer that shapes and forms such attitudes and responses. It is more also than simply "an image of man," as Maurice Friedman sees it: "as a direction of movement which shapes the raw material of the given into authentic personal and human existence."[2] It is the source of such "an image of man" or an "image of totality." Man is already a purposive being in having such myths to live by. The influence of such myths upon us denies only some of our goals and plans; it does not deny purposive being that can order and reorder such goals and plans. This metamodel refuses to identify these images of man with man himself, just as it denies the identity of one's model of existence with existence itself by certain claims to ultimacy.

When man is directed by images of himself and images of totality, this is outward directionality even when conceived subjectively or existentially. The process of reaching out has been completely externalized and a substitute form of directionality has been accepted as the guide. What is needed is not a descriptive or concrete model of man, or even an ideal or normative one. What is needed is a metamodel to account for such model-making prowess in participation. Man's purposive nature already mediates the "process of reaching out" or the "process of reaching in," or the "process of reaching up or down." Such acts of self-transcendence presuppose a purposive being whose general directionality is the basis for such directionally specific trips. Unless ontological self-direction is the basis for such intentional, goal-directed experiences, there is no way to legislate among

[2] Friedman, *To Deny Our Nothingness*, 11.

the different models of goal-directed designs for living and relativism sets in with paralyzing force. If responsibility is left totally to the responder as its caretaker, the same paralysis sets in. The "responder" is already a "type" required by systems of totality to be operational in existence. The responder is a spawn of totalisms unless he is meaningfully related to the human orderer that makes claims on responsibility. Unless the human potential is seen in terms of the perspective of the human orderer, it falls prey to systems of totality.

What has this volume contributed to the clarification of the crisis? What have I added to the theory of responsibility by connecting its source to the human orderer who is able to show "responsibility for" his creations in response-relationships? I have added a "reality-claim" to the practice of "responsibility to." Without such a reality-claim, responsibility can have no seriousness. Man's claims on responsibility are thus of the nature of reality-claims. These are participatory-claims about response-actions.

Totalistic schemes of responsibility, on the other hand, are concerned with a real responder in a real totality. Such responses are responses to reality or to other responses of reality qua reality. The totalist is never satisfied with reality-claims which attest to the seriousness of human participation in response-actions. He moves beyond these reality-claims to reality *qua* reality through the postulate of real unity underlying such a transition. But to prove his point, he cannot stop short of omniscience, and neither is he free of the problems of relativism. As a ludicrous figure, the totalist has his head in the clouds of absolute participation while his feet are in the quicksand of relativism. The sense of crisis is intensified by his totalistic claims on responsibility in the framework of absolute participation.

"Responsibility for," then, is a phrase which requires the human orderer to be part of the participatory situation as claimant therein. In the matrix of participation, man makes claims for the "responsible response." This saves responsibility from externality, from being a fiction, from being an ornament in society. Responsible response-functions is what this volume is about. These are man's reality-claims about his role in participation when he functions in terms of response-acts. As a reality-claim (which is more than simply the reality sense or reality of responsibility), the human orderer functions in the capacity of "responsibility for" in situations of response-actions. Purposive being as ontologically self-directing is not disconnected from such response-actions. Before man can be "answerable" in terms of the response-function of "responsibility to," he must have an autonomy as a human orderer prior to being a responder in some system of totality. Without his capacity to be "responsible for," the answerer is either an empty responder or an external actor open to the call of totality(s). Man is between "responsibility for" and "responsibility to" giving meaning to both showing his concern for the "responsible response." Such phrases are not complementary phases of an ongoing totality. The phenomenal dimension of responsibility is connected with its ontological source in the phrase "responsibility for." Unless this is acknowledged, the sense of crisis cannot be clarified. In man's claims on responsibility, he exercises reality-claims in participation for his response-actions. This makes responsibility an integral aspect of the theory of man rather than an integral theory of some totality that is beyond the boundaries of human participation.

In terms of this standard for responsibility, let us see what happens to Reich's perspective in *The Greening of America*, which in my view deepens the crisis rather than clarifies it. The book fails in its reflections on the social crisis on three counts. One, instead of being a reply to the question, "How can our society be changed?," the author shifts gears to reply to another question: "How can our inner attitudes to society be changed?" "The revolution by consciousness," one that is without violence, is also one without responsibility. Ignoring the political structures, as Reich does, to concentrate on an inward life-style, without a life-style in responsibility, is essentially an irresponsible view. The difficulty derives from Reich's model of human participation.

The best statement of his participatory view is: "Every form of consciousness is a reaction to a way of life that existed before, and an adaptation to new realities."[3] The model of participation is that of action-reaction in the who-to-whom relationship. Consciousness III is either a reaction to basic actions, to social forms, or it is a reaction to previous reactions, such as Con I and Con II. The model of participation is not adequate to bring off the revolution by consciousness. Reich is thus forced to appeal to a new term from another orbit of meaning and participation, which is "transcendence." This is solving the problem outside his restricted theoretical framework. Inner self-transcendence is required for the inner life-style changes which the category of "reaction" cannot produce. Such transcen-

[3] Charles A. Reich, *The Greening of America* (New York, Bantam, 1971), 20–21.

317

dence derives from libertarian philosophies and not from the model of action-reaction participation. This is tantamount to saying that Reich cannot even bring off the revolution by consciousness without going beyond his theoretical structure, let alone facing up to the real issue he posed for himself: "How can our society be changed?"

The third and most basic defect of the volume is his inability to show "responsibility for" the personal responsibility which Con III bears. The new life-style is one of spontaneity, immediacy, and feeling. Such self-expression can only show *responsibility to*, to one's feelingful life *but it cannot show responsibility for the new life-style of the counterculture.* If all that is necessary, for the present, is to "describe a new way of life" and no more in terms of social planning, etc., he cannot make a reality-claim for that new life-style. It remains a fiction, as Con III. He now has a feelingful responder, rather than an institutional responder, but a responder nonetheless. *He cannot show "responsibility for" that would clarify the social crisis and combine a new life-style with a new life-style in responsibility.* When he further recommends that youth be the model for adults, he does not even ponder the perils that beset such a program in terms of the stages of life.

Charles Reich's problem in *The Greening of America* was examined in Chapter I, "Youth's Discovery of Responsibility in Spontaneity." Just because one experiences the "full responsibility of his feelings" does not make one responsible, for one can never show "responsibility for" such feelings. Just because it feels right does not make it right. Just because it feels good does not make it good. The sense of obligation is not born in feelingful awareness; it comes from man's purposive life. The young radical would teach the world new standards, but he will not take "responsibility for" the newly enunciated criteria or their consequences. The 1970's attest to this impotence in the New Left movement. Charles Fried, in evaluating the "cultural revolution," writes: "At most they are a deep symptom of the malaise which Reich insists exists."[4] What it amounts to in the final analysis is that with all their emphasis on feeling as the civilizer of men, they can no more show "responsibility for" than the culture they left behind—and for precisely the same reason. Their life-style is not that of a purposive being that is capable of self-direction and ontological obligatoriness. If the young radicals cannot manifest "responsibility for," what is the

---

[4] Philip Nobile (ed.), *The Con III Controversy* (New York, Pocket Books, 1971), 99.

point of the cultural revolution? They have lost their claim on responsibility by giving primacy to feeling in their newly sought life-style. That "each responds with himself" is beside the point once it is seen that he has chosen another totality to live by, that of nature mysticism. For he has now become a "responder" in a new totality. As a responder he is not his own but belongs to the totality to which he has committed himself. What this suggests is the heightening of the crisis of responsibility rather than the lessening of it. The point is to transcend it to have a vital personal and cultural life.

How can the crisis of responsibility be overcome or transcended, to use an old Hegelian term (*Aufhebung*) which Marx took over to speak of human emancipation from alienation? In this volume I have given only a partial answer to this overriding issue: combining "responsibility for" with "responsibility to" in a healthy theory of human responsibility. What gives my partial solution a measure of health is the view of man as a purposive being in existence. He is more than a submerged "responder" in some system of totality. He is capable of self-direction. Even from the analytic point of view, McPherson states that the main problems of responsibility depend for their solution on a theory of man. He states:

What is involved here is a question of fundamental attitudes towards human beings. Perhaps the strongest consideration against the view that responsibility can be dispensed with lies in our attitude towards human beings—as persons to be respected rather than things to be manipulated. We have already come to much the same conclusion in the previous chapter [where he discusses "Human Action and Free Will"]. There are arguments to be brought against aspects of the views which treat people as creatures that only behave and never act, that are never properly to be held responsible for anything they do, who do not have free will. Over and above such arguments, however, as we saw, there is the question: are we content to think of people in this way?[5]

Although McPherson accepts both the descriptive and ascriptive aspects of responsibility in relation to actions, and although he exhibits much common sense in the passage above, it is clear to me, at least, that we cannot establish the source or sources of responsibility on the level of actions. The model of *human agency* breaks down by being simply an abstraction holding out as the real source of specific actions. This will not do. For this and other reasons I was obliged to go below the level of actions to deal with the source or sources of responsibility. Yet it is only a partial solution to

[5] T. McPherson, *Social Philosophy* (New York, Van Nostrand Reinhold, 1970), 77.

the crisis. A complete solution to the crisis can be had only if we can account for the *human genesis* and meaning of totalities, which have been considered as the alleged sources of responsibility. But this requires separate argumentation and a new volume.

Just such a manuscript is now in process, one which will hold man accountable for systems of responsibility. *Search Without Idols* concerns itself with the human genesis of totalities, how they are the projections and human productions from man's search for wholeness. When totalities are viewed as models of wholeness, supported by *human* reality-claims and not as things-in-themselves, as *Others* without or within experience, making totalitarian claims upon human life, they come to function as tentative and functional guides of life rather than as something given, to be discovered as a find. Once this is demonstrated, as we hope to do, totalities will no longer be considered as the sources of human responsibility. Man will take "responsibility for" such world-building himself as a purposive being and as purpose-bearing institutions in society. What this amounts to is that totalities, as meaning discourse, belong to a theory of man rather than being viewed as integral aspects of reality itself.

Philosophers as totalists have contributed a great deal to the perpetuation of the crisis of responsibility. Religious and secular totalities have also aggravated the problem. They have mistakenly related the concept of totality with reality rather than with a theory of man. When the human genesis of these totalities is revealed, their objectification and reification exposed, they will no longer function as the alleged sources of human responsibility. Up to now man has refused to accept "responsibility for" such world-building. One need not stand on holy ground, on some real neutral world-totality, to expose the projective nature of such totalities. For they relate significantly to man's search for wholeness, which in essence is a search without idolatrous totalities.

Unless modern man masters the source of human responsibility, "the treachery of the imponderables," as Allen Tate reminds us, will be an "impossible burden" to bear. The real source of *human responsibility* is man's capacity for self-direction and the taking of full "responsibility for" his search for wholeness. To seek for sources outside of man for *human* responsibility, above or below man, is to initiate a course of action that is self-defeating in its pursuit. Are we content to think about the sources of responsibility in this way?

If the diagnosis of the crisis in this volume is correct, then it is necessary to reevaluate our stand on totalities. They have a human origin and man must take "responsibility for" such total systems of responsibility. Otherwise we are left with irresponsible life-worlds.

In these reflections on the crisis of responsibility, the concern was with the contemporary scene. The predicament of modern man has an intensity about it that is both frightening and demoralizing. Yet in a sense the crisis is a chronic one and has been with us since the inception of Western civilization. Athens, Jerusalem, and modern science, the three basic determinants of modern culture, have generated totalities to obscure the source of responsibility. The phrase "responsibility for" has been taken out of the realm of human obligation and made into a matter of fact. Compton's endorsement of the Aristotelian view is to the point. He writes: "We may say that someone is responsible for an action or for an event not as an obligation but as a fact, meaning that he performed it or brought it about."[6] When a person's "responsibility for" comes with the fact or after the fact, the "evaluative context" is prior to man as a purposive being. Compton continues: "To be an agent is to make a situation one's own in various ways: through analysis and responsive involvement if it can be affected by one's acts; through awareness and then acceptance or protest, if it cannot. Agency is a power, a power to shape events."[7]

This volume has revealed a deeper meaning of "responsibility for" that is rooted in our attitude toward human beings, toward what we are, rather than toward acts already done. This brings the matter right back to the realm of responsibility, where man is himself *responsible for the evaluative context*. The "human agent" is not a power that lays itself on the line or shapes this. Human agency is an abstraction, a model of man, used to justify specific concrete acts. As a model of man, it has failed to give good account of itself as "responsibility for." It is itself in need of justification.

But more importantly, what has made the problem of responsibility a crisis in Western civilization is the objectification and reification of totalities right from the beginning of our religious, philosophical, and scientific traditions. In this sense we have always been confused on responsibility because we have bifurcated "responsibility for" from "responsibility to." This crisis has reached frightening proportions in our day.

[6] J. J. Compton, "Responsibility and Agency," *Southern Journal of Philosophy* (Spring/Summer, 1973), 83–89.
[7] *Ibid.*, 89.

Index

The paper on which this book is printed bears the watermark of the University of Oklahoma Press and has an effective life of at least three hundred years.

Randall Library – UNCW

BJ1451 .H67   NXWW
Horosz / The crisis of responsibility : man as the

304900204692$